FOURTH EDITION: 1445/2024

Contemplating over the Qur'ān

BOOK TWO

Prepared by:
Abu Suhailah Umar Quinn

Contributors:
Umm Suhailah Khadijah Taylor

Copyright © 2024 by ThaqafaPress.

All rights reserved. No part of this publication may be reproduced, distributed, or transmitted in any form or by any means, including photocopying, recording, or other electronic or mechanical methods, without the prior written permission of the publisher, except in the case of brief quotations embodied in critical reviews and certain other noncommercial uses permitted by copyright law.

ISBN: 979-8320825397 (Paperback)

First printing edition Ramadan 1445 / March 2024.

Thaqafa Press

المحتويات

Table of Contents

Table of Contents 3

Day 10: Sūrah Yunus 9

Day 11: Sūrah Hud 21

Day 12: Yusuf & al-Ra'd 35

Day 13: Ibrahīm & al Hijr 54

Day 14: al-Nahl & al Isrā' 68

Day 15: al Kahf & Maryam 88

Day 16: Taha & Anbiyā' 105

Day 17: Al Hajj & al Mu'minūn 119

Day 18: al-Nūr & al Furqān 132

Day 19: The TawaSīn: al-Shu'arā', al-Naml, & al Qasas 146

Day 20: Dhawāt al Mīm: 'Ankabūt -al-Sajdah 170

Day 21: Ahzāb - Fātir 188

Day 22: Yāsīn - Sād 203

Day 23: al-Zumar - Fussilat 216

Day 24. al-Shūrā - al Ahqāf 231

Day 25: Muhammad - Dhāriyāt 248

Day 26: Al-Tūr - al Hadīd 261

Day 27: Mujādilah - Tahrīm 276

Day 28. Juz' Tabārak 292

Day 29: Juz' Ammā 311

بسم الله الرحمن الرحيم

INTRODUCTION

بسم الله الرحمن الرحيم

The Qur'ān is miraculous and full of wonders. Its wordings, meanings, eloquence, structure, cohesion, impact on the listener, and effect on their heart and behavior are miraculous and wondrous. Allah's speech is unlike any other in its beauty and content. The purpose of this book is to provide the average reader with a framework for better understanding the *Qur'ān* in general, and the main themes and overall content of each *Surah*, in particular. Such comprehension usually requires a degree of focus and attention that is rare in today's world. At times it can be difficult for the average Muslim—especially if they do not have a strong grasp of the Arabic language—to closely follow what each Surah contains of beliefs, stories of the Prophets, rulings, and admonitions regarding how one should behave as a Muslim.

For this year's edition (1445), we have made significant changes to the book's format to increase its readability and expand its content into two volumes, substantially expanding the scope of the book to include further insights on how to contemplate, comprehend, and act upon the *Qur'ān*. The pages normally reserved for note-taking and answering questions in previous editions have been removed. Instead you, the reader, are advised to have a stand-alone journal for recording benefits. We have added several features, the most important of which is a page-by-page guide to the main insights, based on the numbering of the *Madinah Muṣḥaf*, in hopes of significantly aiding the reader in comprehending and applying the Qur'ān to their daily lives.

We have also enhanced the study questions, carefully choosing hundreds of contemplation questions, drawing from the concise abridgment of Tafsir of Ibn Kathir as well as Tafsir al-Sa'di, as their English translations are widely available in Muslim households.

Along with providing a framework for focused contemplation, the number of letters in each *Surah* has been retained to serve as additional encouragement since a believer is rewarded with ten good deeds for every letter of Qur'ān recited. We have kept the *Taḥzīb* (daily allocation) of the Qur'an at 29 days, allowing the book to serve as a guide during Ramaḍān or any other month, as the duration of the month can either be 29 or 30 days depending on the sighting of the new moon.

Section 02

The Suwar of Second Greatest Length

Day 10: Yunus
Day 11: Hūd
Day 12: Yusuf and Ra'd
Day 13: Ibrāhīm and al Ḥijr
Day 14: al-Naḥl and al Isrā'
Day 15: al Kahf and Maryam
Day 16: Ṭaha and al Anbiyā'
Day 17: al Ḥajj and al Mu'minūn
Day 18: al-Nūr and al Furqān
Day 19: al-Shu'arā', al-Naml, al Qaṣaṣ

<u>Day 10: Sūrah Yunus</u>

The *Qur'ān* reading for **day ten** is the entirety of *Sūrah Yunus*. The chapters *Yunus, Hūd,* and *Yūsuf* contain many stories from the *Qur'ān* that are used to invite the disbelievers to Islam.

سُورَةُ يُونُس

YUNUS (10)

Jonah

Sūrah Yunus (Chapter 10) focuses primarily on believing in Allah's wise control of all things by way of divine decree and preordainment (*qaḍā wal qadar*), one of the pillars of faith in Allah (سُبْحَانَهُ وَتَعَالَىٰ). Among the purposes of this Sūrah is to confront the deniers of revelation with arguments and evidence, encouraging them to believe and warning them against unbelief.

VERSES
109

WORDS
1,832

LETTERS
9,900

REVEALED IN
MAKKAH

REVEALATION ORDER
51

It is the third Makkan Sūrah in sequence of the Muṣḥaf, preceded by Sūrah al An'ām and Sūrah al 'Arāf. It is said to have been around the 51st revealed (between Sūrah al Isrā' and before Sūrah Hūd) in the tenth or eleventh year of Prophethood, shortly before the Hijrah. It is the first in the Muṣḥaf named after a Prophet. The story of Yunus is found toward the end. It serves a dual purpose of condemning the disbelievers while comforting the believers in the final portion of the Makkan phase of the da'wah. This is evident at the beginning of the Sūrah and its conclusion.

Allah gives glad tidings that the righteous have *qadam-ṣidq* (precedence of honor) with Allah; He demonstrates that the people of falsehood will ultimately and belatedly admit to the truth, at which point it is usually too late and will not avail them; it concludes with a tremendous passage, *"Say: if you are in doubt about my religion, then..."*

Verse 5 encourages reflection on the natural world. Yet, as highlighted towards the end, signs and cautions prove futile for those who deny faith (refer to verse 101).

The Sūrah elaborates throughout on how the allure of material life leads to negligence, acting as a primary factor for disbelief and immoral behavior. Alongside this, it contrasts that against the path of the believer, his enlightenment, and his rewards (refer to verses 6-10), indicating that the lure of the temporal world motivates the denial of life hereafter, thereby rejecting the foundational beliefs in monotheism and divine revelation. It notes that disbelievers sarcastically demand the swift arrival of divine chastisement.

Some distinct features of the Sūrah include:

1. It is the first Sūrah in the Qur'ānic arrangement named after a prophet.

2. It contains one of the five challenge verses regarding the Qur'ān's inimitability.

3. The word "the truth (*al ḥaqq*)“ is repeated 21 times.

4. It uniquely mentions what Pharaoh said as he was drowning.

Burhān al-Dīn Al-Biqā'ī (d. 885 AH رَحِمَهُ ٱللَّهُ) stated:[1]

”ومقصودها: وصف الكتاب بأنه من عند الله، لما اشتمل عليه من الحكمة وأنه ليس إلا من عنده سبحانه، لأن غيره لا يقدر على شيء منه. وذلك دالّ بلا ريب على أنه واحد في ملكه، لا شريك له في شيء من أمره.

"Its intended purpose is to describe the book as from Allah, due to the wisdom it contains, and that it could only be from Him (سُبْحَانَهُۥ وَتَعَالَىٰ) as none other could produce anything like it. This indicates He is One in His dominion, with no counterpart in His command whatsoever.

وتمام الدليل على هذا: قصة قوم يونس عليه السلام، بأنهم لما آمنوا عند المخايل كشف عنهم العذاب، فدل قطعاً على أن الآتي به إنما هو الله الذي آمنوا به“.

The complete proof of this is the story of the people of Yunus (عَلَيْهِ ٱلسَّلَامُ) who, when they believed at the last moment, were spared from punishment, undoubtedly showing that it was Allah they had believed in."

The Sūrah also discusses disbelievers' religious views, directs attention to Allah's universal signs, narrates some stories for lessons and caution, especially that of Mūsā with Pharaoh, touches upon human nature, describes life in this world, moves to describe the impactful spectacles of the Day of Judgment and what follows it in terms of affirming resurrection, and discusses the Qur'ān and its effect on souls and its deniers.

Its connection to the preceding Sūrah is that the previous one ended with the message of the Prophet (صَلَّى ٱللَّهُ عَلَيْهِ وَسَلَّمَ), and this one concludes similarly, with the former focusing on the

[1] See Maṣā'id al-Naẓr and Naẓm al-Durar.

hypocrites' conditions and actions at the time of the Qur'ān's revelation, and this one on the disbelievers and their statements about the Qur'ān.

The Sūrah begins and ends with an emphasis on revelation and divine wisdom (verses 1 and 109), highlighting that the essence of wisdom lies in following Allah's revelation.

The main topics of the blessed Sūrah in brief:

1. Observing the universe and its phenomena that naturally indicate the truth of its Maker's Divinity and thus His exclusive right to be worshipped.

2. Examples of profound vicissitudes and trials witnessed by people whose implications they overlook.[2]

3. Examples from the fates of past deniers, warning those who deny to expect a similar fate.[3]

A Broader Overview of the Sūrah:[4]

- It opens by affirming prophethood and illustrating the falsehood of the disbelievers' claims regarding the Prophet (ﷺ) and the Qur'ān, mentioning their recompense in the hereafter. It begins with affirming Muhammad's (ﷺ) message through the inability of the polytheists to produce something like the Qur'ān. This is subtly indicated by the disjointed letters at the beginning of the Sūrah,[5] followed by: "*These are the verses of the wise book*" [Yunus: 1], pointing to its miraculous nature as evidence of its divine origin. The command explicitly addresses this later: "*Produce a Sūrah like it*" [Yunus: 38]. The discussion proceeds to affirm Muhammad's (ﷺ) message and refute the polytheists' claim that Allah would not send a human messenger.

- It then transitions to affirming Allah's exclusive right to be worshipped through His creation and management of the world, leading to the rejection of partners in His divinity and the polytheists' excuse that their idols intercede with Allah. It details the positioning of the sun and moon for the benefit of creation, criticizes those content with the fleeting world over eternal bliss, praises the believers in their quest for paradise, addresses the disbelievers' impatience for punishment, examines Allah's trial of His creation through their stewardship of the earth, and

---

[2] verses 12, 21, 23, 31.

[3] verses 13, 14, 71, 74, 90, 91.

[4] The broader summaries of each section are adapted from a number of sources, such as *Al Muyassar fil-Tafsīr*, and the synopses of Fayrūz Abādī in *Baṣā'ir Dhawil-Tamyīz* and Ibn 'Ashūr in *al-Taḥrīr wal-Tanwīr*.

[5] as seen in the opening of Al-Baqarah and multiple other Sūrahs.

mentions the disbelievers' failure to comprehend Allah's speech, attributing it to fabrication and discrepancy.

- It also points to the invalidity of idols and their worshippers, highlights Allah's favor on His servants with salvation from destruction on land and sea, compares worldly life to rain's descent and the emergence of plants and foliage, calls creation to the abode of peace, details the humiliation of disbelievers at the resurrection, outlines the outcomes of both obedience and sin, clarifies that truth is singular while everything else is falsehood. It substantiates resurrection and judgment with clear proof and argument.

- It explains the benefit of the Qur'ān's descent from Allah, instructs mankind to express joy and happiness through prayer and the Qur'ān, distinguishes between the allies of Allah and the criminals, consoles the Prophet (صَلَّىٱللَّهُعَلَيْهِوَسَلَّمَ) with some events from the story of Mūsā and the Israelites' encounter with Pharaoh's people. It mentions the obliteration of the Egyptians' wealth, the Israelites' sea escape, the Pharaohs' demise, and the salvation of Yunus's people through sincere faith at the brink of despair, and emphasizes the Prophet's (صَلَّىٱللَّهُعَلَيْهِوَسَلَّمَ) patience against the polytheists' harm in its conclusion.

- Overall, this blessed Sūrah addresses a significant problem among humans, answers many of their questions, and removes doubts and confusion about belief in Allah, the Last Day, His names and attributes, the reward and punishment, etc., through reflection on the universe and Allah's wisdom and good management in it. This leads to the realization and truth that Allah is wise and does not act in jest. All His actions, commands, and prohibitions are based on wisdom and being the Wisest of judges.

As is typical of Meccan Sūrahs, this chapter delves into three core topics: (1) faith in divine revelation, including the scriptures and prophets; (2) accurate understanding of belief in Allah; and (3) the belief in resurrection and subsequent judgment. It adeptly employs three primary strategies for imparting meaningful lessons through deduction:

(1) Straightforward reasoning that resonates with innate human sensibilities.

(2) Narratives of past communities and their acceptance or rejection of truth, highlighting stories of Prophets like Noah, Mūsā, and Yunus. These narratives illustrate Allah's omnipotence, His unwavering support for the believers, and His retribution towards transgressors. The Sūrah concludes with guidance for the Prophet Muhammad ﷺ to stay true to the revelations received and to remain patient amid adversity.

(3) The use of metaphors to visually represent spiritual truths. The Sūrah emphasizes how worldly attachment greatly hinders spiritual faith, presenting a potent analogy to describe the fleeting nature of worldly existence.

BRIEF SŪRAH SUMMARY

Verses 1-14	It begins with the individual letters and the mention of the Qur'ān. That is followed by the affirmation of Muhammad's ﷺ prophethood and then the Oneness of Allah and His exclusivity in creating. That is followed by the affirmation of resurrection and judgment in the hereafter. That is interspersed with the simple logical evidence of each and a reminder of what befalls those who belied the Messenger and the reminder to take lesson of divine power at land and at sea.
Verses 15-18	Their hopelessness for divine reward compels them to deny the Qur'ān and request that it be changed.
Verses 19-24	People's faith or lack thereof during the changes of circumstance in life. Verse 24 contains a very important parable about the similitude of the worldly life.
Verses 25-30	The reward and punishment in the hereafter.
Verses 31-36	Establishes belief in Allah's Oneness & The Hereafter with simple proofs that appeal to human nature.
Verses 37-44	It contains one of the five verses of challenge as relates to the irreplaceability of the Qur'ān.
Verse 57	Around halfway into the Sūrah, Allah describes believing in it (the Qur'ān) as the greatest source of happiness due to its possessing four attributes of perfection.
Verses 62-70	The Reward of Allah's allies, contrasted with the punishment of His enemies for their lying without proof.
Verses 71-74	The Story of Nuḥ in brief.
Verses 75-93	The Story of Mūsā & Fir'awn. It is the single place in which Fir'awn's words at the time of drowning are quoted.
Verses 94-100	The Greatness of the Qur'ān and a brief mention of the salvation of the people of Yunus as they saw the approach of divine punishment. This is the single nation mentioned in the Qur'ān as being spared at the last moment. Otherwise, the evidence and warnings most often prove to be of no avail for disbelieving peoples. This very hopeful and exceptional occasion in this Sūrah is the reason why it is named after Yunus. Otherwise, the fuller details and elements of the story of Yunus are found elsewhere in the Qur'ān, such as in Sūrah al-Nisā and Sūrah al-Ṣaffāt.

CONTEMPLATE, COMPREHEND, APPLY

Contemplation Insights from page 208 [Yusus 1-6]

- Affirming the prophethood of the Prophet Muhammad (صَلَّى ٱللَّهُ عَلَيْهِ وَسَلَّمَ) and that his sending is reasonable and without cause for astonishment.
- Glad tidings for the people of faith and righteous deeds for what is prepared for them with their Lord. A lack of scruples among the disbelievers concerning lying and deception.
- The creation of the heavens and the earth and all within them, the management of affairs, the timing of the seasons, and the alteration of night and day are all significant signs indicating the divinity of Allah (سُبْحَانَهُۥ وَتَعَالَىٰ).
- Intercession on the Day of Resurrection will not occur except for those whom Allah permits and whose speech and action He approves. Do not seek intercession from the living or the dead in what Allah alone can do, but seek it from Him who grants intercession only with His permission.
- Allah's control of the sun's movement and the moon's phases help people regulate the calendar, days, and years.

Contemplation Insights from page 209 [Yunus 7-14]

- Forgetting the hereafter is the beginning of heedlessness. Whatever Allah decrees around you of events, news, and trials is a reminder for you, so beware of being heedless of them.
- Faith is one of the reasons for divine guidance; strive to increase your faith to gain more guidance from Allah.
- Allah's kindness to His servants in not answering their prayers for harm against themselves or their children.
- Illustrating the human condition of praying in hardship and turning away in ease, warning against embodying this behavior.
- The destruction of previous nations was due to their sins and injustice.

Contemplation Insights from page 210 [Yunus 15-20]

- Combining disobedience and a lack of fear of Allah are signs of a heart's illness. Continually remembering the hereafter protects a person from falling into sin
- Had this Qur'ān not been revealed to us, we would have been among the most ignorant of people; therefore, we must fulfill the rights of this great book
- The gravity of fabricating lies about Allah, altering His words as the Yahūd did with the Torah.
- Benefit and harm are in the hands of Allah alone, without anyone else.

- The falseness of the polytheists' claim that their gods intercede for them with Allah.
- Following desires and differing over religion is the cause of division.

Contemplation Insights from page 211 [Yunus 21-25]

- Improvement of conditions after hardship and constriction can lead to heedlessness and distance from Allah, except for those who remain cautious,
- Know that every act of tyranny and injustice you commit comes back to you, and its consequences return to you. Allah is swifter in plotting against those who plot against His believing servants.
- A person's injustice is ultimately against themselves and harms no one but themselves.
- The reality of this worldly life is highlighted by its fleeting nature and the temporariness of its pleasures.
- Paradise is the abode of the believer, offering eternal bliss and protection from misfortunes and worries.

Contemplation Insights from page 212 [Yunus 26-33]

- The most incredible bliss a believer aspires to is beholding the face of Allah (سُبْحَانَهُ وَتَعَالَى).
- The power of Allah is manifested, and He is capable of everything.
- Acknowledging Allah's Lordship while associating partners in worship is invalid; acknowledgment of Lordship and exclusivity in worship must be combined.
- If Allah decrees disbelief for a people due to their sins, they will not believe. Beware of transgression; it leads to levels of degradation, the lowest of which causes death in disbelief, Allah forbid.

Contemplation Insights from page 213 [Yunus 34-42]

- Allah alone, without any partners, guides us to success.
- The emphasis is on seeking evidence, proof, and guidance to reach knowledge and truth, abandoning illusions and assumptions.
- No one can produce a single verse like the noble Qur'ān until the Day of Judgment. Read the verses challenging the disbelievers and ponder their incapacity.
- The folly of the polytheists and their denial of what they do not understand or contemplate. One must verify matters and not hastily accept or reject something before fully understanding it.

Contemplation Insights from page 214 [Yunus 43-53]

- It is humans who lead themselves to their destruction; Allah is free from any injustice.
- Life is but an hour; make it fruitful with obedience.
- The messenger must convey the message while Allah takes care of their reckoning and punishment with His wisdom, which might be hastened during the messenger's life or postponed until after their death.
- Benefit and harm are in the hands of Allah (تَبَارَكَ وَتَعَالَىٰ); no one among the creation can bring harm or benefit to themselves or others. If the Messenger (صَلَّى ٱللَّهُ عَلَيْهِ وَسَلَّمَ), who is the noblest of creation, does not possess the ability to benefit or harm himself, then what about those below him?
- Faith will not benefit one at the sight of death.

Contemplation Insights from page 215 [Yunus 54-61]

- Whoever does not regret their sins and shortcomings today will face greater regret on the Day of Judgment. The magnitude of the punishment awaiting the polytheists with Allah is such that they would wish to ransom it with everything on earth, but it will not be accepted from them.
- To gauge your love for Allah, reflect: Is your joy greater with worldly possessions, knowledge, and righteousness? The Qur'ān is a healing for the believers from the diseases of desires and doubts, with its guidance and intellectual and transmitted proofs. The believer should rejoice in the blessing of Islam and faith more than any worldly gain.
- Allah meticulously observes His servants, their actions, thoughts, and intentions.
- Beware of speaking about Allah without knowledge, as it is a path to loss.

Contemplation Insights from page 216 [Yunus 62-70]

- Allah's guardianship is for those who believe in Him, comply with His commands, avoid His prohibitions, and follow His Messenger (صَلَّى ٱللَّهُ عَلَيْهِ وَسَلَّمَ). The allies of Allah will have no fear nor grief on the Day of Resurrection, and they receive glad tidings in this world through good visions or at the time of death.
- All might belong to Allah alone, and He is the sovereign; whatever is worshipped besides Allah holds no truth. If you face harm, aggression, and evil speech, do not grieve or be concerned; Allah will honor His religion and those obedient to Him.
- The encouragement to reflect on Allah's creation as it leads to faith in Him and His oneness.
- The prohibition of lying about Allah (تَبَارَكَ وَتَعَالَىٰ) and its perpetrator will not succeed, and among the greatest lies is attributing a child to Him.

Contemplation Insights from page 217 [Yunus 71-78]

- A believer's weapon against his enemies is trusting in Allah. Only Allah (تَبَارَكَ وَتَعَالَىٰ) can save a believer from the harm of creation, so seek refuge in Him alone.
- Persisting in disbelief and denying the messengers seals the hearts, making them never believe. Beware of rejecting the truth, for its rejection may seal your heart, leaving no path to repentance.
- The state of the messengers' enemies is the same; they always describe guidance as magic or a lie. False accusations are a method used by the people of falsehood, oppression, and corruption from ancient times to modern times.
- A sorcerer never succeeds.

Contemplation Insights from page 218 [Yunus 79-88]

- Corrupt deeds will vanish even if they seem strong, while righteous deeds remain, benefitting their doer and others.
- The youth are more inclined towards truth than others; do not neglect them in your call, no matter how much frivolity and playfulness are present among them (verse 83).
- Trusting in Allah, His victory, and relying on Him should be qualities of a firm believer. Relying on Allah (تَبَارَكَ وَتَعَالَىٰ) to bear the burden of calling to Allah (تَبَارَكَ وَتَعَالَىٰ) and obeying Him is obligatory.
- The importance of supplication and its association with those who rely on Allah.
- The significance of prayer and its mandatory status in all divine religions under all circumstances.
- The legitimacy of supplicating to Allah against the oppressor.

Contemplation Insights from page 219 [Yunus 89-97]

- It is obligatory to remain steadfast in faith and not follow the criminals' path.
- Repentance is not accepted from those who seek it at the moment of death or when facing punishment. Hasten to repentance; the end of its acceptance may come unexpectedly to you.
- The Jews and Christians were aware of the Prophet Muhammad's ﷺ characteristics, but pride and stubbornness prevented them from believing.

Contemplation Insights from page 220 [Yunus 98-106]

- Faith is the reason for elevating its holder to the highest ranks and enjoying life in this world.
- No one can force another to believe, as belief is subject to the will of Allah alone. Remember that guidance and faith are in the hands of Allah (تَبَارَكَ وَتَعَالَىٰ); had He willed, He would have made all people believers.

- Repentance is accepted before the punishment occurs, and the signs are witnessed. Signs and warnings do not benefit those who persist in disbelief and continue in it.
- It is obligatory to be steadfast in the true religion and to avoid polytheism and false religions altogether.

Contemplation Insights from page 221 [Yunus 107-109]

- The good and the bad, benefit and harm, are in the hands of Allah alone.
- It is mandatory to follow the Book and the Sunnah, be patient in the face of harm, and await Allah's relief.
- Be patient in obeying Allah and avoiding sins, for those who follow the revelation will face challenges, especially in times of trial.

CONTEMPLATION STUDY QUESTIONS

Verse 3: Why did Allah not create the heavens and the earth all at once? What are the two conditions required for intercession? *[Al-Sa'dī]*

Verse 5: What is the importance of contemplation and reflection on Allah's cosmic creations? *[Al-Sa'dī]*

Verse 8: Mention a sign of being content with worldly life. *[Ibn Kathīr]*

Verse 8: The verse mentioned an impediment that prevents benefiting from the Qur'ānic signs; what is it? *[Al-Sa'dī]*

Verse 9: What do we benefit from adding the gardens to bliss? *[Al-Sa'dī]*

Verse 10: We know that obligations are lifted from people on the Day of Judgment, so how do these acts of worship emanate from them? *[Al-Sa'dī]*

Verse 15: Speech benefits a person only if it is accompanied by honesty. Explain this from the verse. What is the reason for the disbelievers' obstinacy? *[Al-Sa'dī]*

Verse 16: What is meant by informing the Prophet's people that he had lived among them for a lifetime before his mission? *[Al-Sa'dī]*

Verse 20: Why did Allah not respond to the polytheists' requests for signs that prove Muhammad's truthfulness (ﷺ)? *[Al-Sa'dī]*

Verse 24: This verse discourages all sins and the pleasures of worldly life. Explain this. [Ibn Kathīr]

Verse 24: When does a person benefit from the Qur'ānic parables? *[Al-Sa'dī]*

Verse 25: Why is Paradise named the Abode of Peace? *[Al-Sa'dī]*

Verse 26: What is the relationship between this verse and the one before? How can a Muslim be among those who did well? Why did Allah specify that nothing of discomfort will affect the face in Paradise? *[Al-Sa'dī]*

Verse 28: Describe the great shock that idol worshippers, shrines, and grave worshippers will experience on the Day of Judgment when judgment is passed between them and what they worshipped. *[Al-Sa'dī]*

Verse 38: What is the relationship between mentioning the detailed explanation of the Book and ending the verse with the attribute of Lordship? *[Al-Sa'dī]*

Verse 39: How should a person deal with the news regarding belief and disbelief? *[Al-Sa'dī]*

Verse 42: Why did the polytheists not benefit from hearing the Qur'ān? *[Al-Sa'dī]*

Verse 42-43: What are the methods of acquiring knowledge? And how can one fully benefit from them in knowing the law of Allah? What is the importance of studying and teaching the prophetic biography? *[Al-Sa'dī]*

Verse 43: Why did Muslims benefit from observing the Prophet's condition and guidance, and why did the polytheists not benefit from it? *[Ibn Kathīr]*

Verse 45: How should one view worldly life in light of this verse? [Ibn Kathīr]

Verse 58: Why did Allah command to rejoice in His bounty and mercy? *[Al-Sa'dī]*

Verse 60: What are the forms of ingratitude for blessings? *[Al-Sa'dī]*

Verse 61: What is the purpose of informing Allah's servants about His knowledge of everything? *[Al-Sa'dī]*

Verse 64: Mention examples of good tidings for the believer in this life and the hereafter. What assures you that there will be no alteration to Allah's words?

Verse 75: Why is the story of Mūsā (عَلَيْهِ السَّلَامُ) with Pharaoh frequently repeated in the Qur'ān? *[Ibn Kathīr]*

Verse 78: The verse demonstrates a tactic used by the people of falsehood in dialogue. Explain it. *[Al-Sa'dī]*

Verse 81: What is the result of corrupt deeds? And what is the result of righteous deeds? *[Al-Sa'dī]*

Verse 83: What is the reason that most of those who believed in Mūsā were youths? *[Al-Sa'dī]*

Verse 88: What was the reason behind Mūsā's supplication against Pharaoh and his people? *[Al-Sa'dī]*

Verse 92: What causes most people not to benefit from Allah's signs despite their frequent exposure to them? *[Al-Sa'dī]*

Verse 94: What ailment has weakened this nation despite having the correct knowledge? *[Al-Sa'dī]*

Verse 98: Why does faith not benefit someone once punishment has come to them? What is the wisdom in specifying about the people of Yunus that their faith benefited them after the punishment? *[Al-Sa'dī]*

Verse 102: Explain Allah's Sunnah regarding those who do not believe in His signs in light of the verse. *[Al-Sa'dī]*

Verse 107: Through the verse, explain how to advise someone who clings to the creation and forgets the Creator. *[Al-Sa'dī]*

Day 11: Sūrah Hud

The Qur'ān reading for day 11 is Sūrah Hūd: A Cause of Both High Hopefulness and Unnerving Fear. Similar to Sūrah Yunus, Sūrah Hūd is said to have been revealed during the last year of the Makkan phase, in between the Isrā' and Mi'rāj (the night journey and heavenly ascension) and the *Hijrah.*

سُورَةُ هُودٍ
HŪD (11)
Hud

VERSES
123

WORDS
1,600

LETTERS
9,567

REVEALED IN
MAKKAH

REVEALATION ORDER
52

Main Themes: Strong exhortation to remain firm in conveying the message; stern rebuke of those who disbelieved and mistreated the Prophet (ﷺ); uprightness and well-balanced worship during adversity.[6] Another correlated and recurring theme of the Sūrah is the invitation to seek forgiveness and its importance for everyone.[7]

The main themes of the Sūrah are primarily an elaboration of what is mentioned in verse 12.

This Sūrah, following Sūrah Yunus, shares its meaning and subject, elaborating on what was summarized in its predecessor.

Both Sūrahs cover the fundamentals of faith, the miracle of the Qur'ān, discussions on resurrection, recompense, rewards, and punishments, with detailed stories of some prophets, highlighting the evident correlation between them.

[6] see verse 112-115.

[7] see verses 3, 52, 61 & 90.

Imām Al Biqā'ī (d. 885 AH رَحِمَهُ ٱللَّهُ) said:

"ومقصودها: وصف الكتاب بالإحكام والتفصيل، في حالتي البشارة والنذارة المقتضى لوضع كل شيء في أتم محاله وإنفاذه، مهما أريد، الموجب للقدرة على كل شيء.

"The purpose of the Sūrah is to describe the Qur'ān as being precise and detailed in both aspects of issuing glad tidings and warnings, necessitating the placement of everything in its most appropriate position and execution, as intended, requiring divine omnipotence over all things.

وأنسب ما فيها لهذاالمقصد ما ذكر في سياق قصة هو عليه السلام من أحكام البشارة والنذارة بالعاجل والآجل والتصريح بالجزم بالمعالجة بالمبادرة الناظر إلى أعظم مدارات السورة {فلعلك تارك بعض ما يوحى إليك} والعناية بكل دابة والقدرة على كل شيء من البعث وغيره المقتضي للعلم بكل معلوم اللازم منه التفرد بالملك".

Most relevant to this purpose is what is mentioned within the context of the story of Prophet Hud (عَلَيْهِ ٱلسَّلَامُ) of rulings on both immediate and future glad tidings and warnings, explicitly affirming the imminence of what they hastened, which looks to one of the greatest focuses of the Sūrah "Perhaps you would leave some of what is revealed to you…" It also emphasizes care for every creature and divine omnipotence in all things, including resurrection and beyond, necessitating knowledge of all that is known, which entails the uniqueness in possessing sovereignty."

The connection of this Sūrah to the previous one:

- This Sūrah encompasses the same core principles of Islam as found in Sūrah Yunus, namely monotheism (*Tawḥid*), prophecy, resurrection, judgment, and recompense. It elaborates on what was summarized in its predecessor, including stories of the prophets and peace be upon them.

- It aligns with the preceding Sūrah's opening and closing and the detailed discussion of the call to faith within it. Both begin with mentioning the Qur'ān following {*Alif Lam Ra*} and mention the Prophet's (صَلَّى ٱللَّهُ عَلَيْهِ وَسَلَّمَ) message, conveying from his Lord, clarifying that the Prophet's (صَلَّى ٱللَّهُ عَلَيْهِ وَسَلَّمَ) role is purely to give glad tidings and to warn.

- Throughout both Sūrahs, there's a challenge to produce something like the Qur'ān and responses to those who claimed that the Prophet (صَلَّى ٱللَّهُ عَلَيْهِ وَسَلَّمَ) fabricated it. Both argue with the polytheists about the fundamentals of faith and conclude by inviting people to what the Prophet (صَلَّى ٱللَّهُ عَلَيْهِ وَسَلَّمَ) brought forth. Then, they included a command for the Prophet (صَلَّى ٱللَّهُ عَلَيْهِ وَسَلَّمَ) to be patient until Allah decrees a judgment between him and the disbelievers, and in the second, to await this judgment from Allah (عَزَّ وَجَلَّ) while steadfastly worshipping and trusting in Him.

- In essence, each Sūrah summarizes what is detailed in the other, along with unique benefits exclusive to each. They agree on the subject matter for the most part but differ in composition and style, leaving no doubt that they are both from the words of the Merciful, who taught mankind eloquence.

The beginning of the Sūrah aligns with its end:

The Sūrah begins (in verse 2) with the command to worship Allah alone: "*That you not worship except Allah. Indeed, I am a warner and bringer of good tidings to you from Him.*"

It similarly concludes (in verse 123) with a command to worship: "*And to Allah belongs the unseen of the heavens and the earth, and to Him return all affairs, so worship Him and rely upon Him. And your Lord is not unaware of what you do.*" This elucidates the wisdom behind the creation of man, which is to worship Allah (عَزَّوَجَلَّ).

Some Distinct Features of Sūrah Hud:

- It includes one of the five challenge verses mentioned in the Qur'ān's miracle.
- It contains the longest story of Noah (عَلَيْهِ السَّلَامُ) in the Qur'ān, elaborating in a manner not found elsewhere.
- The name of Hud (عَلَيْهِ السَّلَامُ) is mentioned five times.
- The Prophet Muhammad (صَلَّى ٱللَّهُ عَلَيْهِ وَسَلَّمَ) said, "Hud has turned my hair gray."

When it was noticed that some of the Prophet's (صَلَّى ٱللَّهُ عَلَيْهِ وَسَلَّمَ) hair had become gray, Allah's Messenger (صَلَّى ٱللَّهُ عَلَيْهِ وَسَلَّمَ) said:

" شَيَّبَتْنِي {هُودٌ} ، وَ {الْوَاقِعَةُ} وَ {الْمُرْسَلَاتُ} ، وَ {عَمَّ يَتَسَاءَلُونَ} ، وَ {إِذَا الشَّمْسُ كُوِّرَتْ} "

"(Sūrah) Hūd and its likes from the *Mufaṣṣal* grey (my hair)." In another wording: "Hūd, as well as al Wāqi'ah, al Mursalāt, 'Ammā Yatasa'alūn (i.e., Sūrah al-Naba'), and Idhā-l-Shamsu Kuwwirat (i.e., Sūrah al-Takwīr), greyed me (i.e., my hair)."

Some scholars have said that the reason for the Prophet Muhammad's (صَلَّى ٱللَّهُ عَلَيْهِ وَسَلَّمَ) hair turning grey from the Sūrahs mentioned is due to their content concerning the Day of Judgment, resurrection, accounting, Paradise, Hell, and what happened to the previous nations. And Allah knows best the intentions of His Prophet (صَلَّى ٱللَّهُ عَلَيْهِ وَسَلَّمَ). Another plausible explanation of this is because the Prophet (صَلَّى ٱللَّهُ عَلَيْهِ وَسَلَّمَ) is addressed directly with a number of stern commandments for himself and then for his nation. Al Qurṭubī (d. 671 AH رَحِمَهُ ٱللَّهُ) says:

فَالْفَزَعُ يُورِثُ الشَّيْبَ وَذَلِكَ أَنَّ الْفَزَعَ يُذْهِلُ النَّفْسَ فَيُنَشِّفُ رُطُوبَةَ الْجَسَدِ، وَتَحْتَ كُلِّ شَعْرَةٍ مَنْبَعٌ، وَمِنْهُ يَعْرَقُ، فَإِذَا انْتَشَفَ الْفَزَعُ رُطُوبَتَهُ يَبِسَتِ الْمَنَابِعُ فَيَبِسَ الشَّعْرُ وَابْيَضَّ، كَمَا تَرَى الزَّرْعَ الْأَخْضَرَ بسقاية، فَإِذَا ذَهَبَ سِقَاؤُهُ يَبِسَ فَابْيَضَّ، وَإِنَّمَا يَبْيَضُّ شَعْرُ الشَّيْخِ لِذَهَابِ رُطُوبَتِهِ وَيُبْسِ جِلْدِهِ، فَالنَّفْسُ تَذْهَلُ بِوَعِيدِ اللَّهِ، وَأَهْوَالِ مَا جَاءَ بِهِ الْخَبَرُ عَنِ اللَّهِ، فَتَذْبُلُ، وَيُنَشِّفُ مَاءَهَا ذَلِكَ الْوَعِيدُ وَالْهَوْلُ الَّذِي جَاءَ بِهِ، فَمِنْهُ تَشِيبُ.

"Fear leads to greying of the hair because it bewilders the soul, drying out the body's moisture. Beneath each hair lies a source (i.e., follicle) from which it sweats. When fear dries up this moisture, the sources dry out, causing the hair to dry and turn white, just as green crops turn white when their watering ceases due to the loss of moisture and drying of their skin. The soul is confounded by the threat of Allah and the horrors reported from Allah, causing it to wither, and that threat and horror dry up its water, leading to greying.

وَقَالَ اللَّهُ تَعَالَى:" يَوْماً يَجْعَلُ الْوِلْدانَ شِيباً " [المزمل: 17] فَإِنَّمَا شَابُوا مِنَ الْفَزَعِ. وَأَمَّا سُورَةُ" هُود" فَلَمَّا ذَكَرَ الْأُمَمَ، وَمَا حَلَّ بِهِمْ مِنْ عَاجِلِ بَأْسِ اللَّهِ تَعَالَى، فَأَهْلُ الْيَقِينِ إِذَا تَلَوْهَا تَرَاءَى عَلَى قُلُوبِهِمْ مِنْ مُلْكِهِ وَسُلْطَانِهِ وَلَحَظَاتِهِ الْبَطْشُ بِأَعْدَائِهِ، فَلَوْ مَاتُوا مِنَ الْفَزَعِ لَحَقَّ لَهُمْ، وَلَكِنَّ اللَّهَ تَبَارَكَ وَتَعَالَى اسْمُهُ يَلْطُفُ بِهِمْ فِي تِلْكَ الْأَحَايِينِ حَتَّى يَقْرَءُوا كَلَامَهُ.

Allah (سُبْحَانَهُ وَتَعَالَى) said: "*On the day when it will turn children grey.*"[8] They turned grey due to fear. As for Sūrah "Hud," when it mentions the nations and the immediate punishment of Allah that befell them, the people of certainty, when they recite it, see in their hearts from His dominion, authority, and swift punishment of His enemies. Had they died from fear, it would have been justifiable. However, Allah (تَبَارَكَ وَتَعَالَى) is gentle with them in those moments so that they can recite His words."

Despite the Sūrah containing such cautions and warnings that gray one's hair, one of its constant themes is *al-tasliyah* (comforting) and *al-tathbīt* (reinforcing) in support of those who invite to Islam and those who adhere to it.

Sūrah Hūd comprises of three main sections:

[i.] The first twenty-four verses set the tone for the Sūrah. Its subject matter is an illustration of the predominant themes of all of the Makkan Suwar: Al-Tawḥīd (Allah's Oneness), Al-Risālah (the miracle of the Qur'an's revelation), and al Ba'th (Judgment Day).

Allah establishes these subjects by the usual method: (1.) reminding of simple logical proofs that appeal to sound human nature and (2.) contrasting the states of those who are receptive and responsive to the da'wah against those who were unreceptive and unresponsive.

The Sūrah begins by hinting at the challenge to produce something like the Qur'an, implied by the disjointed letters at its start. It highlights the Qur'an's significance, forbids worshipping anything besides Allah, and presents the Prophet Muhammad (صَلَّى ٱللَّهُ عَلَيْهِ وَسَلَّمَ) as a warner to the disbelievers of a great punishment and a bearer of good tidings of delightful enjoyment at a specified time for the believers.

[8] Al-Muzzammil: 17.

It affirms resurrection, Allah's knowledge of people's secret realities, Allah's governance over all living beings, the creation of all worlds from non-existence, and the ultimate return of people to Him for judgment and recompense.

It aims to reinforce the Prophet (صَلَّى ٱللَّهُ عَلَيْهِ وَسَلَّمَ), comfort him against what the disbelievers say, and refute their demands for signs according to their whims. It challenges them to produce something similar to the *Qur'ān* while emphasizing that it alone is sufficient proof of their failure, resulting in their loss in the Hereafter.

[ii.] The bulk of the Sūrah is its second section (verses 25-99), which builds on this initial foundation by mentioning in detail the stories of a number of the Prophets, namely, Nuḥ, Hūd, Ṣāliḥ, Ibrāhīm, Lūṭ, Shu'ayb, and Mūsā. The primary objectives of these stories are demonstrating the unified da'wah of the Messengers, providing comfort and solace to the Prophet ﷺ during a trying time of vulnerability, and issuing a stern warning to the disbelievers who had grown more obstinate in their opposition. These stories account for most of the Sūrah. It recounts the story of Islamic monotheism throughout history, from Noah to Muhammad (عَلَيْهِمُ ٱلسَّلَامُ) to affirm that it came with one truth that none other than Allah should be worshiped. It depicts how the Messengers encountered rejection, disbelief, mockery, harm, and threats with certainty, steadfastness, and patience. This serves as validation of Prophet Muhammad's prophethood (صَلَّى ٱللَّهُ عَلَيْهِ وَسَلَّمَ) and the truth of his call by narrating the stories of previous nations and the details of each story while exhibiting the most exemplary degree of noble character imaginable.

It contrasts the fates of the believers and disbelievers, mentions the predecessors from Noah's people, and details the consequences they faced, including 'Ad, Thamud, Ibrāhīm, the people of Lut, Madyan, and the message of Mūsā, highlighting the lessons and warnings in their stories. It shows that the polytheists' deities could not save them, emphasizing that these historical accounts are a lesson for those who follow their way and that the downfall of the misguided stems from their disregard for divine punishment in the afterlife, indicating that the Arab polytheists are headed towards the same fate.

This Sūrah uniquely details the flood event and seeks to comfort the Prophet Muhammad (صَلَّى ٱللَّهُ عَلَيْهِ وَسَلَّمَ) by referring to the dissent among Mūsā's people regarding the Torah, advising the Prophet and his followers to remain steadfast in their divine mission, not to lean towards the disbelievers, and to persist in prayer, patience, and calling towards righteousness, for there is no destruction with righteousness. It includes moral lessons, encourages establishing prayer, and provides warnings and insights, emphasizing the importance of steadfastness and the futility of opposing divine guidance. The version of the story of Nuḥ in Sūrah Hūd is the longest in the Qur'ān, even longer than that of Sūrah Nuḥ.

This Sūrah shows that the Prophets were mocked for having few followers and supporters. Abu Hurayrah reported from the Prophet (ﷺ) that He said about the statement of Lūṭ (conveyed by Allah in Sūrah Hūd, verse 80):

{لَوْ أَنَّ لِي بِكُمْ قُوَّةً أَوْ آوِي إِلَى رُكْنٍ شَدِيدٍ}

"If I only had strength to deal with you or had a strong pillar to resort to." He said:

" كَانَ يَأْوِي إِلَى رُكْنٍ شَدِيدٍ إِلَى رَبِّهِ عَزَّ وَجَلَّ "

"He did resort to a strong rukn (i.e., source of support); (he resorted) to his Lord."

Then the Prophet ﷺ said:

" فَمَا بَعَثَ اللهُ بَعْدَهُ نَبِيًّا إِلَّا فِي ثَرْوَةٍ مِنْ قَوْمِهِ "

"So Allah did not send a Prophet after Lūṭ except amongst a tharwah of his people."

The narrator, Muḥammad bin 'Umar, said: "Tharwah means a large number of people and protection." Ibn Qutaybah said: "Al-Tharwah is having numerical support and might by way of one's kinfolk."

The context of the stories in the Sūrah was fully explained in its first two verses: the call to tawḥīd, glad tidings for the believers, and warning for the disbelievers. A recurring theme of the Prophets' call was: "Have taqwā of Allah and obey me." The story of Nūḥ begins with this exact statement (verses 25-26), as do those of Hūd (verse 50), Ṣāliḥ (verse 61), and Shu'ayb (verse 84). After these stories, the Sūrah mentions the divine retribution against the disbelievers (verse 102).

[iii.] The third section of Sūrah Hūd (verses 100-123) is its conclusion. These verses contain essential advice to the Prophet (ﷺ) and his nation after him when facing tough challenges and harsh circumstances. These directives are found in verses 112-115 and are, in summary, steadfastness, avoiding tyranny, being mindful of Allah's watchfulness, not inclining to the oppressors, maintaining prayer, and patience. By steadfastness and staying the course, one does not falter and lose hope. By not transgressing, one does not resort to recklessness or unsanctioned violence. By not inclining towards the oppressors, one is not enamored by their wealth or status and does not imitate their evil customs.

CONTEMPLATE, COMPREHEND, APPLY

Contemplation Insights from Page 221 [Hud 1-5]

- An aspect of the Qur'ān's miraculous nature is that found in the disjointed letters that open many Sūrahs, and the Arabs could not produce a Sūrah like it, "Alif, Lam, Ra. [This is] a Book whose verses are perfected and then presented in detail from [One who is] All-Wise and Ever-Acquainted."
- The verses of the Qur'ān are precise, without defect or falsehood, and the rulings within them have been detailed completely.
- It is necessary to hasten to repentance and regret sins to achieve the desired and escape from the feared.

Contemplation Insights from Page 222 [Hud 6-12]

- The vastness of Allah's knowledge and His provision for the sustenance of His creations, including humans, animals, and others.
- Clarification of the purpose of creation is to test the servants through compliance with Allah's commands and avoidance of His prohibitions.
- The importance of not being deceived by Allah's respite towards those who disobey Him, as He may seize them suddenly when they least expect it.
- Explanation of the human condition in times of ease and hardship and the commendation of the believer's stance, characterized by patience and gratitude.
- In the sight of his Lord, a servant is valued by his good deeds, not wealth.

Contemplation Insights from Page 223 [Hud 13-19]

- Allah's challenge to the polytheists to produce ten Sūrahs, like that of the Qur'ān, out demonstrates their inability to do so.
- If a disbeliever is given what he desires from this world, nothing awaits him in the Hereafter but the Fire.
- The great injustice of fabricating lies about Allah and the severe punishment for it on the Day of Resurrection.

- Avoid delving into speaking about the religion without knowledge, for it reaches the extent of lying about Allah.

Contemplation Insights from Page 224 [Hud 20-28]

- The disbeliever does not benefit from his hearing and sight in a way that leads to faith, as if these senses were non-existent for him, unlike the believer.
- Allah's norm with the followers of the messengers is that they are often selected from the poor and the weak due to their absence of arrogance, in contrast to their opponents, who are the nobles and leaders. Do not scorn anyone in your call due to their social or material status.
- The arrogance of the nobles and leaders and their contempt for those beneath them are often evident. Pay more attention to guiding the influential, for they can lead to the guidance of their followers. Misguiding others is a reason for the multiplication of punishment; beware of leading others to disobedience.

Contemplation Insights from Page 225 [Hud 29-37]

- The contentment of the caller to Allah and the fact that he seeks reward from Him alone.
- The prohibition of expelling the poor believers and the obligation to honor and respect them. The call to Allah has principles and constants that cannot be compromised, no matter how lenient we are with our opponents.
- Among the causes of victory, provision, and protection is caring for the weak; even prophets, if they wronged the weak, would not be safe from Allah's punishment.
- Allah alone knows the unseen.
- The legitimacy of arguing and debating with the disbelievers.
- No one can avert or remove it when punishment descends on denying nations.

Contemplation Insights from Page 226 [Hud 38-45]

- Illustration of the polytheists' habit of mocking and ridiculing the prophets and their followers.
- Allah's norm among people is that most do not believe. Do not be saddened if few heed your advice or if many oppose you; for the prophets before you spent their long lives in calling [to Allah], and only a few believed.

- There is no refuge from Allah except to Him, and no one can prevent His decree except Him (سُبْحَانَهُ وَتَعَالَى). Kinship and lineage do not benefit those who do not believe in Allah. No matter how great worldly means may seem, they do not benefit the disobedient when Allah intends to punish him.

Contemplation Insights from Page 227 [Hud 46-53]

- Prophets do not have the power to intercede for those who disbelieve in Allah, even if they are their children. Do not be saddened if Allah does not answer some of your worldly requests; withholding them might be better for you.
- The contentment of the caller to Allah and his disinterest in what people possess are closer to acceptance.
- The virtue of seeking forgiveness and repentance is that they are reasons for the rain to be sent down and for the increase in offspring and wealth.
- 2. Patience and piety are the reasons for victory over those who have wronged you; Allah's promise usually comes at the end of matters after the test and trial are realized.

Contemplation Insights from Page 228 [Hud 54-62]

- One of the methods of the polytheists in deterring people from the messengers is accusing them of being foolish or insane.
- The weakness of the polytheists is in their plotting and enmity, as they are subdued and overpowered under Allah's command and authority.
- Signs of Lordship from creation and inception necessitate exclusivity in worship and the abandonment of everything other than Allah therein.
- Trusting in Allah instills courage in the believer's heart and is the reason for success in this life and the hereafter.
- Arrogance and stubbornness are among the worst character traits in humans.

Contemplation Insights from Page 229 [Hud 63-71]

- The stubbornness and arrogance of the polytheists, as they did not believe in the sign of Prophet Salih, were among the greatest signs.
- The desirability of giving glad tidings to the believer of what is better for him.

- The legitimacy of greeting someone when entering upon them, and the obligation to respond.
- The obligation to honor the guest.
- The caller to Allah should be clear about what he is calling to; this is by verifying issues before speaking about them.
- The believer knows that the good he experiences through guidance, righteousness, and piety is a favor and mercy from Allah.
- The one who invites you to disobedience will not be able to avert Allah's punishment from you, so adhere to obeying Allah.

Contemplation Insights from Page 230 [Hud 72-81]

- The virtue and status of Allah's friend, Ibrāhīm, and his family.
- The legitimacy of arguing on behalf of someone who hoped to have faith before being taken to the ruler.
- The heinousness and ugliness of the actions of the people of Lut.
- When Allah's decree comes, no one can repel it.
- If the friend of the Merciful was abundant in repentance and turning back to Allah, what about us who fall short in repentance and turning back?
- Do not despair of having righteous offspring.

Contemplation Insights from Page 231 [Hud 82-88]

- Among Allah's norms is the destruction of the wrongdoers with the severest and most dreadful punishments. Major sins are not all the same; some incur more severe punishment than others.
- The prohibition of shortening measures and weights and depriving people of their rights states that a small lawful profit is better and more blessed than a large unlawful one.
- The necessity of being content with what is lawful, even if it is little.
- The virtue of enjoining what is right and forbidding what is wrong, and the obligation to act according to what Allah commands and to abstain from what He prohibits.

Contemplation Insights from Page 232 [Hud 89-97]

- Condemnation of the ignorant who do not understand what the prophets brought from the signs.
- Denunciation and folly of those occupied with people's orders, turning away from Allah's commands.
- The role of kinship in supporting the call and the callers.
- The expulsion of the polytheists from Allah's mercy.
- The intensification of crises signals the approach to their resolution.
- Despite his ignorance and tyranny, Pharaoh's followers' example demonstrates the severity of the trial of following the wrong leaders; let correct evidence lead you, not merely the words of men.

Contemplation Insights from Page 233 [Hud 98-108]

- Warning against following leaders of evil and corruption and explaining the misfortune of their followers in both worlds. The reward is the same as the deed; as a tyrant leads his people in falsehood, he will precede them to the punishment on the Day of Judgment.
- Allah is exalted above any injustice in the destruction of the people of shirk (polytheism) and sins. Qur'ānic stories are not for entertainment but for remembrance and warning.
- The deities of the polytheists will not benefit their worshipers on the Day of Judgment, nor will they repel the punishment.
- The division of people on the Day of Judgment into one happy, eternally dwelling in paradise, and one wretched, eternally dwelling in the fire.

Contemplation Insights from Page 234 [Hud 109-117]

- The obligation of steadfastness in the religion of Allah. A person is not considered steadfast in Islam until his actions align with what is prescribed in the Qur'ān and Sunnah, distancing himself from his desires.
- Avoid injustice and the unjust as much as possible. This warns against leaning towards the unjust disbelievers, whether through compromise or affection.
- Clarification of Allah's ruling that good deeds erase bad deeds.

- Encouragement to have a community of virtuous individuals who enjoin what is right forbid corruption and evil, and they are a protection from Allah's punishment.
- Among the causes of deviation is indulgence in luxury and ease.

Contemplation Insights from Page 235 [Hud 118-123]

- The vastness of Allah's knowledge and His provision for the sustenance of His creations, including humans, animals, and others.
- Clarification of the purpose of creation, which is to test the servants through compliance with Allah's commands and avoidance of His prohibitions.
- The importance of not being deceived by Allah's respite towards those who disobey Him, as He may seize them suddenly when they least expect it.
- Explanation of the human condition in times of ease and hardship and the commendation of the believer's stance, characterized by patience and gratitude.
- 1. Avoid places of dispute and division, and aim to unite with the believers and the righteous on the Sunnah and the community, "And they will continue to differ, except those upon whom your Lord has mercy."

CONTEMPLATION STUDY QUESTIONS

Verse **1**: What can be inferred from the Book being sent down from the All-Wise, the All-Aware? [*As-Sa'di*]

Verse **7**: What is the difference between "doing more work" and "doing better work"? And why was the latter formulation chosen? [*As-Sa'di*]

Verse **12**: This verse benefits the people of Da'wah (Islamic calling). Can you explain it? [*As-Sa'di*]

Verse **13**: Why can no one produce the likes of this Qur'ān?

Verse **14**: What does the expression "know that" indicate? [*As-Sa'di*]

Verse **15**: How can it be deduced that this verse is specifically about the polytheists? [*As-Sa'di*]

Verse **29**: The caller to Allah has no right to exclude the poor from his call; explain this. [*As-Sa'di*]

Verse **40**: Why did Allah command Noah to carry on the ark a pair of every kind? [*As-Sa'di*]

Verse **43**: In times of hardship, do we rely on the means or the Cause, who is Allah?

Verse **46**: Islam and faith are conditions for relatives to benefit from each other. In the Hereafter, explain this. [*Ibn Kathir*]

Verse **46**: A person may pray for something, and it is better not to be answered; explain this through the verse. [*As-Sa'di*]

Verse **48**: What are the causes of salvation from loss in the Hereafter? [*As-Sa'di*]

Verse **49**: Allah blessed the offspring of those with Noah on the ark; what is the manifestation of this blessing? [*As-Sa'di*]

Verse **61**: Why did Allah pair His name "the Near" with "the Responder"? [*As-Sa'di*]

Verse **62**: The scholar and the caller combine religion and good character, which is explained through this verse. [*As-Sa'di*]

Verse **69**: What do we benefit from the angels starting with the greeting of peace? [*As-Sa'di*]

Verse **71**: Why was Sara happy and laughed at the news of the angels? [*Ibn Kathir*]

Verse **73**: Why should not the wife of Ibrāhīm be astonished by the decree of Allah? [*As-Sa'di*]

Verse **75**: What are the most notable qualities of Ibrāhīm that we should follow? [*As-Sa'di*]

Verse **83**: A purpose of prayer is mentioned in the verse; clarify it. [*As-Sa'di*]

Verse **88**: Why, after informing them that he wanted to make reforms, did he follow it with: "And my success is not but through Allah"? [*As-Sa'di*]

Verse **89**: In this verse, there's a method of preaching followed by Shu'ayb with his people; what is it? [*As-Sa'di*]

Verse **91**: Why did Shu'ayb's people not understand his words? Is it permissible for a Muslim to pursue worldly means that protect their religion? [*As-Sa'di*]

Verse **94**: Allah mentioned three characteristics of Shu'ayb's people's punishment; how do you reconcile these verses? [*Ibn Kathir*]

Verse **97**: Why were Pharaoh's elite and the nobles of his people specifically mentioned, although Mūsā was sent to all the people?

Verse **98**: Why is Pharaoh leading his people on the Day of Resurrection? [*Ibn Kathir*]

Verse **101**: What is the state of those who seek refuge in others than Allah? [*As-Sa'di*]

Verse **106**: What is meant by describing the state of the people of Hell as having "zafir" (sighing) and "shahiq" (intense breathing)?

Verse **110**: The skeptics of the Qur'ān are likened to the Jews; explain this through the verse. [*As-Sa'di*]

Verse **112**: What is the reason for mentioning the command to remain steadfast after mentioning those who oppose and are hostile to the Prophet? [*Ibn Kathir*]

Verse **113**: This verse contains a severe threat to the oppressors; how can we deduce that? [*As-Sa'di*]

Day 12: Yusuf & al-Ra'd

The Qur'ān reading for day twelve is Sūrah Yūsuf and Sūrah al-Ra'd.

سُورَةُ يُوسُفَ
YUSUF (12)
Joseph

VERSES
110

WORDS
1,996

LETTERS
7,176

REVEALED IN
MAKKAH

REVEALATION ORDER
53

Main Theme of the Sūrah: The outcome of patience following the example of prophets like Yaqūb and Yūsuf, peace be upon them, during trials and their eventual victorious outcomes. It promises empowerment after a manifest trial as a confirmation and promise to the Prophet Muhammad (ﷺ) and the believers.

Al-Biqā'i (d. 885 AH رَحِمَهُ ٱللَّهُ) said:

"ومقصودها: وصف الكتاب بالإبانة لكل ما يوجب الهدى لما ثبت فيما مضى ويأتي في هذه السورة من تمام علم منزله غيباً وشهادة، وشمول قدرته قولاً وفعلاً.

"Its purpose is to describe the book as clarifying everything that necessitates guidance, proven in what has passed and will be mentioned in this Sūrah from the perfection of knowledge revealed both unseen and witnessed, and the encompassment of His power in word and deed.

وهذه القصة كما ترى أنسب الأشياء لهذا المقصود، وأدل عليه مما في آخرها، فلذلك سميت سورة يوسف".

As you see, this story is the most suitable for this purpose and more indicative of it than what is mentioned at its end. Therefore, it is named Sūrah Yūsuf."

Distinctive Features of Sūrah Yūsuf:

- It uniquely contains the story of Prophet Yūsuf (ﷺ).
- The name of Yūsuf (عَلَيْهِ ٱلسَّلَامُ) is mentioned 25 times.
- It consists of the longest story in the Qur'ān, spanning over 97 verses.

- Neither Paradise nor Hell is mentioned in it.
- Umar ibn Al-Khattab (رَضِيَ ٱللَّهُ عَنْهُ) used to recite it in the Fajr prayer.

It's connection to the previous Sūrah: as both Sūrahs delve into the stories of prophets, this Sūrah includes the story of Yūsuf with the finest arrangement, most precise expression, and most remarkable description. Throughout its narration, it supports the Messenger in his major cause, as he knew nothing about Yūsuf, drawing the world's attention to the universe and its signs and lessons, to the instincts within humans like the love for offspring, jealousy and envy among brothers, deceit and trickery by some, and the ensuing regret, referring to the then Egyptian society. All this with a strong style, eloquent expression, and precise depiction.

The opening of this Sūrah is similar to the opening of Sūrah Hud, namely the letters *{Alif Lam Ra}*, except that the Qur'ān here is described as 'clear,' and in Hud, its verses are described as 'precise and detailed.' This is because the place of this Sūrah is a story of a prophet who experienced the vicissitudes of time, between misfortune and fortune, all of which were good examples. The subject of Sūrah Hud was the fundamentals of religion and the affirmation of revelation, prophecy, resurrection, and recompense, along with the varied stories of prophets, so it was described with wisdom. And as for the end, Sūrah Hud concluded with {And each [story] We relate to you from the news of the messengers}, and this began with {We relate to you, [O Muhammad], the best of stories}.

Correlation Between the Beginning and the End of the Sūrah:

It starts with: "We relate to you, [O Muhammad], the best of stories." It concludes with: "There was certainly in their stories a lesson for those of understanding ...". This is to clarify that Allah narrates stories only for the sake of benefit, lesson, and wisdom and that His stories are the truth.

Some of the Most Important Lessons of Sūrah Yūsuf:

Affirming the prophethood of Prophet Muhammad (صَلَّى ٱللَّهُ عَلَيْهِ وَسَلَّمَ) and the truth of his call by revealing the details of the stories of those before him. This story served as consolation to the Prophet Muhammad (صَلَّى ٱللَّهُ عَلَيْهِ وَسَلَّمَ) through the hardships Yaqūb and Yūsuf, peace be upon them, faced from their people. The Prophet Muhammad (صَلَّى ٱللَّهُ عَلَيْهِ وَسَلَّمَ) suffered less from the enmity of other disbelievers than he did from his kinfolk, such as his uncle Abu Lahab, Nadir bin Harith, and Abu Sufyan bin Harith bin Abdul Muttalib, though the latter embraced Islam later and was true to his Islam (رَضِيَ ٱللَّهُ عَنْهُ). Such harm from relatives is more dangerous than the abuse of strangers.

Nadir bin Harith and others misled Quraysh by claiming that the Qur'ānic stories about nations were ancient myths Muhammad had written down. Nadir frequented Hira, learning the tales of the military heroes of Persia, and narrated them to Quraysh, enchanting them with his style, claiming to tell better stories than Muhammad and that what the Qur'ān narrated was no different than ancient tales. How these stories were dramatically narrated misled them into thinking they were more satisfying to the listener. Thus, this Sūrah came in a storytelling style challenging them to compete, despite summarizing much of the story from anything not significantly impactful for the lesson. Although it omits parts not crucial for its lessons, it conveys facts about the history and culture of ancient civilizations, their laws, government systems, punishments, commerce, the enslavement of foundlings, the enslavement of thieves, prison conditions, and the monitoring of granaries.

Yūsuf's (عَلَيْهِ ٱلسَّلَامُ) story is recited day and night. It is an eternal testament to his (عَلَيْهِ ٱلسَّلَامُ) patience, tolerance, honesty, justice, wisdom, knowledge, forgiveness, and kindness. It contains lessons for all segments of society, leaders and subjects, male and female, young and old. This Sūrah is a great honor for him, a clear sign of his infallibility, and a practical example for all to emulate.

A core lesson of this story is showing the horrible outcome of envy, that it is purely evil. In the story's beginning, Yaqūb warned Yūsuf of his brothers' potential envy and plotting. Much later, Yaqūb's (عَلَيْهِ ٱلسَّلَامُ) strong reliance on Allah did not prevent him from taking the proper safeguards, as he feared envy for his sons and said, "Do not enter through one gate but enter through different gates."

Another essential lesson from this Sūrah is the praiseworthy outcome of chastity. Yūsuf the Truthful (عَلَيْهِ ٱلسَّلَامُ) is a perfect example of his chastity, exemplifying the highest ideals of purity and self-guarding that no person can achieve except through sincerity and true faith, being mindful of Allah's ever-watchfulness over all matters, private and public. It presents the best role model, narrating the story of a young man, the most beautiful in form and perfect in build, alone with a woman of position and authority, his female master, and he her slave; she is so captivated by his beauty that she debases herself to him and betrays her husband, soliciting him. Normally, women are sought, not the seekers. Despite his youth, he hears her enticement. He wisely refrains, retaining his purity and showing the best example of sincerity for Allah, preserving the trust of his master who had treated him well, saying, "*Indeed, he is my master who has made my residence comfortable. Indeed, the wrongdoers do not succeed.*"

Another main lesson is the outcome of patience (Ya'qūb and Yūsuf) and the outcome of lying and scheming (the brothers of Yūsuf, the wife of the 'Aziz). Suffice it as evidence of his patience that his brothers envied him and threw him into the depths of the well. He was then found by a caravan, sold as a slave, schemed against by 'Azīz's wife, and then thrown into prison. He remained patient against his brothers' harm, the wife's scheme, and the other women's conspiracy because he knew the corruption of indecency and the benefits and advantages of justice and kindness, preferring the higher over the lower, choosing imprisonment in this world over sinning. Ultimately, Allah saved him, elevated his status, humiliated the 'Aziz and his wife, the women admitted his innocence, Allah empowered him on the earth, and his end was victory, sovereignty, governance, and the ultimate success is for the God-fearing, as Allah says, "*And thus We established Yūsuf in the land, to settle therein wherever he wished. We touch with Our mercy whom We will, and We do not allow the reward of the good-doers to be lost (56). And surely, the reward of the Hereafter is better for those who believed and feared Allah (57).*"

This Sūrah also highlights the merit of dream interpretation and that a disbeliever may have dreams interpreted (the 'Aziz of Egypt, the young men in prison). It establishes that some visions may foretell future events, a foundation of prophecy and part of ancient wisdom. Dream interpretation is a knowledge bestowed by Allah to whom He wills of His righteous servants. It discusses the envy that exists among relatives. It highlights Allah's subtle mercy towards His chosen servants. Note that Yūsuf (عَلَيْهِ ٱلسَّلَامُ) used the talent Allah bestowed upon him to interpret dreams to invite to Allah, not for worldly gains. This story highlights the merit of knowledge in general since Yūsuf (صَلَّى ٱللَّهُ عَلَيْهِ وَسَلَّمَ) combined the knowledge of Yaqūb's law and how to manage governmental matters.

This story reminds us that trials are ongoing occurrences, predestined by Allah for subtle wisdom. This story highlights the danger of despair and losing hope in Allah's mercy in many obvious ways. For example, as the trials increased on Yaqūb (عَلَيْهِ ٱلسَّلَامُ), especially after being informed about the loss of Benyamin, his good thoughts about his Lord and his certainty in the nearness of relief increased, saying, "*It may be that Allah will bring them to me altogether.*" "*Allah is dominant over His affair,*" regardless of what the creatures intend.

The story also highlights the virtues of forgiveness and benevolence, characteristic of the righteous. It shows that it is often easier to ask for forgiveness from the young than from the elders: Yūsuf, when his brothers asked him to forgive them, said, "No blame upon you today," and when they asked Yaqūb, he said, "I will ask forgiveness for you from my Lord."

Additionally, the mention of benevolence (*ihsān*) and its derivatives recur several times throughout the Sūrah in which Yūsuf went above and beyond what was asked of him: (1.) Yūsuf invited the two young men in prison to worship Allah alone and did not limit himself to interpreting the dreams {37-41}. (2.) He did not just interpret the dream of the 'Aziz of

Egypt but added something from himself (verse 49). (3.) He did not blame his brothers or take them to task but forgave and pardoned them (verse 92). This indicates that benevolence is one of the best moral virtues, elevating its bearer to the ranks of faith, elevating his soul and spirit, and ensuring happiness never leaves him.

His justice, honesty, knowledge, and wisdom were manifested when he took charge in Egypt during the seven lean years that consumed the crops and offspring. His wisdom, justice among people, treating them equally, and steering them on the straight path without deviation or inclination towards desires spared the country from famine and certain destruction.

BRIEF SŪRAH SUMMARY

I.	The jealousy and plotting of his brothers who cast him into a well and sold him as a slave to a trade caravan.
II.	The plotting of 'Aziz's wife to seduce him and that becoming common knowledge amongst the local women. His ultimate imprisonment and preferring that to the *fitnah* of the women.
III.	Yūsuf's interpretation of dreams while imprisoned and his inviting of the prisoners to making worship sincere for Allah without partners. His gift of dream interpretation became a means to leave prison and to be exonerated, after which he was made the treasurer of the land.
IV.	The four times that Yūsuf met his brothers, leading to being reunited with his father and making amends with his brothers.
V.	A concluding passage full of important lessons and directives.

CONTEMPLATE, COMPREHEND, APPLY

Contemplation Insights from Page 235 [Yūsuf 1-4]

- Explaining the wisdom behind the Qur'ānic stories, which affirm the heart of the Prophet Muhammad ﷺ and admonish the believers.
- The exclusivity of Allah in knowing the unseen, with no one sharing in this knowledge.
- The wisdom behind revealing the Qur'ān in Arabic is that the Arabs should understand it to convey it to others.
- The Qur'ān contains the best of stories. One does not benefit from the Noble Qur'ān without listening attentively and desiring to benefit, "Indeed, We have sent it down as an Arabic Qur'ān that you might understand."
- Narrating meaningful stories is an effective educational and pedagogical method, "We relate to you the best of stories."

Contemplation Insights from Page 236 [Yūsuf 5-14]

- The affirmation of visions (dreams) in Sharia and the permissibility of their interpretation.
- There is legitimacy in concealing some truths if revealing them leads to harm. It is especially wise to conceal matters from those likely to be envious.
- Explaining the virtue of the lineage of Ibrāhīm and their selection over people with prophecy.
- Favoritism towards one of the children in love leads to enmity and envy among siblings.
- Jealousy is natural, but if a person surrenders to it, Shayṭān uses it to lead the person to envy and then to crime.
- No one is to be blamed for loving their child.

Contemplation Insights from Page 237 [Yūsuf 15-22]

- Demonstrating the danger of envy, which led Yūsuf's brothers to plot against him and conspire to kill him.
- The legitimacy of basing judgments on circumstantial evidence.
- Faith in predestination instills patience during calamities.

- From Allah's planning for Yūsuf and His kindness to him, the heart of the Aziz of Egypt was inclined with fatherly affection after Shayṭān had veiled brotherly affection from his brothers.
- Excellence in worship leads to Allah's preservation, support, and empowerment.

Contemplation Insights from Page 238 [Yūsuf 23-30]

- The horror of betraying a benefactor in their family and wealth, which Yūsuf mentioned among the reasons for rejecting immorality.
- This explains the prophets' infallibility and Allah's protection of them from falling into evil and indecency. Keeping Allah's attributes in mind is a barrier between a servant and falling into sin. Know Allah in times of ease by obeying Him and turning to Him so He knows and preserves you in times of hardship.
- The obligation to resist indecency, flee from it, and free oneself from it. The consequences of adultery and immorality are disappointment, loss, and public disgrace.
- The legitimacy of basing judgments on circumstantial evidence.

Contemplation Insights from Page 239 [Yūsuf 31-37]

- Demonstrating the beauty of Yūsuf (عَلَيْهِ السَّلَامُ), which was the reason for the women's infatuation with him.
- Yūsuf's preference for prison over disobeying Allah. Worldly suffering and hardship are better than fleeting pleasure followed by eternal punishment.
- From Allah's planning for Yūsuf (عَلَيْهِ السَّلَامُ) and His kindness towards him was teaching him the interpretation of dreams and making it a reason for his exit from the ordeal of prison.
- Ignorance is not in the lack of information but rather in the abundance of engaging in sins.

Contemplation Insights from Page 240 [Yūsuf 38-43]

- The obligation to follow the religion of Ibrāhīm and to disassociate from polytheism and its people.
- Utilizing opportunities to call towards Allah, as Yūsuf (عَلَيْهِ السَّلَامُ) did in prison. The caller to Allah should be gentle with those he calls, not making them feel inferior or despised.
- His statement, "Are many lords better or Allah, the One, the Prevailing?" proves that these Egyptians were followers of a heavenly religion but were people of polytheism.

- All deities worshipped besides Allah are merely names without any real entity; they have no share in the divinity and worthiness of worship.
- Seek refuge in Allah from the plots of Satan; he is keen to make you forget your religious and worldly needs, "But Shayṭān made him forget the mention of his Lord, so he stayed in prison for some years."

Contemplation Insights from Page 241 [Yūsuf 44-52]

- Part of Yūsuf's excellent manners was his reference to the women's incident without specifically mentioning Aziz's wife.
- Yūsuf's (عَلَيْهِ السَّلَامُ) excellence in interpreting dreams.
- The legitimacy of exonerating oneself from falsely attributed accusations and pursuing fact-finding to establish the truth. Truth must prevail eventually.
- The virtue of honesty and speaking the truth, even if it is against oneself. The outcome of righteousness is good, while the consequence of sins and immorality is disgrace.
- The value and nobility of knowledge; for it, the king elevated Yūsuf to his royal court.

Contemplation Insights from Page 242 [Yūsuf 53-63]

- Among the believer's enemies is his soul, which is inclined toward evil; thus, monitoring and straightening its wrongs is obligatory. Admitting one's sins is one of the causes for their forgiveness and is a sign of sincere repentance and turning back to Allah.
- Knowledge and trustworthiness are required of those undertaking a position that can reform public affairs. It is necessary to be fair to the wronged, support them, and bring the truth and trustworthiness closer, even if they are weak or foreign.
- What is in the Hereafter from Allah's favor is indeed better, more lasting, and superior for the people of faith.
- It is permissible for a man to seek a position, praise himself if needed, and intend for goodness and reform.
- With patience comes dignity after humiliation and injustice.

Contemplation Insights from Page 243 [Yūsuf 64-69]

- The command to take precautions and be wary of those from whom betrayal is feared: a believer should not be bitten from the same hole twice.

- Among the means of caution is ensuring by taking reinforced oaths and permitting the swearing of oaths by those feared for safeguarding deposits and trusts.
- It is permissible for the one demanding an oath to make exceptions for matters he believes are beyond the oath-taker's capacity.
- Taking precautions from potential harm is part of adopting means. The wise person is wary of the evil eye and envy and acts upon the means without exaggeration.
- Strive to take the means, but do not rely on them; depend on Allah, for to Him belong all matters.
- Obey and consult your parents, seek their permission, for good lies in what they command.

Contemplation Insights from Page 244 [Yūsuf 70-78]

- The permissibility of stratagems to establish justice, provided they do not harm others.
- It is permissible for the owner of a lost or needed item to set a reward for whoever assists in its recovery, specifying its amount and nature.
- Overlooking harm and keeping grievances private is a noble character trait.
- Demonstrating Allah's excellent management of His allies.
- When Allah loves a servant, He grants him understanding and knowledge.
- Knowing that Allah is aware of His servants, their plots, and what they describe eases the impact of people's words and makes one take pride in and rely on Allah (عَزَّوَجَلَّ).

Contemplation Insights from Page 245 [Yūsuf 79-86]

- Punishing an innocent person for another's crime is not permissible, so another person cannot be substituted for the criminal.
- Beautiful patience is that in which a complaint is made to Allah alone.
- A believer must have complete certainty that Allah will relieve his hardship.
- Turn to Allah first before turning to others, especially in times of hardship, "Perhaps Allah will bring them all to me."
- Crying or feeling sad in the face of calamities does not contradict certainty and steadfastness. Love and longing for a child is not contrary to faith, nor is it a flaw or deficiency in men, but it may be a test.

Contemplation Insights from Page 246 [Yūsuf 87-95]

- In his good thoughts, the greatness of Yaqūb's knowledge of Allah did not change despite the succession of calamities and the passing of years. Never despair of Allah's mercy and forgiveness for your sins; Allah is Merciful and Generous.
- It is characteristic of a sincere repenter to seek forgiveness from Allah, to admit their fault, and to ask for pardon from those harmed.
- One attains the greatest levels through piety and patience in this life and the hereafter.
- Accepting an offender's apology and refraining from revenge, especially when able to retaliate, and not reproaching them for their past actions.
- Three qualities made the outcome favorable for Yūsuf: piety, patience, and goodness.
- Forgiving wrongdoers are among the traits of prophets; do not just forgive those who wrong you, but pray for them, benefiting them in this life and the hereafter.

Contemplation Insights from Page 247 [Yūsuf 96-103]

- Honoring and respecting parents is obligatory, including rushing to bring them news that brings joy.
- Beware of Satan's insinuation and those who seek to sow discord between loved ones to separate them.
- No matter how high a servant may rise in his religion or worldly life, it all comes back to Allah's favor and grace. One way to show gratitude to Allah is to remember your state before receiving the blessing.
- Asking Allah for a good end, safety, and success on the Day of Judgment and joining the company of the righteous in Paradise.
- The consideration lies in compliance with the Sharia, not in the minority or majority. Sometimes, the lack of response from those invited is a trial and test from Allah for the caller to Allah.

Contemplation Insights from Page 248 [Yūsuf 104-111]

- From Allah's grace, He informs His prophets of unseen matters for purposes and wisdom.
- A caller to Allah does not have the power to turn people's hearts towards obedience, and most of creation is not among those guided.

- Those who turn away from Allah's universal signs and evidence of His Oneness spread throughout the universe are condemned.
- Preaching to Allah with insight distinguishes the da'wah of the prophets and their followers from others. This verse, 'Say, "This is my way; I invite to Allah with insight, I and those who follow me,"' mentions some pillars of da'wah, including:
    - Having an accurate methodology.
    - The methodology is based on knowledge.
    - The presence of a caller to Allah.
    - The presence of invitees: "and those who follow me."
- A caller to Allah does not seek worldly reward for his da'wah; he is keen on the reward in the Hereafter, "And you do not ask them for a reward for it."
- Do not be oblivious to Allah's signs scattered across the heavens and the earth, "And how many a sign within the heavens and earth do they pass over while they, therefrom, are turning away."

CONTEMPLATION STUDY QUESTIONS

Verse **2**: Why was the Qur'ān revealed in Arabic? [*Ibn Kathir*]

Verse **3**: Why is the story of Yūsuf considered one of the best? What do you think of those who add to the story of Yūsuf additions that are not in the Qur'ān or the Sunnah? [*As-Sa'di*]

Verse **5**: If Allah blesses you with a bounty, when should you display it? And when should you conceal it? [*Ibn Kathir*]

Verse **7**: Why did the verses specifically benefit the questioners? [*As-Sa'di*]

Verse **9**: The verse mentions a trick of Shayṭān against the righteous; what is it? A single sin may lead to multiple sins. Discuss this through the verses. [*As-Sa'di*]

Verse **16**: What evidence indicated the lie of Yūsuf's brothers? [*As-Sa'di*]

Verse **18**: Explain some types of beautiful patience. [*Ibn Kathir*]

Verse **19**: What is the significance of ending the verse with, "*and Allah is Knowing of what they do*"? [*Ibn Kathir*]

Verse **23**: Which of the two calamities was greater and more rewarding for Yūsuf: his ordeal with his brothers or with his master's wife? And why? What factors helped Yūsuf avoid sin? [*As-Sa'di*]

Verse **23**: It turns out that sincerity prevents the domination of Satan; as Allah said: "Thus, to avert from him evil and immorality. Indeed, he was one of Our devoted servants." [*Ibn Taymiyyah*]

Verse **25**: What do we learn from Yūsuf's escape from the place of sin? [*As-Sa'di*]

Verse **30**: How dangerous is succumbing to love outside of marriage? [*As-Sa'di*]

Verse **33**: If a person is given a choice between committing a sin and facing a worldly punishment, what should they choose? [*As-Sa'di*]

Verse **37**: The caller to Allah must be astute and alert to the appropriate times for preaching. Explain this from the verse. Does worship only pertain to times of ease and not times of hardship? [*As-Sa'di*]

Verse **38**: What are the greatest blessings of Allah upon you? [*As-Sa'di*]

Verse **38**: What does the statement that most people do not give thanks imply to you? [*Ibn Kathir*]

Verse **41**: Why didn't Yūsuf specify who would give his lord wine and who would be crucified? [*Ibn Kathir*]

Verse **42**: Explain Allah's wisdom in His decree through this verse. Does seeking help from created beings in matters they are capable of contradicting strong faith? [*As-Sa'di*]

Verse **57**: What is the significance of piety and faith in reaching the hereafter? [*As-Sa'di*]

Verse **64**: When is suspicion prohibited? [*As-Sa'di*]

Verse **69**: After clarifying that Yaqūb's strategy avails nothing, Allah said, "And indeed, he was knowledgeable." What is a benefit of this statement here? [*As-Sa'di*]

Verse **70**: What are permissible tricks, and what is forbidden from this verse? [*As-Sa'di*]

Verse **76**: If Allah wishes well for His allies, none can overturn His decree; explain that through the verse. [*As-Sa'di*]

Verse **79**: How did Yūsuf extricate himself from lying when he wanted to take his brother? [*As-Sa'di*]

Verse **83**: Allah mentioned beautiful patience, beautiful forgiveness, and beautiful abandonment; beautiful patience is that with no complaints, beautiful abandonment is that with no harm, and beautiful forgiveness is that with no reproach. [*Ibn Taymiyyah*]

Verse **86**: When does complaining contradict patience? [*As-Sa'di*]

Verse **87**: What is the benefit of having a good opinion of Allah and not despairing of His mercy? [*As-Sa'di*]

Verse **100**: Why did it mention that the discord caused by Shayṭān was from him and his brothers, although it came only from his brothers?

سُورَةُ الرَّعۡدِ
RA'D (13)
The Thunder

VERSES
43

WORDS
855

LETTERS
3,506

REVEALED IN
MAKKAH

REVEALATION ORDER
96

It is understood to have been revealed around the same time as Sūrah Yūsuf and, therefore, revealed for a similar purpose.

Main Themes: No matter how much the enemy plots, calm your heart with Allah's remembrance (*Dhikr*); the truth will prevail. The Sūrah demonstrates the power of the truth. It reminds us of Allah's magnificence and power in many ways. It reminds us of His frightening signs for those who reject the truth (such as the thunder). All this is to affirm the truth and His promise to His allies while threatening His enemies.

Allah informs us of how He changes people's conditions for better or worse according to their changes (see verse 11).

The Sūrah seamlessly connects with the preceding one: Allah pointed out in Sūrah Yūsuf that there are numerous signs in the heavens and the earth that people pass by while ignoring them. This Sūrah elucidates and details those signs, mentioning monotheism in a rhetorical question about the superiority of scattered lords over Allah, the One, Almighty Deity. This continues the monotheistic call, mentioning Allah's attributes and providing solace for the Prophet Muhammad (ﷺ).

The relation of this Sūrah to the preceding one is multifaceted:

1. Allah summarized the heavenly and earthly signs in the previous Sūrah, then elaborated on them here in several places.

2. He hinted at the proofs of monotheism in Sūrah Yūsuf and then detailed the evidence more thoroughly here.

3. Both Sūrahs narrate stories of past peoples with their messengers, the trials they faced, and how Allah seized them with His mighty power, inscribing disgrace upon the

disbelievers, ensuring victory for His messengers and the believers. This serves as a consolation for His messenger (ﷺ) and fortification of his heart.

4. The Qur'ān is described at the end of the previous Sūrah and the beginning of this one, emphasizing its truthfulness and noting that most people do not believe.

The alignment of the beginning and end of the Sūrah:

The Sūrah begins by mentioning in the first verse that most people do not believe.

It ends by discussing the disbelievers and their denial of the Prophet's prophethood in the last verse.

This highlights that they do not possess the truth or believe in it despite its strength and clarity.

A Broader Overview of the Sūrah:

- Like all Makkan chapters, Sūrah al-Ra'd focuses primarily upon the three fundamental subject matters of the Qur'ān—al-Tawḥīd, the trueness of the Prophet's (ﷺ) message, and the Hereafter. Its primary focus is Tawḥīd. It demonstrates the truthfulness of the Messenger (ﷺ) regarding what was revealed to him about the uniqueness of Allah in divinity and resurrecting the dead for judgment while repudiating the statements of the deniers. Therefore, their statements are narrated five times throughout the Sūrah from the beginning to the end. He contrasts the obstinacy of polytheists in their demands for signs as per their specifications with the certainty of believers and the good Allah has prepared for them.

- It commands us to observe and contemplate the signs of Allah in the universe and deduce His exclusive right to be worshipped (سُبْحَانَهُۥ وَتَعَالَىٰ). It extends an invitation to contemplate over the vast universe: the heavens and earth, sun and moon, night and day, the mountains that stabilize the earth, the rivers that water the vegetation. All of these are blessings and for our benefit. It outlines the diversity of Allah's vast creation. It elaborates on Allah's knowledge: what the wombs conceal and reveal, what people do privately and publicly, etc. It reminds us that Allah gives and takes, bestows, and withholds what He wills, as He wills when He wills.

- It thoroughly refutes the claims of polytheists and their denial of resurrection, threatening them with the fate that befell similar nations before them, including heavenly punishment, while reminding them of Allah's blessings upon people, affirming that Allah alone is worthy of worship over their deities, that Allah is the Knower of secrets and that the idols know nothing nor can they bestow any blessing. It establishes the belief in the Hereafter in several verses throughout. It establishes and reasserts the truth of the Prophets' message throughout the entire Sūrah. (see verses 1, 7, 19, 27, 30, 36, 38, 43.)

- It provides two powerful similitudes to illustrate truth's power against falsehood's fragility. It then extolls the virtue of employing reason, followed by ten virtuous characteristics of intelligent believers and their immense reward. Immediately after that, it contrasts that with the opposite characteristics of the disbelievers and what they are threatened with in terms of punishment.

- The central theme of Sūrah Al-Ra'd revolves around the potency of truth. A related objective of the Sūrah is demonstrating Divine power through some manifestations, affirming the concepts of divine promise and warning, and elucidating Allah's natural law of change and transition. The Sūrah concludes with Allah's guarantee that Islam will continue to spread and that the truth shall prevail. (verse 41). Thus, the message of this blessed Sūrah is: do not be deceived by appearances; instead, we should look into their essences and actualities, for truth is luminous, and falsehood is murky.

- In summary, the blessed Sūrah clarifies that truth is strong, clear, and firm, even if not yet evident to many people or comprehended in their hearts, and that falsehood is weak, brittle, and defeated, even if it appears dominant to people. This theme is interspersed with moral lessons, warnings, parables, and similitudes.

CONTEMPLATE, COMPREHEND, APPLY

Contemplation Insights from Page 249 [Ar-Ra'd 1-5]

- Engage with the Qur'ān and learn its sciences, which is the path to truth. The truth is indicated by correct evidence, not by the number of followers.
- Affirmation of Allah's power, marveling at His creation of the heavens without pillars supporting them, despite their immense creation and expanse. Marveling at divine power in how Allah creates immense plants from small seeds and nourishes them with the same water, their fruits vary in size, color, and taste.
- Allah's creation of massive trees from tiny seeds, previously non-existent, refutes the disbelievers' denial of resurrection. Bringing back to life the scattered and decomposed body parts on the earth is relatively easier than bringing something non-existent into existence.
- Only those with intellect take heed of Allah's signs.

Contemplation Insights from Page 250 [Ar-Ra'd 6-13]

- The vastness of Allah's forgiveness and His patience with human folly, as they defy His messengers and prophets, yet He provides for them, spares them, and is patient. A warner must convey the message, not to guide hearts to faith.
- Allah's extensive knowledge of what is in the darkness of the womb, knowing the fate of the semen in the womb, whether it will develop into a male or female, its health, sustenance, lifespan, and whether it will be wretched or blessed.
- The immense care of Allah for humans, affirming the existence of angels guarding and protecting them and others like the recording angels.
- A great divine universal law: blessings do not disappear except by sins. Allah changes the condition of a servant for the better when He sees them following the guidance, as guidance to success is linked to following the path shown by the signs. To improve your condition and increase Allah's blessings in this life and the hereafter, start by changing yourself, steering clear of sins, disobedience, and their doers.

Contemplation Insights from Page 251 [Ar-Ra'd 14-18]

- Demonstrates the misguided invocation of polytheists, likening their state to one stretching his hand for water but not reaching it, not truly drinking despite such an act, for not adopting a correct means to do so.
- One method of clarification in the Qur'ān is through parables, which bring the abstract closer to the tangible, providing a mental image that aids in understanding the intended meaning. Hearts are like valleys; they vary in capacity, and each receives the good according to its capacity. A principle that never changes is truth, which remains even if people think it will disappear, and falsehood, which vanishes no matter how inflated it becomes.
- Affirms that all beings prostrate to Allah willingly or unwillingly, as dictated by their innate disposition to submit to Him.

Contemplation Insights from Page 252 [Al-Ra'd 19-28]

- This is an encouragement towards a set of moral virtues that lead to Paradise, including maintaining ties, fearing Allah, fulfilling promises, patience, spending in His way, repelling evil with good, and warning against the opposite. Patience can be observed by both the righteous and the wicked, but the patience that is rewarded is that which is sought to gain Allah's pleasure.

- Affirming that the provision is in Allah's control, and neither His expansion nor restriction of someone's provision should be cause for joy or sorrow, as it's not indicative of His pleasure or displeasure with the servant.
- Guidance is not necessarily linked to the sending down of signs and miracles, as suggested by the disbelievers.
- Not everything that makes you happy in this world benefits you in the Hereafter. The abundance or scarcity of provision is not a sign of Allah's satisfaction or anger towards a servant.
- One of the effects of the Qur'ān and remembrance on a believing servant is that it brings tranquility to the heart.

Contemplation Insights from Page 253 [Ar-Ra'd 29-34]

- The primary purpose of every revealed book and messenger is guidance, not the descent of signs, which is at Allah's discretion.
- Consolation for Prophet Muhammad ﷺ, with the knowledge that previous prophets faced similar disbelief and rejection from their communities. If faced with mockery for your faith and righteousness, ignore their foolishness, do not grieve, and know Allah will vindicate you. Remember that your Prophet ﷺ faced more than this; endure seeking Allah's pleasure.
- Shayṭān can lead some servants astray to the extent of beautifying their sinful actions and corruption. Know that the arrogant, the oppressors, and the wicked, no matter how they appear to be in bliss, are in punishment, for Allah has promised them torment in this life.

Contemplation Insights from Page 254 [Ar-Ra'd 35-42]

- Encouragement towards Paradise by describing its features, such as the flowing rivers, perpetual provision, and shade.
- Emphasize learning and spreading the Arabic language; it's the foundation for understanding the Qur'ān.
- The danger of following whims after receiving knowledge as it leads to Allah's punishment. Beware of embracing the disbelievers' doubts and arguments; doing so can lead Allah to forsake you because you turned away from His commands.
- Messengers are humans with spouses and offspring, and our Prophet Muhammad ﷺ was no exception, sharing similarities with them in this regard.
- Strive to convey the message to people; guidance lies in Allah's hands.

CONTEMPLATION STUDY QUESTIONS

Verse 2: Why were the sun and the moon specifically mentioned? *[Ibn Kathir]*

Verse 2: How can a person attain certain knowledge in matters of belief? *[Al-Sa'dī]*

Verse 5: Comparing the Creator to the creation is a reason for the misguidance of the polytheists. Explain this through this verse. *[Al-Sa'dī]*

Verse 6: Explain how Allah's benevolence and forgiveness reach His servants despite their oppression. *[Al-Sa'dī]*

Verse 6: What is the benefit of mentioning His forgiveness and severe punishment in the same context? [*Ibn Kathir]*

Verse 12: How should recognition of Allah's (سُبْحَانَهُ وَتَعَالَىٰ) complete control over atmospheric phenomena (like the rain, clouds, lighting, thunder) affect the believer? *[Al-Sa'dī]*

Verse 15: How do all in the heavens and the earth prostrate? [*Al-Sa'dī]*

Verse 20: When is a servant considered among the people of understanding? [*Al-Sa'dī]*

Verse 23: Why did Allah gather parents, spouses, and righteous offspring in Paradise? *[Ibn Kathir]*

Verse 26: When is rejoicing in worldly matters blameworthy? [*Al-Sa'dī]*

Verse 32: What is the danger of feeling secure from punishment while persisting in sins?

Day 13: Ibrahīm & al Hijr

The Qurā'n reading for **day 13** is *Sūrah Ibrāhīm* and *Sūrah al Ḥijr*.

سُورَةُ إِبْرَاهِيمَ

IBRĀHĪM (14)

Abraham

VERSES
52

WORDS
831

LETTERS
3,434

REVEALED IN
MAKKAH

REVEALATION ORDER
70

Main Themes: Constantly remember Allah and be grateful. Establishing the responsibility to convey the truth and to warn those who turn away from divine punishment. "*This is a great conveyance for humankind.*" *(verse* 52.)

The *Sūrah* begins by mentioning that the Qurā'n was revealed to remove people from compounded darkness to the light. It ends by mentioning that the *Qurā'n* is conveyed as a warning.

Its overarching theme is to demonstrate the unity of the message brought by the messengers and how it was their role to diligently move people from the darkness of polytheism to the light of monotheism, despite their people's rejection, and to affirm the Prophet Muhammad (ﷺ), and to warn the oppressors. The Sūrah is named after the father of the prophets, Ibrahim (عَلَيْهِ السَّلَامُ), who was a nation unto himself in preaching, inviting to Islamic monotheism, and in gratitude for blessings. The Sūrah encompasses all of this. Sūrah *Ibrāhīm* is unique in that it does not speak about the Prophets individually, but rather, it speaks about them with their nations collectively throughout.

Imam Al-Biqā'ī (d. 885 AH رَحِمَهُ ٱللَّهُ) asserts that:[9]

"ومقصودها: التوحيد، وبيان أن هذا الكتاب غاية البلاغ إلى الله، لأنه كافل ببيان الصراط الدال عليه، المؤدي إليه. وأدل ما فيها على هذا المرام: قصة إبراهيم عليه السلام.

[9] Naẓm al-Durar; Maṣā'id al-Naẓr.

The purpose of this Sūrah is monotheism and to clarify that this book is the ultimate means of communication with Allah, as it guarantees guidance to the path that leads to Him, which is signified by the story of Ibrahim (عَلَيْهِ ٱلسَّلَامُ).

أما التوحيد: فواضح. وأما أمر الكتاب: فلأنه من جملة دعائه لذريته الذين أسكنهم عند البيت المحرم، ذرية إسماعيل عليه السلام: (رَبَّنَا وَابْعَثْ فِيهِمْ رَسُولًا مِنْهُمْ يَتْلُو عَلَيْهِمْ آيَاتِكَ وَيُعَلِّمُهُمُ الْكِتَابَ وَالْحِكْمَةَ وَيُزَكِّيهِمْ)".

Its being about monotheism is evident. Regarding the book, it is part of his (عَلَيْهِ ٱلسَّلَامُ) supplication for his offspring who settled near the Sacred House, the progeny of Ismail (عَلَيْهِ ٱلسَّلَامُ): "Our Lord, send among them a messenger from themselves who will recite to them Your verses and teach them the Book and wisdom and purify them."

It is an extension of what is in Sūrah Ar-Ra'd, as it both clarifies what was summarized there and summarizes what it had clarified. Both discuss the Qur'ān and the universal signs, the affirmation of resurrection, analogies for truth and falsehood, and the discussion of the disbelievers' plots and their outcomes.

Its relation to the preceding Sūrah is from multiple aspects:

- Allah mentioned in the previous Sūrah that He revealed the Qur'ān as an Arabic judgment without specifying its wisdom, which is explicitly mentioned here.
- In the previous Sūrah, it was mentioned: "And it is not for any messenger to bring a sign except by Allah's permission." Here, it is mentioned that the messengers said: "It was not for us to bring you authority except by the permission of Allah."
- There, the command for the Prophet Muhammad (صَلَّى ٱللَّهُ عَلَيْهِ وَسَلَّمَ) to rely on Allah was mentioned, and here, it recounts the command for his brothers, the messengers, to rely on Allah (سُبْحَانَهُ وَتَعَالَىٰ).
- The previous Sūrah included the representation of truth and falsehood in similitude form, and this one also consists of that.
- There, the raising of the sky without pillars, the spreading of the earth, and the subjugation of the sun and the moon were mentioned, and similar things are discussed here.
- The plots of the disbelievers were mentioned there, and something similar is discussed here, along with some additional descriptions not discussed there.

BROADER OVERVIEW OF THE SŪRAH

- The Sūrah begins by alerting to the Qur'ān's miraculous nature, highlighting its status, and that it was revealed to guide people out of misguidance and acknowledging that it was shown in the Arabic language. It glorifies Allah, who revealed it and warns those who disbelieved in it and the one it was revealed to. It awakens the obstinate by stating that Muhammad (صَلَّىٰ اللَّهُ عَلَيْهِ وَسَلَّمَ) was not unique among messengers and that being human does not conflict with his message from Allah, like other messengers.

- It then draws a parallel with the mission of Mūsā (عَلَيْهِ السَّلَامُ) to Pharaoh to improve the condition of the Children of Israel, reminding his people of Allah's favors and the necessity of gratitude and admonishing them with what befell the people of Noah, Aad, and those after them and the denial faced by their messengers.

- It discusses the fate of the deniers, establishing evidence for Allah's uniqueness in His sole right to be worshipped with signs of His creation, mentioning resurrection, warning the disbelievers against being deceived by their leaders and nobles who enacted Satan's scheme, and how they will disown them on the Day of Gathering, describing their condition and that of the believers that day. It mentions the oration of Shayṭān on Judgment Day and his disowning of his followers.

- It discusses the superiority of the monotheistic statement of Islam, the corruption of the doctrine of disbelief, then marvels at the condition of a people who denied Allah's favor and led those who followed them to ruin through polytheism, contrasting their state to that of the believers.

- It lists some of His (عَزَّوَجَلَّ) favors on people preferentially, then collectively. It reminds both groups of Ibrahim's (صَلَّىٰ اللَّهُ عَلَيْهِ وَسَلَّمَ) condition so that all know who is following Ibrahim's path and who is turning away from it among the residents of Makkah at that time, warning them against being ungrateful for the blessings.

- It warns them of what occurred those unjust before and affirms the Prophet (صَلَّىٰ اللَّهُ عَلَيْهِ وَسَلَّمَ) with the promise of victory. It concludes with comprehensive words from His saying: "This [message] is a notification to the people" to the end of the Surah.

BRIEF SŪRAH SUMMARY

Verses 1-27	The first half of the *Sūrah* is focused on the Messengers, their message and the disbelieving nations.
Verses 28-52	The second half of the *Sūrah* is focused on showing gratitude for Allah's greatest blessing, which is the message of Islam. It establishes the evidences for *Tawḥīd* and provides the example of *Ibrāhīm;* it concludes with the mention of severe punishment for disbelief and oppression *(verses 42-52).*

CONTEMPLATE, COMPREHEND, APPLY

Contemplation Insights from Page 255 [Ibrahim 1-5]

- The purpose of revealing the Qur'ān is guidance, taking people from the darkness of falsehood to the light of truth. Whenever you are confused about something and do not know its truth, promptly read the Qur'ān; perhaps Allah (عَزَّوَجَلَّ) will guide you to the truth and righteousness.
- Messengers are sent with the language of their people for better understanding and acceptance.
- Facilitation of understanding and learning is a characteristic of the religion. The role of messengers is summarized in guiding people and leading them from darkness to light. Guidance only occurs with Allah's permission, help, and success (عَزَّوَجَلَّ).

Contemplation Insights from Page 256 [Ibrahim 6-10]

- One means of calling to Allah is reminding those called of Allah's blessings upon them, especially if it is linked to a significant blessing, like victory over an enemy or salvation from them.
- Allah (عَزَّوَجَلَّ) promises to increase His blessings for His servants' gratitude, and His warning is severe for those who are ungrateful.
- The disbelief of servants does not harm Allah at all, as their belief does not add anything to Him; He is Self-Sufficient and praiseworthy.

Contemplation Insights from Page 257 [Ibrahim 11-18]

- Prophets and messengers are humans who are descendants of Adam, but Allah favored them with the message and chose them from among the descendants of Adam.
- A caller aiming for change should expect significant challenges, including expulsion, banishment, and verbal and physical harm. Know that one of the most important duties of a caller to faith is certainty in Allah's promise and good reliance on Him.
- The callers and the righteous are promised victory and succession on the earth after they were weak and oppressed, and this was realized for the Companions and the Successors. May Allah be pleased with them.
- It explains the nullification of the good deeds of the disbelievers due to their disbelief.

Contemplation Insights from Page 258 [Ibrahim 19-24]

- It shows the bad end of both the follower and the followed if they unite upon falsehood. The stance of the weak against the arrogant on the Day of Judgment teaches you not to compromise in matters of religion, urging you to follow the divine law, not individuals. Be obedient and refrain from sins before a day comes when patience or panic will not avail.
- It shows that Shayṭān is humankind's greatest enemy, a weak, defeated liar who cannot protect himself or his followers on the Day of Judgment.
- Iblis confesses that Allah's promise is true, and the promise of Shayṭān is nothing but lies.
- The word of monotheism is likened to a fruitful, high-branched, firmly rooted tree.
- The greatest wish of the polytheists on the Day of Judgment is guidance, so strive for it in this world as long as you can.

Contemplation Insights from Page 259 [Ibrahim 25-33]

- The word disbelief is likened to the creeping bitter apple tree, which does not rise to a great height, produces nothing sweet, and does not last.
- Steadfastness is required in this life, and the hereafter is a grace from Allah; whoever Allah makes steadfast in this world, He will make steadfast in the hereafter. On the other hand, injustice by a servant is a reason for Allah's misguidance; thus, avoid injustice, especially against the vulnerable: women, orphans, servants, employees, and the poor.
- The link between the command to perform prayers and zakat, along with the mention of the Hereafter, signifies that these acts are among the means of salvation on that day.

- The wise recognize the fleeting nature of worldly pleasures, which are bound to perish, so they do not let them distract from the deeds of the Hereafter.
- Listing some great blessings indicates the enormity of some humans' disbelief and denial of Allah's favors (سُبْحَانَهُ وَتَعَالَى).

Contemplation Insights from Page 260 [Ibrahim 34-42]

- You cannot enumerate Allah's blessings upon you, let alone be thankful for them, but let your tongue always be moist with the remembrance and gratitude of Allah.
- The virtue of Mecca, for which the Prophet Ibrahim prayed. Preserving the country's security is one of the first wishes of the righteous and the callers to Allah.
- No matter how elevated one's status in obedience and servitude, one should fear for oneself and one's offspring from both the apparent and subtle shirk.
- Ibrahim's prayer indicates that no matter how exalted a person's status, he remains in need of Allah (سُبْحَانَهُ وَتَعَالَى).
- The relationship between faith and monotheism is more important than the ties of kinship and lineage. Among the methods of upbringing is praying for one's children for righteousness, good belief, and success in performing religious rites.

Contemplation Insights from Page 261 [Ibrahim 43-52]

- Depicting spectacles of the Day of Judgment, where creation is panicked, fearful, weak, and terrified, with the Earth and the heavens changing. While an oppressor may be strong in his tyranny in this life, he will be resurrected on the Day of Judgment fearful and panicked, with his heart shattered from fear.
- The Qur'ān describes the severe punishment and humiliation that befall those who sin and disbelieve on the Day of Judgment. The ancient ruins of punished nations remind people of the eradication punishment that befell nations before us.
- During one's lifetime in this world, one has the liberty to strive in obedience, for Allah will not provide another opportunity if one is resurrected on the Day of Judgment.
- Allah will not break His promise to His messengers and allies; victory and empowerment will surely come to them.

CONTEMPLATION STUDY QUESTIONS

Verse 1: What is implied by attributing the straight path to the names of Allah: "The Almighty" (Al-Aziz) and "The Praiseworthy" (Al-Hamid)? *[Al-Sa'dī]*

Verse 4: How does this verse prove the importance of learning Arabic? *[Al-Sa'dī]*

Verse 10: Why did the messengers denounce the doubt in the existence of Allah (سُبْحَانَهُ وَتَعَالَىٰ)? *[Ibn Kathir]*

Verse 12: What are the highest and most complete levels of reliance on Allah? *[Al-Sa'dī]*

Verse 18: This verse explains the danger of being lenient with heresies and polytheistic practices. *[Ibn Kathir]*

Verse 22: What is the outcome of Iblis's speech to the punished in the fire? *[Ibn Kathir]*

Verse 22: What is the characteristic of those upon whom Satan's authority is established? Satan's authority was denied in one verse and affirmed in another, so how do you reconcile between them? *[Al-Sa'dī]*

Verse 27: Explain how Allah fortifies a servant in the Hereafter. *[Al-Sa'dī]*

Verse 31: What is meant by establishing prayer in this verse? *[Al-Sa'dī]*

Verse 35: What are the forms of Allah responding to Ibrahim's (عَلَيْهِ السَّلَامُ) prayer? *[Al-Sa'dī]*

Verse 36: Explain the prophets' mercy towards their people through this verse, and what can a caller to Allah learn from this? *[Al-Sa'dī]*

Verse 37: Why did Ibrahim specifically emphasize prayer among all acts of worship when he prayed for his offspring? *[Al-Sa'dī]*

Verse 42: What can be understood from people keeping their eyes open, without blinking or moving them, on the Day of Judgment? *[Al-Sa'dī]*

Verse 43: Why can't the wrongdoers avert their gaze or close their eyes on the Day of Judgment? *[Ibn Kathir]*

Verse 51: Why is Allah's account described as swift? *[Ibn Kathir]*

سُورَةُ الحِجْرِ

AL ḤIJR (15)

The Rocky Tract

VERSES
99

WORDS
654

LETTERS
2,760

REVEALED IN
MAKKAH

REVEALATION ORDER
54

Some say *Sūrah al Ḥijr* was approximately the 54th in order of revelation, before *Sūrah al An'ām* and after *Sūrah Yūsuf* in the period between the year of sadness and the *Hijrah*. Others surmise that it was revealed around the fourth year of prophethood because it contained the command to boldly proclaim.

It is similar to *Sūrah al A'rāf* in key aspects: it issues multiple threats to the polytheists; they both contain the story of Ādam and Iblīs; they both conclude with the final abodes of the people of truth and falsehood.

Main Themes: Allah's protection of His religion. The greatest method of preserving the religion found in the Sūrah is by warning the deniers of divine punishment through the depiction of destroyed nations, serving as a warning to the addressed and as a conforming affirmation of divine support for the Prophet and the believers. The Prophet is further comforted by Allah, mentioning the blessing of the Qur'ān. See the concluding verses *(87-95).*

A recurring theme is that the *Dhikr* (Allah's remembrance, which is Islām as a whole) is safeguarded, and those who safeguard it are safeguarded. Stubbornness and arrogance are the greatest causes of disbelief. It mentions the story of Ādam and Iblīs along these lines as an illustration of the initial manifestation of haughty rejection. It then proceeds to mention important examples of nations that followed Shayṭān in rebellion.

Relevance of the name to the theme: The barrier (*ḥijr*, also translated as a rocky track) in the *Sūrah* refers to the dwellings of Thamud (verse 80). The name is said to be relevant to the main theme because a barrier (*Hijr*) preserves what is inside it, and most of the Sūrah talks about Allah's preservation of His religion and creation.

Reflecting on this blessed Sūrah reveals that its beginning, middle, and end discuss preservation:

1. Allah's preservation of His Book (verse 9).

2. Allah's preservation of the heavens from eavesdropping devils (verses 16-17).

3. The preservation of sustenance in the divine treasuries (verse 21).

4. Preservation of rainwater on Earth (verse 22).

5. Allah's protection of Adam and his sincere believers from his progeny (verses 39-40).

6. Allah's protection of Ibrahim and his nephew when He saved them and destroyed their people.

7. Allah's protection of Shu'ayb and Salih, peace be upon them when He saved them and destroyed their people.

8. Allah's protection of His Messenger (ﷺ) from those who mock him (verse 95).

- Burhān al-Dīn al Biqā'ī (d. 885 AH رَحِمَهُ ٱللَّهُ) says:

"ومقصودها: وصف الكتاب بأنه في الذروة من الجمع للمعاني الموضحة للحق من غير اختلاف أصلًا.

"Its primary objective is describing the book as being the utmost standard in compiling conceptual meanings that elucidate the truth without any discrepancies whatsoever.

وأشكل ما فيها وأمثله وأشبهه في هذا المعنى: قصة أصحاب الحجر فإن وضوح آيتهم عندهم وعند كل من شاهدها، أي سمع بها وصحت عنده كوضوح ما دل عليه مقصود هذه السورة في أمر الكتاب عند جميع العرب، لاسيما قريش.

The most representative, exemplary, and illustrative matter representing this meaning is the story of the people of the Rocky Tract (*Aṣḥāb al Ḥijr*). The clarity of their sign to them and to everyone who witnessed it—meaning those who heard about it and knew of its veracity—is as clear as this Sūrah indicates regarding the (clarity of) Book for all Arabs, especially Quraysh.

وأيضاً آيتهم في غاية الإيضاح للحق، والجمع لمعانيه الدائرة على التوحيد، المقتضى للاجتماع على الداعي".

For their sign (i.e., the *Qur'ān*) is the utmost standard in clarifying the truth and assembling its meanings, which revolve around monotheism, necessitating uniting in support around the inviter (i.e., the Prophet ﷺ)."

Like the rest of the Meccan Sūrahs, it revolves around discussing the polytheists' beliefs and ideas and what follows from proving resurrection and illustrating signs of Allah's power or reminding humans of their initial creation, their relationship with the unseen—such as the world of angels and jinn—then mentioning the stories of some prophets, and concluding the Sūrah by addressing the Prophet Muhammad (ﷺ).

Its relation to the previous Sūrah from numerous aspects:

1. It began similarly to its predecessor, describing the clear book.

2. It explained the conditions of the disbelievers on the Day of Resurrection, wishing they were Muslims, as the previous one did.

3. Each of them describes the heavens and the earth.

4. Each of them has detailed stories about Ibrahim (عَلَيْهِ ٱلسَّلَامُ).

5. Each consoles the Messenger of Allah (صَلَّىٱللَّهُعَلَيْهِوَسَلَّمَ) by mentioning what previous messengers endured from their nations and the outcome favoring the righteous.

The Alignment of the Beginning and End of the Sūrah: The Sūrah begins by mentioning the Noble Qur'ān (verse 1), and it concludes with the command to steadfastly worship until death (verse 99) because the greatest means of preserving the servant and stabilizing him in worship is the Qur'ān.

Broader Overview of Sūrah al Ḥijr:

- It opens with disjointed letters, hinting at the challenge of the Qur'ān's inimitability and highlighting the Qur'ān's excellence and guidance. It then warns the polytheists of the regret they will feel for not embracing Islam. It rebukes them for being preoccupied from guidance by their immersion in desires. It warns them of destruction at the appointed time of threat determined by Allah in His knowledge.

- It consoles the Messenger (صَلَّىٱللَّهُعَلَيْهِوَسَلَّمَ) for the disbelief of those who have not believed what they say about him and their demands from him, showing that this is the habitual response of deniers to their messengers. It illustrates that divine supernatural signs and warnings are ineffective for them, even if they were to witness the miraculous signs as they demand, and that Allah protects His Book from their schemes. Then, it establishes proof against them with the grandeur of Allah's creation and the blessings found within themselves. It mentions the resurrection and the evidence for its possibility.

- It transitions to the creation of humankind and the honor Allah bestowed upon this species. It narrates the story of Satan's disbelief. Then, it mentions the stories of Ibrahim, Lut, the companions of the thicket (*al Aykah*), and the companions of the Rocky Tract.

- It concludes by affirming the Messenger (صَلَّىٱللَّهُعَلَيْهِوَسَلَّمَ) 's anticipation of the moment of victory, his overlooking those who harm him, his entrusting their affairs to Allah, his engaging with the believers, and his affirming that Allah is sufficient for him against his enemies.

- This includes discussions on the creation of the jinn, their eavesdropping on the discourses of the angels, the conditions of the righteous, encouragement towards forgiveness, and warnings of punishment.

BRIEF SŪRAH SUMMARY

Verses 1-15	The universal constant law of Allah in dealing with the arrogant disbelievers. In the middle of this passage (verse 9), Allah guarantees to protect His religion.
Verses 16-25	The religion is preserved by being established on simple logical arguments, so these verses present some of Allah's signs in the creation.
Verses 26-48	The story of Ādam.
Verses 49-84	The destruction of past nations and the reasons for their collapse. (the peoples of Luṭ, al *Aykah*, al *Ḥijr*).
Verses 85-99	This universe has not been created without purpose. Be patient. Allah will suffice you against those who mock. Worship your Lord until the certainty of death arrives.

CONTEMPLATE, COMPREHEND, APPLY

Contemplation Insights from Page 262 [Al-Hijr 1-15]

- The Glorious Qur'ān perfectly encompasses all aspects of guidance with clarity and explanation.
- Disbelievers typically focus on materialistic aspects, immersing themselves in desires and whims, deceived by false hopes, and preoccupied with worldly life over the hereafter.
- The destruction of nations is predetermined at a specific date, fixed in time, with no delay or advancement, and Allah does not hasten for anyone's haste.
- Allah (عَزَّوَجَلَّ) has taken upon Himself the preservation of the Holy Qur'ān from any change, alteration, addition, or omission until the Day of Judgment.

Contemplation Insights from Page 263 [Al-Hijr 16-31]

- A servant should reflect on the sky and its adornment and use it to deduce the existence of its Creator.
- None but Allah controls all sustenance and decrees; His treasuries are in His hands. According to His wisdom and mercy, He gives to whom He wills and withholds as He wills.
- The earth is created flat and spread out to suit human life, stabilized with mountains so it doesn't shake with its inhabitants, and it contains various plants of known proportions according to wisdom and benefit.
- The command for angels to prostrate to Adam is an honor for humanity.

Contemplation Insights from Page 264 [Al-Hijr 32-51]

- The verses indicate the virtue of righteous people visiting and gathering together, exhibiting good manners, and facing each other without turning away.
- Servants should always keep their hearts between fear and hope, desire and awe.
- All angels prostrated to Adam in a gesture of salute and honor, except Iblis, who refused and was arrogant.
- Iblis has no authority over those whom Allah has guided and chosen; he cannot lead them into sin that prevents them from Allah's forgiveness.

Contemplation Insights from Page 265 [Al-Hijr 52-70]

- Teaching the etiquette of hosting guests with greetings and peace upon arrival.
- Those blessed by Allah with guidance and profound knowledge cannot succumb to despair from Allah's mercy.
- Allah commanded Lut and his followers not to look back during the destruction of Lut's people to prevent them from feeling pity for them.
- Lut's people's insistence on committing indecency with the guests is evidence of their corrupt nature and the extent of their indecency.

Contemplation Insights from Page 266 [Al-Hijr 71-90]

- If Allah intends to destroy a town, its people's evil and tyranny increase, and when their time expires, they receive the punishment they deserve.
- It is disliked to enter places of punishment, including the graves of disbelievers; if one enters such places or graves, they should hasten.
- A believer's gaze does not covet the adornments of the world when they know the Lord (عَزَّوَجَلَّ).
- A believer should distance themselves from polytheists, not grieve if they do not believe, be close to believers, humble towards them, and love them even if they are poor.

Contemplation Insights from Page 267 [Al-Hijr 91-99]

- Allah's care and protection in safeguarding the Prophet ﷺ from the harm of the polytheists.
- Glorification, praise, and prayer remedy worries, sorrows, and ways out of crises and hardships.
- Muslims are required to continuously perform obligatory acts of worship, such as prayer until death comes unless they are overtaken by unconsciousness or loss of memory.

CONTEMPLATION STUDY QUESTIONS

Verse 7: Their demand for angels to come is an act of injustice and ignorance. Clarify this. *[Al-Sa'dī]*

Verse 9: What is the significance of describing the Qur'ān as "Dhikr"? *[Al-Sa'dī]*

Verse 16: How do the stars and constellations in the sky increase a believer's faith? *[Al-Sa'dī]*

Verse 19: Believing that the earth's provisions will not suffice for people in the future is a form of bad assumption about Allah. Explain this concerning the verse. *[Al-Sa'dī]*

Verse 26: Why is the creation of humans linked with the creation of jinn? *[Ibn Kathir]*

Verse 30: What is the purpose of detailing the story of Adam's creation and Iblis's stance? *[Al-Sa'dī]*

Verse 33: To what extent can arrogance and envy lead its owner? *[Ibn Kathir]*

Verse 36: What is the wisdom behind Allah accepting Iblis's prayer? *[Al-Sa'dī]*

Verse 39: Who is exempt from Iblis's deception? *[Al-Sa'dī]*

Verse 49: How should a believer react knowing Allah is Forgiving and merciful? *[Al-Sa'dī]*

Verse 50: What should be the state of a Muslim's heart in this worldly life? *[Al-Sa'dī]*

Verse 80: How did the people of Al-Hijr deny all messengers when they only denied Saleh? *[Ibn Kathir]*

Verse 85: Is there any form of overlooking that is not noble? What is it? *[Al-Sa'dī]*

Verse 95: Allah promised His Messenger ﷺ to suffice him against the mockers. How is this promise realized, and what is the ruling on those who mock the Messenger of Allah? (صَلَّى ٱللَّهُ عَلَيْهِ وَسَلَّمَ)? *[Al-Sa'dī]*

DAY 14: AL-NAHL & AL ISRĀ'

The *Qurā'n reading* for **day 14** is *Sūrah al-Nahl* and *Sūrah al Isrā'*. The common theme between them is Allah reminding them of his general blessings and inviting them to the special blessing of guidance and faith so that they may enjoy His gracious reward in both worlds. This method summarizes the entire *da'wah* of the *Qur'ān.*

سُورَةُ النَّحۡلِ

AL-NAḤL (16)

The Bees

VERSES	128
WORDS	2,840
LETTERS	7,707
REVEALED IN	MAKKAH
REVEALATION ORDER	70

Main Themes: Affirming Allah's divinity (i.e., exclusive right to be worshipped) and lordship (i.e., exclusive ability to create, own, and control all things) by enumerating His blessings upon His creation. To remind them of the blessings that point to their Bestower, obliging loving servitude to Him and warning against denying His blessing. It is named after its 68th verse about the honey bee.

The relation of the name to the main theme: Because bees are among Allah's amazing creations, endowed with wondrous abilities, producing various blessings for His servants (honey, pollen, etc.), fitting the overall meaning of the Sūrah, which is to enumerate blessings.

The Sūrah is also called Sūrah Al-Ni'am (The Blessings) for enumerating Allah's blessings within it. It is considered Meccan, and its discussion revolves around mentioning blessings, demonstrating manifestations of divine power, and debating with the polytheists about their beliefs while addressing the Day of Judgment and what it entails.

Al-Biqā'ī (d. 885 AH رَحِمَهُ ٱللَّهُ) said:

"ومقصودها: الدلالة على أنه تعالى تام القدرة والعلم، فاعل بالاختيار منزه عن شوائب النقص

"The purpose of the Sūrah is to demonstrate that Allah is perfect in power and knowledge, acting by choice, exalted above any imperfection.

وأدل ما فيها على هذا المعنى: أمر النحل، لما ذكر من شأنها في دقة الفهم، في ترتيب بيوتها على شكل التسديس، ترتيباً لا يصل إليه أكابر المهندسين، إلا بعد تكامل كبير، وقانون يقيسون به ذلك التقدير

The clearest evidence for this within the Sūrah is the command to the bees, who have a remarkable understanding of arranging their hives in hexagonal shapes, a configuration not achieved by the greatest of engineers without significant advancement, and a law by which they measure that estimation.

وذلك على وجه هو أنفع الوجوه لها، وفي رعيها، وسائر أمرها، من اختلاف ألوان ما يخرج منها، من أعسالها وشموعها، وجعل الشمع نوراً وضياء، والعسل بركة وشفاء، مع أكلها من كل الثمار، النافع منها والضار، وغير ذلك من الأسرار، ووسمها بالنعم واضح في ذلك".

This arrangement is the most beneficial for them in their foraging and all their affairs, including the variation in colors of what they produce, from their honey and waxes, making wax a source of light and illumination and honey a source of blessing and healing, despite their consumption of all types of fruits, both beneficial and harmful, among other mysteries. (The Sūrah) being described as one of the blessings is clear, and Allah knows best."

Recognizing Allah's blessings with humble gratitude necessitates that a person: (1.) Single out Allah with worship so His blessings can be enjoyed forever in the next life, a command reiterated throughout the Sūrah. (2.) Freely enjoy what is lawful while abstaining from the limited number of prohibited things. Verse 96 reminds us that worldly blessings are temporary and Allah's reward is eternal, so we must be patient and grateful. (3.) Treat others with justice, kindness, and similar aspects of good character, as elaborated upon in Verses 90-92, some of the most comprehensive verses in the *Qur'ān*. They instruct people to be just and gracious, just as they would like to be treated with justice and graciousness, and to avoid every type of evil. These themes are focused upon throughout the *Sūrah*. Collectively, they illustrate the method of inviting to Allah. As such, the *Sūrah* concludes with the most concise and comprehensive verse in the *Qurā'n* about *da'wah* (verse 125).

The connection between it and the previous Sūrah:

The end of the preceding Sūrah mentioned the mockers and deniers and mentioned death, saying: "*We will surely question them all,*" which aligns with the beginning of this Sūrah, "*The command of Allah is coming, so do not hasten it,*" and also, the statement at its end, "*Worship your Lord until certainty (death) comes to you,*" ties closely with "*The command of Allah has come.*"

The beginning of Sūrah al-Naḥl connects to its end in several important ways:

The Sūrah begins with Allah's command to His messengers to warn the people (verse 2). It concludes with a description of the warning method (verse 125). It also starts with the command to fear Allah (verse 2). It ends with a statement about the outcome of righteousness: "*Indeed, Allah is with those who fear Him and those who are doers of good* (verse 128)." It is among the greatest blessings for creation to have Allah with them in guidance and support when they fear Him.

The Main Topics of the Sūrah:

- Illustrating Allah's blessings upon His creation in this world and the hereafter, with revelation (the message) being the foremost, requiring creation to accept and be grateful for these blessings.
- Detailing some of these blessings makes creation feel, showing that Allah is close to them and immensely kind to them. There are 23 tremendous blessings mentioned in Sūrah al-Naḥl: Twelve in the beginning, seven in the middle, and four after that:

1. The revelation of the message of *Tawḥid (verse 2).*
2. The blessing of the world being created for a great purpose *(verse 3).*
3. The blessing of humankind being created from sexual fluids, despite which he disbelieves in the next life *(verse 4).*
4. The blessing of livestock (*verses 5 & 7).*
5. The blessing of riding animals and all other modes of transport *(verse 8).*
6. The blessing of intellect to recognize benefit from harm and by which to seek guidance *(verse 9).*
7. The blessing of rain for people, animals, plants, etc. *(verses 10-11).*
8. The subjugation of the day and night, and the sun, moon, and stars for our many uses *(verse 12).*
9. The generality of good produce yielded from the earth *(verse 13).*
10. The ocean and the goodness it contains *(verse 14).*
11. The stabilizing of the earth with mountains *(verse 15).*
12. The natural landmarks that aid in travel *(verse 16).*
13. The blessing of water *(verse 65).*
14. The blessing of milk *(verse 66).*
15. Good sustenance from dates and grapes *(verse 67).*
16. The blessing of honey and the amazing process by which it is made *(verses 68-69).*
17. The blessing of life and death *(verse 70).*
18. The blessing of varying degrees of wealth *(verse 71).*
19. The blessing of marriage and reproduction *(verse 72).*
20. The blessing of the physical senses and sound mind *(verse 78).*
21. The blessing of the sky and birds *(verse 79).*

22. The blessing of home and furnishings *(verse 80).*
23. The blessing of shelter from the elements through shade, caves, and clothing *(verse 81).*

- It explains how those who do not believe in the hereafter deny Allah's blessings through arrogance and denial. It explains many ways that people deny blessings (see verses 53, 54, 58, 73, 101, 103). Verse 112 is a key closing verse highlighting the main theme of the *Sūrah.* It mentions the similitude of the city that showed ingratitude for Allah's favors.
- Presenting a series of legal rulings related to migration, jihad, commanding justice and goodness, and forbidding immorality, evil, and breaking promises.
- Presenting a model for the grateful, exemplified by Ibrāhīm (عَلَيْهِ ٱلسَّلَامُ), who was a nation unto himself. We then are told of the reward of patience and righteousness *(see verses 120-124).*

Concluding Summary of Sūrah al-Naḥl:[10]

The Sūrah abounds in multiple evidences of Allah's exclusive right to worship, proofs of the falseness of polytheism and its vile nature, evidence of Muhammad's prophethood, the revelation of the Qur'ān to him, and that Islam's legislation is based on the religion of Ibrāhīm (عَلَيْهِ ٱلسَّلَامُ).

It establishes belief in resurrection and recompense, beginning with the warning that the punishment of Allah, which the polytheists mock, is near. It then rebukes the polytheists for their steadfastness in polytheism and denial. The Sūrah moves on to disprove the belief in polytheism, starting with reminding of Allah's creation of the heavens and the earth, the celestial bodies, and the various creatures on Earth, including the changing times of day and night. The Sūrah specifically mentions bees and their benefits as an example. It highlights the Qur'ān's exalted status, protected from Satan's reach, and debunks the polytheists' claims against the Qur'ān. It argues for the possibility of resurrection as a re-creation similar to the creation of existing beings.

It warns of the fate that befell nations that engaged in polytheism and denied their prophets—punishment in this world and the hereafter, contrasting this with the bliss of those who were pious, believed, endured the harm of the polytheists, and migrated for the sake of Allah after being oppressed.

It warns against apostasy from Islam and allows for dissimulation by those forced into disbelief. It commands abiding by the foundations of Sharia, including justice, kindness, mutual support, fulfilling promises, prohibiting indecency, evil, tyranny, and the breaking of covenants, with the corresponding recompense for good deeds in both this life and the hereafter.

It includes moral lessons, cosmic proofs, encouragement for gratitude, reminders of wholesome sustenance, the beauty of creation, knowledge of time, navigation signs in land and sea, and parables.

It contrasts actions with their opposites, warns against falling into Satan's traps, alerts us to the consequences of ingratitude for blessings, and then offers a call to repentance. The key to the method of

[10] Adapted from al-Taḥrīr.

Islamic da'wah is to invite to Allah's way with wisdom. It reassures and promises support from Allah to His messenger.

CONTEMPLATE, COMPREHEND, APPLY

Contemplation Insights from Page 267 [Sūrah Al-Naḥl 1-6]

- Allah called revelation a "spirit" because it is with it that souls are enlivened.
- Allah has granted us control over cattle and beasts, subduing them for us, and permitted us to utilize and benefit from them out of His mercy towards us.

Contemplation Insights from Page 268 [Al-Naḥl 7-14]

- It's a sign of Allah's greatness that He creates what no human knows at any time He wills.
- Allah created the stars as ornaments of the sky, for navigation in the darkness of land and sea, and for determining times and calculating periods.
- Praising and thanking Allah, who bestowed what sustains our lives and aids us in living better.
- Allah's favor upon us includes subjugating the sea to obtain food (fish), extracting pearls and corals for transportation and trade, and defending the nation from the harm of invaders and colonial aggressors.

Contemplation Insights from Page 269 [Al-Naḥl 15-26]

- The verses include a significant variety of Allah's blessings upon His servants, both general and detailed, inviting them to thank and remember Him.
- Human nature involves oppression and boldness in committing sins and neglecting the rights of their Lord, ungrateful for His blessings except for those whom Allah guides.
- Equating the misleader with the misled in the crime of misguidance, for without his misguidance, the misled might have been guided by reflection or by asking those who advise rightly.
- Allah's sudden seizing of the criminals inflicts more terror, unlike what comes gradually.

Contemplation Insights from Page 270 [Al-Naḥl 27-34]

- The virtue of the people of knowledge is that they speak the truth in this world and on the Day of Testimony, and their words are considered by Allah and His creation.
- Part of the angels' manners towards Allah is attributing knowledge to Him without saying, "Indeed, we know what you were doing," indicating that they knew only because Allah taught them.
- From Allah's generosity and existence, He grants the people of Paradise all they wish for, even reminding them of delights they hadn't thought of.
- Deeds are the basis for entering Paradise and being saved from Hell, ultimately by Allah's mercy and favor upon the believers, not by their power and strength.

Contemplation Insights from Page 271 [Al-Naḥl 35-42]

- The wise person learns and takes heed from what befell the misguided deniers, seeing how their end was destruction, ruin, torment, and annihilation.
- The wisdom behind resurrection and accountability is to manifest the truth in people's differing views regarding resurrection and everything else.
- Patience is due to suppressing the self, and reliance is about turning away from creation and towards the truth.
- The reward for those who emigrated, leaving their homes and wealth, bore hardships, and relied on their Lord is a better abode, a noble station, a satisfying life, abundant provision, victory over enemies, and dominion over lands and people.

Contemplation Insights from Page 272 [Al-Naḥl 43-54]

- The wrongdoer should feel ashamed before Allah for receiving His blessings at all times while his sins ascend to his Lord at every moment.
- Those who disbelieve and deny engaging in various sins should fear Allah's punishment, catching them unawares.
- All blessings, whether material like sustenance, safety, health, or moral like security, prestige, and position, are from Allah.
- In times of hardship, humans find no refuge but in Allah, earnestly supplicating to Him, knowing no one else can relieve distress.

Contemplation Insights from Page 273 [Al-Naḥl 55-64]

- Among the ignorance of the polytheists is attributing daughters to Allah (عَزَّوَجَلَّ) while claiming sons for themselves, their aversion to daughters, their faces darkening with sorrow and grief at the birth of a daughter. One of them hiding from the community because of the intense sadness, shame, and dishonor brought about by the birth of a daughter.
- The respite given to disbelievers without hastening their punishment, which allows them to believe and repent, comes from the Sunnah of Allah.
- The primary mission of the Prophet (صَلَّىٱللَّهُعَلَيْهِوَسَلَّمَ) is to elucidate what is in the Qur'ān and clarify matters of religion and law disputed among people of different beliefs and whims, thus establishing the argument against them.

Contemplation Insights from Page 274 [Al-Naḥl 65-72]

- Allah made for His servants benefits and provisions from the fruits of palm trees and grapevines, which people consume fresh and preserved as food and drink.
- The creation of the small bee and what comes from its belly of delicious honey of varying colors according to the differences in its land and pastures is evidence of Allah's perfect care and complete kindness to His servants, showing He alone deserves to be loved and called upon.
- Among the great favors of Allah to His servants is granting them spouses for tranquility and granting them children from their spouses, who are a source of joy, assistance, and numerous benefits.

Contemplation Insights from Page 275 [Al-Naḥl 73-79]

- Allah's profound wisdom in distributing sustenance among His servants, making some wealthy, some poor, and some of moderate means, is to ensure the world's functioning, people's coexistence, and mutual assistance.
- The examples in the verses demonstrate the misguidedness of polytheists and the invalidity of idol worship, as the essence of a deity is to be an owner capable of managing affairs, benefiting those who worship him, and commanding righteousness and justice.
- Among His favors and manifestations of His power is creating people from their mothers' wombs knowing nothing, then providing them with means of knowledge and understanding, such as hearing, sight, and hearts.

Contemplation Insights from Page 276 [Al-Naḥl 80-87]

- The verses indicate the permissibility of benefiting from wool, fur, and hair in all states, including their use in homes and furnishings.
- The abundance of blessings calls for increased gratitude from the servants and praise for Allah (عَزَّوَجَلَّ).
- The most truthful and just of witnesses in every nation are the messengers, whose testimony finalizes the judgment when they bear witness.
- Allah's statement about garments that protect you in battle suggests the permissibility of preparing for jihad to assist in fighting enemies.

Contemplation Insights from Page 277 [Al-Naḥl 88-93]

- For the disbelievers who obstruct Allah's way, there is a doubled punishment due to their corruption in the world through disbelief and disobedience.
- The earth never lacks people of righteousness and knowledge, who are the guides of guidance, successors of the prophets, and scholars, the protectors of the prophets' laws.
- These verses outlined the pillars of the Muslim community in private and public life for individuals, groups, and the state.
- The prohibition against bribery and taking money to break a covenant.

Contemplation Insights from Page 278 [Al-Naḥl 94-102]

- Righteous deeds coupled with faith make life good.
- The path to safety from the evil of Satan is seeking refuge with Allah and seeking His protection from Satan's evil.
- Believers should make the Qur'ān their leader, nurtured by its sciences, adopt its morals, and be illuminated by its light, for it will straighten their religious and worldly affairs.
- The abrogation of rulings in the Qur'ān during the time of revelation is for wisdom, considering benefits, incidents, and changing human conditions.

Contemplation Insights from Page 279 [Al-Naḥl 103-110]

- Being forced against one's will into uttering disbelief outwardly is permitted while the heart remains secure in faith.
- Apostates deserve Allah's wrath and punishment for preferring worldly life over the hereafter, being deprived of Allah's guidance, and having their hearts, hearing, and sight sealed by Allah, rendering them heedless of the severe punishment awaiting them on the Day of Judgment.
- Allah has decreed forgiveness and mercy for those who believed, migrated after they were persecuted, and persevered in striving.

Contemplation Insights from Page 280 [Al-Naḥl 111-118]

- The recompense is proportional to the deed, as the inhabitants of the village who extravagantly enjoyed the blessings were replaced with their opposites: the eradication and deprivation of these blessings, leading them to experience severe hunger after satiety, fear, and panic after security and tranquility, and scarcity in livelihood after sufficiency.
- The obligation to believe in Allah and His messengers, to worship Allah alone, to be grateful for His numerous blessings and favors, and that divine punishment is inevitably upon everyone who disbelieves in Allah, disobeys Him and denies His blessings upon them.
- Allah has forbidden us only the impurities out of His grace and to keep everything detestable from us.

Contemplation Insights from Page 281 [Al-Naḥl 119-128]:

- Allah's mercy requires accepting the repentance of His servants who commit sins, including disbelief and disobedience, then repent and reform their deeds, upon which Allah forgives them.
- Muslims are encouraged to take Prophet Ibrahim as a role model.
- Callers to the religion of Allah should follow these three methods: wisdom, good admonition, and arguing in the best way.
- Punishment is proportional without excess.

CONTEMPLATION STUDY QUESTIONS

Verse 8: Why doesn't the verse mention eating as one of the benefits of these items? How does the Qur'ān mention the unseen blessings through this verse? *[Al-Sa'dī]*

Verse 8: What is the relation between the two mentioned verses? *[Ibn Kathīr]*

Verse 18: Why does the verse end with the attributes of being Forgiving and Merciful? *[Al-Sa'dī]*

Verse 19: What practical benefit does knowing that Allah is aware of what you conceal and what you reveal provide? *[Ibn Kathīr]*

Verse 27: What is the virtue of the people of knowledge mentioned in the verse?

Verse 28: How do you reconcile the disbelievers' denial of their deeds on the Day of Judgment with their admission of them? *[Al-Sa'dī]*

Verse 29: Hell has seven gates, so through which gate will the people of Hell enter? *[Al-Sa'dī]*

Verse 29: The disbeliever goes through two stages of punishment after death; what are they? *[Al-Sa'dī]*

Verse 32: How do you make yourself "pure" at the time of death? *[Al-Sa'dī]*

Verse 43: The verse indicates a virtue for the people of knowledge. Explain it. The best scholars are those closest to the Qur'ān and elaborate on this through the verse. *[Al-Sa'dī]*

Verse 47: The best scholars are those closest to the Qur'ān; elaborate on this through the verse. *[Al-Sa'dī]*

Verse 56: Explain the folly of the polytheists in dedicating acts of worship to partners other than Allah. *[Al-Sa'dī]*

Verse 56: What is meant by informing them that they will be asked about what they fabricate? *[Ibn Kathīr]*

Verse 61: The harm of sin from an individual reflects on the entire community; explain this through the verse.

Verse 66: What is the lesson from milk coming out from the bellies of cattle? *[Ibn Kathīr]*

Verse 67: What are the lessons that the wise can derive from the existence of various fruits? *[Al-Sa'dī]*

Verse 67: What is the appropriateness of ending the verse mentioning intellect? *[Ibn Kathīr]*

Verse 69: Why did Allah (عَزَّوَجَلَّ) say "therein is healing" and not "the healing"? *[Ibn Kathīr]*

Verse 78: Why were these three organs specifically mentioned? *[Al-Sa'dī]*

Verse 79: Why were the believers specifically mentioned benefiting from creational signs? *[Al-Sa'dī]*

Verse 81: Why is heat specifically mentioned rather than cold in this verse? *[Al-Sa'dī]*

Verse 81: Some scholars call Sūrah Al-Naḥl "The Chapter of Blessings"; what is the reason for this naming? *[Ibn Kathīr]*

Verse 81: When blessings are abundant on a person, what is their duty towards them? *[Al-Sa'dī]*

Verse 84: Why are those who disbelieved not permitted to offer excuses? *[Al-Sa'dī]*

Verse 96: What can the wise Muslim derive from this verse? *[Al-Sa'dī]*

Verse 97: Why does Allah condition good deeds with faith in this verse? *[Al-Sa'dī]*

Verse 98: This verse mentions an effective method to ponder the Qur'ān; what is it? *[Ibn Kathīr]*

Verse 99: What authority is denied to Satan over those who believe? *[Ibn Kathīr]*

Verse 106: If the conditions of coercion are met, then Allah's mercy is broader than restricting His servants; explain this from the verse. *[Al-Sa'dī]*

Verse 106: Why is the sin of apostasy from Islam greater than the sin of original disbelief? *[Ibn Kathīr]*

Verse 107: The verse indicates a major reason for the apostasy of many apostates; what is it? *[Ibn Kathīr]*

Verse 115: What is the rationale behind the prohibition of certain foods? *[Al-Sa'dī]*

Verse 116: How does the verse indicate the prohibition of innovations in religion? *[Ibn Kathīr]*

Verse 119: Why is the sinner described as ignorant? *[Ibn Kathīr]*

Verse 125: How should arguing in the best manner be conducted? *[Al-Sa'dī]*

سُورَةُ الإِسْرَاء
AL ISRĀ' (17)
The Night Journey

VERSES
111

WORDS
1,533

LETTERS
6,460

REVEALED IN
MAKKAH

REVEALATION ORDER
50

The Prophet ﷺ would not go to bed without reciting *Sūrah al Isrā'* and *Sūrah al-Zumar*.[11] It was revealed in the tenth year of the prophethood after the deaths of Khadījah and Abū Ṭālib, which is called the year of sadness because a loss of support left the Muslims extremely vulnerable in Makkah. It is thought to have been revealed after *Sūrah al Qaṣaṣ* and before *Sūrah Yunus*.

After mentioning the night journey, the *Sūrah* mentions the transfer of trust for the message from *Banu Isrā'īl* to this most excellent nation *(verses 2-3)*. The reasons for that transfer were the Israelites' failings. This is mentioned in some detail, beginning with verse 4.

Main Themes: The lofty status of the Qur'ānic message and the excellence of the Messenger. The Prophet's ﷺ status is mentioned in verse 1; the perfection of his message is mentioned in verse 9; the beautiful outcome awaiting him on Judgment Day is mentioned in verse 79. The *Sūrah* highlights that continuous blessing and divine honor are in store for those who hold fast to the truth. Gratitude brings a perpetual increase and Divine Honor. The highest such examples of this were *Isra'* and the revelation of the *Qur'ān*.

It is named al Isrā' because it begins with the mention of the Isra' incident, one of the remarkable miracles that Allah (سُبْحَانَهُۥ وَتَعَالَىٰ) exclusively bestowed upon His Prophet (صَلَّى ٱللَّهُ عَلَيْهِ وَسَلَّمَ), involving the transition of the book and the message from the Children of Israel to the nation of the Prophet (صَلَّى ٱللَّهُ عَلَيْهِ وَسَلَّمَ).

This Sūrah addresses the Islamic creed in its various aspects. It speaks about the Messenger and his message, the Qur'ān and its guidance, and the people's stance towards it; then, it addresses human behavior and the foundations of a healthy Islamic society. It distinguished

[11] Reported by Ahmad; see Ṣaḥīḥ al Jāmi' 4874.

itself by exalting Allah above what the polytheists claim. It includes stories about the Children of Israel and mentions part of Adam's story, initiating the discourse on Al-Isra'.

The relevance of this Sūrah to Sūrah Al-Naḥl is from several aspects:

1 As Allah mentioned the dispute of the Jews about the Sabbath in Sūrah Al-Naḥl, here He mentioned the Sabbath law prescribed for them in the Torah. Ibn Jarir (رَحِمَهُ ٱللَّهُ) reported from Ibn Abbas (رَضِيَ ٱللَّهُ عَنْهُ) that he said, "The entire Torah is in fifteen verses from Sūrah Bani Israel."

2 After commanding His Prophet (صَلَّى ٱللَّهُ عَلَيْهِ وَسَلَّمَ) to be patient and prohibiting him from feeling saddened and constrained by their schemes in the previous Sūrah, His honor and high status with his Lord are mentioned here.

3 As the previous Sūrah mentioned many blessings to the extent it was named Sūrah of Blessings, specific and general blessings are also mentioned.

4 There, it was mentioned that from the bellies of bees comes a drink of varying colors, a healing for people, and here it is mentioned, "And We send down from the Qur'an what is a healing and a mercy to the believers."

5 As that Sūrah commanded to give to the relatives, so does this Sūrah, with the addition of giving to the needy and the traveler.

The connection between its beginning and end:

The Sūrah starts by mentioning the Qur'an, "Indeed, this Qur'an guides to that which is most upright."

It also ends with mentioning the Qur'an, "And with truth, We have sent it down, and with the truth it has descended." This reaffirms the importance of the Qur'an, illustrating its status and value.

The Presentation of the Main Theme:

1. The book transitions and the message from the Children of Israel to the new nation (verses 2, 3).

2. The negligence of the Children of Israel regarding their book (verse 4).

3. The receiving of the Qur'an by the nation of Muhammad (صَلَّى ٱللَّهُ عَلَيْهِ وَسَلَّمَ) (verse 9).

4. All commands of the Holy Qur'an are consistent with human nature, such as honoring parents, kindness to relatives and orphans, prohibiting wastefulness and stinginess, prohibiting the killing of children and self without right, prohibiting fornication, the sanctity of people's wealth especially orphans, keeping promises, equity in weight and measure, humility In the span of 17 verses, Allah issues around 14 commandments and prohibitions (verses 23-39).

5. Demonstrating the unmatchable value of the Qur'an (verses 45, 58, 60, 73, 78, 79).

6. The Qur'an is healing and mercy (verse 82).

7. The magnificence and majesty of the Qur'an (verses 88, 89).

8. The purpose of the revelation of the Qur'an (verses 105, 106).

9. An invitation to believe in the Qur'an and not to neglect it as previous nations neglected their books {verses 107-109}

Broader Overview of the Sūrah:

The foundation upon which the purposes of this Sūrah are built is affirming Muhammad's prophethood, that the Qur'an is divine revelation, highlighting its excellence and the excellence of whom it was revealed to, mentioning it is a miracle, refuting the objections of the polytheists about it and its bringer, and their failure to comprehend it, hence their disregard for it, and invalidating their denial of the Prophet's night journey to Al-Masjid Al-Aqsa.

It starts with the miraculous event of Iṣrā' as a prelude to comparing Islamic law with the Mosaic law. By doing so, Allah symbolized that he had granted Muhammad (ﷺ) greater virtues than before and had completed his station of merit and virtue. He granted him access to al Aqṣā, the sacred place held in the highest esteem by previous prophets, indicating his nation would renew its glory and that Allah had empowered him in prophecy and law, despite the desolation of Al-Masjid Al-Aqsa at the time of this Sūrah's revelation.

The Sūrah highlights Allah's uniqueness in divinity and uses the alternation of night and day and the blessings therein to establish monotheism. It reminds us of the favors Allah made subservient to people, indicates His sole ability to organize creation, necessitates gratitude to the benefactor alone, and purifies Him of having counterparts, such as the daughters attributed to Him by the polytheists.

It reveals the virtues of Islamic law and its wisdom, teaches Muslims the etiquettes of dealing with their Lord and each other, and being mindful of Allah in public and private lives. It includes parables, healing and mercy warnings, and examples that combine knowledge and wisdom.

CONTEMPLATE, COMPREHEND, APPLY

Contemplation Insights from Page 283 [Al-Isra 1-7]

- His saying: "the furthest masjid," is an indication of that land's eventual inclusion under the rule of Islam, for a masjid is a place of worship for Muslims.
- Illustrating the virtue of gratitude, and following the grateful among the prophets and messengers.
- It is from Allah's wisdom and His Sunnah to send upon the corrupt those who prevent them from corruption to fulfill Allah's wisdom in reform.
- A warning for this nation against committing sins, lest they be afflicted with what befell the Children of Israel, for Allah's Sunnah is one; it does not change or shift.

Contemplation Insights from Page 283 [Al-Isra 8-17]

- Those guided by the guidance of the Qur'ān are the most complete, upright, and guided people in all their affairs.
- A warning against praying for evil upon oneself, one's children, or one's wealth.
- The alteration of night and day, their increase and decrease, their alternation between them, the brightness of the day and the darkness of the night—all are evidence of Allah's oneness, existence, and the perfection of His knowledge and power.
- The verses establish personal responsibility as an act of justice from Allah and mercy to His servants.

Contemplation Insights from Page 284 [Al-Isra 18-27]

- It is incumbent upon a person to do what they are capable of doing in terms of good deeds and to intend to do what they are incapable of so that they may be rewarded for that.
- The blessings in this world should not be taken as evidence of Allah's pleasure, for the world may be granted even though its end may be Allah's punishment.
- Being kind to parents is a mandatory and obligatory duty, and Allah has associated gratitude to them with gratitude to Him due to their immense favor.
- Islam prohibits wastefulness, which is spending money in ways other than its rightful use.

Contemplation Insights from Page 285 [Al-Isra 28-38]

- The high moral standard is to gently turn away relatives, promise them a good connection when able, and apologize to them acceptably.
- Allah is more merciful to the children than their parents; hence, He forbade parents from killing their children out of fear of poverty, and He guaranteed to provide for everyone.
- The verses indicate that the right to execute capital punishment belongs to the guardian, and it can only be carried out with his permission; if he forgives, the right to retaliate is dropped.
- From Allah's kindness and mercy, the orphan commands their guardians to preserve and protect their wealth and to improve and grow it until they reach maturity.

Contemplation Insights from Page 286 [Al-Isra 39-49]

- Claiming that angels are Allah's daughters is a great fabrication and a sin of immense magnitude before Allah (عَزَّوَجَلَّ).
- Most people do not increase [in faith] upon seeing Allah's signs except in aversion because they despise the truth and love what they were upon of falsehood.
- There is no creature in the heavens and the earth, but it glorifies Allah with praise, so it behooves a servant not to be outdone by the creatures in glorification.
- From Allah's forbearance with His servants is that He does not hasten to punish them for their negligence and misdeeds, for His mercy precedes His anger.

Contemplation Insights from Page 287 [Al-Isra 50-58]

- Good speech is a call to all beautiful manners and righteous deeds, for whoever masters their tongue controls all their affairs.
- Allah distinguished among prophets some over others with knowledge and wisdom.
- Allah only wants what is good for His servants and commands them according to their best interests.
- A sign of Allah's love is the servant's effort in every act that brings them closer to Allah and their competition in closeness through the sincerity of all their deeds to Allah and their advice.

Contemplation Insights from Page 288 [Al-Isra 59-66]

- Out of Allah's mercy for people, He does not send down the signs that the deniers demand so as not to hasten their punishment if they deny them.
- Allah tested the servants with Satan, who invites them to disobey Allah through his whispers and actions.
- Among the ways Satan shares with humans in their wealth and children are neglecting to mention Allah's name over food, drink, and during sexual intercourse, and not disciplining the children.

Contemplation Insights from Page 289 [Al-Isra 67-75]

- Humans are ungrateful for blessings except for those whom Allah guides.
- Every nation will be called to its religion and its book, whether they acted upon it or not, and Allah does not punish anyone except after the proof has been established against them and they opposed it.
- The hostility of the criminals and deniers towards the messengers and their successors is evident due to the truth they carry, not because of their selves.
- Allah protected the Prophet from the means of harm and people, thus stabilizing him and guiding him to the straight path, and his successors have similar protection according to their following of him.

Contemplation Insights from Page 290 [Al-Isra 76-86]

- The verses indicate the great need of the servant for Allah to make him steadfast, and he should constantly beseech his Lord to make him steadfast in faith.
- When the truth appears, falsehood vanishes, and falsehood only prevails in times and places where the people of truth become lazy.
- The healing in the Qur'ān is general, for healing hearts from doubts, ignorance, corrupt opinions, deviations, and ill intentions.
- The verses indicate that if a person is asked about something that is not in the asker's best interest, it's better to avoid answering and instead guide them to what they need and what benefits them.

Contemplation Insights from Page 291 [Al-Isra 87-96]

- Allah has clarified to people in the Qur'ān everything that can be a lesson, warning, command, prohibition, and stories, hoping they would believe.

- The Qur'ān is the word of Allah and the eternal miracle of the Prophet, and no one can bring something like it.
- Out of Allah's mercy to His servants, He sent them a human messenger, for they could not bear to receive the message directly from angels.
- Among Allah's testimonies to His Messenger are the signs He supported him with and His victory over his adversaries.

Contemplation Insights from Page 292 [Al-Isra 97-104]

- Allah alone is singular in guiding and leading astray; whoever He guides is truly guided, and whoever He leads astray and forsakes, there is no guide for them.
- The abode and resting place of disbelievers is Hell; whenever its fire subsides, Allah increases its flames.
- The necessity of holding firmly to Allah when faced with threats from tyrants and oppressors.
- Tyrants and oppressors resort to using power and force when confronted with the people of truth because they cannot face them with evidence and clear arguments.

Contemplation Insights from Page 293 [Al-Isra 105-111]

- Allah revealed the Qur'ān encompassing truth, justice, the perfect law, and ruling.
- It is permissible to weep during prayer out of fear of Allah.
- The supplication or reading in prayer should be done moderately, between loud and silent.

CONTEMPLATION STUDY QUESTIONS

Verse 1: Was the Prophet's Night Journey (Isra) with his soul only or with his soul and body? Explain. *[Ibn Kathīr]*

Verse 1: What is the wisdom behind describing the Prophet as a servant in this context? *[Al-Sa'dī]*

Verse 8: How can you benefit from such verses when you read a verse from the Qur'ān about another nation? *[Al-Sa'dī]*

Verse 14: Discuss the perfection of Allah's justice through this verse. *[Al-Sa'dī]*

Verse 17: What does it mean that Allah has destroyed many nations after the people of Noah? *[Ibn Kathīr]*

Verse 18: In Hell, there is psychological and physical punishment. Explain this in light of this verse. *[Al-Sa'dī]*

Verse 24: We often hear that a teacher is a second father. What rights does this teacher deserve? *[Al-Sa'dī]*

Verse 30: What is the significance of ending this verse with the All-Knowing and All-Seeing attributes? *[Ibn Kathīr]*

Verse 31: Who is more merciful to you? Your Lord, or your parents? And why? *[Ibn Kathīr]*

Verse 32: What is the difference between "Do not approach adultery" and "Do not commit adultery"? Which is more emphatic and stronger in prohibition? What reasons made adultery deserving of being described as a grave sin? *[Al-Sa'dī]*

Verse 46: What are the signs of having a veil or cover over the heart? *[Al-Sa'dī]*

Verse 47: What is the best way to benefit from the Qur'ān when hearing its verses? *[Al-Sa'dī]*

Verse 51: Asking the polytheists about the time of the Day of Judgment is a misplaced question. Why? *[Al-Sa'dī]*

Verse 53: What is the difference between good speech and better speech, and which were we commanded with? The devil enters into your conversation with people; how do you handle that? *[Al-Sa'dī]*

Verse 57: How important are hope and fear in a believer's life? *[Ibn Kathīr]*

Verse 73: What caused the polytheists to oppose the Prophet ﷺ? And how can a caller benefit from this? *[Al-Sa'dī]*

Verse 74: These verses indicate the intense need of the servant for Allah to affirm him. Explain. *[Al-Sa'dī]*

Verse 75: Why is a mistake from the Prophet ﷺ, a scholar, or a caller to Allah if it occurs greater than a mistake from others? *[Al-Sa'dī]*

Verse 90: Why did Allah not respond to the requests of the polytheists? *[Ibn Kathīr]*

Verse 92: Why did the Prophet ﷺ not pray to his Lord to drop the sky in fragments on these stubborn deniers who requested that? *[Ibn Kathīr]*

Verse 102: Mūsā, being truthful and trusted, said: "You know what these [signs] have been sent down by none but the Lord of the heavens and the earth as clear [evidence]." This indicated that Pharaoh knew that Allah sent the signs, despite being one of Allah's most defiant and oppressive creations, due to the corruption of his intention and purpose, not because of his lack of knowledge. *[Ibn Taymiyyah: 4/248]*

Verse 106: What is the best way to read the Qur'ān for someone who wants to contemplate it? *[Al-Sa'dī]*

DAY 15: AL KAHF & MARYAM

The Qur'ān reading for day 15 is Sūrah al Kahf and Sūrah Maryam. The main theme of the former is dealing with trials of every variety, while the main theme of the latter is leaving behind a legacy after one's death.

سُورَةُ الكَهْفِ

AL KAHF (18)

The Cave

VERSES	110
WORDS	1,577
LETTERS	6,360
REVEALED IN	MAKKAH*
REVEALATION ORDER	69

It is said to have been revealed mostly in Makkah, with a few verses in Madinah.

✦ Main Themes: When greatly blessed, expect to be tested and tried. Safeguarding oneself from trials.

The blessed Sūrah mentions various trials a person may face, including trials of wealth, authority, knowledge, and religion. It is named after the People of the Cave (Ahl al-Kahf) because they encountered the greatest of these trials: the trial of faith. This story exemplifies the challenges believers may face in preserving their faith amidst pressures and threats to their belief system. It illustrates the significance of steadfastness, reliance on Allah, and seeking divine protection against such trials.

There are many examples of da'wah and resilience in the face of various types of trials in this Sūrah:

- Young people invited their king and people to the truth despite being tried religiously (verses 9-29).
- A friend invited his companion to attribute his blessings to Allah so that he would not be destroyed by the trial of wealth (verses 32-44).

- Between the first two and last two of these stories, we find the story of the chief cause of all fitnah and evil, Iblīs, who is driven by his ancient enmity for the children of Ādam (verse 50).
- A teacher invites his student to patience, the trial of learning knowledge (verses 60-80).
- A king invites his subjects to the truth despite the trial of leadership and authority (verses 83-101).

Burhān al-Dīn al Biqā'ī (d. 885 AH رَحِمَهُ ٱللَّهُ) said:

ومقصودها: وصف الكتاب بأنه قيم، لكونه زاجراً عن الشريك الذي هو خلاف ما قام عليه الدليل في "سبحان "، من أنه لا وكيل دونه، ولا إله إلا هو وقاصًا بالحق أخبار قوم قد فضلوا في أزمانهم، وفق ما وقع الخبر به في سبحان، من أنه يفضل من يشاء، ويفعل ما يشاء.

"Its primary objective is to demonstrate the Qur'an's characteristic as an authoritative guide, emphasizing its role in admonishing against associating partners with Allah—a concept that directly opposes what (Surah al Isrā') proved, which is that there is no wakīl (guardian to be entrusted) or deity in truth besides Him. It narrates truthful accounts of various peoples distinguished in their times, as was reported in (Surah al Isrā'), showing that Allah distinguishes whom He chooses and does as He wills.

وأدل ما فيها على هذا المقصد: قصة أهل الكهف، لأن خبرهم أخفى ما فيها من القصص، مع أن سبب فراقهم لقومهم الشرك، وكان أمرهم موجباً بعد طول رقادهم للوحدانية، وإبطال الشرك

The story of the People of the Cave (Ahl al-Kahf) is presented as a prime example of the Qur'an's purpose. Despite the obscurity of their story among the Qur'an's narratives, their separation from their people due to idolatry and their long sleep, which ultimately reaffirms the principle of monotheism and the rejection of polytheism, encapsulates the message the Qur'an aims to convey."

The Sūrah discusses the Noble Qur'ān and its impact, then narrates the story of the People of the Cave with its lessons. It follows with beneficial directives, setting a practical example for those deluded by worldly life and its allure while reminding people of the Day of Judgment. Amidst this, there are judgments, verses, directives, and warnings. Then, it moves on to the story of Mūsā with Al-Khidr and a discussion in response to those who asked about the soul and Dhul-Qarnayn. The Sūrah concludes magnificently with discourse about the believers and the inexhaustible words of Allah.

The connection between this Sūrah and the previous one (Al-Isra) is highlighted from several aspects:

1 Sūrah Al-Isra opens with glorification (*Tasbih*), and this Sūrah begins with praise (*Tahmid*), both of which are often linked in speech, as in "So glorify the praises of your Lord" and similar phrases like "*SubhanAllah wa biHamdihi*" (Glory be to Allah and His is the praise).

2 The conclusion of the previous Sūrah and the beginning of this one are similar in that both praise Allah.

3 The previous Sūrah mentions, "And you have been given of knowledge but little," addressing the Jews. Here, the story of Mūsā, the prophet of the Children of Israel, with Al-Khidr, is mentioned, which demonstrates the vastness of Allah's knowledge that is beyond count, serving as evidence for the statement made previously.

4 The previous Sūrah states, "So when the promise of the Hereafter comes, We shall bring you all together." Then this is detailed here with, "So when the promise of my Lord comes, He will make it level, and the promise of my Lord is true," leading to the presentation of Hell to the disbelievers on that Day, as mentioned in verse 100.

The beginning and end of the Sūrah contain the mention of the Qur'ān's status: It starts by praising Allah for sending down the Book to His servant without any crookedness, and it concludes with the mention of the Qur'ān, emphasizing the inexhaustibility of Allah's words. Given the Sūrah's discussion on trials, it is fitting that it both begins and ends with references to the Qur'ān, as it protects against all kinds of trials, the last of which is the trial of the antichrist.

Al-Suyuti (رَحِمَهُ ٱللَّهُ) said in 'Hashiyah Abi Dawud': Al-Qurtubi (رَحِمَهُ ٱللَّهُ) stated:[12]

اختَلَف المتأوّلون في سبب ذلك، فقيل: لِمَا في قصّة أصحاب الكهف من العجائب والآيات، فمن وَقَفَ عليها لم يَستغرب أمر الدجّال، ولم يَهِلْهُ ذلك، فلم يُفتن به.

"The interpreters have disagreed about the reason for this. It has been said: Due to what is in the story of the People of the Cave from wonders and signs, whoever comes upon it will not find the matter of the Dajjāl (Antichrist) strange, nor will it alarm him, thus he will not be tempted by him.

وقيل: لقوله تعالى: {لِيُنْذِرَ بَأْسًا شَدِيدًا مِنْ لَدُنْهُ} [الكهف: 2] تمسّكًا بتخصيص البأس بالشدّة واللدنية، وهو مناسب لما يكون من الدجّال من دعوى الإلهيّة، واستيلائه، وعِظَم فتنبّه، ولذلك عظّم النبيّ صلى الله عليه وسلم أمره، وحذّر منه، وتعوّذ من فتنبّه، فيكون معنى الحديث أن من قرأ هذه الآيات وتدبّرها، ووقف على معناها حَذِرَهُ، فأَمِنَ منه.

It has also been said: Due to Allah's saying: {To warn of severe punishment from Him} [Al-Kahf: 2], paying special attention to the punishment being specified as severe directly from Him, which is appropriate for what comes from the Dajjāl in terms of claiming divinity, his domination, and the greatness of his tribulation. Therefore, the Prophet (H) magnified the seriousness of his matter, warned against him, and sought refuge from his temptation. Hence, the meaning of the hadith is

[12] Al Baḥr al Muḥīṭ al-Thajjāj fī Sharḥ Sahih al-Imam Muslim bin al-Hajjaj" (16/387).

that whoever recites these verses, contemplates them, and understands their meaning will be wary of him and thus be safe from him.

وقيل: إن ذلك من خصائص هذه السورة كلّها، فقد روي: "من حفظ سورة الكهف، ثم أدركه الدجّال لم يُسلّط عليه"، وعلى هذا يجتمع رواية من روى من أول سورة الكهف مع رواية من روى من آخرها، ويكون ذكر العشر على جهة الاستدراج في حفظها كلّها. انتهى كلام السيوطيُّ".

And it has been said: That this is among the specific characteristics of this Surah as a whole. It has been narrated: 'Whoever memorizes Surah Al-Kahf and then encounters the Dajjal will not be subjected to him.' Based on this, the narration of those who narrated from the beginning of Surah Al-Kahf and the narration of those who narrated from its end come together, and mentioning the ten is on the aspect encourages to memorize it all. This concludes the words of al-Suyuti."

Broader Outline of the Sūrah:

- It begins with praising Allah for sending down the Book, highlighting the Qur'ān's significance as a favor from Allah towards the polytheists and their instructors from the People of the Book. It integrates a warning to those stubborn individuals who attributed a son to Allah and offers glad tidings to the believers, as well as consoling the Prophet (ﷺ) regarding their statements when revelation was delayed, following Allah's Sunnah (custom) with His allies by showing His displeasure towards negligence in observing perfect manners.
- It discusses the polytheists' infatuation with worldly life and its adornments, which do not purify souls, and moves to the story of the People of the Cave, as asked about. It warns them against Satan and his enmity towards Adam's progeny to keep them wary of his schemes.
- Before presenting the story of Dhul-Qarnayn, it brings forth a more significant narrative, the story of Mūsā and Al-Khidr, peace be upon them both. This is because both stories involved journeys for a noble purpose: Dhul-Qarnayn embarked on extending his dominion, and Mūsā sought knowledge. Mentioning Mūsā's story also indirectly criticizes the scholars of the Children of Israel, who were preoccupied with the tale of a king not from their people or religion, neglecting a narrative from their prophet's life.
- Included are digressions about guiding the Prophet and affirming the truth in his messages, highlighting that his constant companions were better than the dignitaries of the disbelievers, along with promises and warnings, comparisons between believers and disbelievers, and illustrations of worldly life's transience and what follows of resurrection and assembly. It reminds us of the fates of nations that deny messengers; it refutes polytheism and threatens its people while promising believers the opposite. It exemplifies Allah's vast knowledge and concludes with affirming the Qur'ān as a revelation from Allah to His messenger, making this conclusion an elegant way to reinforce the introduction.

BRIEF SŪRAH SUMMARY

Verses 1-8	The description of the *Qur'ān* and the sadness of the Prophet ﷺ for those who did not believe.
Verses 9-26	The story of *Aṣḥāb al Kahf*
Verses 27-31	Being kind to the poor and vulnerable amongst the believers; the believers reward and the disbelievers punishment in the hereafter.
Verses 32-44	Story of two men: one was proud of his religion and the other was deluded by worldly status.
Verses 45-59	A discussion about this world and the next, and about the incident of Ādam and Iblīs.
Verses 60-82	The story of Mūsā and Khaḍr.
Verses 83-101	The story of Dhul Qarnayn.
Verses 102-110	Concluding verses.

سُورَةُ مَرْيَمَ
MARYAM (19)
Mary

VERSES
98

WORDS
762

LETTERS
3,802

REVEALED IN
MAKKAH

REVEALATION ORDER
44

It is said to be the 44th in order of revelation. It was revealed before the Hijrah to Abyssinia. The Sūrah is distinguished by starting directly with stories without an introduction. Ja'far ibn Abi Talib (رَضِيَ اللَّهُ عَنْهُ) recited the opening of this Sūrah to the Negus of Abyssinia, which led to his conversion to Islam.

✦ Main Themes: The truth of the Hereafter; Leaving the religion as a legacy for one's offspring; Allah's perfect mercy with the creation and their complete need of Him; Allah's freedom of needing anything, let alone a son or helper.

The Sūrah aims to affirm the principle of monotheism for Allah, denying any partners or offspring associated with Him, and to establish the reality of resurrection for judgment. It utilizes stories as a means to achieve these ends.

Additionally, the Sūrah presents various spectacles of the Day of Judgment and addresses the arguments of those who deny the resurrection.

The name al-Raḥmān appears 16 times in this Sūrah (*see verses 18, 26, 44, 45, 58, 61, 69, 75, 78, 85, 87, 88, 91, 92, 93, 96*) The word mercy is mentioned ten times throughout beginning with the very first ayah.

It begins by mentioning Allah's ability to create children with or without fathers and concludes by mentioning that Allah does not need offspring. It contains the story of Maryam, the birth of 'Isā, and the story of Ibrāhīm inviting his father to Islam.

Examples of leaving the religion as a legacy for one's offspring:

(1.) Zakariya (see verses 2-15); (2.) Maryam (see verses 16-34); (3.) The opposite of this scenario is also mentioned in the story of Ibrahīm with his father (verses 41-50); (4.)

Despite the refusal of Ibrāhīm's father, Allah caused the legacy of Tawḥīd to be inherited from Ibrāhīm through 'Isḥāq and Ya'qūb. (5.) When this legacy was in jeopardy, Allah revived it with Mūsā (see verse 58).

After relating multiple stories of the prophets' legacy of guidance being preserved by their believing offspring, Allah (who is free of needing any person to preserve His religion) exalts and praises Himself for being free from needing offspring and warns that even the mere suggestion to the contrary is enough to destroy the universe itself, had it not been for his patience (see verse 90).

The name of the Sūrah highlights the virtue of Maryam (عَلَيْهَاالسَّلَامُ), as she is considered the best of the women of the worlds, as mentioned in a hadith where Fatimah (رَضِيَ اللَّهُ عَنْهَا)is referred to as the leader of the women of Paradise, except for Maryam bint Imran.13

The beginning and the end of the Sūrah are aligned in the concept of du'ā: The concept of du'ā (supplication) has two meanings: du'ā in the sense of worship, which includes faith and righteous deeds, and du'ā in the sense of asking, which involves requesting one's needs from Allah. The Sūrah starts with the mention of the du'ā of asking and concludes with the mention of du'ā as worship: "Indeed, those who believe and do righteous deeds the Most Merciful will appoint for them affection." As a whole, the Sūrah, from beginning to end, underscores the significance of religion in a believer's life and the perpetual need for devotion across generations.

The interconnection and appropriateness of this Sūrah succeeding the previous one is due to the extraordinary stories within both. Just as the preceding Sūrah includes wondrous tales like those of the People of the Cave, Mūsā's journey with Al-Khidr, and Dhul-Qarnayn, this Sūrah encompasses remarkable accounts of Yahya's birth to an old, fading man and a barren, elderly woman, and Isa's birth without a father. The shared element of these unusual and astonishing stories makes the placement of this Sūrah immediately after the other suitable.

A Broader Outlook at the Sūrah:

- The purpose of the Sūrah appears to be a response to the Jews for their heinous statements about Maryam and her son, clarifying the purity and sanctity of the family of Imran in goodness. It emphasizes the disgrace of those who attribute a partner or a child to Allah, contradicting the evidence in "Subhan" (Glory be to Him) that there is no agent or god but Him.

[13] This hadith was reported by Ahmad (authenticated in Sahih Al-Jami: 3181).

- It highlights a group of prophets and messengers from the ancestors and relatives of these families, criticizing some of their descendants from among the People of the Book and the polytheists who did not follow in their footsteps of goodness and made outrageous statements by attributing a child to Allah.
- It includes the story of Zakariya's honor when Allah answered his prayer by granting him a child despite his old age and his wife's barrenness. It mentions the miracle of Maryam's pregnancy and the sanctity of her child as a precursor to the prophecy of Isa ('Īsā) (عَلَيْهِ ٱلسَّلَامُ).
- The Sūrah also purifies Ibrahim, Ishaq, Ya'qub, Mūsā, Ismail, and Idris (عَلَيْهِمُ ٱلسَّلَامُ) describes Paradise and its people, recounts the denial of resurrection by the polytheists, and warns the polytheists that they will regret their worship of idols.
- It promises victory to the Messenger over his enemies, condemns attributing a child to Allah, and highlights the Qur'ān and its Arabic nature as a bearer of glad tidings for its allies and a warning of destruction for its opponents, similar to the fate of previous generations.
- The Sūrah repeats the attribute of the Most Merciful throughout, indicating its objective to affirm Allah's attribute of mercy and to counter the polytheists who denied this attribute, as Allah recounts in Sūrah Al Furqān.

BRIEF SŪRAH SUMMARY

Verses 1-50	The story of Zakariyya and Yaḥyā followed by the story of Maryam and 'Isā.
Verses 51-65	The story of Ibrahīm with his father, notice the soft tone of Ibrāhīm in inviting his father to Islam in contrast to the harsh tone of his father; negligence of the prayer causes people to become consumed in sin and desires. *(verse 59)*
Verses 66-98	The Day of Judgment and a rebuttal of those who deny it; the greatest cause of true love and acceptance by others is belief and righteous deeds. *(verse 96).*

CONTEMPLATE, COMPREHEND, APPLY

Contemplation Insights from Page 293 [Al-Kahf 1-4]

- It is obligatory to praise Allah (عَزَّوَجَلَّ) for His bounties and great favors.
- Only He who deserves praise should be praised; otherwise, the praise would be false and deceitful.
- The significance of the Holy Qur'ān and its immunity from excess, deficiency, and deviation in everything it presents.
- Clarifying the mission of the Qur'ān's mission is to bring glad tidings to the people of faith and warn the people of polytheism and disbelief.

Contemplation Insights from Page 294 [Al-Kahf 5-15]

- Those who call to Allah must convey the message to the best of their ability, relying on Allah in this matter. If people are guided, that is a blessing; if not, they should not grieve or despair.
- In knowing the duration of the Companions of the Cave's stay, Allah's complete power, wisdom, and mercy are recognized.
- The verses indicate the importance of fleeing with one's religion and migrating from family, children, relatives, friends, homelands, and wealth for fear of trials.
- It is crucial to focus on youth education, for they have the purest hearts, the cleanest souls, and the most enthusiasm. They are the foundation on which the revival of nations is built.

Contemplation Insights from Page 295 [Al-Kahf 16-20]

- It's by Allah's wisdom and power that He turned them on their sides, left and right, so that the earth would not corrupt their bodies. This is a lesson from Allah to His servants.
- It's permissible to keep dogs for necessity, hunting, and guarding.
- Humans benefit from the company of the righteous and associating with good people, even if they are of lesser status. The dog's mention is preserved because it kept company with people of virtue.
- The verses indicate the legitimacy of agency and the importance of good governance and tactfulness in dealing with people.

Contemplation Insights from Page 296 [Al-Kahf 21-27]

- Building masjids over graves, praying in them, and constructing upon them is not permissible in our religion.
- The story establishes proof of Allah's power over resurrection and bringing bodies out of graves for judgment.

- The verses indicate that commendable argumentation and debate should be conducted in the best manner.
- Sunnah and Islamic manners require attributing future events to the will of Allah.

Contemplation Insights from Page 297 [Al-Kahf 28-34]

- The virtue of keeping the company of the righteous, striving to be with them and mix with them even if they are poor, for in their company are countless benefits.
- Frequent remembrance of Allah with attentive hearts leads to blessings in lifespans and times.
- Faith and good deeds are the basis for reward and salvation, as Allah has stipulated rewards for them in this world and the hereafter.

Contemplation Insights from Page 298 [Al-Kahf 35-45]

- Believers should not submit to the arrogance of wealthy disbelievers. Instead, they should advise and guide them to believe in Allah, acknowledge His Oneness, and be grateful for His blessings.
- Anyone impressed by their wealth or children should attribute the blessing to its giver by saying, "Whatever Allah wills, there is no power except with Allah." When Allah wants good for His servant, He hastens the punishment in this world.
- It is permissible to pray for the destruction of wealth if it leads to tyranny, disbelief, and loss.

Contemplation Insights from Page 299 [Al-Kahf 46-53]

- Servants should increase in performing the enduring good deeds, which are every righteous act, whether said or done, that remains for the Hereafter.
- Servants must remember the terrors of the Day of Judgment and work for that day to escape its horrors and enjoy the paradise and pleasure of Allah.
- Allah (عَزَّوَجَلَّ) honored our Father Adam (عَلَيْهِالسَّلَامُ) and all of humanity by commanding the angels to bow to him at the beginning of creation as a gesture of greeting and honor.
- The verses urge taking Satan as an enemy.

Contemplation Insights from Page 300 [Al-Kahf 54-61]

- The greatness, majesty, and universality of the Qur'ān because it contains every path leading to beneficial knowledge, eternal happiness, and protection from evil.
- One of Allah's wisdom and mercy is that sending those who argue the truth with falsehood is among the greatest reasons for the clarity of truth, the identification of falsehood, and the corruption of falsehood.
- The verses warn those who abandon the truth after knowing it that they might be prevented from it afterward, which is a terrifying deterrent.

- The virtue of seeking knowledge and the merit of traveling to meet the virtuous and scholars, even in far-off lands.
- "Hūt" is used for small and large fish in the Qur'ān.

Contemplation Insights from Page 301 [Al-Kahf 62-74]

- A person's servant should be intelligent, insightful, and wise to accomplish what he wants.
- Allah's aid descends upon a servant according to their adherence to the commanded duties, and those who comply with Allah's command receive support not given to others.
- Proper manners with a teacher and the student should address them most kindly.
- Forgetfulness does not entail accountability, is not subject to an obligation, and is not attached to a ruling.
- A learned scholar learns knowledge in which he is not an expert from someone who is, even if they are far below him in overall knowledge.
- Attributing knowledge and other virtues to Allah (عَزَّوَجَلَّ), acknowledging this, and thanking Allah for them.

Contemplation Insights from Page 302 [Al-Kahf 75-83]

- It is obligatory to deliberate and verify before judging anything.
- Matters are judged based on their apparent aspects, and worldly rulings regarding wealth, blood, etc., are tied to these appearances.
- Committing lesser harm can prevent greater harm, and the greater of two benefits should be chosen even if it means missing the lesser one.
- It is important for companions not to part ways until they have made excuses and sought forgiveness from each other.
- Manners towards Allah in speech involve attributing goodness to Him and not attributing evil to Him. Allah protects a righteous servant in his person and his progeny.

Contemplation Insights from Page 304 [Al-Kahf 98-110]

- Affirming resurrection and gathering of jinn and humans in the Day of Judgment's plane with the second blowing of the trumpet.
- The greatest losers on the Day of Judgment are those whose efforts in worldly life went astray while they thought they were doing well in worshiping others besides Allah.
- Allah's words, knowledge, wisdom, and secrets are infinite; if the seas and their like were ink, it would not suffice to write them down.

SŪRAH MARYAM INSIGHTS

Contemplation Insights from Page 305 [Maryam 1-11]

- Weakness and incapacity are among the most beloved means of drawing closer to Allah; they signify the repudiation of one's power and strength and the attachment of the heart to the power and strength of Allah.
- It is recommended that people mention the blessings of Allah upon them and what befits humility in their supplication.

Contemplation Insights from Page 306 [Maryam 12-25]

- Patience in fulfilling religious obligations is required.
- Honoring parents has a high status and is significant to Allah, who has associated it with His gratitude.
- Despite Allah's perfect power in the magnificent signs shown to Mary, He made her work with causes to reach the dates from the palm tree.

Contemplation Insights from Page 307 [Maryam 26-38]

- The command to Maryam to remain silent indicates the virtue of silence in some situations. Vowing silence is not permissible in our religion.
- What the Qur'an has informed us about the creation of 'Īsā is the absolute truth without doubt, and anything else claimed is false and not befitting the messengers.
- In this world, the disbeliever is deaf and blind to the truth, but he will see and hear in the Hereafter when he sees the punishment, which will not benefit him then.

Contemplation Insights from Page 308 [Maryam 39-51]

- Since Ibrāhīm's separation from his people was shared with Sara, mentioning their shared gift and grandchild was appropriate. Then, Ismail was mentioned independently, even though Allah granted him before Ishaq.
- Manners, gentleness, and kindness in conversing with parents and choosing the best names to address them are emphasized.
- Sins prevent the servant from Allah's mercy and close its doors to them, while obedience is one of the biggest reasons to attain His mercy.
- Every good doer deserves genuine praise according to their goodness, and Ibrāhīm and his progeny are among the leaders of the good doers.

Contemplation Insights from Page 309 [Maryam 52-64]

- The caller to Allah always needs supporters to assist him in his call.
- Affirmation of the attribute of speech for Allah.
- Keeping promises is praiseworthy, a trait of prophets and messengers, while its opposite, breach of promise, is blameworthy.
- Angels are messengers of Allah with revelation and do not descend upon prophets and messengers among humans except at Allah's command.

Contemplation Insights from Page 310 [Maryam 65-76]

- Believers should engage in what they are commanded and continue upon it as much as possible.
- The crossing of all creations over the fire - meaning crossing the Sirat, not entering the fire - is an inevitable matter.
- The criteria of religion and its correct concepts differ from the perceptions of the ignorant and common people.
- Those who are deeply engrossed in misguidance and entrenched in disbelief are left by Allah in their tyranny of ignorance and disbelief until their delusion prolongs, making their punishment more severe.
- Allah fortifies the believers with guidance, increases them in provision and support, and sends down signs as a reason for increasing certainty as a reward for them.

Contemplation Insights from Page 311 [Maryam 77-95]

- The verses indicate the folly of the disbeliever, the naivety of his thinking, and his wishful thinking of sweet illusions, while he will find the complete opposite in the afterlife.
- Allah has loosed demons upon the disbelievers to further entice and tempt them into evil and to lead them from obedience to disobedience.
- People of virtue, knowledge, and righteousness will intercede by Allah's permission on the Day of Resurrection.

Contemplation Insights from Page 312 [Maryam 96-98]

- Reflect on the past nations that Allah destroyed; do you hear any of them or see any trace of them? "And how many a generation before them have We destroyed? Can you find a single one of them [now] or hear [even] a whisper of them?"

CONTEMPLATION STUDY QUESTIONS

Sūrah Al-Kahf Questions

Verse 1: What is the practical benefit for a Muslim from knowing Allah's praise for Himself? *[Al-Sa'di]*

Verse 2: What is the source of glad tidings for the believer? *[Al-Sa'di]*

Verse 6: This verse contains a significant benefit for da'wah (Islamic missionary work); explain it. *[Al-Sa'di]*

Verse 13: Which age groups are most likely to accept the call to truth? *[Ibn Kathīr]*

Verse 1: When is it legislated for a Muslim to isolate from people and flee with their religion? *[Ibn Kathīr]*

Verse 17: If you want guidance, from whom should you seek it? *[Al-Sa'di]*

Verse 18: Allah (عَزَّوَجَلَّ) is capable of protecting the people of the cave from the earth without turning them, so why did He make them turn? *[Al-Sa'di]*

Verse 19: What is the Shariah etiquette when asked about something you do not know? Is a person commanded to stay away from the best of foods? *[Al-Sa'di]*

Verse 21: Mention three brief benefits from the People of the Cave story. *[Al-Sa'di]*

Verse 22: What is the best method for a student of knowledge when confused or halted on some scientific issues? *[Ibn Kathīr]*

Verse 22: Mention some issues related to a fatwa (Islamic legal opinion) derived from this verse. *[Al-Sa'di]*

Verse 24: What is the relationship between remembering Allah and forgetting? *[Al-Sa'di]*

Verse 28: How does the verse indicate the legitimacy of the morning and evening remembrances? What is the harm of loving the worldly life in the Hereafter? A person must follow others in some religious matters or worldly matters, so who must we follow, and who must we leave? *[Al-Sa'di]*

Verse 34: What is the ultimate wish of a disbeliever, and what can a Muslim benefit from this? *[Ibn Kathīr]*

Verse 36: Is there a correlation between the giving of the world and the giving of the Hereafter? *[Al-Sa'di]*

Verse 40: What is the best and most complete blessing for a Muslim?

Verse 41: Explain how the punishment that afflicted the owner of the two gardens might have been better for him.

Verse 42: Explain how the punishment that afflicted the owner of the two gardens might have been better for him. *[Al-Sa'di]*

Verse 46: Mention some of the enduring good deeds. *[Al-Sa'di]*

Verse 47: What is the implicit threat in Allah's statement: "And you see the earth barren"? *[Ibn Kathīr]*

Verse 48: What is meant by Allah's statement: "Indeed, you have come to Us as We created you the first time"? *[Al-Sa'di]*

Verse 50: Was the prostration of the angels to Adam a prostration of worship, or what was it? *[Ibn Kathīr]*

Verse 50: Explain the ignorance and stubbornness of some of Adam's children through this verse. *[Ibn Kathīr]*

Verse 54: Is arguing with scholars and students of knowledge good? And what reason causes a person to argue frequently with the people of truth? *[Al-Sa'di]*

Verse 57: There is a difference between those who turn away from the truth while knowing it and those who are ignorant; discuss this in light of this verse. *[Al-Sa'di]*

Verse 62: This verse alerts to some etiquettes in dealing with servants; explain them. *[Al-Sa'di]*

Verse 63: Why is forgetting attributed to Satan, although it is decreed by Allah (عَزَّوَجَلَّ)? *[Al-Sa'di]*

Verse 66: Why did Mūsā ask Al-Khidr to teach him righteousness and not any knowledge? *[Al-Sa'di]*

Verse 72: Why did Mūsā not have patience with the actions of Al-Khidr? *[Ibn Kathīr]*

Verse 79: Scholars have derived an important principle from this verse: what is it? *[Al-Sa'di]*

Verse 80: A Muslim is afflicted with sorrows and calamities, so how should they deal with them? Your good deeds might benefit your offspring; explain this through the verse. *[Ibn Kathīr]*

Verse 84: What is our position on what Allah and His Messenger have remained silent about? *[Al-Sa'di]*

Verse 86: The believers are the most merciful of people towards creation; explain this through the verse. *[Ibn Kathīr]*

Verse 88: What is the sign of success for a righteous leader? *[Al-Sa'di]*

Verse 100: Why is Hell displayed to the disbelievers in the open spaces on the Day of Resurrection before they enter it? *[Ibn Kathīr]*

Verse 101: What is the reason that made those who hate the religion unable to hear the verses of the Qur'ān in a way that they could benefit from? *[Al-Sa'dī]*

Sūrah Maryam Questions

Verse 4: In the story of Zakariyyā (عَلَيْهِ ٱلسَّلَامُ), there is an explanation of an effective means among the means of supplication; what is it? *[Al-Sa'dī]*

Verse 5: Did the Prophet of Allah, Zakariyyā (عَلَيْهِ ٱلسَّلَامُ), fear for his wealth to be taken after his death by heirs who are not his sons, as the people of the world do today? And do prophets inherit? *[Ibn Kathīr]*

Verse 15: Why were these three instances specifically mentioned with peace upon Prophet Yahya (عَلَيْهِ ٱلسَّلَامُ)? *[Ibn Kathīr]*

Verse 18: What is the best way to repel an aggressor? *[Ibn Kathīr]*

Verse 21: The story of Maryam (عَلَيْهَا ٱلسَّلَامُ) and her son (عَلَيْهِ ٱلسَّلَامُ) makes hearts cling to Allah without worldly causes. Explain that. *[Al-Sa'dī]*

Verse 25: It is derived from the verse that the servant must seek means in seeking sustenance. Explain that. *[Ibn Kathīr]*

Verse 26: Why was Maryam (عَلَيْهَا ٱلسَّلَامُ) commanded not to speak to anyone about 'Īsā? *[Al-Sa'dī]*

Verse 27: How did Maryam (عَلَيْهَا ٱلسَّلَامُ) dare to come to her people carrying 'Īsā although she was not married? *[Al-Sa'dī]*

Verse 30: Why was the first thing 'Īsā (عَلَيْهِ ٱلسَّلَامُ) said: "Indeed, I am the servant of Allah"? *[Al-Sa'dī]*

Verse 45: Being gradual in calling to faith is one of the most important matters a caller must be keen on; how do we benefit from this matter from the story of Ibrāhīm (عَلَيْهِ ٱلسَّلَامُ)? *[Al-Sa'dī]*

Verse 43: How can a caller benefit from this verse in his communications with people when inviting them? *[Al-Sa'dī]*

Verse 47: How should the manners of a caller to Allah be if faced with harm and bad speech? *[Al-Sa'dī]*

Verse 48: What does a caller do if he does not find acceptance from those he invites? *[Al-Sa'dī]*

Verse 55: Why were relatives specifically mentioned here? *[Al-Sa'dī]*

Verse 58: What is gained from adding the verses to the name of Allah, "The Most Merciful"? *[Al-Sa'dī]*

Verse 59: The specification of prayer in the verse alerts us to an important matter: what is it? *[Ibn Kathīr]*

Verse 61: What is gained from coupling the mention of gardens with His name, "The Most Merciful," in this verse? *[Al-Sa'dī]*

Verse 71: Why does the one contemplating the Qur'ān not fear crossing the Fire? *[Al-Sa'dī]*

Verse 73: People often consider worldly blessings proof of Allah's love for them; what is your opinion on this? *[Al-Sa'dī]*

Verse 85: What do the righteous expect from their Lord on the Day of Resurrection when they are gathered to Him? *[Al-Sa'dī]*

Verse 86: This verse illustrates the grim situation of the polytheists on the Day of Resurrection; explain it. *[Al-Sa'dī]*

Verse 87: What is the reason for naming faith in Allah and His messengers a covenant? *[Al-Sa'dī]*

Verse 91: The mountains and trees are more sensible than some humans; explain that through the verse. *[Ibn Kathīr]*

Verse 96: What benefit does a Muslim gain from the love of the righteous for him? *[Al-Sa'dī]*

DAY 16: TAHA & ANBIYĀ'

The Qur'ān reading for day 16 is Sūrah Ṭaha and Sūrah al Anbiyā'. Sūrah Ṭaha highlights how the Qur'ān is the key to all success. Sūrah al Anbiyā' provides an essential key for that success by showing the unity of the Prophets and Messengers in their message.

سُورَةُ طه

ṬAHA (20)

Taha

VERSES
135

WORDS
1,641

LETTERS
5,240

REVEALED IN
MAKKAH

REVEALATION ORDER
45

✦ Main Themes: Comforting the Prophet (ﷺ) and the believers by demonstrating that Qur'ān is the cause of success for whoever follows it; misery is the plight of those who oppose it.

The Sūrah begins and ends with this theme. Read and reflect on verses 2 and 124.

Most of this Sūrah is about the story of Mūsā. It mentions Allah's special care for Mūsā and the difficulties he endured to show the Prophet (ﷺ) that Allah is with him. It mentions the salvation of the Pharaoh's sorcerers after they believed (see verses 70-73). It mentions the story of the Samiri, who introduced the worship of the Golden Calf among the Children of Israel. The Sūrah is among those that extensively discuss the story of Mūsā (عَلَيْهِ ٱلسَّلَامُ), covering his story in 90 verses.

The Sūrah serves as a roadmap to reach true happiness and avoid misery.

- The Sūrah mentions the story of Mūsā (عَلَيْهِ ٱلسَّلَامُ) and the severe hardships he faced in his call to the Children of Israel. This example is repeated often throughout the Qur'ān due to its many lessons and benefits.
- The Sūrah mentions the happiness of Pharaoh's magicians when they believed and affirmed their faith, evidenced by their steadfastness despite Pharaoh's threats (verses 70-73).

- The Sūrah presents another model, this time that of Adam and Eve. It illustrates that those who obey Allah find happiness, and those who disobey Him find misery (115-127).
- The blessed Sūrah concludes by mentioning the most important reason one attains contentment: the pinnacle of tranquility and happiness (verse 130).

The relation of this Sūrah to the previous one:

1. Since Sūrah Maryam narrated the stories of several prophets and messengers, some in detail and conciseness, like the story of Ibrāhīm (عَلَيْهِ ٱلسَّلَامُ), and others in a summarized form, like the story of Mūsā (عَلَيْهِ ٱلسَّلَامُ), and then referred to the rest of the prophets in general... Here, it elaborates on the story of Mūsā, which was briefly mentioned before, covering it comprehensively. Then, it details the story of Adam (عَلَيْهِ ٱلسَّلَامُ), which was not mentioned in Sūrah Maryam except by name.

2. It is narrated from Ibn Abbas that this Sūrah was revealed after its predecessor.

3. The beginning of this Sūrah is connected to the end of the previous Sūrah and matches in meaning, as it was mentioned at the end of that Sūrah that the Qur'ān was made easy in its clear Arabic language, to be glad tidings for the righteous, and a warning to the contrarians. The beginning of this Sūrah reinforces this meaning.

The consistency between the beginning and the end of the Sūrah: The blessed Sūrah begins by affirming that the Qur'ān is a source of happiness, not misery (verse 2). It concludes by stating that those who turn away from the Qur'ān will suffer misery and not find happiness (verse 124). This emphasizes the importance, value, and status of the Qur'ān, and following it is the cause of success.

A Broader Overview of the Sūrah:

- Challenging with the Qur'ān by mentioning the disjointed letters at its opening. Highlighting that it is a revelation from Allah for guiding those inclined to guidance, with the majority of it focused on this aspect.
- Emphasizing the greatness of Allah and affirming the message of Muhammad (صَلَّى ٱللَّهُ عَلَيْهِ وَسَلَّمَ) as parallel to the message of the greatest messenger before him, whose mention was widespread among the people. It illustrated the revelation of the Qur'ān to Muhammad (صَلَّى ٱللَّهُ عَلَيْهِ وَسَلَّمَ) with the speech of Allah to Mūsā (عَلَيْهِ ٱلسَّلَامُ).
- Expanding on Mūsā's upbringing, Allah's support for him, and his victory over Pharaoh with evidence and miracles, diverting Pharaoh's plots against him and his followers. Allah's deliverance of Mūsā and his people, the drowning of Pharaoh, and the honors Allah bestowed upon the Children of Israel upon their departure from the land of the Copts.
- The story of the Saimiri and his making of the calf, which the Children of Israel worshipped in Mūsā's absence, implied that the outcome of Muhammad's (صَلَّى ٱللَّهُ عَلَيْهِ وَسَلَّمَ) mission would lead to the victory over his opponents, just as Mūsā's (عَلَيْهِ ٱلسَّلَامُ) mission did.

- Then, it shifts to warning those who turned away from the Qur'ān and did not benefit from its examples and warnings. It reminds people of Satan's enmity towards man, as illustrated in the story of Adam's creation. It outlines the dire consequences in the hereafter for those who let Satan lead them, warning them of the severe punishment in this world.
- Consoling the Prophet (صَلَّى ٱللَّهُ عَلَيْهِ وَسَلَّمَ) regarding what they say and quickening him in the religion. It is interspersed with the affirmation of resurrection, the magnificence of the Day of Judgment, and the events and horrors that precede it.

BRIEF SŪRAH SUMMARY

Verses 1-18	Introduction: The status of the message, the *Qur'ān* and of the Messenger ﷺ.
Verses 9-98	The detailed story of Mūsā, beginning with Allah speaking to him and ending with the story of the Golden Calf. A key benefit of this story is that disobeying the Messenger puts a person at great risk of trials and tribulation *(see verses 85-97).*
Verses 99-135	The threat of eventual and ultimate punishment of the disbelievers and the fact that the end result will favor the righteous. The concluding verses contain many matters to comfort the Prophet ﷺ and provide him with solace.

سُورَةُ الأَنبِيَاء
AL ANBIYĀ' (21)
The Prophets

VERSES
112

WORDS
1,168

LETTERS
4,890

REVEALED IN
MAKKAH

REVEALATION ORDER
71

It is said to be around the 71st Sūrah revealed, in between Sūrah al-Sajdah and Sūrah al-Naḥl.

- Main Themes: The sending of Messengers as a mercy to mankind; a reminder about the unified da'wah, worship, and du'a of the Prophets. It mentions the names of 16 Prophets, more than any other Sūrah except al An'ām.

The longest story narrated in Sūrah al Anbiyā' is the story of Ibrāhīm in his youth destroying the idols. The story of Ibrāhīm is mentioned at length because he is the father of the Prophets who succeeded him.

It aims to affirm the belief in Islam within the hearts of the polytheists by addressing their statements, refuting them with threats and warnings, and drawing attention to the universe and its contents as evidence of its Creator. Then, it presents the stories of some prophets as lessons and warnings. Both at the beginning and the end, it depicts various spectacles of the Day of Judgment with a strong and impactful style.

It begins and ends with the mention that the Qur'ān is a reminder, but in the first verses, it mentions that the disbelievers hear to no avail (verses 1-2), and at the end of the Sūrah, it is said to be for a people who are devout in worship (verse 106).

The words worship and *dhikr* and their derivatives are repeated throughout. Remembrance of Allah and His religion is a source of solace for the righteous and a stern rebuke and source of anger for the disbelievers.

It includes the mention of 16 prophets. It contains the supplications of the prophets (عَلَيْهِمُ السَّلَامُ). It uniquely mentions the supplication of Dhul-Nun "There is no deity except

You; exalted are You. Indeed, I have been of the wrongdoers." (Verse 87) which, when recited by a Muslim in any distressing situation, Allah responds to their supplication.

In demonstrating the main theme of the Sūrah, which is sending messengers to people as a mercy from Allah, it addresses the following topics:

1. Alerting people from their heedlessness and the nearing of the Hour (verses 1-2).

2. Warning the disbelievers about what happened to those who denied and mocked the messengers before them (verses 12-15, 39-41).

3. Presenting signs of Allah's power in His creation to affirm His Oneness and Right to be worshipped (verses 30-33).

4. Reviewing the nation of the prophets (عَلَيۡهِمُ ٱلسَّلَامُ) and stating that it is one nation (verses 48-92).

5. Displaying the reality of the hereafter through a series of spectacles from the Day of Judgment (verses 97-104).

Its relevance to the preceding Sūrah: The preceding Sūrah concluded by highlighting how people are preoccupied with the transient pleasures of the world, which Allah has made a trial for them. It also instructed the Prophet not to covet these pleasures but to focus on prayer and patience, emphasizing that the ultimate success is for the righteous. This Sūrah begins similarly to how the previous one ended by mentioning that people are heedless of the Hour and the reckoning. It states that when they hear the Qur'ān, they listen to it while they play, and their hearts are distracted from comprehending it.

A Broader Overview of the Sūrah:

- Warning about the resurrection, affirming its occurrence, and its happening is imminent. Establishing evidence for it through the creation of the heavens and the earth from nothing and the creation of beings from water.
- Warning against denying Allah's book and His messenger. Reminding that this messenger (صَلَّى ٱللَّهُ عَلَيۡهِ وَسَلَّمَ) is like the messengers before him, bringing the same message as the previous messengers. Mentioning many stories of the prophets (صَلَّى ٱللَّهُ عَلَيۡهِ وَسَلَّمَ).
- Highlighting the significance of the Qur'ān as a grace from Allah to those it addresses and the status of the Messenger of Islam as a mercy to the world.
- It reminds them of what befell previous nations due to denying their messengers. Allah's promise to those who deny is inevitable, and its delay should not deceive them. It warns them not to be deluded by the delay, as those before them were until sudden punishment came upon them. It also mentions signs of the Hour, like the release of Gog and Magog.

- Reminding them of the evidence of the creation of the heavens and the earth for the Creator. Indicating that there is a life after this life that is more perfect and just, where every soul will be rewarded for what it has earned, and truth will prevail over falsehood.
- This creation's evidence points to the oneness of the Creator, as this order cannot be maintained with multiple gods. Sanctifying Allah from partners and children and arguing for the oneness of Allah. That all creations are destined to perish, followed by a reminder of the great grace upon them, which is the grace of preservation.
- Then, it transitions to mentioning the messengers and prophets. Comparing their situations and the situations of their nations to Muhammad (ﷺ) and his people's situations. How Allah supported the messengers against their nations and answered their prayers. That all messengers came with Allah's religion, which is one in its fundamentals but was distorted by those who strayed.
- Praising the messengers and those who believed in them. Promising that the outcome is for the believers, in the best of this world and the hereafter, and that Allah will judge between the two groups with truth, supporting His messengers in spreading His law.

BRIEF SŪRAH SUMMARY

Verses 1-33	*Tawḥīd* and a repudiation of doubts surrounding it. The evidences of Allah's power as proof of His Oneness *(v. 30-33).*
Verses 34-92	The message and the Messengers. The followers of the Prophets are like a single nation (*verses 48-92).*
Verses 93-112	The Day of Judgment and the Hereafter.

CONTEMPLATE, COMPREHEND, APPLY

Contemplation Insights from Page 312 [Taha 2-12]

- The revelation of the great Qur'ān is not for exhausting oneself in worship or experiencing severe hardship; rather, it is a book of reminder benefiting those who fear their Lord.
- Allah paired creation and command, as creation does not depart from wisdom; likewise, He does not command or prohibit except what is just and wise.
- The husband must spend on the family (the wife) for food, clothing, accommodation, and heating during cold times.

Contemplation Insights from Page 313 [Taha 13-37]

- Listening attentively to important matters, especially the revelation from Allah, is obligatory.
- The first revelation to Mūsā included two foundational beliefs: acknowledgment of Allah's oneness and belief in the Day of Resurrection (Judgment Day) and the most important obligation after faith, which is prayer.
- Cooperation among the callers to Allah is necessary for the success of their mission; thus, Allah made Mūsā's brother Harun a prophet to assist him in conveying the message.
- A caller to Allah must possess the skill of making the message understandable to the audience.

Contemplation Insights from Page 314 [Taha 38-51]

- Allah's complete care for His messenger Mūsā, the prophets, and their successors varies according to their status with Allah.
- General guidance for creations includes each creature striving for its benefits and repelling harm.
- The virtue of enjoining good and forbidding evil is highlighted, and this should be done gently with those in power and guaranteed protection.
- Allah alone possesses knowledge of the unseen, past, present, and future.

Contemplation Insights from Page 315 [Taha 52-64]

- The emergence of various types of plants from the earth is a clear sign of Allah's power and the existence of the Creator.
- The verses present two logical pieces of evidence for the resurrection: the revival of plants from the dead earth and the creation of accountable beings.
- Pharaoh stubbornly disbelieved; he saw the signs directly, not just by hearsay, and was convinced by them deep within.

- Mūsā chose the day of the festival so that Allah's word would be exalted, His religion would be evident, and disbelief would be suppressed in front of everyone at the "general assembly" to spread the news.
- Debating is legitimate to reveal the truth and negate falsehood, "He said, 'Your appointment is the day of the festival, and let the people assemble when the sun has risen high.'"
- Engage in debates only with knowledge, insight, and witnesses, "He said, 'Your appointment is the day of the festival, and let the people assemble when the sun has risen high.'"
- Callers to Allah and students of knowledge should primarily cooperate to convey the message to others and spread the religion, "So gather your plan, then come in a line."

Contemplation Insights from Page 316 [Taha 65-76]

- A magician will fail, no matter where he comes from on Earth or what tactics he employs. He will not achieve his aims with magic, whether good or bad.
- Faith can work wonders; the magicians' faith was firmer than mountains, so they disregarded worldly punishment and were not concerned by Pharaoh's threats.
- Tyrants habitually threaten severe punishment to those who uphold the truth and persist in doing so to humiliate and demean them.

Contemplation Insights from Page 317 [Taha 77-87]

- It's a divine tradition to exact vengeance on criminals in a way that satisfies the believers' hearts, clears their grievances, and soothes their souls.
- A tyrant is a curse upon himself and his people; he leads them astray from guidance and does not direct them to any good or salvation.
- Blessings require preservation and gratitude combined with more blessings, and denial of them incurs Allah's wrath and descent.
- Allah is always forgiving those who repent from polytheism, disbelief, and disobedience, believe in Him, perform righteous deeds, and remain steadfast until death.
- Although haste is generally disapproved of, it is praiseworthy in religious matters.

Contemplation Insights from Page 318 [Taha 88-98]

- Deceiving people by distorting the truth is the way of those astray.
- Commendable anger arises when the sacred boundaries of Allah are violated.
- The verses establish a principle of disavowing those who engage in heresies and sins and avoiding their company.
- The verses necessitate contemplation to recognize Allah through His effects in the universe.

Contemplation Insights from Page 319 [Taha 99-113]

- The Qur'ān is a reminder and warning for nations, communities, and individuals and dignity and pride for humanity.
- Intercession will not benefit anyone except by the permission of the Most Merciful and His approval of the intercessor's speech.
- The Qur'ān encompasses the best judgments acknowledged by reason and innate disposition for their goodness and perfection.
- Among the etiquettes of dealing with the Qur'ān are receiving it with acceptance, submission, reverence, being guided by its light to the straight path, and engaging in its learning and teaching.
- The regret of the criminals on the Day of Judgment for having squandered many times, being heedless, turning away from what benefits them, and engaging in what harms them.

Contemplation Insights from Page 320 [Taha 114-125]

- Etiquette in acquiring knowledge requires that the learner be patient and listen attentively until the speaker or teacher has finished their connected speech.
- Adam forgot, and so did his progeny, not remaining firm on their resolve, yet he hastened to repent, and Allah forgave him. Whoever resembles his father has not been wronged.
- The virtue of repentance, as Adam was better after his repentance than before.
- The constrained life in this world, the Barzakh, and the hereafter for the disbelievers and those astray.

Contemplation Insights from Page 321 [Taha 126-135]

- One of the aids in enduring the harm from those who turn away is to invest in moments of excellence in glorifying Allah's praise.
- If one finds themselves aspiring to the transient adornments of this world and leaning towards it, they should balance between its fleeting beauty and the everlasting bliss of the hereafter.
- It is incumbent upon one to establish prayer properly and, if faced with a concern, to pray and command their family to pray, emulating the Prophet (ﷺ).
- The beautiful and praiseworthy end, Paradise, is for the pious.

SŪRAH AL ANBIYĀ' INSIGHTS

Contemplation Insights from Page 322 [Al-Anbiya 1-10]

- The proximity of the Day of Judgment necessitates preparation for it.
- Being preoccupied with amusement diverts the heart from the truth.
- Allah's encompassing knowledge of what His servants issue in speech or action.
- The disbelievers' varying stance towards the Prophet (ﷺ) indicates their confusion and instability.
- Allah supports His messengers and believers with aid and victory over their enemies.
- The Qur'ān is an honor and might for those who believe in and act upon it.

Contemplation Insights from Page 323 [Al-Anbiya 11-24]

- Oppression is a cause of destruction for individuals and communities.
- Allah did not create anything in vain; He is transcendent above all frivolity.
- The triumph of truth and the vanquishing of falsehood is a divine tradition.
- Refuting the creed of polytheism with the argument of mutual hindrance.

Contemplation Insights from Page 324 [Al-Anbiya 25-35]

- Exalting Allah above having offspring.
- The status of angels with Allah: they are worshipful servants He created for His obedience, not characterized by maleness or femaleness, but as honored servants.
- The heavens and the earth were created according to the divine norm of gradual progression, conjoined and separated.
- Trials can come through both adversity and prosperity.

Contemplation Insights from Page 325 [Al-Anbiya 36-44]

- Demonstrating the disbelief of those who mock the Messenger through speech, action, or gesture.
- Hastiness is human nature, while patience is a commendable trait.
- None can protect another from Allah's punishment except Allah Himself.
- The fate of falsehood is to vanish while the truth remains.

Contemplation Insights from Page 326 [Al-Anbiya 45-57]

- Acknowledging sin benefits only when accompanied by repentance before it's too late.
- Affirming justice for Allah and negating injustice from Him.
- The importance of strong evidence in calling to Allah.
- The harm of blind imitation.
- A gradual change in correcting wrongs, starting with the easiest first, as Ibrahim began changing his people's wrongdoings with speech and reasoning before moving to action.

Contemplation Insights from Page 327 [Al-Anbiya 57-72]

- It is permissible to use stratagems to reveal the truth and invalidate falsehood.
- Adherents of falsehood cling to arguments they believe are in their favor, yet these arguments are against them.
- Harshness in speech is a means of changing wrongdoings, provided it does not lead to greater harm.
- Resorting to the use of force is evidence of incapacity to confront with reasoning.
- Allah supports His believing servants and rescues them from trials in ways they least expect.

Contemplation Insights from Page 328 [Al-Anbiya 73-81]

- Doing good, prayer, and zakat are common themes in divine laws.
- Committing grave sins leads to annihilating punishment.
- Righteousness is a path to entering Allah's mercy.
- Supplication is a means of escape from distress.

Contemplation Insights from Page 329 [Al-Anbiya 82-90]

- Righteousness leads to mercy.
- Turning to Allah is a way to unveil distress.
- The virtue of desiring offspring to continue one's legacy.
- Acknowledging one's sins, feeling desperate for Allah, complaining about one's condition to Him, and obeying Allah in prosperity are reasons for answering prayers and alleviating distress.

Contemplation Insights from Page 330 [Al-Anbiya 91-101]

- Emphasizing chastity and its virtues.
- The consistency of divine messages in monotheism and the fundamentals of worship.

- The opening of Gog and Magog's barrier is one of the major signs of the Hour.
- Failure to prepare for the Day of Judgment leads to suffering its horrors.

Contemplation Insights from Page 331 [Al-Anbiya 102-112]

- Righteousness leads to empowerment on Earth.
- The mission of the Prophet (صَلَّى ٱللَّهُ عَلَيْهِ وَسَلَّمَ), his law, and his Sunnah is mercy for all worlds.
- The Prophet (صَلَّى ٱللَّهُ عَلَيْهِ وَسَلَّمَ) does not possess knowledge of the unseen.
- Allah's knowledge encompasses everything that emanates from His servants, whether spoken or acted upon.

CONTEMPLATION STUDY QUESTIONS

Surah TaHa Questions

Verse 14: Why was prayer specifically mentioned in remembrance even though it is part of worship? *[Al-Sa'dī]*

Verse 25: In this verse, there is an encouragement for callers to ask Allah to remove their heavy worries before starting their call, explain this. *[Al-Sa'dī]*

Verse 28: This verse explains a manner from the manners of the prophets' supplication to their Lord for their worldly needs; what is it? *[Al-Sa'dī]*

Verse 41: How does the verse indicate the virtue of Mūsā, peace be upon him? *[Al-Sa'dī]*

Verse 54: Who benefits from the effects of Allah's blessing and His power, understanding its purposes? *[Al-Sa'dī]*

Verse 58: Why did Pharaoh accuse Mūsā of coming to expel Pharaoh and his people from their land? *[Al-Sa'dī]*

Verse 64: Why did the magicians advise each other to come in a row? *[Al-Sa'dī]*

Verse 66: The confidence of the people of falsehood in themselves does not shake the believer's confidence in his Lord; explain this through the verse. *[Al-Sa'dī]*

Verse 67: As is the requirement of human nature, otherwise he is certain of Allah's promise and His victory. *[Al-Sa'dī]*

Verse 72: If you face pleasure from the forbidden pleasures of this world, this verse guides you on how to get rid of this desire. Explain this.

Verse 82: The verse mentions three reasons for forgiveness. What are they? *[Al-Sa'dī]*

Verse 86: The prophets and callers are the most compassionate people towards the nation; explain this through this verse. [Ibn Kathir]

Verse 94: Why did Harun call Mũsā "O son of my mother" although he is his brother? [Ibn Kathir]

Verse 97: Why did Mũsā dispose of the calf in this way? *[Al-Sa'dī]*

Verse 99: Why is the Qur'ān called a reminder? *[Al-Sa'dī]*

Verse 104: What does the information about the criminals benefit the person? *[Al-Sa'dī]*

Verse 114: What etiquette can a student of knowledge extract from this verse? This verse includes an important means to acquiring beneficial knowledge; what is it? *[Al-Sa'dī]*

Verse 127: In this verse, there is an important means to acquiring beneficial knowledge; what is it? *[Al-Sa'dī]*

Verse 131: Moments pass for a Muslim where they desire to be among the indulged and luxurious in this worldly life, how should one deal with these moments? *[Al-Sa'dī]*

Verse 132: How should one command their family and others to pray? And why was prayer specifically commanded and perseverance upon it emphasized over other acts of worship? *[Al-Sa'dī]*

Surah Al Anbiyā' Questions

Verse 7: What are the community's rights over scholars and students of knowledge? *[Al-Sa'dī]*

Verse 10: When does this book become a reason for our honor, dignity, and elevation? *[Al-Sa'dī]*

Verse 18: What is the best way to invalidate the misconceptions of the polytheists and those with corrupt intellects? *[Al-Sa'dī]*

Verse 19: When is a servant closest to his Lord? *[Al-Sa'dī]*

Verse 24: What is the reason for the misguidance of many people? *[Al-Sa'dī]*

Verse 27: Why is it a characteristic of the angels that they do not speak ahead of Allah, the Exalted? *[Al-Sa'dī]*

Verse 29: Why is claiming divinity described as oppression? *[Al-Sa'dī]*

Verse 34: Some say that Al-Khidr is eternally living in this world. What do you think? *[Al-Sa'dī]*

Verse 36: What is the wisdom behind mentioning haste after mentioning those who mock the Messenger of Allah (صَلَّىٰ ٱللَّهُ عَلَيْهِ وَسَلَّمَ)? *[Al-Sa'dī]*

Verse 45: What is the reason behind comparing the disbelievers to the deaf? How can one prepare to benefit from the Book of Allah (عَزَّوَجَلَّ)? *[Al-Sa'dī]*

Verse 49: Why did Allah specifically mention the righteous? *[Al-Sa'dī]*

Verse 49: What is the wisdom behind associating fear with the unseen? *[Al-Sa'dī]*

Verse 58: Why did the Exalted describe the idol with the phrase "a big one for them"? *[Al-Sa'dī]*

Verse 63: What was Ibrāhīm's (عَلَيْهِ ٱلسَّلَامُ) intention with this question? *[Al-Sa'dī]*

Verse 68: What method do those incapable of finding evidence for their claims resort to? *[Al-Sa'dī]*

Verse 73: What can be learned from Allah's favor upon Ibrāhīm (عَلَيْهِ ٱلسَّلَامُ) and his offspring by making them leaders? And what blessing does a Qur'ān memorizer and a student of knowledge feel when reading this verse? Why were prayer and almsgiving specifically mentioned when they are included in the general term of good deeds? *[Al-Sa'dī]*

Verse 79: When is a ruler, judge, teacher, or parent excused for their mistake? Why did Allah endow Dawud (عَلَيْهِ ٱلسَّلَامُ) with the miracle that mountains and birds would glorify Allah with him? *[Al-Sa'dī]*

Verse 84: What makes Ayyūb (عَلَيْهِ ٱلسَّلَامُ) and his story a reminder for the worshippers? - Ibn Kathīr

Verse 86: When is a person described as righteous? *[Al-Sa'dī]*

Verse 87: This supplication contains three matters that warranted Yunus's salvation from the belly of the whale. What are these three matters? *[Al-Sa'dī]*

Verse 88: This verse indicates an ideal way to escape difficulties. - Ibn Kathīr

Verse 91: The story of Maryam and 'Īsā is often mentioned alongside the story of Yaḥyā and Zachariah (عَلَيْهِمَا ٱلسَّلَامُ). Why is that? *[Al-Sa'dī]*

Verse 92: How are all messengers and their followers one nation? *[Al-Sa'dī]*

Verse 97: What causes the disbelievers' eyes to stare in horror on the Day of Judgment? *[Al-Sa'dī]*

Verse 98: What is the wisdom behind idols entering the fire? *[Al-Sa'dī]*

Day 17: Al Hajj & al Mu'minūn

The Qur'ān reading for day 17 is Sūrah al Ḥajj and Sūrah al Mu'minūn. The recurring theme of these chapters is revering Allah by honoring what He has made of great importance and the invitation to worship Allah alone and adorn oneself with the qualities of righteousness.

سُورَةُ الحَجّ

AL ḤAJJ (22)

The Pilgrimage

VERSES	98
WORDS	1,291
LETTERS	5,175
REVEALED IN	MADINAH
REVEALATION ORDER	103

It is estimated to be the 103rd Sūrah revealed, having been revealed between Sūrah al-Nūr and Sūrah al Munāfiqīn. It contains two places of prostration.

✦ Main Themes: Revering Allah and His legislated rituals that afford special attention to honored places and times, one of the greatest of which is the Ḥajj. (verses 30, 32).

Its beginning and ending are similar: it begins by mentioning spectacles of sheer magnificence as relates to Allah's *ayāt* (signs)and the Day of Judgment. Its final verses reinforce this theme (verses 77-78).

It begins with the command to have Taqwā (verse 1) and concludes with the command to enact the greatest characteristics of Taqwā (verse 78).

It includes discussions on resurrection and some of its spectacles, then discusses the polytheists and their stance regarding the Sacred masjid. This leads to discussions about the Kaaba and the rites of Hajj, followed by discussions on the deniers and their ends as a lesson. The Sūrah concludes with signs of Allah in the universe and parables about the deities. The main points it establishes are:

- Evidence for resurrection, the coming of the Hour, and the initial creation, the sending down of rain on dead earth to revive it with plants, and that Allah is the truth and capable of all this.

- Mentioning the state of the disbelievers on the Day of Judgment and the severe punishment they will face in the most degrading and humiliating forms, and the state of the believers and the bliss they will enjoy in the most beautiful dwellings, finest clothing, and adornments.
- Legislating the rulings related to Hajj and the sacrificial offerings, encouraging the veneration of the sacred rites, and reminding the polytheists of the benefits bestowed by Allah in legislating Hajj for them and how they should conduct themselves during this rite.
- Legislating fighting in Islam and the permission to combat enemies to repel oppression and aggression, promising divine support for the believing fighters in His cause, and His promise of ultimate victory over those who tempted them and unjustly expelled them from their homes.
- Recounting the stories of destroyed cities due to their oppression and tyranny to demonstrate Allah's sunnah (way) in punishing the disbelievers, to console His Messenger ﷺ over his people's rejection, and to reassure the Muslims of the favorable outcome awaiting the patient.
- Affirming Allah's deservingness of worship and uniqueness by mentioning creational signs and divine blessings, His exclusivity in creation, and His bringing life to an end.

The unique distinctions of this Sūrah are that it is the only Sūrah named after one of the five pillars of Islam, it contains two prostration verses, and it includes the verse that grants permission to fight after enduring years of persecution (verse 39).

The beginning of this Sūrah is related to the previous one because Allah (عَزَّوَجَلَّ) mentioned in the prior Sūrah the condition of the wretched and the blessed, as well as the great terror which will occur on the Day of Judgment. The polytheists of Mecca denied the resurrection and disbelieved in it due to the delay of punishment upon them. Therefore, this Sūrah was revealed as a warning to them to instill fear with its mention of the earthquake of the Hour, its severe terror, and what is prepared for its deniers. It also serves to alert them about the resurrection by discussing their development in creation and the shaking and trembling of the earth, which brings forth vegetation.

BROADER OVERVIEW OF THE SŪRAH

- Urging people to fear Allah and be wary of the Day of Judgment and its terrors.
- Arguing against polytheism and addressing polytheists to cease their obstinacy in acknowledging Allah's sole right to be worshipped and disputing this out of following satanic whispers. It emphasizes that devils cannot offer them any protection or aid in this world or the hereafter. It highlights the polytheists' argument against monotheism as baseless and a mere diversion to mislead others.
- Questioning their doubt in the resurrection for judgment, which is a confirmed fact without any doubt, wondering how they doubt it due to the supposed impossibility of revival after death,

without considering that Allah created man from dust, then from a sperm-drop, then and developed him through stages.

- Allah sends down water to the dead earth, reviving it and bringing forth various vegetation types. Allah is capable of all this, so He can certainly resurrect the dead, being powerful over everything. Their dispute over the denial of resurrection stems from ignorance and arrogance against complying with the Prophet's (صَلَّى ٱللَّهُ عَلَيْهِ وَسَلَّمَ) message.
- He described polytheists as indecisive in their religion and hesitant in following Islam. He criticized polytheists for their arrogance in straying from Ibrāhīm's way, whom they claim to follow and consider themselves the protectors of his religion. Yet, they deviate from the core of the religion. He reminded them of the benefits of Hajj as legislated by Allah, which they have ungratefully denied.
- Comparing their reception of Islam's call to that of past nations who rejected their prophets' calls, leading to their punishment. They are warned that similar punishment could befall them and not to be deceived by its postponement, as it's merely a respite from Allah as was given to previous nations. Comforting the Prophet (صَلَّى ٱللَّهُ عَلَيْهِ وَسَلَّمَ) and believers, warning them about Satan's attempts to corrupt hearts against the messengers' calls. However, Allah secures His religion and nullifies Satan's whispers. Hence, unbelievers turn away and deny the Qur'ānic verses.
- It highlights the Qur'ān and those who receive it with fear and patience while describing disbelievers as hating the Qur'ān and resenting its messenger. It praises believers, stating that Allah made following the true faith easy for them and named them Muslims. It permits Muslims to fight and assures them of victory and empowerment on Earth.
- The Sūrah concludes by reminding people of Allah's blessings on them and that Allah chose certain creations from angels and people. Allah turns towards the believers with guidance that brings them closer to Him. Allah is their protector and helper.

BRIEF SŪRAH SUMMARY

Verses 1-24	*Taqwā*, the characteristics of the righteous and the categories of people who fail to abide by *Taqwā* and their recompense: some argue against Allah without any knowledge and follow every rebellious devil (v. 3); some harbor doubt about the Day of Judgment (v. 5) ; some outright reject without any guidance or evidence (v. 7) ; some worship Allah with instability, and may leave Islam if tested (v. 11). Along with contrasting between the believers and the disbelievers, this passage contains the simple logical evidences for the truth of *Tawḥīd*, the Prophethood and the Day of Judgment. Understanding this opening passage fills the believers heart with awe and humility for Allah, and therefore contains a place of *Sajdah* (v. 18). Verse 18 shows that humility for Allah raises a person and arrogance and denial of the truth is the guaranteed cause of humiliation.
Verses 25-41	*Verses 25-41:* The story of the building of the *Ka'bah* and Allah's invitation to all of mankind for the pilgrimage; the tremendous status of *al Ḥajj* and the similitude of *Tawḥīd* and disbelief; The concluding verses of this passage (Verses 38-41) contain the first instance of permission for the believers to fight in defense of the sanctities of the religion against the hostility of the transgressors
Verses 42-66	Allah will exact retribution in this world and the next against those who harm the believers. In Verses 58-65, Allah guarantees to guide, help and provide for those who flee from persecution or defend themselves against transgression. It is the longest unbroken sequence of verses that are concluded with Allah's beautiful names.
Verses 67-78	Establishing Tawḥīd and correct beliefs and invalidating polytheism and disbelief. This final section contains a second Sajdah. *Sūrah al Ḥajj* is the only *Sūrah* that contains two places of prostration.

سُورَةُ المُؤْمِنُون
AL MU'MINŪN (23)
The Believers

VERSES
118

WORDS
1,840

LETTERS
4,800

REVEALED IN
MAKKAH

REVEALATION ORDER
74

Its unique distinction is that it opens with eleven verses describing the believers and their reward. Also, the Prophet (ﷺ) began the morning prayer with it in Mecca on the day of the conquest.

Main Themes: No person will ever succeed without abiding by the qualities of faith; commending the believers on their excellent traits; stern criticism of the disbelievers by mentioning their final abode. It contains the commendable traits of the believers in three places. Al Imām Abū Isḥāq al-Shāṭibī (d. 790 AH رَحِمَهُ ٱللَّهُ) wrote:[14]

غَلَبَ عَلَى نَسَقِهَا ذِكْرُ إِنْكَارِ الْكُفَّارِ لِلنُّبُوَّةِ الَّتِي هِيَ الْمَدْخَلُ لِلْمَعْنَيَيْنِ الْبَاقِيَيْنِ، وَإِنَّهُمْ إِنَّمَا أَنْكَرُوا ذَلِكَ بِوَصْفِ الْبَشَرِيَّةِ تَرَفُّعًا مِنْهُمْ أَنْ يُرْسَلَ إِلَيْهِمْ مَنْ هُوَ مِثْلُهُمْ، أَوْ يَنَالَ هَذِهِ الرُّتْبَةَ غَيْرُهُمْ إِنْ كَانَتْ؛ فَجَاءَتِ السُّورَةُ تُبَيِّنُ وَصْفَ الْبَشَرِيَّةِ وَمَا تَنَازَعُوا فِيهِ مِنْهَا، وَبِأَيِّ وَجْهٍ تَكُونُ عَلَى أَكْمَلِ وُجُوهِهَا حَتَّى تَسْتَحِقَّ الِاصْطِفَاءَ وَالِاجْتِبَاءَ مِنَ الله تعالى؛

"The structure of the Sūrah predominantly focuses on the denial of prophecy by the disbelievers, which serves as an entry point to the remaining themes. They denied this based on humanity, elevating themselves above the notion that someone like them could be sent to them or that someone else could attain such a status if possible. Thus, the Sūrah clarifies the nature of humanity and what they disputed about it, and how it can be in its most perfect form to deserve selection and choice by Allah (عَزَّوَجَلَّ)."

The relationship between this Sūrah and the one before it can be seen from several perspectives:

1. Allah concluded the previous Sūrah by addressing the believers, commanding them to establish prayer, give zakat, and do good deeds, promising them success. This promise of success is realized at the beginning of this Sūrah.

[14] al Muwāfaqāt 4/270.

2. In both Sūrahs, the initial creation is discussed as evidence for the resurrection and final judgment.

3. Each Sūrahs includes stories of past prophets and their nations, providing lessons for present and future generations.

4. In each, proofs of the Creator's existence and His Oneness are presented.

The Connection Between its Beginning and End: The Sūrah begins by mentioning that the believers are successful (verse 1) and closes by mentioning that the disbelievers will not prosper (verse 117). In the beginning, it mentions the creation of man (verse 12), and at the end, it mentions that he was not created without purpose (verse 115).

In establishing the main theme of contrasting the characteristics of the believers and the devastating outcomes of disbelief, the Sūrah discusses several topics:

- Describing the characteristics of the believers (verses 1-9).
- Mentioning the reward of the believers (verses 11-12).
- Presenting the history of believers across generations (verses 23-50).
- Additional characteristics of the believers (verses 57-61).
- Establishing the argument against disbelievers with logical evidence (verses 78-91).
- The fate of believers and disbelievers (verses 99-111).
- Praying for forgiveness and mercy is a sign of dependence on Allah, among believers' greatest traits (verse 118).

BROADER OVERVIEW OF THE SŪRAH

- This Sūrah revolves around affirming monotheism, invalidating polytheism, and undermining its principles while highlighting faith and its laws. It begins with glad tidings for believers of great success due to their spiritual and intellectual virtues, which purify the soul and straighten conduct.
- It then describes the creation of humans, their origin, and progeny, indicating Allah's sole right to be worshipped due to His unique creation of humans and their development. It urges contemplation on one's formation and eventual non-existence after life. This creation signifies the affirmation of resurrection after death, emphasizing that Allah did not create creation aimlessly or in jest.

- The Sūrah moves on to reflect upon the creation of the heavens and its evidence of Allah's wisdom and gratitude for Allah's creations based on water, essential for life in animals and plants, demonstrating the intricacies of creation, benefits from livestock, including transportation, and the utilization of benefits for humanity, including tools for thought and observation. It mentions sailing ships, transitioning to the story of Noah and the flood.
- It proceeds to remind us of the prophets' missions to guide us towards monotheism and righteous actions, the rejection and criticism by their communities, and the punishment of the deniers as examples for those turning away from Muhammad's call, praising those who believed and feared Allah.
- It alerts the polytheists that their situation mirrors that of previous nations; they're liable to face what befell the denying past nations. Allah has shown them aspects of punishment, hoping they cease their stubbornness, yet they persisted in their polytheism due to satanic whispers. They're reminded that they acknowledge Allah's sole lordship when asked, yet they don't act upon this acknowledgment and will regret their disbelief at death and on Judgment Day.
- They knew the Prophet (ﷺ), were intimately aware of his truthfulness, integrity, and sincere advice, and were not seeking personal gain but Allah's reward. So, they have no excuse for their polytheism and denial of the message but are merely following their desires and turning away from the truth.
- The Sūrah concludes by instructing the Prophet to overlook their poor treatment, respond with what is better, and seek forgiveness for believers, and that is the great success the Sūrah opened with.

BRIEF SŪRAH SUMMARY

Verses 1-11	The qualities and reward of the believers.
Verses 23-50	The believers throughout history.
Verses 57-61	Additional qualities of the believers
Verses 78-98	Establishing the proof against the believers.
Verses 99-111	The final abode of the believers and of the unbelievers.
Verses 118	One of the greatest qualities of the believers is making du'a for Allah's forgiveness and mercy.

CONTEMPLATE, COMPREHEND, APPLY

Contemplation Insights for Page 332 [Al-Hajj 1-5]

- The necessity of preparing for the Day of Judgment with the provision of piety.
- The intensity of the horrors of the Day of Judgment where a nursing mother forgets her infant, a pregnant woman drops her load, and people lose their minds.
- Gradation in creation is a divine practice.
- The initial creation is evidence of the possibility of resurrection.
- The phenomenon of rain and its subsequent growth of the earth is tangible proof of the resurrection of the dead.

Contemplation Insights for Page 333 [Al-Hajj 6-15]

- Causes of guidance are knowledge that leads to the truth, a guide who directs them to it, or a book they trust that guides them.
- Arrogance is a trait that prevents success in truth.
- From Allah's justice, He does not punish except for a sin.
- Allah supports His prophet and His religion, even if the disbelievers dislike it.

Contemplation Insights for Page 334 [Al-Hajj 16-23]

- Guidance is in Allah's hand; He grants it to whom He wills among His servants. Do not grieve over the disobedient and the deniers, and contemplate the great blessing of guidance that Allah has distinguished you with
- Allah's watchfulness over everything from the actions and conditions of His servants.
- All creations submit to Allah by destiny, and believers obey Him.
- Punishment is destined for the disbelievers and the disobedient, while mercy is affirmed for the believers and the obedient.

Contemplation Insights for Page 335 [Al-Hajj 24-30]

- The sanctity of the Sacred House requires extra caution against sins therein more than anywhere else.
- The Sacred House of Allah is a refuge for the hearts of believers at all times and places.
- The benefits of Hajj return to people, both worldly and in the hereafter.
- Gratitude for blessings necessitates kindness towards the weak.

Contemplation Insights for Page 336 [Al-Hajj 31-38]

- Using parables to make abstract concepts tangible is a great educational purpose.
- The virtue of humility.
- Kindness leads to happiness.
- Faith is a reason for Allah's defense of the servant and His care for him.

Contemplation Insights for Page 337 [Al-Hajj 39-46]

- Affirming Allah's attributes of strength and dignity.
- Affirming the legitimacy of Jihad to protect places of worship.
- Establishing religion is a reason for Allah's support for His believing servants.
- Heart blindness prevents contemplation of Allah's signs.

Contemplation Insights for Page 338 [Al-Hajj 47-55]

- Luring the oppressor into further oppression to punish him with a greater punishment is a divine norm.
- Allah preserves His book from alteration and distortion and deflects the devil's minions' schemes away from it.
- Hypocrisy and heartlessness are two deadly diseases.
- Faith is the fruit of knowledge, and humility and submission to Allah's commands are the fruit of faith.

Contemplation Insights for Page 339 [Al-Hajj 56-64]

- The status of migration in Islam and its virtues.
- The permissibility of retaliation in kind.
- Allah's support for the wronged may come in this world or the hereafter.
- Affirmation of the high attributes of Allah, such as knowledge, hearing, sight, and supremacy, in a manner befitting His Majesty.

Contemplation Insights for Page 340 [Al-Hajj 65-72]

- Among Allah's blessings to people is the subjugation of what is in the heavens and the earth for them.
- Affirmation of the attributes of compassion and mercy for Allah (عَزَّوَجَلَّ).
- Allah's encompassing knowledge of what is in the heavens and the earth and between them.

- Blind following is the reason the polytheists cling to their association of partners with Allah.

Contemplation Insights for Page 341 [Al-Hajj 73-78]

- The importance of using parables to clarify meanings is a noble educational method.
- The incapacity of idols to create the slightest thing proves their incapacity to create anything else.
- Associating partners with Allah stems from not magnifying Allah properly.
- This affirms Allah's attributes of power and might and the importance of the believer contemplating their meanings.

SŪRAH AL MU'MINŪN INSIGHTS

Contemplation Insights from Page 342 [Al Mu'minūn 1-17]

- For success, there are various causes worth knowing and adhering to.
- Gradual progression in creation and legislation is a divine norm.
- Allah's encompassing knowledge of His creations.

Contemplation Insights from Page 343 [Al Mu'minūn 18-27]

- Allah's kindness to His servants is evident in sending down rain and facilitating its benefits.
- Highlighting the status of the olive tree.
- The idolaters' belief in the divinity of stones and their denial of human prophethood is a testament to their foolishness.
- Allah's support for His messengers is confirmed when their nations deny them.

Contemplation Insights from Page 344 [Al Mu'minūn 28-42]

- - The obligation to praise Allah for His blessings.
- Indulgence in worldly pleasures leads to negligence or arrogance towards the truth.
- The consequence for the disbeliever is regret and loss.
- Injustice leads to estrangement from Allah's mercy.

Contemplation Insights from Page 345 [Al Mu'minūn 43-59]

- Arrogance is a barrier to receiving the truth.
- Pure food contributes to the heart's and action's righteousness.
- Monotheism is the creed of all prophets and their message.

- Allah's blessings on the wicked are not an honor but a form of delusion.

Contemplation Insights from Page 346 [Al Mu'minūn 60-74]

- The believer's fear of their good deeds is not being accepted.
- Lifting obligation beyond one's capacity is a mercy to the servants.
- Luxury is a barrier to steadfastness and a cause of destruction.
- The human mind's inability to grasp many benefits.

Contemplation Insights from Page 347 [Al Mu'minūn 75-89]

- The disbelievers' disregard for blessings or calamities that befall them is evidence of their corrupted nature.
- Ingratitude for blessings is a trait of disbelievers.
- Adherence to blind imitation prevents reaching the truth.
- Acknowledgment of God's lordship, without acknowledgment of His divinity, does not save one.

Contemplation Insights from Page 348 [Al Mu'minūn 90-104]

- The stability of the universe's order is evidence of Allah's Oneness.
- Allah's encompassing knowledge of everything.
- Treating the wrongdoer with kindness is a noble Islamic ethic with a significant impact on the opponent.

CONTEMPLATION STUDY QUESTIONS

Verse 1: Why was the mention of the Lord specified here among all other names and attributes of Allah? *[Al-Sa'dī]*

Verse 2: Why was the nursing mother specifically mentioned here? *[Al-Sa'dī]*

Verse 9: Why is the punishment for turning away upon hearing the Qur'ān being humiliated? And why is this humiliation in this world before the hereafter? *[Ibn Kathīr]*

Verse 11: What is the aspect of the loss for the apostate in this world? What causes a person's faith to be on the edge, threatened with extinction? *[Al-Sa'dī]*

Verse 18: Why were these creational signs specifically mentioned over others? How do creations prostrate to Allah (عَزَّوَجَلَّ)? *[Ibn Kathīr]*

Verse 22: Why are the people of Hell told while they are being tormented: "Taste the punishment of burning"?

Verse 23: What's the reason for talking about the attire of the people of Paradise? *[Ibn Kathīr]*

Verse 27: In the verse, there is an aspect of the Qur'ān's miracle related to informing about the unseen; clarify that. *[Al-Sa'dī]*

Verse 30: How can a Muslim earn immense reward without doing anything with his limbs? *[Al-Sa'dī]*

Verse 40: The Mujahideen have virtues over Muslims; clarify that. *[Al-Sa'dī]*

Verse 53-54: People are divided into three categories in the face of doubts: what are they? *[Al-Sa'dī]*

Verse 57: How does Allah reward the criminals according to their deeds? *[Al-Sa'dī]*

Verse 60: What is implied by describing Allah (عَزَّوَجَلَّ) as Oft-Pardoning and Forgiving? *[Al-Sa'dī]*

Verse 62: Why is Takbir (saying "Allahu Akbar") a slogan for major acts of worship? *[Al-Sa'dī]*

Verse 65: What is the reason for ending the verse with the attributes of being Full of Kindness and Merciful? *[Al-Sa'dī]*

Verse 67: The verse guides how to confront and clarify those who attack certain Islamic rulings. *[Al-Sa'dī]*

Verse 72: In the verse, there is consolation for the oppressed believers and a threat to the oppressors; explain it. *[Ibn Kathīr]*

Verse 78: Is Jihad limited to using weapons to fend off enemies? *[Al-Sa'dī]*

Sūrah Al-Mu'minoon Questions

Verse 2: Why is humility specifically mentioned over other pillars and duties of prayer? *[Al-Sa'dī]*

Verse 5: How does one recognize the deficiency within oneself to complete it? *[Al-Sa'dī]*

Verse 18: What is the wisdom behind sending down water in measure? *[Ibn Kathīr]*

Verse 18: There is an alert to a method by which people recognize the reality of the blessing; what is it? *[Al-Sa'dī]*

Verse 34: Explain the contradiction and conflict in their speech. *[Al-Sa'dī]*

Verse 35: What mistake did these people commit, for which they denied the resurrection? *[Al-Sa'dī]*

Verse 40: What makes the son of Maryam and his mother a sign? *[Ibn Kathīr]*

Verse 51: What is the relationship between good, lawful food and righteous deeds? *[Ibn Kathīr]*

Verse 56: Why does Allah (عَزَّوَجَلَّ) extend the criminals with wealth and children? *[Al-Sa'dī]*

Verse 61: The race towards good deeds may reach the point of hardship; how does the verse address this issue? *[Al-Sa'dī]*

Verse 66: The verse indicates that applying Sharia is the optimal way for progress and advancement; explain that. *[Al-Sa'dī]*

Verse 68: What benefit is there in urging them to contemplate? *[Ibn Kathīr]*

Verse 77: Neglecting the warning necessitates a punishment after that; explain that through the verse. *[Al-Sa'dī]*

Verse 96: How to repel evil from humans, and how to repel evil from the devil? *[Al-Sa'dī]*

Verse 102: In light of this verse, Explain the value of increasing good deeds. *[Ibn Kathīr]*

Verse 106: Explain the danger of despair dominating a person. *[Ibn Kathīr]*

Verse 116: Why was the creation's account aimless followed by saying: "So high [above all] is Allah"? *[Al-Sa'dī]*

Day 18: Al-Nūr & Al Furqān

The *Qurā'n* reading for **day 18** is *Sūrah al-Nūr* and *Sūrah al Furqān.* The focus of *Sūrah al-Nūr* is one of purifying the believing community from sexual immorality and indecency. Sūrah al Furqān focuses on defending the truth and inculcating righteous character traits.

سُورَةُ النُّورِ
AL-NŪR (24)
The Light

VERSES
64

WORDS
1,316

LETTERS
5,680

REVEALED IN
MADINAH

REVEALATION ORDER
102

It is said to be the 100th *Sūrah* revealed after *Sūrah al Ḥashr,* following the events of the battle of *Banū Muṣṭaliq* after Sha'bān in the year six after *Hijrah.* Many features distinguish it: The only Sūrah that begins with a verse explicitly stating it is a Sūrah. It features the verses about the slander incident, consisting of 16 verses. The term "light" appears more frequently in this Sūrah than in any other, occurring seven times. It contains the "verse of veiling," where 25 pronouns are gathered in one verse. Umar bin Al-Khattab (رَضِيَ اللهُ عَنْهُ) recommended teaching this Sūrah to women.

Main Themes: Chastity and safeguarding reputations; persevering in the purity of Muslim society by setting legal parameters to curb sexual immorality. This purity and protection come on account of divine guidance (light). Religion is a spiritual light, guiding believers to purity and turning them far away from their opposites.

It begins by mentioning the punishment of those who oppose laws related to fornication (verse 2) and closes by mentioning the punishment of those who oppose the Messenger's command in general (verse 63). Opposing the light of guidance afflicts a person with calamities and punishments in this life and the hereafter.

The relevance of this Sūrah to the preceding one can be seen from two perspectives:

1. In the previous Sūrah, it was stated, "And those who guard their private parts (verse 5)," and here, it mentions detailed laws concerning those who do not preserve their chastity, regarding the fornicator and the fornicatress, and related issues such as slander, the story of the slander (*Al-Ifk*), the command to lower the gaze which leads to fornication, the order for those unable to marry to remain chaste, and the prohibition against forcing girls into prostitution.

2. A series of commands and prohibitions are mentioned here After stating in the previous Sūrah that He did not create us but with the purpose of commands and prohibitions.

In establishing the main topic, the Sūrah addresses several points:

1. Criminalizing adultery and slandering chaste women due to its grave impact on society.

2. Exonerating the Mother of the Believers, Aisha (رَضِيَ ٱللَّهُ عَنْهَا), from false accusations.

3. Measures for protecting society from indecency:

- Warning against spreading indecency (verse 19).
- Commanding men and women to lower their gaze (verses 30-31).
- Prohibiting the display of adornment except to mahrams (verse 31).
- Encouraging the marriage of young single men and women, even if they are poor (verse 32).
- Outlining the etiquettes of seeking permission to enter (verses 58-59).
- Warning against following the footsteps of Satan (verse 21).

4. The rectification of society begins with the Houses of Allah and prayer (verses 36-37).

5. Outlining the etiquettes of hospitality and hosting (verse 61).

6. Explaining the reasons for Allah granting succession and empowerment on Earth (verses 55-56).

BROADER OVERVIEW OF THE SŪRAH

- This Sūrah encompasses various regulations regarding men's interaction with women, including etiquette in mixing and visiting.

- It was first revealed in response to the issue of marrying a woman known for adultery, initiated by clarifying the punishment for adultery. It addresses the punishment for those who slander chaste women. It covers the ruling on li'an (mutual cursing).
- It discusses the exoneration of Aisha (رَضِيَ ٱللَّهُ عَنْهَا) from the slander spread by the hypocrites, their punishment, and those who participated in spreading the rumor. It warns against the desire to spread indecencies among believers. It commands forgiveness in the face of harm, referencing the case of Mistah ibn Uthatha.
- It includes regulations on seeking permission before entering inhabited and uninhabited homes and the manners of Muslims in social interactions. It promotes spreading greetings of peace.
- It encourages marrying off slaves and maids and incentivizes their manumission through a contractual agreement where they compensate their owners. It prohibits prostitution, which was widespread in the pre-Islamic era. It commands chastity.
- It criticizes the conditions of the hypocrites and hints at their malicious intentions towards the Prophet (صَلَّى ٱللَّهُ عَلَيْهِ وَسَلَّمَ). It warns against falling into Satan's traps.
- It presents parables to guide faith and misguide disbelief. It highlights the status of the houses of worship and their caretakers. It includes a description of Allah's greatness, creations, and favors upon people.
- It concludes with a description of what Allah has prepared for the believers, acknowledging that Allah is aware of everyone's inner thoughts, that the return is to Him, and that He holds the reward.

BRIEF SŪRAH SUMMARY

Verses 1-26	Laws related to illicit sexual relations or accusations of such. The story of the slander against 'Aā'ishah.
Verses 27-34	The preventative means against illicit sexual relations; the specific etiquettes of entering the homes of others; lowering one's gaze; the rulings of ḥijāb.

Verses 35-46	Connecting Allah's laws to our belief about Him; the parable of those who frequent and support the masājid in comparison to those in delusion and the darkness of misguidance; the mention of Allah's creational signs and how the creation glorify him.
Verses 47-57	Contrasting between the Munāfiqūn who enjoy slander and the obedient believers who are suited to be given authority in the earth.
[v.] Verses 58-64	Etiquettes of children seeking permission to enter; etiquettes when speaking to the Prophet (H)

Al Imām al-Sa'dī (d. 1376 AH رَحِمَهُ ٱللَّهُ) brings an amazing benefit about a recurring statement, "**Were it not for Allah's grace and mercy**," throughout this *Sūrah*:[15]

" لولا فضل الله ورحمته لما شرع لعباده الأحكام،

"Were it not for Allah's grace and mercy, He would not have legislated the laws for His servants.

ولولا فضله ورحمته لما فصَّلها وبيَّنها،

Were it not for His grace and mercy, He would not have detailed and explained (His ayāt).

ولولا فضله ورحمته وأن الله تواب حكيم لما وضَّح ما يحتاج إليه العباد ويسَّره غاية التيسير،

Were it not for His grace and mercy and that Allah is surely al-Tawwāb (the Acceptor of Repentance) and All-Wise, He would not have clarified what the servants need and made it easy for them (to carry out).

ولولا فضله ورحمته لما شرع أسباب التوبة والمغفرة، ولما تاب على التائبين،

Were it not for His grace and mercy, He would not have legislated the means of repentance and forgiveness and would not accept the repentance of the penitent.

ولولا فضله ورحمته لما زكَّى منكم من أحد أبدًا،

Were it not for His grace and mercy, He would never have purified and nurtured you.

ولكن الله يزكي من يشاء، والله سميع عليم، كما فصل ذلك في صدر سورة النور ".

However, Allah purifies and nurtures whom He wills, and Allah is All-Hearing, All-Knowing, as He explained in detail in the opening section of Sūrah al-Nūr."

---

[15] in al Mawāhib al-Rabbāniyyah. This statement is found in verses 10, 14, 20, and 21 of this Sūrah, accounting for four of the six times it is mentioned in the Qur'ān, the other two being in verses 82 and 113 of Sūrah al-Nisā'.

سُورَةُ الفُرْقَانِ
AL FURQĀN (25)
The Criterion

VERSES
77

WORDS
892

LETTERS
3,783

REVEALED IN
MAKKAH

REVEALATION ORDER
42

Main Themes: The *Qur'ān* is a criterion between truth and falsehood and a decisive victory for the people of truth against the people of falsehood. Supporting the Prophet (ﷺ) and the *Qur'ān* after the continuing onslaught of the polytheists. It manifests the truth of his prophethood and disproves the criticisms of the disbelievers. It shows that they are unimportant and that what they worship is futile. It concludes by mentioning the commendable characteristics and rewards of the honored servants of al-Rahman.

Burhān al-Dīn al Biqā'ī (d. 885 AH رَحِمَهُ ٱللَّهُ) said:

"ومقصودها: إظهار شرف الداعي صلى الله عليه وسلم بإنذار المكلفين عامة بما له سبحانه من القدرة الشاملة، المستلزم للعلم التام، المدلول عليه بهذا القرآن المبين، المستلزم لأنه لا موجود على الحقيقة سوى من أنزله فهو الحق، وما سواه باطل.

"The purpose of this surah is to display the nobility of the caller, the Prophet (ﷺ), by warning all those morally accountable about Allah's encompassing power, which implies complete knowledge proven by this clear Qur'ān. This implies that the only true existence is from Him who revealed it; He is the truth, and everything else is falsehood.

وتسميتها بالفرقان، واضح الدلالة على ذلك، فإن الكتاب ما نزل إلا للتفرقة بين الملتبسات، وتمييز الحق من الباطل، ليهلك من هلك عن بينة. ويحيى من حي عن بينة، فلا يكون لأحد على الله حجة، ولله الحجة البالغة".

Naming it "Al Furqān" (The Criterion) signifies this, as the Book was revealed to distinguish between ambiguities, to separate truth from falsehood, so that those who perish do so with clear evidence. Those who live do so with clear evidence. Thus, no one can argue against Allah, and to Allah belongs the ultimate proof."

It begins by mentioning the reality of the people of Shirk and closes by mentioning the attributes of the righteous (verses 63-76).

It is distinct in many ways: the phrase *Tabārak*, "Blessed is He," appears most frequently, three times; it includes fourteen verses towards its end that are considered comprehensive verses describing the servants of the Most Merciful; and it contains the eighth prostration verse of the Qur'ān.

The core objectives of the surah include:

- Highlighting the Qur'ān and its guidance, expressing gratitude towards its guidance, highlighting the Messenger (صَلَّى ٱللَّهُ عَلَيْهِ وَسَلَّمَ) to whom the Qur'ān was revealed, mentioning the proofs of his truthfulness and his detachment from worldly desires, and stating that he follows the path of other messengers. This serves to strengthen the Messenger (صَلَّى ٱللَّهُ عَلَيْهِ وَسَلَّمَ) in his call and to console him regarding the opposition from his people.
- Affirming resurrection, promising reward to the righteous in the afterlife, warning of punishment for the polytheists, detailing the disgrace they will face on the Day of Judgment, and the regret and sorrow they will experience for denying the Messenger (صَلَّى ٱللَّهُ عَلَيْهِ وَسَلَّمَ) their polytheism and following the misguided.
- Proving the oneness of Allah (عَزَّ وَجَلَّ) by mentioning various wonders of His creation in the universe, including natural phenomena and human creation, clarifying that He has no son or partner, and refuting the divinity of idols and their claim of angels being the daughters of Allah (سُبْحَانَهُ وَتَعَالَىٰ).
- Describing the characteristics of the servants of the Most Merciful, whom Allah has distinguished with noble morals and steadfastness in this life on His law, mentioning the great reward prepared for them in the gardens of bliss, and hinting at a near punishment that will befall the deniers.

There are many parallels connecting this Sūrah and the previous one:

This surah is related to the previous one in several ways:

1. Allah *concluded the previous surah* by affirming His ownership of everything in the heavens and the earth, managing it according to His profound wisdom and general benefit, with a beautiful order and arrangement. He also mentioned that He would hold His servants accountable on the Day of Judgment for their good or bad deeds. *This surah begins by* highlighting His transcendence in His essence, attributes, and actions, and His love for the best of His servants by revealing the Qur'ān to them as a guide and a bright lamp.

2. *The previous surah was concluded* with the believers' need to follow the Prophet (صَلَّى ٱللَّهُ عَلَيْهِ وَسَلَّمَ), praising them for doing so and warning them against disobeying his command for fear of sedition and painful punishment. *This surah opens* with praise for the Prophet (صَلَّى ٱللَّهُ عَلَيْهِ وَسَلَّمَ), the revelation of the Book to him for guidance towards the path of righteousness, and condemning those who deny his prophethood by claiming he is bewitched, eats food, and walks in the markets, among other allegations.

3. Both surahs describe clouds, the sending of rain, and the reviving of the earth after that. The previous surah says, "Do you not see that Allah drives clouds?" and this one says, "He is the one who sends the winds as heralds of good news."

4. Each surah describes the disbelievers' deeds on the Day of Judgment as worthless, saying in the first, "*The deeds of those who disbelieve are like a mirage in a desert,*" and in this surah, "*And We shall turn to whatever deeds they did, and We shall make them into scattered dust.*"

5. The original creation of humans is described in both surahs. The first says, "*Allah created every living creature from water,*" and the second, "*He is the one who created a human being from water and made him related by lineage and marriage.*"

BROADER SŪRAH OVERVIEW

It begins with glorifying Allah (عَزَّوَجَلَّ) and initiating praise for Him, describing Him with divine and unique attributes. It includes emphasis on the Qur'ān, its noble origin, and its guidance, along with gratitude towards people for its guidance and direction away from perils, highlighting the Prophet's (صَلَّىٰٱللَّهُعَلَيۡهِوَسَلَّمَ) status.

The surah is founded on three main pillars:

The first pillar Affirms that the Qur'ān is revealed from Allah, emphasizing the messenger it was revealed upon (صَلَّىٰٱللَّهُعَلَيۡهِوَسَلَّمَ) evidence of his truthfulness and elevated status above worldly desires, following the path of other messengers, including how his people received his call with denial.

The second pillar is establishing resurrection and recompense, warning about the consequences in the hereafter, promising rewards there for the righteous, and warning the polytheists about their regretful state on that day due to their denial of the messenger and their polytheism, following their leaders of disbelief.

The third pillar is arguing for the oneness of Allah, His uniqueness in creation, absolving Him of having a son or partner, negating the divinity of idols, and refuting their claim of the angels being Allah's daughters.

Each of these three pillars starts with"Blessed is He who." Al-Tibi (رَحِمَهُٱللَّهُ) mentioned that the focus of this surah is on the Prophet's (صَلَّىٰٱللَّهُعَلَيۡهِوَسَلَّمَ) mission to warn all humanity of what lies ahead and behind them, which is why its introduction glorifies the One who revealed the Criterion to His servant to be a warner to all worlds.

It mentioned the wonders of Allah's creation, combining arguments and reminders, followed by reinforcing the Prophet's (صَلَّىٰٱللَّهُعَلَيۡهِوَسَلَّمَ) commitment to his mission and his resistance against the disbelievers. It set examples through the missions of previous messengers and what they faced from their people, like the people of Mūsā, Noah, Aad, Thamud, the Companions of the Rass, and the people of Lut.

It encouraged reliance on Allah, praised the believers in Him, commended their traits and moral qualities, and hinted at an imminent punishment that would befall the deniers.

BRIEF SŪRAH SUMMARY

Verses 1-22	The false claims of those who cast doubts about the *Qurā'n;* people are a trial for each other (verse 20).
Verses 23-62	Some spectacles of Judgment Day; those who disregarded the *Qur'ān* and the complaint of the Messenger ﷺ about them; this is followed by the mention of the previous nations and the mention of
Verses 63-77	Description of Allah's righteous servants.

CONTEMPLATE, COMPREHEND, APPLY

Contemplation Insights from Page 350 [Al-Nur 1-10]

- Paving the way for discussing significant matters by indicating their importance.
- An adulterer loses respect and mercy in a Muslim community.
- Social isolation of adulterers is a means to shield the community from them and a deterrent against adultery.
- Diversifying the punishment of slander to include both physical (punishment) and moral (rejection of testimony and branding as corrupt) penalties highlights the gravity of this act.
- Adultery is not proven except with evidence; claiming it without evidence is considered slander.

Contemplation Insights from Page [Al-Nur 11-20]

- Hypocrites focus on undermining trust centers in the Muslim community by spreading false accusations.
- Hypocrites may entice some believers to participate in their actions.
- Honoring Umm al-Mu'minin Aisha (رَضِيَ اللَّهُ عَنْهَا) by exonerating her above the seven heavens.
- The necessity of verification towards rumors.

Contemplation Insights from Page [Al-Nur 21-27]

- Temptations and whispers of Satan call to commit sins, so believers should beware.
- Success in repentance and good deeds is from Allah, not the servant.
- Forgiving and overlooking the misdeeds of others is a reason for the forgiveness of sins.
- Slandering chaste individuals is among the major sins.
- The legitimacy of seeking permission is to protect sight and maintain the sanctity of homes.

Contemplation Insights from Page [Al-Nur 28-31]

- Permission is not required to enter public buildings.
- Men and women must lower their gaze from what is unlawful for them.
- Wearing the hijab is mandatory for women.
- Using means of provocation is prohibited.

Contemplation Insights from Page [Al-Nur 32-36]

- Allah limited the reasons for slavery (through war), expanded the reasons for emancipation, and encouraged it. Freeing oneself from slavery through the contract of emancipation and assisting slaves financially for their freedom prevents slaves from becoming a despised class resorting to immorality.
- A believer's heart is illuminated with natural disposition and divine guidance.
- The masjids are houses of Allah on earth established for His worship; they must be kept away from physical and moral impurities.
- Among the beautiful names of Allah is "The Light," which encompasses the attribute of light for Him (سُبْحَانَهُ وَتَعَالَى).

Contemplation Insights from Page [Al-Nur 37-43]

- Balancing worldly engagements with acts for the Hereafter is essential for a believer.
- The work of a disbeliever is null due to the lack of the condition of faith.
- Disbelievers are discordant from the creatures of Allah that glorify Him in obedience.
- All stages of rain are from the creation and decree of Allah.

Contemplation Insights from Page [Al-Nur 44-53]

- The diversity of creation is proof of Allah's power.
- Among the characteristics of hypocrites is turning away from Allah's decree unless it is in their favor, their heart disease and doubt, and their suspicion of Allah.
- Obedience to Allah and His Messenger and fear of Allah are reasons for success in both worlds.
- Swearing falsely is a known behavior among hypocrites.

Contemplation Insights from Page [Al-Nur 54-58]

- Following the Messenger (صَلَّى ٱللَّهُ عَلَيْهِ وَسَلَّمَ) is a sign of guidance.
- The caller to Allah must exert effort to call Allah, and the results are in Allah's hands.
- Faith and good deeds are the cause of empowerment on Earth and security.
- Teaching slaves and children about asking for permission at times when people's privacies are exposed.

Contemplation Insights from Page [Al-Nur 59-61]

- Elderly women may set aside some of their clothing as there is no fear of temptation from them.
- Caution in religion is the behavior of the pious.

- Excuses lead to a reduction in obligations.
- The Muslim community is of mutual support, solidarity, and brotherhood.

Contemplation Insights from Page [Al-Nur 62-64]

- Islam is a religion of order and etiquette; adhering to these etiquettes brings blessings and goodness.
- The status of the Messenger of Allah (ﷺ) requires honoring and respecting him more than others.
- The ominous consequences of opposing the Sunnah of the Prophet (ﷺ).

SŪRAH AL FURQĀN INSIGHTS

Contemplation Insights from Page 359 [Al Furqān 1-2]

- Emphasizing Allah's sovereignty and knowledge over everything. Manifestations of Allah's Lordship that necessitate His Divinity include the bestowal of good upon creation, sovereignty, power, knowledge, and wisdom.

Contemplation Insights from Page 360 [Al Furqān 3-11]

- Describes the true God characterized by creating all things and controlling benefit, death, and resurrection, in contrast to the incapacity of idols for any of these.
- Affirming Allah's attributes of forgiveness and mercy.
- Highlighting that prophethood does not negate humanity.
- The Prophet's (ﷺ) humility is living as people do.

Contemplation Insights from Page 361 [Al Furqān 12-20]

- Combining warnings of Allah's punishment with encouragements of His reward.
- Worldly pleasures lead to forgetting Allah.
- The humanity of messengers is a mercy for easy interaction.
- Variations in people's fortunes as a divine test.

Contemplation Insights from Page 362 [Al Furqān 21-32]

- Disbelief prevents the acceptance of good deeds.
- The danger of bad companionship.
- The harm in abandoning the Qur'ān.

◆ The wisdom in revealing the Qur'ān in stages to comfort and facilitate understanding and action for the Prophet (ﷺ).

Contemplation Insights from Page 363 [Al Furqān 33-43]

◆ Disbelief in Allah and denial of His signs lead to the destruction of nations.

◆ The absence of faith in resurrection leads to a lack of caution.

◆ Mocking the people of truth is the behavior of disbelievers.

◆ The danger of following whims.

Contemplation Insights from Page 364 [Al Furqān 44-55]

◆ The disbeliever descends to a level lower than animals because he disbelieves in Allah.

◆ The phenomenon of shadow is a sign from Allah's signs indicating His power.

◆ Varying arguments and proofs is a successful educational method.

◆ Calling others to Allah with the Qur'an is a form of jihad in the way of Allah.

Contemplation Insights from Page 365 [Al Furqān 56-67]

◆ The caller to Allah does not seek reward from the people.

◆ The attribute of ascension (Istawa) is affirmed for Allah in a manner befitting His Majesty.

◆ Al-Raḥmān (The Most Merciful) is a name of Allah that no one else shares, indicating one of His attributes: mercy.

◆ Helping the servant by alternating night and day to catch up on missed obedience in one of them.

◆ Attributes of the Most Merciful servants include humility, forbearance, obedience to Allah in the absence of people, fear of Allah, and maintaining moderation in spending and other matters.

Contemplation Insights from Page 366 [Al Furqān 68-77]

◆ Characteristics of the Most Merciful's servants include avoiding polytheism, refraining from unjustly taking lives, staying away from adultery, avoiding falsehood, being mindful of Allah's signs, and praying.

◆ Sincere repentance necessitates abandoning sin and engaging in obedience.

◆ Patience leads to entry into the highest levels of Paradise.

◆ Allah does not need anyone's faith; rather, it is they who benefit from their belief.

CONTEMPLATION STUDY QUESTIONS

Sūrah An-Nur Questions

Verse 2: What is the mercy prohibited in this verse? *[Ibn Kathīr]*

Verse 2: What is the benefit of people witnessing the punishment? *[al-Sa'dī]*

Verse 3: This verse clarifies the enormity of the sin of fornication; explain that. *[al-Sa'dī]*

Verse 9: Why is the woman specifically associated with anger in the case of li'an (oath of condemnation)? *[Ibn Kathīr]*

Verse 15: What is the danger of belittling some sins? *[al-Sa'dī]*

Verse 22: Discuss the principle "The recompense is of the same kind as the action" through this verse. *[Ibn Kathīr]*

Verse 30: Mention two benefits of lowering the gaze. *[al-Sa'dī]*

Verse 31: What is the juristic principle derived from this verse? *[al-Sa'dī]*

Verse 37: What is learned from describing the mosque attendees as "men"? [Ibn Kathīr]

Verse 37: Why does the verse end with "they fear a Day in which the hearts and eyes will [fearfully] turn about"? *[al-Sa'dī]*

Verse 39: What causes the deeds to be voided on the Day of Judgement? *[Ibn Kathīr]*

Verse 46: This verse contains a doctrinal benefit; mention it. *[al-Sa'dī]*

Verse 50: Satisfaction with the Sharia is a blessing from Allah; explain that through the verse. *[al-Sa'dī]*

Verse 54: Is there any path to guidance other than obedience to the Messenger of Allah ﷺ? *[al-Sa'dī]*

Verse 55: Why did Allah describe those who disbelieved after empowerment as transgressors? *[al-Sa'dī]*

Verse 56: Why were prayer and almsgiving specifically mentioned among the commands that require obedience to the Messenger? What do you think of someone who hopes for Allah's mercy while neglecting their prayer and almsgiving, disobeying His Messenger? *[al-Sa'dī]*

Verse 61: What is the ruling if someone mentioned in the verse does not forgive eating from his house? Which is better, gathering or separating, when eating? The statement "yourselves" indicates the strength of the bond among Muslims; explain that. *[al-Sa'dī]*

Sūrah Al Furqān Questions

Verse 6: Why does this verse end with "Indeed, He is ever Forgiving and Merciful"? *[Ibn Kathīr]*

Verse 12: Why did the fire become angry at its people? *[al-Sa'dī]*

Verse 13: This verse describes types of torment for the disbelievers; explain them. *[al-Sa'dī]*

Verse 26: What is learned from attributing the ownership of the Day of Judgment to His name, "the Most Merciful"? *[al-Sa'dī]*

Verse 33: Through this verse, Explain a bit of the wisdom of a preacher and a teacher. *[al-Sa'dī]*

Verse 43: How can one worship one's desires? *[Ibn Kathīr]*

Verse 44: Why are cattle deemed more guided than disbelievers? *[al-Sa'dī]*

Verse 62: How does the variation of night and day serve as a reason to thank Allah (عَزَّوَجَلَّ)? *[al-Sa'dī]*

Verse 70: Through the verse: Highlight the immense virtue of sincere repentance. *[Ibn Kathīr]*

Verse 74: Praying for the righteousness of spouses and offspring implies something; what is it? *[al-Sa'dī]*

Day 19: The TawaSīn: al-Shu'arā', al-Naml, & al Qasas

The *Qurā'n* reading for **day 19** is the *ṬawāSīn: al Shu'ara', al-Naml & al Qaṣaṣ*. All three begin with the letters Ṭā Sīn. They are said to have been revealed sequentially and have a singular style and subject matter.

All focus on the main themes of the Makkan chapters: (1.) *Tawḥīd*; (2.) The revealed message and the prophethood; (3.) the hereafter. They begin with introductory verses about the excellence of the *Qurā'n*. They then mention numerous stories that are followed by concluding passages. (seven stories in al-*Shu'ara'*; four stories in *al Naml*; two stories in *al Qaṣaṣ*).

سُورَةُ الشُّعَرَاءِ

AL-SHU'ARĀ' (26)

The Poets

VERSES 227

WORDS 1,279

LETTERS 5,540

REVEALED IN MAKKAH

REVEALATION ORDER 47

Main Themes: Providing comfort and support for the Prophet (صَلَّى ٱللَّهُ عَلَيْهِ وَسَلَّمَ) during significant hardships in Makkah. It did this by mentioning Allah's might in both showing mercy to the believers and punishing the disbelievers. It concisely refutes a number of the slanders of the disbelievers against the Prophet (صَلَّى ٱللَّهُ عَلَيْهِ وَسَلَّمَ).

It tells the story of seven prophets (Mūsā, Ibrāhīm, Nūḥ, Hūd, Ṣāliḥ, Luṭ, and Shuayb—in that order). *"Have Taqwā of Allah and obey me." "Indeed within that is a great sign, and most of them are not believers; indeed your Lord is All-Might, Ever-Merciful."* It begins *(verse 1)* and ends *(verse 192)* by mentioning the *Qurā'n's* revelation. Verses 4 and 227 both mention the descent of Allah's punishment for the wicked. It has some powerful verses about the day of Judgment *(87-89)*.

The objectives of the surah include:

- The surah discusses the prophets and messengers Allah sent to guide humanity throughout the ages and presents some events between the prophets and their people. In these narratives, the surah affirms monotheism, resurrection, and judgment and illustrates the condition and fate of those who deny these truths.

- Highlighting the Qur'ān, challenging the disbelievers' inability to produce anything like it, providing evidence that it is from Allah, refuting the disbelievers' criticisms of the Qur'ān, clarifying that it is neither poetry nor the words of devils, and warning the polytheists of Allah's wrath.
- Commanding the Prophet (ﷺ) to place his trust in Allah in his mission and all matters, charging him with the task of warning the people, and stating that his responsibility is merely to convey the message.

The connection of this surah to the preceding one can be understood in several ways:

- It elaborates and details some of the topics mentioned in its predecessor.
- Both begin with the praise of the Noble Qur'ān.
- Both conclude with a warning to those who deny the truth.

The surah's beginning and end are congruent in several aspects:

- It starts with mentioning the Qur'ān, "These are the verses of the clear Book," and concludes with the statement, "And indeed, it is a revelation from the Lord of the worlds," reaffirming the Qur'ān's divine origin.
- It also opens with a warning to the wrongdoers: "If We wish, We could send down to them from the sky a sign…" and ends with a warning to the wrongdoers: "And those who have wronged will know to what kind of return they will be returned," emphasizing the consequences of their actions.
- This structure highlights that the Qur'ān is the truth in all of its information and proofs because it is from Allah, the truth. In contrast, poets are often associated with misguidance and injustice, using their talent away from the truth.

BROADER OVERVIEW OF THE SŪRAH

Firstly, the Sūrah highlights the Qur'ān, addressing their inability to challenge it and consoling the Prophet (ﷺ) regarding his people's disregard for the monotheism the Qur'ān calls them towards. It also includes threatening them for exposing themselves to Allah's wrath and setting examples for them through the fate of nations that denied their prophets and turned away from Allah's signs.

It's believed that this surah was revealed after the disbelievers requested miraculous signs. Thus, it begins with consoling the Prophet (ﷺ) and reinforcing his resolve by reminding him that what he faces from his people is the tradition of the messengers before him with their nations, like Mūsā, Ibrāhīm, Noah, Hud, Salih, Lut, and Shu'aib. Hence, every argument presented to the disbelievers concludes with the statement that *"in these are signs, yet most of them do not believe, and that your Lord is indeed the Almighty, the Merciful,"* thus setting the record against them that the signs of monotheism and the truthfulness of the messengers are abundant and sufficient for those seeking the truth, but most of the people will not believe, and that Allah possesses the might to inflict punishment on them and is merciful towards His messengers, aiding them against their enemies.

Each of these stories rightly concludes with what was concluded in its counterpart, for repeating these stories reinforces their meanings in souls, and the more they are repeated, the deeper they settle in hearts and understanding, becoming more resistant to forgetfulness. This repetition and reiteration were also due to the disbelievers' hard-heartedness and refusal to heed the truth, so they were frequently admonished and reminded, hoping to open a listening ear or enlighten a mind.

Furthermore, the surah emphasizes the Qur'ān, bringing the testimony of the People of the Book to it, refuting their criticisms of the Qur'ān, and denying it being poetry or the words of devils. It commands the Prophet (ﷺ) to warn his closest kin, stating that his only duty is to convey the message. It includes proof of monotheism and the sanctity of the Qur'ān from being considered poetry or the words of devils. The core message is that the Prophet's (ﷺ) role is merely to deliver the message, interspersed with arguments demonstrating the Qur'ān's truth.

BRIEF SŪRAH SUMMARY

Verses 1-19	Introductory verses
Verses 10-191	Story of Mūsā (10-68); Ibrāhīm (69-104); Nuḥ (105-122); Hūd (123-140); Ṣāliḥ (141-159); Luṭ (160-175); Shu'ayb (176-191)
Verses 192-227	Concluding verses

سُورَةُ النَّمْلِ
AL-NAML (27)
The Ants

VERSES
93

WORDS
1,317

LETTERS
4,799

REVEALED IN
MAKKAH

REVEALATION ORDER
48

Main Theme: Gratitude for blessing knowledge-based guidance and its role in establishing a society. It begins (verses 1-2) and ends (verse 92), mentioning the guidance of the Qur'ān. Al Biqā'ī (d. 885 AH رَحِمَهُ اللَّهُ) said:

"فالمقصود الأعظم منها: إظهار العلم والحكمة، كما كان مقصود التي قبلها: إظهار البطش والنقمة.

"The primary aim of this Sūrah is to demonstrate knowledge and wisdom, as the primary focus of the preceding Sūrah was to showcase divine might and retribution.

"وأدل ما فيها على هذا المقصود: ما للنمل من حسن التدبير وسداد المذاهب في العيش، ولاسيما ما ذكر عنها سبحانه من صحة القصد في السياسة، وحسن التعبير عن ذلك القصد، وبلاغة التأدية".

The most evident indication of this aim within the Sūrah is seen through the story of the ants. Their exceptional management and sound living strategies, especially as Allah mentioned, including their accurate intention in governance, excellent expression of those intentions, and eloquence in their communication exemplify this purpose.

Through these narratives, the Sūrah emphasizes the significance of wisdom, foresight, and articulate communication in leadership and governance, illustrating these concepts through human examples and within the natural world, thus highlighting the universal application of divine wisdom and knowledge. The Sūrah, being named after the ants, reflects humanity, endowed with reason and understanding, underscoring the potential for even greater organization and achievement within human societies. The story showcases some miraculous aspects of Allah's creation. It serves as a metaphorical lesson for humans, encouraging them to use their intellect and comprehension to improve their lives and the societies they inhabit.

Sūrah An-Naml is distinguished by its portrayal of dialogues between humans and other earthly creatures such as the ant, the hoopoe, the jinn, and other beings. These interactions highlight the Qur'ān's emphasis on the universality of communication and understanding across different forms of creation, demonstrating the wisdom and knowledge granted by Allah to His prophets, in this case, Sulaymān (عَلَيْهِ ٱلسَّلَامُ). This Sūrah beautifully illustrates the interconnectedness of all living beings and the importance of recognizing and respecting the wondrous signs of Allah in every aspect of creation.

This overarching theme is highlighted in the very first story great Algerian scholar, 'Abd al Ḥamīd b. Bādīs (d. AH رَحِمَهُ ٱللَّهُ) said:

قد ابتدأ الحديث عن الملك العظيم بذكر (العلم)، وقدمت النعمة به على سائر النعم، تنويهًا بشأن العلم، وتنبيهاً على أنه هو الأصل الذي تنبني عليه سعادة الدنيا والأخرى، وأنه هو الأساس لكل أمر من أمور الدين والدنيا،

"The discourse on the great dominion (of Dawud and Sulaymān) begins by emphasizing knowledge and prioritizing this blessing above all others, highlighting its significance. It serves as a reminder that knowledge is the foundation upon which the happiness of this world and the hereafter is built. It is the basis of all matters about religion and worldly affairs.

وأن الممالك إنما تنبني عليه وتشاد، وأن الملك إنما ينظم به ويساس، وأن كل ما لم يبن عليه فهو على شفا جرف هار، وأنه هو سياج المملكة ودرعها، وهو سلاحها الحقيقي، وبه دفاعها، وأن كل مملكة لم تحم به فهي عرضة للانقراض والانقضاض

Knowledge is the only thing that establishes and strengthens kingdoms, organizes governance and administration, and keeps anything not based on it on the brink of collapse. Knowledge acts as a kingdom's protective barrier and shield and is its true weapon. A kingdom defends itself through knowledge, and any kingdom not fortified by it is vulnerable to extinction and downfall.

فأما الممالك التي تبنى على السيف فبالسيف تهدم، وما يشاد على القوة فبالقوة يؤخذ. وإنما أعلى الممالك وأثبتها ما بني على العلم، وحمي بالسيف. وإنما يبلغ السيف وطره ويؤثر أثره، إذا كان العلم من ورائه".

... The sword demolishes kingdoms built upon the sword, and what is established on strength is seized by strength. The highest and most stable kingdoms are those built upon knowledge and protected by the sword. The sword achieves its purpose and leaves its mark only when knowledge stands behind it."

Gratitude for guidance as the ultimate aim of civilizational superiority is delineated in the *Sūrah* through several key themes:

1. The Ultimate Aim: Expressing gratitude for blessings by utilizing them in ways that please the Ever-Merciful (verse 19).

2. Knowledge is highlighted as the most essential foundational element (verse 16).

3. Scientific Excellence is crucial for advancement (verse 44).

4. Military Power: Recognized as necessary for safeguarding civilization (verse 37).

5. The story of the Hoopoe exemplifies Every citizen's belief in the ultimate goal (verses 22-26).

6. Acknowledging Allah's Power in Creation: Demonstrating divine omnipotence through the universe's wonders (59-64).

These elements underscore that civilizational superiority is not merely about material wealth or power but involves a comprehensive approach that includes spiritual fulfillment, the pursuit of knowledge, scientific achievement, robust defense capabilities, collective belief in a higher purpose, and acknowledgment of divine power and grace.

The relevance of this Sūrah to the one preceding it is multifaceted:

1. This Sūrah continues the previous one by adding the stories of Prophets Dawud and Sulaymān, enriching the narrative with further examples of divine messages and miracles.

2. It provides detailed accounts and expansions on stories mentioned briefly in the preceding Sūrah, such as those of Prophets Lut and Mūsā, deepening the understanding of their trials and the lessons to be learned from them.

3. Both Sūrahs emphasize the Qur'ān's divine origin, affirming it as a revelation from Allah, thereby reinforcing its authority and authenticity. The shift from dismissing the idea that demons brought down the revelation at the end of the previous Sūrah to affirming the Qur'ān as a revelation from the Lord of the Worlds at the opening of Sūrah al-Naml serves to reinforce the sacred and unassailable nature of the Qur'ānic message.

4. They both offer solace and consolation to Prophet (صَلَّى ٱللَّهُ عَلَيْهِ وَسَلَّمَ) for the opposition and hardship he faces from his people, encouraging perseverance in the face of rejection and disbelief.

The alignment between the beginning and the end of the surah:

It begins by mentioning the Qur'ān as a clear book of guidance and good news for the believers. It concludes with a reminder of the Qur'ān's role in guiding individuals, stating that those who follow its guidance do so for their benefit, and those who stray do so to their detriment. This reinforces that the Qur'ān is the key to prosperity in this world and the hereafter, highlighting its central role in guiding humanity towards righteousness and success.

BROADER OVERVIEW OF THE SŪRAH

- The primary objectives of this Sūrah include the opening that points to the Qur'ān's miraculous nature through its eloquent composition and profound meanings, as indicated by the separated letters at its beginning. It highlights the significance of the Qur'ān as guidance for those whom Allah facilitates guidance, excluding those who deny its divine origin.

- It challenges people with the knowledge contained within it, including the stories of the prophets. It reflects on the rule of the greatest kingdom bestowed upon a prophet, which is the kingdoms of

Dawud and Sulaymān, peace be upon them, and Sulaymān's knowledge about the conditions of birds and the greatness his kingdom reached in civilization.

- It mentions the most famous nation among the Arabs that was given strength, the nation of Thamud, and refers to a great Arab kingdom, Sheba. This subtly implies that the prophecy of Muhammad (صَلَّى ٱللَّهُ عَلَيْهِ وَسَلَّمَ) is a message accompanied by the governance of the nation, followed by a kingdom, which is the Caliphate of the Prophet. It suggests that Islamic governance will establish a future kingdom for the nation, as Sulaymān's kingdom was established for the Children of Israel.
- It argues against the idolaters about the falsity of their religion, the invalidity of their gods, the falsehood of their priests and diviners, and the custodians of their idols. It establishes the concept of resurrection, the horrors preceding the Day of Judgment, and its signs.
- It asserts that the Qur'ān is a guardian over the previous scriptures. It also deals with the idolaters, informing them that the role of the messenger is to continue delivering the Qur'ān and warns them that they will witness true signs. Allah is fully aware of their actions.

BRIEF SŪRAH SUMMARY

Verses 1-6	Introduction; the final abode of the believers and disbelievers in summary.
Verses 6-58	The story of Mūsā (verses 7-14) Dāwūd and Sulaymān (verses 15-44); Ṣāliḥ (45-53); Luṭ (54-58).
Verses 59-93	Conclusion: The details of the introduction, beginning with five verses about Allah's Oneness (verses 59-64); the perfect knowledge of Allah as relates to the hereafter and this world (verses 65-75); the guidance of the Qur'ān in conveying to the Israelites much of what they differ about; what people will see on the day of gathering of the final judgment for the believers and disbelievers.

سُورَةُ القَصَصِ

AL QAṢAṢ (28)

The Stories

VERSES
88

WORDS
1,441

LETTERS
5,800

REVEALED IN
MAKKAH

REVEALATION ORDER
49

It was revealed at a time when the Muslims were vulnerable in Makkah as a means to boost the morale of the believers and provide them with solace.

Main Themes: Manifesting Allah's Power and His Universal Way of aiding the vulnerable believers and destroying the tyrannical disbelievers as a deterrent for all other disbelievers. The Sūrah is distinct in many ways:

(1.) Its detailed narration of the story of Mūsā (عَلَيْهِ ٱلسَّلَامُ) followed by Sūrahs Al-A'raf and Taha. It provides a comprehensive account of his life, from infancy to his prophethood, making it one of the richest sources of his story in the Qur'ān. It delves deeply into the life of Mūsā, offering insights into his struggles, leadership, and interactions with Pharaoh from infancy.

(2.) Its Exclusive Mention of Qarun's Story: Qarun (Korah), a wealthy man from Mūsā's people, was infamous for his immense riches and subsequent downfall due to his arrogance and rejection of Mūsā's teachings.

(3.) Sūrah Al-Qasas is distinguished by its narration of Mūsā accidentally killing an Egyptian man, his subsequent flight to Midian, and his marriage there. These events are crucial to understanding Mūsā's early life, moral dilemmas, and the divine nurturing leading up to his becoming a prophet.

From the objectives of the surah:

- The surah details the story of Mūsā, illustrating how Pharaoh's kingdom was lost due to Allah's care for His allies and His abandonment of His enemies in the conflict between truth and falsehood.

- It challenges the disbelievers with the Prophet's (صَلَّى ٱللَّهُ عَلَيْهِ وَسَلَّمَ) knowledge of these stories despite being illiterate, having never read or written, nor mingled with the People of the Book. It warns them of the adverse consequences of polytheism, challenges them with the miraculous nature of the Qur'ān, refutes their excuses for disbelief if they were to believe, warns them of the fate that befell denying nations before them, criticizes their pride over Muslims due to their power and blessings, for such is the transient enjoyment of this world, whereas for Muslims, what is with Allah (تَبَارَكَ وَتَعَالَىٰ) is better and everlasting.

- It mentions the creational signs that prove Allah's Oneness, the blessings He has placed in the universe for His servants, and reminds the disbelievers of what will occur to them on the Day of Recompense.
- It uses the example of Qarun among Mūsā's people to demonstrate how tyranny can manifest through power and wealth, leading to his ultimate destruction and ruin.
- It outlines the foundations of goodness and happiness in this life and the hereafter, consoles the Prophet (صَلَّى ٱللَّهُ عَلَيْهِ وَسَلَّمَ), strengthens him, and promises his return to his homeland and dominion over his enemies.

Sūrah Al-Qasas's relation to the preceding Sūrahs can be discerned through three primary aspects:

1. Expansion of Previously Summarized Narratives: Allah elaborates on the story of Mūsā, briefly touched upon in the preceding Sūrahs. This detailed account includes his upbringing by Pharaoh, the decree to kill the sons of the Israelites, which led to Mūsā being cast into the river, his killing of an Egyptian, his escape to Midian, his marriage there, and his divine appointment. This narrative depth provides a fuller understanding of Mūsā's trials, leadership, and prophethood.

2. Detailed Discussion on the Day of Judgment: While the previous Sūrahs briefly touched upon the disbelievers' questioning of the Day of Judgment, Sūrah Al-Qasas delves deeper into this topic, offering a more comprehensive exposition that underscores the inevitability and significance of the Last Day.

3. Further Elaboration on the Fates of Previous Nations: The Sūrah revisits the fate of previous communities, such as the people of Prophet Salih and Lut, expanding on their stories to highlight the consequences of their actions. It contrasts those who brought forth good deeds with those who perpetrated evil, underscoring the moral lessons and divine justice that pervade their stories.

These thematic connections and narrative continuities demonstrate the Qur'ān's cohesive and interconnected nature, with each Sūrah building upon and complementing the messages of the others.

The connection between the Sūrah's beginning and ending:

Both the beginning and the end mention the promise of Allah. *It starts with* the divine promise to Mūsā's mother, assuring her of her son's safety and his future prophethood, demonstrating Allah's meticulous care and plan for His messengers from their very early moments. *The end of the Sūrah mirrors this beginning* with a promise to Prophet (ﷺ), assuring his eventual victorious return, reinforcing the message that Allah's promise is the ultimate truth, and He is the supporter of His allies.

This structural symmetry not only underscores the certainty of Allah's promises but also serves as a reassurance to believers of all times. It reinforces the concept of divine justice and the eventual triumph of righteousness over tyranny and falsehood. Sūrah Al-Qasas, therefore, serves as a powerful reminder of Allah's sovereignty, the importance of steadfast faith, and the inevitability of divine support for the righteous, setting a clear distinction between the paths of guidance and misguidance.

BROADER OVERVIEW OF THE SŪRAH

- This Sūrah narrates a detailed story of Prophet Mūsā (عَلَيْهِ السَّلَامُ) and Pharaoh, enriching what was summarized in previous Sūrahs such as Sūrah Ash-Shu'ara and Sūrah An-Naml. It elaborates on Mūsā's upbringing within Pharaoh's household and the subsequent downfall of Pharaoh's reign. This Sūrah provides a more comprehensive account of Mūsā's life, from his upbringing to the moment he received the divine message, and briefly summarizes events that followed since those were detailed in other Sūrahs like Al-A'raf and Al-Shu'ara.
- The purpose of detailing these narratives is to offer lessons and admonitions, allowing the disbelievers to understand Allah's tradition in sending messengers and dealing with nations that deny their messages.
- It challenges the disbelievers with the knowledge given to the Prophet (ﷺ) despite his being unlettered and not having been in the company of the People of the Book. This revelation serves as a stern warning to the disbelievers about the consequences of polytheism and provides a compelling warning.
- The Sūrah refutes the disbelievers' demands for miracles similar to those given to Mūsā, like turning a staff into a serpent, and criticizes their rejection of Mūsā as well. It challenges them with the inimitability of the Qur'ān alongside the guidance of the Torah.
- It discredits their excuses, warns them about the fate of nations that denied Allah's messengers, and presents arguments for Allah's oneness. The Sūrah emphasizes the temporary nature of worldly gains compared to the eternal rewards awaiting believers.

- In essence, Sūrah Al-Qasas comforts and reinforces the Prophet (صَلَّى ٱللَّهُ عَلَيْهِ وَسَلَّمَ), reminding him and the believers of Allah's promise to empower the oppressed and grant victory to the faithful. The detailed recounting of Mūsā's mission is intended to draw parallels between the experiences of past prophets and those of the Prophet (صَلَّى ٱللَّهُ عَلَيْهِ وَسَلَّمَ) and his followers, offering them insight, encouragement, and a clear demonstration of divine support and the eventual triumph of faith.

BRIEF SŪRAH SUMMARY

Verses 1-50	The story of Mūsā with Fir'awn is fifty verses. The birth and suckling of Mūsā, his accidental killing of a man, his service of his father-in-law for ten years as dowry for his wife are only mentioned in *Sūrah al Qaṣaṣ.*
Verses 51-75	It is followed by 25 verses as commentary;
Verses 76-83	The story of Qārūn
Verses 83-88	That is followed by five verses of commentary.

CONTEMPLATE, COMPREHEND, APPLY

Contemplation Insights from Page 367 [al-Shu'arā' 1-19]

- The concern of Prophet (صَلَّى ٱللَّهُ عَلَيْهِ وَسَلَّمَ) for guiding people.
- Affirmation of Allah's attributes of dignity and mercy.
- The importance of patience and eloquence for a caller to Allah.
- Prophets call for liberation from servitude to other than Allah.
- Pharaoh's objection to Mūsā's mission due to a past killing incident, which Mūsā acknowledged, indicating it wasn't a valid argument for Pharaoh's disbelief.

Contemplation Insights from Page 368 [al-Shu'arā' 20-39]

- Previous mistakes and blessings of a caller to Allah do not negate his right to invite others.
- Taking protective measures against enemies does not contradict faith in Allah.
- Allah's creation signifies His sovereignty and unity.
- Weak arguments often lead to violence.
- Inciting the public against religious people is a tyrant's tactic.

Contemplation Insights from Page 369 [al-Shu'arā' 40-60]

- The relationship between the people of falsehood is based on material interests.
- His Lord's promise confirmed Mūsā's confidence in victory over the magicians.
- The magicians' belief demonstrated that Allah controls hearts.
- Tyranny and injustice lead to the loss of kingdoms.

Contemplation Insights from Page 370 [al-Shu'arā' 61-83]

- Allah supports His believing servants with victory, backing, and rescue from hardships.
- Affirmation of Allah's attributes of dignity and mercy.
- The danger of blind imitation.
- A believer's hope in their Lord is immense.

Contemplation Insights from Page 371 [al-Shu'arā' 84-111]

- The importance of keeping the heart free from diseases like envy, ostentation, and vanity.
- Blaming misguides does not excuse the misguided.

- Denying one messenger is like denying all messengers.
- Ibrahim's story concludes by returning to the Day of Judgment and wrapping the narrative neatly.

Contemplation Insights from Page 372 [al-Shu'arā' 112-136]

- The superiority of those who believe first, even poor or weak.
- The divine tradition of destroying wrongdoers and saving believers.
- The danger of being deluded by worldly life.
- The obstinacy of falsehood adherents and their persistence in it.

Contemplation Insights from Page 373 [al-Shu'arā' 137-159]

- The succession of blessings with disbelief is a lure to destruction.
- Reminding of blessings is hoped to lead to faith and a return to Allah by the servant.
- Sins are the cause of corruption on earth.

Contemplation Insights from Page 374 [al-Shu'arā' 160-183]

- Homosexuality is a deviation from the natural disposition and a great evil.
- It is a trial for a caller to Allah that his family members may be among the disbelievers or the disobedient.
- Without faith, Earthly relationships do not benefit one when divine punishment descends.
- The obligation to give full measure and the prohibition of shortchanging.

Contemplation Insights from Page 375 [al-Shu'arā' 184-206]

- The deeper a Muslim delves into Arabic, the more capable they can understand the Qur'ān.
- Arguing against the polytheists with the acknowledgment of impartial People of the Book that the Qur'ān is from Allah.
- The worldly blessings disbelievers enjoy are a lure, not an honor.

Contemplation Insights from Page 376 [al-Shu'arā' 207-227]

- Affirmation of divine justice, negating any injustice from Him.
- Sanctification of the Qur'ān from any closeness of the devils.
- The importance of gentleness and kindness for callers to Allah.
- The quality of poetry: its good is good, and its bad is bad.

SŪRAH AL-NAML INSIGHTS

Contemplation Insights Page 377 [Al-Naml 1-13]

- The Qur'ān is guidance and good news for the believers. It illustrates the miraculous nature of the Qur'ān, composed of letters like Ta and Sin; humanity cannot produce its like.
- Maintain prayer in its pillars, obligations, and conditions, and with humility to benefit from this Qur'ān's verses.
- Disbelief in Allah makes one worse than animals, leads to the following falsehood in actions and words, and results in confusion and turmoil.
- Allah safeguards His messengers and protects them from all harm.

Contemplation Insights Page 378 [Al-Naml 14-22]

- Smiling is the laughter of dignified people.
- Gratitude for blessings is the conduct of prophets and the righteous towards their Lord.
- Apologizing for the righteous in their absence.
- Governance includes penalizing the deserving and accepting the excuses of those justified.
- Knowledge may exist among the lesser-known that is not found among the more prominent.

Contemplation Insights Page 379 [Al-Naml 23-35]

- The hoopoe's condemnation of the people of Saba for their disbelief and idolatry shows that faith is innate in all creatures.
- Investigating the accused and verifying their arguments.
- It's legitimate to uncover information about adversaries.
- Letters should ideally begin with "Bismillah."
- Displaying the believer's dignity before those who deny the truth is essential.

Contemplation Insights Page 380 [Al-Naml 36-44]

- The dignity of faith shields the believer from being affected by the world's trivialities.
- Rejoicing in material things and relying on them is a characteristic of disbelievers. The standards of the people of the Hereafter differ from those of worldly people; hence, they do not rejoice in worldly life as its people do. The greatest blessing is the religion of Islam, and the world is fleeting.
- A believer's consciousness is always mindful of Allah's blessings.
- Testing an opponent's intelligence to deal with them appropriately.

- Demonstrating superiority over an opponent to influence them.
- Contemplate the combination of Richness and Generosity attributes of Allah in verse 40.

Contemplation Insights Page 381 [Al-Naml 45-55]

- Seeking forgiveness for sins is a reason for Allah's mercy.
- Superstition about people and things is not a trait of believers.
- The end of conspiring against the righteous is grim.
- Public declaration of sin is worse than concealing it.
- Condemning the actions of the wicked is obligatory.
- Do not pay attention to the mockers; mockery is the tactic of the ignorant and weak.
- Trustworthiness is the emblem of true messengers and sincere callers to Allah across all nations and ages.
- Beware of obeying the extravagant in sin; their path leads to ruin.

Contemplation Insights Page 382 [Al-Naml 56-63]

- Opponents of truth resort to violence when confronted with irrefutable evidence. Indulging in a sin habitually desensitizes one to its ugliness.
- Allah's universal norm is to save His allies and annihilate His enemies
- Marital bonds without faith are of no avail on Judgment Day.
- Reminding of Allah's blessings reinforces the belief in monotheism.
- Every distressed person, whether believer or disbeliever, is promised relief by Allah if they call upon Him.

Contemplation Insights Page 383 [Al-Naml 64-76]

- Claiming knowledge of the unseen is disbelief, as Allah exclusively possesses this knowledge.
- Disbelief in the Hereafter emboldens one to commit sins.
- Reflecting on the fate and conditions of previous nations is a path to salvation.
- Allah's comprehensive knowledge encompasses all actions of His servants.
- The Qur'ān corrects the deviations and alterations of the Children of Israel in their scriptures.
- Following the guidance of the Qur'ān is protection against disagreement and division.

Contemplation Insights Page 384 [Al-Naml 77-88]

- The importance of reliance on Allah (تَبَارَكَ وَتَعَالَى).
- Guiding people and showing mercy are among the purposes of the Qur'ān.

- The Prophet (صَلَّى ٱللَّهُ عَلَيْهِ وَسَلَّمَ) is affirmed to be upon clear truth.
- Guidance and success are at Allah's discretion, not the Prophet's (صَلَّى ٱللَّهُ عَلَيْهِ وَسَلَّمَ).
- Sleep signifies death, and awakening signifies resurrection.

Contemplation Insights Page 385 [Al-Naml 89-93]

- Faith and good deeds are the keys to security from dread on the Day of Judgment.
- Disbelief and disobedience lead to the Fire.
- Prohibiting murder, injustice, and hunting in the sacred precincts.
- Allah (تَبَارَكَ وَتَعَالَىٰ) may guide a person to Himself just by hearing the Qur'ān being recited.

SŪRAH AL QASAS INSIGHTS

Contemplation Insights from Page 385 [Al-Qasas 1-5]

- Affirms the miraculous nature of the Qur'ān as a clear sign that it is truly the book of Allah.
- Confirms the prophethood of Muhammad (صَلَّى ٱللَّهُ عَلَيْهِ وَسَلَّمَ) through this divine revelation.
- Warns against oppression, tyranny over people, and spreading corruption on earth.
- Believers benefit from what is recited to them for the life of their hearts.
- Establishes the principle that precautions do not avert fate.
- Prohibits enforcing a limit on the number of children a citizen can have.
- One of Allah's ways is to destroy the wrongdoers when they arrogate themselves over the reformers, disunite their word, or strive to weaken or kill them.

Contemplation Insights from Page 386 [Al-Qasas 6-13]

- Allah's providence saves His righteous servants from the scheming of their enemies.
- The scheming of the oppressor leads to their destruction.
- The strength of mothers' affection towards their children. Blessings come with trials; Allah (تَبَارَكَ وَتَعَالَىٰ) promises Mūsā's mother relief and a great favor, making her son a messenger. Patience during calamities is a gift from Allah, so ask Allah for it.
- The legitimacy of using lawful stratagems to escape the oppression of the oppressor.
- The fulfillment of Allah's promise is inevitable. Empowerment on earth requires patience, preparation, and effort.

Contemplation Insights from Page 387 [Al-Qasas 14-21]

- Acknowledging wrongs is part of the etiquette of supplication.
- Commendable gratitude leads a servant to obey his Lord and avoid His disobedience.
- The importance of initiating advice, especially if it can save a believer from destruction.
- The necessity of taking means of escape and supplicating to Allah for salvation.
- Excel in your worship, and Allah (تَبَارَكَ وَتَعَالَىٰ) will grant you wisdom and knowledge.
- Beware of Satan; he is an enemy to mankind.
- Goodness includes promptly offering help and advice to people.

Contemplation Insights from Page 388 [Al-Qasas 22-28]

- Seeking refuge in Allah (تَبَارَكَ وَتَعَالَىٰ) is the way to salvation in this world and the Hereafter.
- The virtue of modesty for women and the honor of believing women who maintain purity and avoid mixing with men. The modesty of a Muslim woman leads to honor and high status.
- Caring for the weak and attending to their needs is characteristic of prophets and their noble traits.
- One reason for accepting supplication is the servant's imploring while manifesting humility and need.
- Women's participation in decision-making and considering their opinion if it is correct is commendable.
- Strength and trustworthiness are qualities of a successful official.
- It is permissible for the dowry to be a service.

Contemplation Insights from Page 389 [Al-Qasas 29-35]

- Fulfilling contracts is the behavior of believers. Prophets are faithful to their word; Mūsā completed and fulfilled the ten-year term.
- Among the righteous attributes are striving for sustenance and diligently solving worldly problems with wisdom and patience.
- Allah's speaking to Mūsā is affirmed as truth.
- A caller to Allah (تَبَارَكَ وَتَعَالَىٰ) needs support.
- Eloquence is important for callers to the faith.

Contemplation Insights from Page 390 [al-Qasas 36-43]

- Rejecting the truth with baseless doubts is the way of the tyrants.
- Arrogance prevents following the truth.
- The bad end of the arrogant is a divine tradition.

- Falsehood has its leaders, callers, forms, and manifestations.
- The believer is confident in Allah's promise of a good outcome for those who obey Him.

Contemplation Insights from Page 391 [al-Qasas 44-50]

- Denial of the Prophet's (صَلَّى ٱللَّهُ عَلَيْهِ وَسَلَّمَ) knowledge of the unseen except what Allah (تَبَارَكَ وَتَعَالَىٰ) revealed to him.
- Knowledge fades over time. Faith and knowledge require regular revision, as the passage of time and longevity lead to forgetfulness.
- Challenging the disbelievers to bring something more guiding than Allah's revelation to His messengers.
- The misguidance of disbelievers is due to following desires, not evidence.
- Muslim actions are based on valid religious evidence. The Book of Allah is the most guiding book.

Contemplation Insights from Page 392 [al-Qasas 51-59]

- The virtue of those among the People of the Book who believe in the Prophet (صَلَّى ٱللَّهُ عَلَيْهِ وَسَلَّمَ) and Islam: they are rewarded doubly.
- Guidance of success is in Allah's hand, not in the messengers or others.
- Following the truth is a means of security, not a cause of fear, as the polytheists claim.
- The danger of luxury on individuals and society.
- From Allah's mercy, He does not destroy the people until after sending messengers as a warning to them.
- The virtue of repelling evil with good and spending from what Allah (تَبَارَكَ وَتَعَالَىٰ) has provided. Make your speech free from harmful and offensive language, even towards disbelievers.

Contemplation Insights from Page 393 [al-Qasas 60-70]

- The wise person prefers the eternal over the transient. Do not let food, clothing, or housing distract you from what is in the Hereafter.
- Repentance erases what came before it.
- The choice belongs to Allah, not His servants; they have no right to object to Him.
- Allah's knowledge encompasses all that is apparent and hidden in His servants' deeds.
- Leaders of misguidance disavow their followers on the Day of Judgment.
- When the correct evidence comes to you, follow it and act upon it. Remember that Allah will ask you how you responded to the messengers.

Contemplation Insights from Page 394 [al-Qasas 71-77]

- The alternation of night and day is one of Allah's blessings that should be thanked. Gratitude to Allah involves using the night for rest and the day for seeking sustenance, all in ways that please Allah without incurring His displeasure.
- Tyranny, as with leadership and sovereignty, can also occur through wealth.
- Being arrogantly joyful is a sin detested by Allah.
- It's necessary to advise those who are feared to be tempted.
- Allah despises those who spread corruption on earth.
- Those who do not believe and are certain today will know the truth when they stand before Allah.

Contemplation Insights from Page 395 [al-Qasas 78-84]

- Everything good and blessed in a person is from Allah in what He created and commands.
- People of knowledge are people of wisdom and salvation from trials; knowledge guides its bearer to correctness. Fitnah is recognized by the knowledgeable when it comes but recognized by all when it leaves.
- Highness and pride on earth and spreading corruption result in destruction and loss. Materialistic people are more susceptible to temptation.
- The expansiveness of Allah's mercy and justice is in doubling the rewards for the believers and not doubling the sins for the disbelievers.

Contemplation Insights from Page 396 [al-Qasas 85-88]

- Prohibiting aiding those in misguidance. Beware of bad companions; they are a reason for deviation from Allah's path.
- Commanding adherence to the monotheism of Allah and avoiding polytheism.
- Beware of bad companions; they are a reason for deviation from Allah's path, "And let them not avert you from the signs of Allah after they have been revealed to you."

CONTEMPLATION STUDY QUESTIONS

Sūrah al-Shu'ara' Questions

Verse 10: Why is the story of Mūsā repeated in the Qur'ān more than others? *[Al-Sa'dī]*

Verses 12-14: What was Mūsā's intention with this supplication? *[Ibn Kathīr]*

Verse 15: Why couldn't Pharaoh overpower Mūsā? *[Al-Sa'dī]*

Verses 27-28: In Mūsā's words, there is a response to Pharaoh's accusation of madness; explain that. *[Al-Sa'dī]*

Verse 29: Explain the method of oppressors when they lose argument and evidence. *[Ibn Kathīr]*

Verses 36-39: Pharaoh wanted to invalidate Mūsā's argument by gathering magicians, but the opposite of his intent occurred; explain that. *[Ibn Kathīr]*

Verse 49: The verse indicates the great obstinacy of Pharaoh; explain that. *[Ibn Kathīr]*

Verse 50: Why weren't the magicians affected by Pharaoh's threats? *[Al-Sa'dī]*

Verses 69-70: Allah (عَزَّوَجَلَّ) commanded His prophet to inform about a specific state of Ibrahim, among all his states, which is the state of calling to Allah; why? *[Al-Sa'dī]*

Verses 100-101: How does this verse encourage taking a righteous friend? *[Ibn Kathīr]*

Verse 106: Why did Allah send messengers from among their people? *[Al-Sa'dī]*

Verse 111: How does the verse indicate their arrogance towards the truth? *[Al-Sa'dī]*

Verse 139: "The recompense is proportional to the deed"; explain this statement through the punishment of 'Ad, the people of Hud. *[Ibn Kathīr]*

Verse 145: What is the sign of the truthfulness of Allah's sincere allies mentioned in the verse? *[Al-Sa'dī]*

Verse 158: Explain the nature of Thamud's punishment to the people of Salih. *[Ibn Kathīr]*

Verse 167: What does the similarity of statements between the criminals of the past and present indicate? *[Al-Sa'dī]*

Verses 187-189: The punishment of Shu'ayb's people was the same kind they asked for as punishment; explain that. *[Al-Sa'dī]*

Verse 192: What is the benefit of describing Allah as the Lord of the worlds in this context? *[Al-Sa'dī]*

Verses 192-195: Discuss the combined virtues in this noble Qur'ān. *[Al-Sa'dī]*

Verse 197: Why is the knowledge of the scholars of the Children of Israel specified as sufficient evidence for the truthfulness of this Qur'ān? *[Al-Sa'dī]*

Verse 214: Does this verse imply that the Prophet's (صَلَّى ٱللَّهُ عَلَيْهِ وَسَلَّمَ) invitation was specifically for his people?

Verse 216: Why was the phrase "if they disobey you" followed after "lower your wing to those who follow you among the believers"? *[Al-Sa'dī]*

Sūrah al-Naml Questions

Verses 2-3: What is the sign of sincerity in someone claiming faith? *[Al-Sa'dī]*

Verse 3: What does faith in the Hereafter entail? *[Al-Sa'dī]*

Verse 14: This verse serves as a warning to those who deny the prophethood of Muhammad (صَلَّى ٱللَّهُ عَلَيْهِ وَسَلَّمَ) even though it speaks of those who denied Mūsā; explain that. *[Ibn Kathīr]*

Verse 15: In light of this verse, explain the effect of blessings on the righteous. *[Al-Sa'dī]*

Verse 16: One of the best inheritances a child can receive from their father is faith, knowledge, and wisdom; explain that through the verse. *[Al-Sa'dī]*

Verse 21: How does the verse demonstrate Sulaymān's purity, patience, and lack of haste? *[Al-Sa'dī]*

Verse 30: What is recommended at the beginning of writing? *[Al-Sa'dī]*

Verse 35: Dealing with wisdom can lead to guidance; explain that from the verse. *[Ibn Kathīr]*

Verse 40: What is the main difference between righteous and ignorant kings? *[Al-Sa'dī]*

Verse 47: What causes of incidents and calamities that befall a person? *[Al-Sa'dī]*

Verse 54: Why is the crime of the people of Lut termed indecency? *[Al-Sa'dī]*

Verse 57: Why was Lut's wife destroyed, and in what way did she support her people? *[Al-Sa'dī]*

Verse 61: Why was a barrier created between the two seas?

Verse 66: What causes disbelievers to precede in committing sins and daring to do so? *[Al-Sa'dī]*

Verse 75: How is reliance related to the Prophet ﷺ being upon clear truth? *[Al-Sa'dī]*

Verse 92: What is the duty of the warners towards the misguided? *[Ibn Kathīr]*

Sūrah al Qasas Questions

Verse 3: Why is the story specified for the believing people? *[Al-Sa'dī]*

Verse 7: Does sending Mūsā' sister to see what happened to him contradict faith in Allah's promise? *[Al-Sa'dī]*

Verse 9: Did Pharaoh's wife benefit from her compassion for Mūsā? *[Al-Sa'dī]*

Verse 10: How is agitation related to the increase and decrease of faith? *[Al-Sa'dī]*

Verse 14: The verse indicates the great reward for kindness; explain how. *[Al-Sa'dī]*

Verse 26: From the verse, how do we deduce the ideal traits for those in charge of public affairs? *[Al-Sa'dī]*

Verse 27: How does the verse indicate the duty in the ethics of business owners and their managers? *[Al-Sa'dī]*

Verse 31: Fear and security of hearts are in Allah's hands; explain that from the verse. *[Al-Sa'dī]*

Verse 34: Being sincere in carrying the burden of calling to faith means seeking to complement one's deficiencies through other means; explain that from the verse. *[Al-Sa'dī]*

Verse 35: Mūsā had a great favor upon Harun; explain it. *[Ibn Kathīr]*

Verse 35: What benefit does this verse offer Mūsā before his mission to Pharaoh? *[Al-Sa'dī]*

Verse 38: How were the minds of Pharaoh's people corrupted? *[Al-Sa'dī]*

Verse 43: Has a nation been eradicated after the destruction of Pharaoh and his people? *[Al-Sa'dī]*

Verse 45: When does the need become evident among people for the presence of a caller to remind and teach them? *[Al-Sa'dī]*

Verse 50: What is the sign of the following desires mentioned in this verse? *[Al-Sa'dī]*

Verse 60: How do you distinguish the wise from the unwise? *[Al-Sa'dī]*

Verse 67: What does the word "perhaps" imply when it comes from Allah (عَزَّوَجَلَّ)? *[Ibn Kathīr]*

Verse 72: The verses prompt contemplation and reflection on Allah's blessing; what is it? *[Al-Sa'dī]*

Verse 81: Why was Qarun punished by sinking into the ground rather than other types of punishment? *[Al-Sa'dī]*

Section 03

The Mathānī (Oft Repeated)

Day 20: al 'Ankabūt, al-Rūm, Luqmān, al-Sajdah
Day 21: al Aḥzāb, Saba', Fāṭir
Day 22: YaSīn, al-Ṣāfāt, Ṣad
Day 23: al-Zumar, Ghāfir, Fuṣṣilat
Day 24: al-Shūrā to the end of al Aḥqāf

DAY 20: DHAWĀT AL MĪM: 'ANKABŪT -AL-SAJDAH

The Qurā'n reading for **day 20** is four chapters of medium length: *Sūrah al 'Ankabūt, Sūrah al-Rūm, Sūrah Luqmān,* and *Sūrah al-Sadjah*. These chapters are called *Dhawāt al Mīm* because they all begin with the individual letters *Ālif Lām Mīm*. They are estimated to have been revealed toward the end of the Makkan phase, especially *Sūrah al-Rūm,* which foretold the victory of Al-Rūm over the Persians in less than ten years (the victory happened in the year of the Treaty of *Ḥudaybiyyah*). The theme of *Sūrah al 'Ankabūt* also matches the circumstances of that part of the Makkan phase.

سُورَةُ العَنكَبُوتِ
AL 'ANKABŪT (29)
The Spider

VERSES
69

WORDS
980

LETTERS
4,165

REVEALED IN
MAKKAH

REVEALATION ORDER
85

It is estimated to be the 85th *Sūrah* in the order of revelation. It was revealed after *al-Rūm* and before al *Muṭaffifeen*, making it one of the last chapters to be revealed in Makkah.

Ibn al Qayyim said:[16]

«فذكر سبحانه في هذه السورة أنه لا بُدَّ أن يمتحن خلقه ويفتنهم؛ ليتبين الصادق من الكاذب، والمؤمن من الكافر، ومَن يشكره ويعبده ممّن يكفره ويعرض عنه ويعبد غيره.

"So, in this Sūrah, Allah mentions that it is necessary to subject His servants to trials and tests to differentiate between those who are truly sincere and those who are insincere, the believer from the disbeliever, and those who thank and worship Him from those who are ungrateful, averse and worship others.

وذكَر أحوالَ المتحَنين في العاجل والآجل، وذكَر أئمةَ المتحَنين في الدنيا وهم الرسل وأتباعهم، وعاقبة أمرهم وما صاروا إليه، ثم ذكَر المتحَنين من أعدائهم ومكذّبيهم، وما صاروا إليه.

[16] Shifā al 'Alīl (vol. 2, p. 268-276, Dār 'Aṭā'āt al 'Ilm, Riyāḍ.

He mentions how people are tested in this world and the next. He mentioned the leaders of those tested in this world, namely, the Messengers and their followers, and what will ultimately become of them and what they eventually reach (i.e., of Allah's reward). Then He mentions those tested by their enemies and deniers and what will ultimately happen to them...

فَمَضْمُونُ هَذِهِ السُّورَةِ هُوَ سِرُّ الْخَلْقِ وَالْأَمْرِ، فَإِنَّهَا سُورَةُ الِابْتِلَاءِ وَالِامْتِحَانِ، وَبَيَانِ حَالِ أَهْلِ الْبَلْوَى فِي الدُّنْيَا وَالآخِرَة، وَمَنْ تَأَمَّلَ فَاتِحَتَهَا وَوَسَطَهَا وَخَاتِمَتَهَا وَجَدَ فِي ضِمْنِهَا أَنَّ أَوَّلَ الْأَمْرِ ابْتِلَاءٌ وَامْتِحَانٌ، وَوَسَطَهُ صَبْرٌ وَتَوَكُّلٌ، وَآخِرَهُ هِدَايَةٌ وَنَصْرٌ، والله المستعان»

"...This *Sūrah* contains the secret of the creation and the command (i.e., the wisdom of the *Qadar* and the revelation). Surely, it is the *Sūrah* of trialing and testing and of explaining the condition of those put to test in the worldly life and the hereafter. Whoever reflects upon its opening section, main body, and conclusion will find that the beginning of the matter is being trialed and tested, the middle is patience and trust, and the conclusion is guidance and triumph. Allah alone is sought for aid." (End of statement)

As a Makkan chapter, it is concentrated on the three main topics of correct belief, the Prophethood, and the Hereafter. Its opening verses address the subject of *Tawḥīd* and correct belief by mentioning how the believer is subjected to trial due to their faith. As for addressing the issue of Prophethood and revelation, that is evident throughout. See verse 18 as a prime example. As for addressing the Hereafter, Allah briefly addresses that in many statements (*see verse 19 as an example).*

Considered to be one of the last chapters revealed in Makkah. It is the only Meccan Sūrah that mentions the *munāfiqīn* (hypocrites). It is also the only Sūrah that mentions the duration that Nūḥ (عَلَيْهِ ٱلسَّلَامُ) stayed amongst his people, inviting them to believe.

Objectives of the Sūrah:

- Demonstrating the polytheists' acknowledgment of Tawhid al-Rububiyyah (Oneness of Lordship), which necessitates Tawhid al-Uluhiyyah (Oneness of Divinity), and expressing astonishment at their condition, they confess that Allah is their Creator and the Creator of all things, yet they have taken powerless partners who cannot benefit or harm or manage any affairs.
- This invalidated the polytheists' creed regarding angels. They considered them to be daughters of Allah and worshipped them despite believing daughters to be lesser in value than sons. Their basis for this belief was merely the tradition of their ancestors, invalidating their claim of following the religion of Ibrahim.
- Clarifying that worldly life is not a measure of Allah's love for a servant, the polytheists found it improbable for the revelation to be sent to Muhammad (صَلَّى ٱللَّهُ عَلَيْهِ وَسَلَّمَ), a poor orphan

and wished that the revelation had come to a significant man of stature and wealth. Thus, the Qur'ān refutes these false worldly values.

- Presenting the story of Mūsā and 'Īsā - peace be upon them - in their call to their people towards monotheism, how their communities divided into factions, and their eventual outcomes; to console the Prophet (ﷺ) regarding the objections raised by the leaders of his people against his selection by Allah for prophethood, their pride in false values, the allure of worldly life, and their contempt for him.
- Warning of the sudden coming of the Hour, depicting the spectacle of the Day of Judgment, describing the state of the believers after entering Paradise, followed by the condition of the criminals in Hell, reminding them that the angels have recorded their deeds and that their suffering in torment is due to their actions.

BRIEF SŪRAH SUMMARY

The beginning *(v. 6)* and end *(v. 69)* of the *Sūrah* mention *al Jihād*. Struggling in the face of adversity is the foundational topic of the *Sūrah*. In exploring this primary theme, the *Sūrah* consists of three sections.

The segments are connected by the presentation of creational evidence that substantiates *Tawḥīd*, such as the heavens and earth, the sending of rain from the sky, and the navigation of ships throughout the sea. This continues until the end of the *Sūrah*.

Verses 1-130	Covers the reality of faith and struggling against oneself; It mentions being tested and tried and the ultimate outcome of the three categories of humankind: the believers, the hypocrites, the disbelievers.
Verses 14-45	Contains the bulk of its verses: it discusses the method of the Prophets in *da'wah*. Despite great trials and the seemingly little fruits of its yield, they were patient with their peoples for long spans of time. It goes on to allude to the nations led by tyrannical unbelievers such as 'Aād, Thamud, Qārūn, Fir'awn and Ḥāmān.
Verses 46-69	Covers the mannerisms of inviting Ahlul Kitāb and debating with them in the best way.

سُورَةُ الرُّومِ
AL-RŪM (30)
The Romans

VERSES
59

WORDS
819

LETTERS
3,534

REVEALED IN
MAKKAH

REVEALATION ORDER
84

The victory of Al-Rūm over the Persians is said to have happened either the same year as Badr or a few years later during the year of the *Bay'ah* (oath of allegiance) of Riḍwān and the *Ṣulḥ* (peace treaty) of Ḥudaybiyyah. It was revealed mostly in the 11th year of the Makkan phase.

Main Themes: Having certainty about the revelation *(see opening and closing verses)*, Allah's Power to change circumstances and grant aid to the believers while forsaking the disbelievers. From the objectives of the surah: It demonstrates the universal truth that the management of matters, conditions, and events belongs to Allah alone; as He (سُبْحَانَهُ وَتَعَالَىٰ) said: {To Allah belongs the command before and after}. Al-Biqā'ī (885 AH رَحِمَهُ ٱللَّٰهُ) said:

ومقصودها: إثبات الأمر كله لله، فتأتي الوحدانية مطلقاً في الإلهية وغيرها، والقدرة على كل شيء فيأتي البعث ونصر أوليائه، وخذلان أعدائه، وهذا هو المقصود بالذات، واسم السورة واضح فيه بما كان من السبب في نصر الروم من الوعد الصادق، والسر المكتوم

"Its purpose is to affirm that Allah decrees everything; thus, absolute monotheism in divinity and beyond is presented, along with the power over everything. This leads to the resurrection, the victory of His allies, and the downfall of His enemies. This very purpose is intrinsic, and the name of the surah reflects it through the cause of the victory of Al-Rūm as promised truly and the concealed secret."

It is centered around the three recurring themes of the Makkan Suwar, which are the integrity of (1.) *Tawḥīd*; (2.) the revelation of the message; (3.) The Day of Judgment.

The objectives of the surah include:

- Demonstrating the Qur'ān's miraculous nature by informing about future events that came to pass, such as Al-Rūm's victory over the Persians after initially being defeated by them, providing reassurance and comfort to the believers with this prophecy.

- Discussing the wonders of creation and life, demonstrating the immense power of Allah through the many signs in the world, establishing evidence for the existence of the great Creator, and drawing attention to Allah's signs, the Almighty and Compeller.
- Speaking on the possibility of resurrection after death using logical and sensory evidence, including the notion that revival is logically simpler than the initial creation and that the revival of the earth after its death by rain is proof of resurrection after annihilation.
- Praising this religion and its virtues, urging the Prophet (ﷺ) and Muslims to adhere to it, giving rights to those entitled to them, and highlighting the condition of the polytheists and their vices.
- Using parables to invalidate polytheism, describing the polytheists as ignorant and neglectful of consideration for the hereafter, failing to take lessons from the destruction of previous nations similar to them in associating partners with Allah, and explaining their state upon resurrection and their excuses for their past deeds.

BRIEF SŪRAH SUMMARY

Verses 1-7	The prophecy of the Roman defeat of Persia
Verses 8-32	Planting Tawḥīd in the heart by way of contemplating Allah's creation. Verses 21-26 contain 12 tremendous evidences for Allah's Oneness and Greatness.
Verses 33-54	The human experience between easy and difficulty, wealth and poverty.
Verses 55-59	The final hour and preparation for it.

سُورَةُ لُقْمَانَ
LUQMĀN (31)
Luqman

VERSES
227

WORDS
1,279

LETTERS
5,540

REVEALED IN
MAKKAH

REVEALATION ORDER
47

Main Themes: Divine Nurturing (التربية الربانية) and following the way of Wisdom (اتباع الحكمة). The words Hikmah and Hakīm are mentioned four times throughout. It contains the story of Luqmān the Wise.

Sūrah Luqmān mentions multiple types of wisdom: the wisdom for Allah's revelation, the wisdom in Allah's creation, and the wisdom of Allah's blessings so that they are appreciated and not neglected.

Objectives of the Sūrah:

- Highlighting the Qur'ān's miracle and its profound meanings, indicating it as guidance and mercy, mentioning a group of wretched ones who turned their backs on the Qur'ān, preferring Satan's music over Allah's verses.
- This demonstrates the stunning evidence of divine power in the precise cosmos, leading to the acknowledgment of the Creator's oneness and criticizing those who worship others besides Allah.
- Outlining a father's duty towards his son through the story of Luqman and his son, encompassing education, guidance, and wise counsel granted by Allah to whom He wills among His servants.
- Mentioning Allah's extensive blessings demands worship and gratitude towards Him, contrasting with the disbelief and ingratitude of those who worship others out of mere tradition.
- Commanding fear of the Day of Judgment when familial ties will not benefit, warning against the devil's traps, the allure of worldly life, and its adornment.

BRIEF SŪRAH SUMMARY

Verses 1-11	The introduction; people are of two types in their response to the *Qur'ān*: (1.) the *Muḥsinūn* (i.e., the righteous) whose attributes and reward is mentioned in brief; (2.) the *Mujrimūn* whose attributes and punishment is mentioned in brief. One of the most important verses to highlight in this section is: *"From the people are those who purchase vain speech to mislead others from Allah's path." (Verse 6)*
Verses 12-19	The advice of Luqmān to his son which contains vital matters of belief, worship, character and etiquette. Luqmān addresses his son by saying, "Oh my son" four times: The *first*: the prohibition against shirk. The *second*: dutifulness to one's parents. The *third*: belief in the day of judgment. The *fourth*: seven essential religious duties: (1.) establishing the prayer; (2.) ordering good and forbidding evil; (3.) being patient with what is difficult; (4.) not being arrogant and conceited; (5.) being humble and tranquil; (6.) being modest in manner of walking; (7.) not being loud and boisterous.
Verses 20-32	Allah's creational signs and blessings alongside the mention of His knowledge and power. In the midst of these reminders there is a call to submit oneself entirely to Allah. The most powerful verse of this passage contains a lofty similitude for Allah's speech (verse 27).
Verses 33-34	A powerful concluding admonition for all of humankind to fear Allah and prepare for Judgment Day. A reminder that Allah alone knows the unseen.

سُورَةُ السَّجْدَةِ

AL-SAJDAH (32)

The Prostration

VERSES
30

WORDS
380

LETTERS
1,518

REVEALED IN
MOSTLY MAKKAH

REVEALATION ORDER
75

It is said to be approximately the 73rd in the order of revelation after *Sūrah al-Nahl* before *Sūrah Nūḥ*.

The Sunnah is recited in the first rak'ah and *Sūrah al Insaan* in the second for *Salatul Fajr* on *Jumu'ah* [Bukhari and Muslim]. It is likewise a *sunnah* to recite *Sūrah al-Sajdah* daily before sleep (*al-Silsilah al-Ṣaḥīḥah* by al Albānī #585).

✦ **Main Themes:** The reality of creation and humankind's states in both worlds. Humility for Allah (الـخضوع لله). The *Sūrah* focuses primarily on belief in the Day of Judgment.

Objectives of the Sūrah:

- Mentioning Allah's signs that serve as evidence of His omnipotence and Oneness, drawing attention to the existence of the One True God through the marvels of creation in the heavens, the earth, and between them, specifically discussing the unique creation of humans, all in the context of refuting the divinity of anything other than Allah.
- Refuting the polytheists' disbelief in resurrection due to their weak reasoning, arguing that revival is easier than initial creation, although both are easy for Allah.
- Describing the disgrace and humility that criminals will face at the gathering ground, their vain wishes for a return to life for rectification, contrasting them with the blissful state of the righteous, praising those who believe in Allah's signs, and detailing the rewards prepared for them.
- Discussing the Day of Judgment, Allah's fair judgment among His creatures, the destruction of denying wrongdoers, the promised victory for believers, and instructing the Prophet (ﷺ) to disregard the disbelievers.

The connection between its beginning and end begins with a lengthy passage about Allah's greatness and ends by mentioning His āyāt in the earth. It covers the revelation and the truth of the Prophet (صَلَّى ٱللَّهُ عَلَيْهِ وَسَلَّمَ) (opening verse) just as it discusses the issue of *tawḥīd* and belief in the day of judgment. Belief in the day of judgment is the main topic of the *Sūrah.*

BRIEF SŪRAH SUMMARY

Verses 1-3	Defending the Qur'ān from doubts and the sending of the Prophet (صَلَّى ٱللَّهُ عَلَيْهِ وَسَلَّمَ) as a mercy to all people.
Verses 4-9	Evidences for Tawḥīd.
Verses 10-14	Segues into the discussion about Judgment Day.
Verses 15-22	The obvious difference between those who believe and those who disbelieve.
Verses 23-25	Be patient and certain, as were the Prophets of old, indeed Allah will judge between all.
Verses 26-30	Evidences for belief and Allah's guarantee to judge between all.

CONTEMPLATE, COMPREHEND, APPLY

Contemplation Insights from Page 396 [Al 'Ankabūt 1-6]

- Allah's divine tradition involves testing and examining the believers.
- Allah is independent of His servants' obedience.
- Emphasizes the significance of striving, as it is in this effort that one's soul finds salvation and escape, "And whoever strives only strives for [the benefit of] himself."

Contemplation Insights from Page 397 [Al 'Ankabūt 7-14]

- Allah forgives sins through good deeds.
- Emphasizing the obligation of being dutiful to parents.
- Believing in Allah necessitates patience in the face of adversity for His sake.
- Whoever initiates a bad precedent will bear its sin and the sin of those who act on it without their sins being diminished.
- It is obligatory to treat parents kindly within the bounds of what is right but not to obey them in matters of wrongdoing, such as polytheism and sins.
- Be wary of leading others into sin, fearing that you will bear the sin of those who participate in it with you.
- Following the example of the prophets in their patience and efforts in inviting to Allah.

Contemplation Insights from Page 398 [Al 'Ankabūt 15-23]

- Idols do not possess the power to provide sustenance and, therefore, do not deserve worship.
- Seeking provision should be directed only towards Allah, who controls sustenance. Allah alone lifts poverty and assigns provision, and no one besides Him possesses this capability; thus, we should directly supplicate to Him.
- The creation of life is evidence of resurrection.
- Entrance to Paradise is forbidden for those who die in disbelief.
- Despairing of Allah's mercy leads to disbelief, punishment, and destruction.

Contemplation Insights from Page 399 [Al 'Ankabūt 24-30]

- Allah's care for His righteous servants includes saving them from their enemies' schemes.
- The virtue of migrating for Allah's sake.
- The esteemed status of Ibrahim and his family with Allah.
- Some rewards being hastened in this world does not mean a decrease in the hereafter's reward.

- The hideousness of engaging in immoral acts in public gatherings.
- When oppressors are unable to prevail with arguments, they resort to force.
- Forgoing something for Allah's sake results in Allah compensating with better in this world and the next, "And We gave him Ishaq and Ya'qūb in addition, and all [of them] We made righteous.

Contemplation Insights from Page 400 [Al 'Ankabūt 31-38]

- Allah's statement, "It has become clear..." indicates the Arabs' familiarity with the dwellings of destroyed peoples and their history.
- Faith and righteous deeds are the reasons for salvation from punishments, and familial or even marital relations without them are useless.
- Emphasizing the importance of ensuring guests' safety and security from aggression.
- The dwellings of those destroyed by punishment serve as a lesson for those who take heed.
- Knowing the truth is not beneficial when desires are followed and preferred over guidance. One of Satan's steps in misleading people is to beautify bad deeds.
- Remembering the Last Day and fearing it is among the greatest aids in abstaining from sins.

Contemplation Insights from Page 401 [Al 'Ankabūt 39-45]

- The importance of using parables: "The example of the spider."
- Various types of punishment in this world.
- Allah is above any form of injustice. From Allah's justice, He does not punish anyone except for their deeds.
- Relying on other than Allah is like grasping at the weakest straws.
- The significance of prayer in correcting the believer's behavior.
- The merit of knowledge leads to benefiting from the examples Allah sets for people.

Contemplation Insights from Page 402 [Al 'Ankabūt 46-52]

- Debating with the People of the Book should be done best.
- Belief in all true messengers and scriptures without differentiation is a condition for the correctness of faith.
- The Noble Qur'ān is the everlasting sign and the permanent proof of the Prophet's (صَلَّىٰ ٱللَّهُ عَلَيْهِ وَسَلَّمَ) truthfulness. Allah's favor upon this nation is His revealing the best book to the best messenger for their guidance.
- A true scholar knows the correct way of worshiping Allah, even if he cannot read or write. The Qur'ān reached the pinnacle of eloquence, even though it was revealed to our Prophet ﷺ, who was illiterate.

Contemplation Insights from Page 403 [Al 'Ankabūt 53-63]

- The disbelievers' haste for punishment is a sign of their folly.
- No one has an excuse for abandoning the monotheistic worship of Allah; if prevented in one land, it is obligatory to migrate to another. The door to migration for the sake of religious safety is always open.
- The virtue of patience and reliance on Allah. Do not worry about provision; Allah, who provides for the creatures without them carrying their sustenance, will suffice you.
- Acknowledging exclusive lordship without acknowledging Allah's divinity does not achieve salvation and faith for its adherent.

Contemplation Insights from Page 404 [Al 'Ankabūt 64-69]

- The polytheists' resorting to Allah in hardship and forgetting their idols, yet associating others with Him with ease, is evidence of their confusion.
- The blessing of security in homelands is great, and preserving it is achieved through righteous deeds and the establishment of Allah's prescribed public rituals.
- Allah's glad tidings are for those who strive against the polytheists and strive against themselves for guidance in His way. Striving in the way of Allah leads to guidance to the truth.
- Allah's glad tidings for those who strive against the polytheists and strive against themselves for guidance to His way, "And those who strive for Us - We will surely guide them to Our ways. And indeed, Allah is with the doers of good."

SŪRAH AL-RŪM INSIGHTS

Contemplation Insights from Page 404 [Al-Rūm 1-5]

- The Qur'ān's foretelling of the unseen is proof that it is from Allah.
- Affirming the correctness of Islam and that it is the true religion through the accuracy of its scripture's revelations of the unseen.
- Indicating that the People of the Book, Jews and Christians, are closer to Muslims than polytheists and atheists, such as Communists, who do not believe in Allah and the Last Day.

Contemplation Insights from Page 405 [Al-Rūm 6-15]

- Knowledge is beneficial for this world, but neglecting what benefits the hereafter is of no use.
- The signs of Allah within ourselves and on the horizon are sufficient to prove His Oneness.
- Injustice is a reason for the destruction of past nations.

- On the Day of Judgment, Allah will elevate the believers and humiliate the disbelievers.

Contemplation Insights from Page 406 [Al-Rūm 16-24]

- Servants' time in prayer and glorification signifies a good end.
- The argument for resurrection is through the renewal of life, where Allah creates the living from the dead and the dead from the living.
- The signs of Allah within ourselves and the horizons only benefit those who utilize their sensory and conceptual faculties bestowed by Allah.

Contemplation Insights from Page 407 [Al-Rūm 25-32]

- All of creation submits to Allah, both forcibly and willingly.
- The evidence of the first creation indicates the resurrection.
- Following desires misleads and leads to tyranny.
- The religion of Islam is a religion of sound nature.

Contemplation Insights from Page 408 [Al-Rūm 33-41]

- Excessive joy in times of blessing and despair in times of hardship are characteristics of disbelievers.
- Giving rights to those entitled to them is a reason for success.
- The eradication of interest and the multiplication of rewards for spending in the way of Allah.
- The impact of sins in the spread of epidemics and environmental destruction is observable.

Contemplation Insights from Page 409 [Al-Rūm 42-50]

- Sending winds, bringing down rain, and ships sailing in the sea: blessings that necessitate thanking Allah.
- The destruction of the wicked and the victory of the believers is a divine tradition.
- The growth of the earth after its dryness is evidence of resurrection.

Contemplation Insights from Page 410 [Al-Rūm 51-60]

- The despair of disbelievers from Allah's mercy when calamity descends.
- Guidance and success are in Allah's hands, not the prophet's (ﷺ).
- Life stages are a lesson for those who reflect.
- Sealing hearts is a consequence of sins.

SŪRAH LUQMAN INSIGHTS

Contemplation Insights from Page 411 [Luqman 1-11]

- Among the fruits of following the Qur'ān that a servant attains are guidance, mercy, and achieving the station of excellence (*iḥsān*). Obedience to Allah leads to success in both this life and the hereafter.
- Prohibiting everything that deviates from the straight path, whether speech or action. Whoever listens to music turns his heart away from loving the Qur'ān.
- Humility aids in following the truth, unlike pride. Pride prevents following the truth.
- Allah's sole authority in creation, challenging disbelievers to show creation by their gods.

Contemplation Insights from Page 412 [Luqman 12-19]

- When Allah (سُبْحَانَهُ وَتَعَالَىٰ) detailed what the mother endures from the effort of pregnancy and childbirth, it indicated the need for more kindness towards her.
- There is no obedience to creation in disobedience to the Creator, which does not contradict showing kindness to parents in matters other than disobedience.
- Follow the path of those who turn to Allah, from the knowledgable who truly know Him.
- Beware of the sins committed in solitude.
- The benefit of obedience and the harm of disobedience return to the servant.
- It's obligatory to take care of children with upbringing and education.
- Islam's manners cover both individual and communal behavior.

Contemplation Insights from Page 413 [Luqman 20-28]

- Allah's blessings are a means to thank and believe in Him, not a means to disbelief.
- Blind imitation and suspending the intellect are harmful, especially in matters of belief.
- The importance of surrendering to Allah, following His commands faithfully, and doing good deeds for His sake. Holding onto religion is the lifeline and safety valve.
- The servant is tasked with conveying Allah's message, but the outcomes are entrusted to Allah.
- The endlessness of Allah's words.

Contemplation Insights from Page 414 [Luqman 29-34]

- The shortening and lengthening of days and nights and the subjugation of the sun and moon are signs of Allah's power, deserving gratitude.
- Patience and gratitude are ways to reflect on Allah's signs.

- Some of today's polytheists are more severe than the Quraysh disbelievers; they associate partners with Allah in both ease and hardship, whereas the Quraysh did so in ease but turned to monotheism in hardship.
- Fear of the Day of Judgment prevents delusion by worldly life and succumbing to demonic whispers.
- Allah's knowledge encompasses all unseen matters. Claiming to know the unseen is disbelief, and whoever claims that prophets or saints know the unseen alleges that the creation shares attributes with the Creator.
- Beware of procrastination and be diligent in deeds, "And no soul knows in what land it will die."

SŪRAH AL-SAJDAH INSIGHTS

Contemplation Insights from Page 415 [As-Sajdah 1-11]

- The purpose of sending messengers is to guide their people to the straight path.
- The attribute of Allah's ascension (Istiwā) is affirmed without likening Him to His creation or embodying Him.
- Polytheists' denial of resurrection despite clear evidence.

Contemplation Insights from Page 416 [As-Sajdah 12-20]

- The belief of disbelievers on the Day of Judgment will not benefit them; it is a time for compensation, not for deeds.
- The danger of being heedless of meeting Allah on the Day of Judgment.
- Among the guidance for believers is the performance of night prayers.

Contemplation Insights from Page 417 [As-Sajdah 21-30]

- The punishment of the disbeliever in this world serves as a means for his repentance.
- The affirmed meeting between our Prophet (ﷺ) and Mūsā (عَلَيْهِ السَّلَامُ) on the night of Isra and Mi'raj.
- Patience and certainty are characteristics of those who lead in faith.

CONTEMPLATION STUDY QUESTIONS

Sūrah al 'Ankabūt Questions

Verse 4: What makes it easy for a servant to commit sins and crimes? *[Al-Sa'dī]*

Verse 13: Is the sin of the one who calls to corruption the same as that of the one who responds to it? Explain this through the verse. *[Ibn Kathīr]*

Verse 13: This verse subtly encourages calling to Allah (عَزَّوَجَلَّ); explain this aspect. *[Al-Sa'dī]*

Verse 14: Is guidance solely through reason, or what else? *[Al-Sa'dī]*

Verse 21: What can a Muslim benefit from Allah's (عَزَّوَجَلَّ) announcement that the return is to Him? *[Al-Sa'dī]*

Verse 24: What does the tyrants' recourse to using force indicate? *[Al-Sa'dī]*

Verse 26: One of the characteristics of Allah's allies is that they are the most merciful of creation towards creation; explain this through the story of Ibrāhīm. *[Al-Sa'dī]*

Verse 43: Why is understanding parables specified for the knowledgeable? *[Al-Sa'dī]*

Verse 46: Arguing with the disbeliever is based on justice and wisdom; explain this through the verse. *[Al-Sa'dī]*

Verse 47: Does anyone who intends well disbelieve in this Qur'ān? *[Al-Sa'dī]*

Verse 52: How is Allah's testimony to the truth of Muhammad's prophecy made? *[Ibn Kathīr]*

Verse 55: Why is the punishment described as enveloping them from above and below? Why are they told this in Hell? *[Ibn Kathīr]*

Verse 56: What is meant by telling the believers that Allah's earth is vast? *[Al-Sa'dī]*

Sūrah al-Rūm Questions

Verse 4: What is the significance of including this sentence in the story of Persia and Rome? *[Al-Sa'dī]*

Verse 7: How do we balance between worldly knowledge and knowledge of the Hereafter? *[Al-Sa'dī]*

Verse 18: What can be learned from Allah's creation of things and their opposites? *[Ibn Kathīr]*

Verse 22: The difference in languages and colors indicates Allah's mercy for those who reflect; how so? *[Al-Sa'dī]*

Verse 22: What can one learn from observing the diversity in human creation? *[Ibn Kathīr]*

Verse 27: The Qur'ān uses logical argumentation, explained through the verse. *[Al-Sa'dī]*

Verse 28: Why is the address specifically to the wise? *[Al-Sa'dī]*

Verse 42: Is traveling the earth for contemplation limited to physical travel? What benefits does one gain from contemplating the fate of those before? *[Al-Sa'dī]*

Verse 45: Does lack of love justify oppression? *[Ibn Kathīr]*

Verse 46: How does a Muslim feel when tasting Allah's mercy? *[Al-Sa'dī]*

Verse 56: The verse indicates the ignorance of disbelievers in this world and the Hereafter, explain. *[Al-Sa'dī]*

Verse 60: Why is patience mentioned before stating that Allah's promise is true? This verse indicates different intellects among those who face trials, explain. *[Al-Sa'dī]*

Sūrah Luqmān Questions;

Verse 1-2: What are people's attitudes towards this wise book? *[Al-Sa'dī]*

Verse 3: Why are these two deeds specifically mentioned over others? *[Al-Sa'dī]*

Verse 6: Does entering this verse mean one has spent money on idle talk? The compensation for these individuals was by their deeds, explain. *[Ibn Kathīr]*

Verse 13: What benefits are the commandments for his son? *[Ibn Kathīr]*

Verse 14: Why did Allah mention the hardship of the mother in raising her child? *[Ibn Kathīr]*

Verse 17: Why was patience commanded after ordering enjoining good and forbidding evil? *[Ibn Kathīr]*

Verse 20: How is gratitude for blessings expressed? *[Al-Sa'dī]*

Verse 33: Why does Allah frequently mention the horrors of the Day of Judgment in the Qur'ān? *[Al-Sa'dī]*

Sūrah al-Sajdah Questions

Verse 1-2: Consider Sūrah As-Sajdah and explain the wisdom behind its recommended recitation on Friday's Fajr. *[Ibn Kathīr]* and *[As-Sa'di]*

Verse 2: What is meant by the attribute of Lordship in the phrase "Lord of the Worlds"? *[Al-Sa'dī]*

Verse 24: From where did Ali bin Abi Talib derive the meaning: "Patience in faith is like the head to the body"? *[Ibn Kathīr]*

Verse 28: What is meant by "victory" in this verse? *[Ibn Kathīr]*

Day 21: Ahzāb - Fātir

The Qurā'n reading for **day 21** is from three chapters: *Sūrah al Aḥzāb*, *Sūrah Saba'*, and *Sūrah al Fāṭir*. *Sūrah al Aḥzāb* discusses Allah's care for the Muslim household and society. It teaches that submission to Allah's commandments is the best way to retain Allah's help and favor when calamity befalls. Similarly, *Sūrah Saba'* mentions mankind's changing circumstances and how *Tawḥīd* and gratitude are necessary to retain His favors. The main theme of *Sūrah Fāṭir* is Allah's vast mercy. So, these three chapters address a similar theme in very different ways.

سُورَةُ الأَحْزَابِ

AL AḤZAB (33)

The Confederates

VERSES
73

WORDS
1,280

LETTERS
5,990

REVEALED IN
MADINAH

REVEALATION ORDER
90

Main Themes: Caring for the Prophet (ﷺ) and defending his honor and household; Surrendering to Allah's commands *(Verses 22, 28-29, 36)*.

The confederation of tribes who rallied against the Muslims at the instigation of the *Yahūd* were the tribes of *Quraysh, Kinānah,* and *Ghatfān* in an army of 10,000. They attempted to storm al Madīnah and laid siege to it for 20-30 days.

Objectives of the Chapter:

- To purify the Islamic community from the remnants of ignorance by abolishing inherited customs such as adoption, Zihar (a form of divorce in pre-Islamic Arabia), and their belief that a wise man has two hearts in his chest.
- Discussion about the Battle of the Confederates, revealing the secrets of the hypocrites, how the forces of evil and aggression rallied against the Muslims, and how Allah's mercy manifested in supporting His allies with troops from Him, fulfilling His promise of victory to them.
- Declaration of several family-related laws; some regulations concerning women, including staying at home, dressing modestly, not displaying adornment, not speaking softly, the waiting period before remarriage after divorce, and the veil, among others.

- Urging the believers to remember Allah and sanctify Him in gratitude for His guidance, following the Prophet (صَلَّى ٱللَّهُ عَلَيْهِ وَسَلَّمَ), honoring his status with Allah and in the higher assembly, and commanding prayers and peace upon him.
- Threatening the hypocrites and the spreaders of sedition with the Prophet's (صَلَّى ٱللَّهُ عَلَيْهِ وَسَلَّمَ) and the believers' dominion over them, discussing the Hour and its horrors, and the fate of disbelievers and hypocrites tasting the torment of Hell and its blazing fire.

BRIEF SŪRAH SUMMARY

Verses 1-8	Verses 1-3 and 7-8 contain tremendous exhortations for the Prophet (صَلَّى ٱللَّهُ عَلَيْهِ وَسَلَّمَ). In between are the correction of a number of erroneous habits related to divorce and adoption followed by the declaration that the Prophet (صَلَّى ٱللَّهُ عَلَيْهِ وَسَلَّمَ) is the spiritual father and his wives are our mothers. Fuḍayl said: "If the Prophets will be asked about their truthfulness, then what about us?" *(verse 8)*
Verses 9-27	Describes how the events of the siege of the confederates was foiled and contrasts the different reactions of the believers and the hypocrites.
Verses 28–34, 37-40 & 49-62	A discussion about the wives of the Prophet, a number of special instructions for them and how Zaynab was married to the Prophet (صَلَّى ٱللَّهُ عَلَيْهِ وَسَلَّمَ) after being released by Zayd. This is followed by rulings related to marriage, the legislation of hijab and an explanation of who is considered a maḥram. This is concluded with a command for all women to cover so as to not be a temptation for men, to protect themselves and to prevent immorality from spreading. This is to safeguard the honor of the Muslims and paralyze
Verses 35-36	Detailed description of believing men & women (10 characteristics followed by the exhortation that there is no option for the believers when commanded except to hear and obey). This segues into the marriage of the Prophet (صَلَّى ٱللَّهُ عَلَيْهِ وَسَلَّمَ) to Zaynab.
Verses 41-44	The benefit and reward of Dhikr
Verses 45-48	The status of the Prophet and his responsibility, it also repeats the same instruction in the beginning of the Sūrah: *"Do not obey the disbelievers and hypocrites;"* along with the command to put his reliance on Allah.
Verses 63-73	The day of judgment between leaders and followers; the command to respect the Prophet (صَلَّى ٱللَّهُ عَلَيْهِ وَسَلَّمَ) and not to be disrespectful; the trust offered to the heavens earth and mountains.

The *Sūrah* contains five instances of Allah directly addressing the Prophet (صَلَّى ٱللَّٰهُ عَلَيْهِ وَسَلَّمَ)

1) Verse 1.
2) Verse 28: *"Say to your wives…"*
3) Verse 45: "*We have sent you as a witness…"*
4) Verse 50: "*We have made your wives lawful for you."*
5) Verse 59, the verse of *ḥijab*.

It also contains six instances of Allah (تَبَارَكَ وَتَعَالَىٰ) summoning the believers:

1) Verse 9: *"Remember Allah's favor upon you when an army came…"*.
2) Verse 41: "*Remember Allah much and often…*".
3) Verse 49: Instruction about divorcing before consummation.
4) Verse 53: Etiquettes for attending the *walīmah.*
5) Verse 69: Protecting the honor of the Prophets.
6) Verse 70: *"Say a straight word…"*

Shaykh al Islām ibn Taymiyyah said about al-tawakkul:[17]

وهذا وَإِنْ كَانَ مَأْمُورًا بِهِ فِي جَمِيعِ الدِّينِ؛ فَإِنَّ ذَلِكَ فِي الْجِهَادِ أَوْكَدُ؛ لِأَنَّهُ يَحْتَاجُ إِلَى أَنْ يُجَاهِدَ الْكُفَّارَ وَالْمُنَافِقِينَ؛ وَذَلِكَ لَا يَتِمُّ إِلَّا بِتَأْيِيدِ قَوِيٍّ مِنْ اللَّهِ؛ وَلِهَذَا كَانَ الْجِهَادُ سَنَامَ الْعَمَلِ وَانْتَظَمَ سَنَامُ جَمِيعِ الْأَحْوَالِ الشَّرِيفَةِ. فَفِيهِ سَنَامُ الْمَحَبَّةِ … وَفِيهِ سَنَامُ التَّوَكُّلِ وَسَنَامُ الصَّبْرِ؛ فَإِنَّ الْمُجَاهِدَ أَحْوَجُ النَّاسِ إِلَى الصَّبْرِ وَالتَّوَكُّلِ

"Although this is something commanded to be done in all of the religions, then as relates to jihād that is more emphasized because it requires striving against the Kuffār and Munāfiqīn, which cannot be completed without strong support from Allah. For this reason, jihād is the pinnacle of deeds and gathers the epitome of all honorable states of the heart, such as the pinnacle of love [as proven by Sūrah al Mā'idah, verse 54]…and the pinnacle of al-tawakkul and patience. Surely, the Mujāhid is the greatest in their need for patience and al-tawakkul."

[17] Majmū' al Fatāwā (28/441).

سُورَةُ سَبَإٍ
SABA' (34)
Sheba

VERSES
54

WORDS
883

LETTERS
3,512

REVEALED IN
MAKKAH

REVEALATION ORDER
58

✦ **Main Themes:** How people respond to blessings and Allah's universal law in changing circumstances: reacting to Allah's blessings with gratitude causes them to be retained *(verses 10, 13, 15)*, reacting to Allah's blessings with aversion and ingratitude causes their departure and such a person is a loser in this world and the next *(verses 1-18, 34-35).*

Another common theme is the doubts of the disbelievers about the Day of Judgment *(verses 3, 7, 29, 53-54)*. Similarly, the *Sūrah* emphasizes in multiple places that only Allah knows the unseen *(verses 3, 7, 29, 53-54).*

The *Sūrah* begins by mentioning how the disbelievers denied the final hour *(verse 3)*. It concludes by mentioning how they will attempt to profess belief in the final hour at a time when it will not benefit them *(verse 53).*

It also opens with a mention of the believers' reward *(verse 4) and concludes* with a mention of the punishment of the disbelievers.

Objectives of the Sūrah:

- The surah discusses the polytheists' denial of the Hereafter and their rejection of resurrection, affirming the resurrection by instructing the Prophet (ﷺ) to swear by it and arguing their denial by drawing attention to Allah's power to create what is greater than them, as evident in the creation of the heavens and the earth around them.
- It explains that gratitude preserves blessings, and ingratitude causes them to disappear, as illustrated by the stories of Sulaymān and the people of Saba.
- It establishes the oneness of God's divinity by presenting proofs of His lordship, negating the worship of anything other than Allah by proving its incapacity to perform the functions of lordship.
- It confirms Allah's knowledge, calling for belief in the Last Day with encouragement and warning, inviting the polytheists to believe in Allah, devote worship solely to Him, and

reflect on the status of this messenger among them, known for his integrity and trustworthiness.

Sūrah Saba' addresses the three main themes of the Makkan Suwar: *Tawḥīd*, the revelation and Prophethood, and the Day of Judgment.

Of these three main subjects, it focuses primarily on *Tawḥīd* & Shirk, namely in its opening verses, verse 22, and verses 40-41 regarding those who claimed to be worshipping angels and were worshipping devils.

Its next greatest priority is the day of judgment. *See Verses 3-5, 7-8, and 31-33* (how they will blame each other when entering the hellfire).

Thirdly, it addresses the issue of prophethood and revelation. *(See Verses 29, 31, 33-34.)*

One way that it does so is by mentioning the stories of some of the Prophets. It mentions parts of the stories of Dāwūd and Sulaymān (it mentions how the *Jinn* were subjected to Sulaymān in refutation of those who worship the *Jinn*).

BRIEF SŪRAH SUMMARY

Verses 1-9	Opening verses clarifying correct beliefs
Verses 10-22	Three stories: Dāwūd; Sulaymān; the people of Saba'
Verses 23-27	5 verses that establish one of the strongest arguments in proof of *Tawḥīd* and warn against Shirk.
Verses 28-45	The wealthy and powerful are most often the greatest opponents of Prophets and their message. It mentions the argument that will happen between the powerful and their followers while entering the fire *(verses 31-33)*. The rejection of the angels on Judgment Day for those who rejected the truth while claiming to worship them. The final verse warns that these disbelievers will be deprived of the pleasures they once enjoyed, just as their predecessors were.

سُورَةُ فَاطِر

FĀṬIR (35)
The Originator

VERSES 45

WORDS 670

LETTERS 3,310

REVEALED IN MAKKAH

REVELATION ORDER 43

It is also called *Sūrah al Malā'ikah.* It is estimated to be around the 43rd *Sūrah* revealed (between *Sūrah al Furqān* and *Sūrah Maryam*), between the open proclamation of the Message (i.e., year 4 of the prophethood) and the *Hijrah* to Abyssinia.

✦ **Main Themes:** Allah's Mercy with His servants and their dire need of Him. It begins and ends by mentioning Allah's Mercy *(verses 2 & 45).* ["*None can withhold or extend His Mercy, save He; if He were to seize people for what they've done, he wouldn't leave a creature on the earth…*"]

Objectives of the Sūrah:

- Discussing the signs of Allah's omnipotence and uniqueness to affirm His sole right to divinity, establishing the truth of the resurrection and judgment day, and highlighting the impotence of creatures idolaters worship.
- Mentioning clear signs of Allah's oneness, such as the diversity in fruits, colors, tastes, mountains, people, animals, and their kinds, forms, and colors, all witnessing Allah's existence, magnificence, and majesty.
- Praising those who fear Allah, purify themselves, and have enlightened insights, who respond to the Prophet's (ﷺ) call, detailing their rewards and warning the deniers with prepared punishment.
- Illustrating the significant difference between believers and disbelievers, the righteous and the wicked, by comparing the blind with the seeing, darkness with light, and life with death.

Sūrah Fāṭir is focused on what all the Makkan chapters establish:

(1.) Allah's Oneness (*al-Tawḥīd*); (2.) the Message of the Prophet (ﷺ) (al-Risālah); (3.) the Hereafter (al Ma'ād). The connecting thread of these three core subjects of the *Qur'ān* is Allah's Mercy, which is the focus of the *Sūrah.* Allah's mercy and blessings are mentioned throughout the *Sūrah (see verses 3, 9, 11, 12, 13, 27, 28, 41, 45).*

Allah's special blessing is dignity for the believer, which can only be achieved by obeying Allah *(see verse 10).*

From Allah's mercy, He presents the creational proofs of His Oneness so that they may be guided *(see verses 9, 12, 13, 27, 28).*

Allah sent a Warner to every nation, and His greatest blessing is the sending of the Prophet (صَلَّى ٱللَّهُ عَلَيْهِ وَسَلَّمَ) *(see verse 24).*

In verse 28, Allah informs us that knowledge of the religion should cause a person to fear Allah. He then mentions many qualities of righteous people. Shortly after that, in Verse 32, the three levels of those Allah chooses are mentioned.

This is one of the most hopeful passages in the *Qurā'n* because it begins by mentioning the believers who wrong their selves as being amongst those chosen for guidance. It is followed by a mention of the disbelievers' punishment and the believers' reward *(Verses 33, 37).*

BROADER OVERVIEW

- The purposes of this surah encompass several key themes, starting with the affirmation of Allah's sole divinity. The surah begins by highlighting the creation as evidence of Allah's unmatched worthiness of praise and His exclusive divinity. It firmly establishes the truthfulness of the Messenger Muhammad (صَلَّى ٱللَّهُ عَلَيْهِ وَسَلَّمَ) in what he conveyed, which aligns with the messages brought by previous messengers, emphasizing the reality of the resurrection and the afterlife.
- The surah serves as a reminder of Allah's bounties upon humanity, including the blessings of creation and sustenance. It points out the futility of worshipping anything besides Allah, as those worshipped by previous generations failed to benefit their devotees. It provides support to the Prophet (صَلَّى ٱللَّهُ عَلَيْهِ وَسَلَّمَ) as he faces opposition from his community, revealing their true motives for shunning the path of Islam, primarily their pride and desire to maintain their social status. The surah warns them of facing a fate similar to past nations who denied their prophets and suffered the consequences. It contrasts the attitude of the disbelievers with that of the believers who embraced Islam with conviction, challenging the former's arrogance and refusal to accept guidance.
- The surah admonishes the disbelievers for their reluctance to welcome the prophethood despite their initial longing for divine guidance, highlighting their pride and rejection once guidance arrived. It alerts them to the inevitability of divine retribution, reminding them of the historical precedents set by the destruction of previous deniers and cautioning them against taking Allah's patience for granted, as His promises are unbreakable.
- Lastly, the surah warns against the snares of Satan and underscores his perpetual enmity towards humankind, urging vigilance against his deceitful temptations.

CONTEMPLATE, COMPREHEND, APPLY

Contemplation Insights from Page 418 [Al-Ahzab 1-6]

- No one is too great to be commanded to do good and forbidden from wrong. Allah commanded His Prophet to fear Him so that no one would avoid advising and reminding.
- Disbelievers and hypocrites are not suitable for consultation in religious matters. Whoever relies on Allah, He will make a way out for him from every hardship.
- This nation is excused for mistakes.
- The Prophet's (صَلَّى ٱللَّهُ عَلَيْهِ وَسَلَّمَ) wishes must take precedence over personal desires.
- The elevated status of the Prophet's (صَلَّى ٱللَّهُ عَلَيْهِ وَسَلَّمَ) wives and their sacredness from marriage after him, as they are considered mothers of the believers.

Contemplation Insights from Page 419 [Al-Ahzab 7-15]

- The station of the messengers with the strongest resolve.
- Allah's support for His faithful servants during hardships.
- The betrayal of hypocrites to believers in times of trial.
- Allah tests His servants to distinguish the truthful from the liars. The Battle of the Trench was among the most difficult and tiresome for Muslims, "There the believers were tested and shaken with a severe shaking."
- The hypocrite is not loyal to the covenant or the Creator, but how with the creation?

Contemplation Insights from Page 420 [Al-Ahzab 16-22]

- Lifespans are predetermined; fleeing from trials and hardships does not extend one's life or delay one's appointed time; rather, it might cause one's sudden demise.
- Characteristics of hypocrites include discouragement and disabling of good deeds, beware of being a barrier to good, and a key to evil.
- The Prophet (صَلَّى ٱللَّهُ عَلَيْهِ وَسَلَّمَ) is the model for believers in his words and actions. Hope in Allah and the Hereafter and constant remembrance of Allah greatly aid in following the Prophet - (صَلَّى ٱللَّهُ عَلَيْهِ وَسَلَّمَ).
- Trusting in Allah and submitting to Him are attributes of the believers.

Contemplation Insights from Page 421 [Al-Ahzab 23-30]

- Allah's commendation for the companions of the Prophet (ﷺ) is a great honor for them. Anyone who reviles them has indeed denied the Qur'ān.
- Allah's power is limitless; He is omnipotent over everything, and nothing is beyond His capability. Allah's help and victory for His servants come unexpectedly if they fear Him.
- The dire consequences of betrayal by the Jews who aided the Confederates.
- The choice of the Prophet's wives (ﷺ) for Allah and His Messenger is proof of their strong faith.

Contemplation Insights from Page 422 [Al-Ahzab 31-35]

- The Qur'ān's guidance for Muslim women includes forbidding soft speech, ordering them to stay at home except when necessary, and forbidding tabarruj (display of beauty).
- The honor of the Prophet's family (ﷺ) and his wives as part of his household.
- The principle of equality between men and women in deeds and recompense, except for what the Shari'ah has exempted for each.

Contemplation Insights from Page 423 [Al-Ahzab 36-43]

- It is obligatory for a believer to surrender to Allah's decree and follow it.
- Allah is aware of what is in the souls.
- Among the virtues of Umm al-Mu'minin Zaynab, bint Jahsh is that Allah married her off above the seven heavens.
- The virtue of remembering Allah, especially in the morning and evening.

Contemplation Insights from Page 424 [Al-Ahzab 44-50]

- Patience in adversity is a trait of a successful caller to Allah.
- It is recommended that a husband give some money to his divorced wife before consummation as a kind gesture.
- The Prophet (ﷺ) has a unique allowance to marry those who offer themselves to him without a dowry.

Contemplation Insights from Page 425 [Al-Ahzab 51-54]

- The high esteem of the Prophet (ﷺ) with his Lord, to the extent that He admonished the companions for staying in his house, which caused him discomfort.
- Affirmation of the attributes of knowledge and forbearance for Allah.
- Modesty is among the morals of the Prophet (ﷺ).
- Protecting the status of the Mothers of the Believers, the wives of the Prophet (ﷺ).

Contemplation Insights from Page 426 [Al-Ahzab 55-62]

- The high status of the Prophet (صَلَّى ٱللَّهُ عَلَيْهِ وَسَلَّمَ) with Allah and His angels.
- The prohibition of harming believers without cause.
- Hypocrisy leads to punishment for those who engage in it.

Contemplation Insights from Page 427 [Al-Ahzab 63-73]

- Allah alone knows the Hour.
- Followers blaming their leaders for misleading them does not absolve them of responsibility.
- Strict prohibition against harming prophets in any way.
- The great trust that humanity has undertaken.

SŪRAH SABA INSIGHTS

Contemplation Insights from Page 428 Sūrah 34 [Saba 1-7]

- The vastness of Allah's knowledge encompasses everything.
- The virtue of people of knowledge.
- The denial of resurrection by polytheists is a rejection of Allah's power who created them.

Contemplation Insights from Page 429 [Saba 8-14]

- Allah honored His prophet Dawud with prophethood and kingship, the subjugation of mountains and birds to glorify and praise Allah with him, and the softening of iron for him.
- Allah's honor to His prophet Sulaymān with prophethood and kingdom.
- The requirement to thank Allah for His blessings.
- Allah's exclusivity in the knowledge of the unseen negates the claims of jinn or others having access to it.

Contemplation Insights from Page 430 [Saba 15-22]

- Gratitude preserves blessings, while ingratitude causes their removal.
- Security is among the greatest blessings Allah bestows on His servants.
- True faith protects from following Satan's temptations by Allah's permission.
- The exposure of the bases of polytheism and its entryways, like claiming that idols have sovereignty, share in God's dominion or can intercede or assist with Allah.

Contemplation Insights from Page 431 [Saba 23-31]

- Be gentle with those called to the truth to avoid them resorting to stubbornness and obstinacy.
- The bearer of guidance is elevated by it, while the follower of misguidance is immersed and belittled by it.
- The Prophet's (ﷺ) message encompasses all humanity and the jinn.

Contemplation Insights from Page 432 [Saba 32-39]

- The disavowal between followers and those followed does not exempt any of them from their responsibility.
- Luxurious living distances one from submitting to the truth and adhering to it.
- A believer benefits from their wealth and children, while a disbeliever does not benefit from them.
- Spending on Allah's cause replenishes wealth in this world, leading to a good reward in the hereafter.

Contemplation Insights from Page 433 [Saba 40-48]

- Blindly following ancestors diverts from guidance.
- Reflection, free from desires, is a means to reach correct conclusions and sound judgment.
- A caller to Allah does not expect reward from people but from the Lord of people.

Contemplation Insights from Page 434 [Saba 49-54]

- The spectacle of the disbelievers' terror on the Day of Judgment is immense.
- The place for benefiting from faith is in this world, for it is the abode of action.
- The creation of angels indicates the greatness of their Creator (سُبْحَانَهُ وَتَعَالَىٰ).

SŪRAH FĀTIR INSIGHTS

Contemplation Insights from Page 434 [Fatir 1-3]

- The magnificent creation of angels signifies the greatness of their Creator.
- Contemplate the grand creation of Allah for the angels, who are utterly humble and submissive to Allah.
- It is obligatory to praise and thank Allah for His blessings. He confirms Muhammad's message and prophethood by stating that He made angels messengers.

Contemplation Insights from Page 435 [Fatir 4-11]

- Consoling the Prophet (ﷺ) with stories of messengers and their people.
- Being deluded by worldly life leads to ignoring the truth.
- Taking Satan as an enemy by adopting means to protect against him through remembrance of Allah, recitation of the Qur'ān, doing obedience, and avoiding sins.
- Establishing the attribute of Highness for Allah.

Contemplation Insights from Page 436 [Fatir 12-18]

- Commanding the sea, alternating night and day, and subjugating the sun and the moon are among Allah's blessings on people, which people become accustomed to and hence overlook.
- The foolishness of idolaters when they invoke inanimate objects that neither hear nor understand.
- Being needy towards Allah is an inherent trait of humans, while richness is an attribute of perfection for Allah.
- Self-purification is the individual's responsibility; it is up to them to protect or ruin it.

Contemplation Insights from Page 437 [Fatir 19-30]

- Denying equality between the truth and its people and falsehood and its followers.
- The large number of messengers before our Prophet is evidence of Allah's mercy and the stubbornness of creation.
- Destroying the deniers is a divine tradition.
- Attributes of faith are a profitable trade, while those of disbelief are a losing transaction.

Contemplation Insights from Page 438 [Fatir 31-38]

- The superiority of Muhammad's nation over all others.
- Differences in believers' faith mean differences in their status in both this world and the hereafter.
- Time is a trust that must be preserved; wasting it leads to regret when it's too late.
- Allah's knowledge encompasses everything.

Contemplation Insights from Page 439 [Fatir 39-44]

- Disbelief is a reason for Allah's disdain, a path to loss and misery.
- Idolaters have no logical or scriptural evidence for their idolatry.
- Allah's planning against the oppressors leads to their destruction, sooner or later.

Contemplation Insights from Page 440 [Fatir 45]

- It's stated that nothing is beyond Allah's power, knowledge, and patience, invoking fear of Him and urging repentance.
- It is forbidden to hasten punishment, as everything has a determined term that will not be expedited.
- Be certain that one's end will not be delayed by a moment.

CONTEMPLATION STUDY QUESTIONS

Surah al Ahzab Questions

Verse 1: Does anyone not need the command to fear Allah and the prohibition against obeying disbelievers and hypocrites?

Verse 7: Is the question about the solemn covenant specific to prophets and messengers? *[Al-Sa'dī]*

Verse 16: Is there evidence in the verse that negates the concept of causality? *[Al-Sa'dī]*

Verse 18: List the types of stinginess mentioned in this verse. *[Al-Sa'dī]*

Verse 22: Does faith increase and decrease? Explain this through the verse. *[Ibn Kathīr]*

Verse 32: Why is the sick heart specifically mentioned? Why is the verse concluded with "and speak a recognized word"? *[Al-Sa'dī]*

Verse 33: The Shia view on the Ahl al-Bayt? *[Ibn Kathīr]*

Verse 35: Why is guarding the private parts mentioned after fasting? *[Ibn Kathīr]*

Verse 37: What should someone who intends to leave his wife be advised? The Prophet (ﷺ) reached the pinnacle of honesty in conveying what was revealed to him; how do you illustrate that from this verse? The verse hints at education through practical application and explains it. *[Al-Sa'dī]*

Verse 45-46: Why were these five characteristics mentioned in describing our Prophet over others? There might be slips in the sincerity of the callers. Explain that through the verse. *[Al-Sa'dī]*

Verse 48: Why did Allah forbid harming disbelievers and hypocrites? *[Al-Sa'dī]*

Verse 50: What is the wisdom behind legislating enjoyment here? *[Al-Sa'dī]*

Verse 52: The verse encourages prioritizing the Hereafter over the worldly life; how so? *[Al-Sa'dī]*

Verse 53: Is demanding people for their rights, legitimized by Sharia, considered against manners and public taste? Sharia's wisdom does not only prohibit the haram but also its means and paths leading to it; briefly explain this through the verse. *[Al-Sa'dī]*

Verse 56: Why did Allah command prayer and peace upon the Prophet after announcing that He and His angels send blessings on him? *[Ibn Kathīr]*

Sūrah Saba Questions

Verse 1: Why is His praise specified in the Hereafter? *[al-Sa'dī]*

Verse 3: Why is Allah described as the Knower of the unseen after mentioning the resurrection? *[Ibn Kathīr]*

Verse 9: Why is benefiting from the signs exclusive to those who turn repentantly to Allah? [al-Sa'dī]

Verse 13: What are the ways of thanking Allah for His blessings? *[Ibn Kathīr]*

Verse 16: Discuss the principle of "the reward is commensurate with the deed" through this verse. *[al-Sa'dī]*

Verse 24: What do you think of those who downplay the differences between sects and religions, seeing everyone as correct? *[Ibn Kathīr]*

Verse 32: Why are the oppressed described as criminals? *[Ibn Kathīr]*

Verse 33: Why do disbelievers not openly express remorse on the Day of Judgment? *[al-Sa'dī]*

Verse 35: Why did disbelievers associate wealth and children with the absence of punishment? *[Ibn Kathīr]*

Verse 40: What is the wisdom behind the angels asking on the Day of Judgment about the polytheists' worship of them? *[Ibn Kathīr]*

Verse 53: Why is the disbelievers' rejection of the truth described as coming from a distant place? *[al-Sa'dī]*

Sūrah Fāṭir Questions

Verse 3: What is the relationship between creation and provision with the unification of worship? *[Ibn Kathīr]*

Verse 5: If you know that the promise of Allah is true, what should you do? *[Al-Sa'dī]*

Verse 10: What benefits does a Muslim gain from knowing that all might belong to Allah? *[Al-Sa'dī]*

Verse 13: What benefit does a person gain from knowing that whatever is invoked besides Allah owns nothing? *[Al-Sa'dī]*

Verse 15: Is people's need for Allah only regarding wealth? Explain some of the aspects of neediness where people need their Lord. *[Al-Sa'dī]*

Verse 27-28: What divine attribute is inferred from the diversity, formation, and colors of creation? *[Al-Sa'dī]*

Verse 29: What is learned from the phrase "seeking a trade that will never perish"? *[Al-Sa'dī]*

Verse 32: Why is the one who races towards good deeds specifically mentioned with "by the permission of Allah"? *[Al-Sa'dī]*

Verse 35: Does a person enter Paradise merely by their deeds? Explain this through the verse. *[Ibn Kathīr]*

Verse 39: The verse mentions what disbelief does to disbelievers; what does faith do for believers? *[Ibn Kathīr]*

Verse 42: Was their oath seeking the truth? *[Al-Sa'dī]*

Day 22: Yāsīn - Ṣād

The Qurā'n reading for **day 22** is *Sūrah YāSīn*, *Sūrah al-Ṣāffāt*, and *Sūrah Ṣād*. All three are Makkan Suwar and focus on planting faith in the heart.

سُورَةُ يسٓ
YĀSĪN (36)
Ya Sin

VERSES
83

WORDS
729

LETTERS
3,020

REVEALED IN
MAKKAH

REVEALATION ORDER
41

Main Theme: Establishing belief about Tawḥīd, the Prophets, and the day of Judgment while establishing the proof against the deniers.

The Sūrah begins and ends with Allah mentioning giving life to what is lifeless. *(12, 79).* Special attention is given to establishing evidence for Judgment in the Hereafter.

The objectives of the Sūrah:

- The divine oath affirms the truthfulness of Muhammad's message, discusses the disbelievers of Mecca who denied the Prophet (صَلَّىٰ ٱللَّهُ عَلَيْهِ وَسَلَّمَ), and clarifies the reward for those who follow the Prophet (صَلَّىٰ ٱللَّهُ عَلَيْهِ وَسَلَّمَ) and benefit from the warning.
- The Qur'ān mentions signs of Allah's power through various spectacles in the universe to prove Allah's oneness and affirm the reality of resurrection and judgment.
- Discussing the Day of Judgment and its horrors, such as the blast of terror and the blast of death, talking about the people of Paradise and the people of Hell, and reminding of what Allah entrusted to their innate nature; avoiding the path of evil and following the caller to goodness.
- Affirming the truthfulness of the Messenger and the Book he brought and consoling him not to be saddened by the disbelievers' sayings, for Allah is aware of their secrets and declarations, including a threat to the opposers.

Broader Overview of the Sūrah:

The surah challenges mankind through the Qur'ān's miracle, marked by the disjointed letters, and further emphasizes this with a divine oath. It highlights the wisdom of the Qur'ān, indicating its highest degree of accuracy and precision. The primary aim is to affirm Muhammad's ﷺ message and elevate the religion he brought forth, which is detailed in the Book revealed by Allah. This aims to guide the community towards righteousness in their worldly lives and ensure their success in eternal life after that. Hence, the religion is depicted as the straight path, reminiscent of its portrayal in Sūrah Al-Fatiha. It points out the role of the Qur'ān in offering salvation to the existent Arabs who had not previously encountered a messenger. Their unfamiliarity with previous messengers readied their hearts for accepting the religion, free from any prior commitments that might make parting difficult or from feeling sufficed by any existing guidance.

Moreover, the surah depicts the reluctance of most to embrace Islam, demonstrating their dire state and their refusal to benefit from guidance. Those who chose Islam are depicted as people of awe, adhering to the religion described as the straight path. An analogy is drawn between those who follow and the townspeople who turned away, linking their situation to those who denied the messengers, similar to Quraysh's rejection. The discussion extends to the consequences faced by both groups - the rejectors faced punishment in this life, whereas the followers were elevated in ranks in the hereafter. Additionally, the surah expands to include communities across generations that rejected the messengers and were consequently destroyed. It expresses sorrow over how individuals squander their chances at success by hastily denying the messengers.

It concludes by arguing for the imminent and undeniable reality of the resurrection, incorporating direct and incidental arguments, and integrating a sense of gratitude within its verses for the blessings described. Interspersed throughout the Sūrah are the simple logical evidence of belief in Allah and the Last Day and the highlighting of the importance of gratitude. Allah consoles His Messenger (صَلَّى ٱللَّهُ عَلَيْهِ وَسَلَّمَ), advising him not to be disheartened by their rejection, for Allah serves as the ultimate exemplar. He created them, and despite their doubts, they are destined to return to Him.

Therefore, the surah stands as a firm establishment of the religion's core principles, ranging from the message's affirmation and the Qur'ān's miraculous nature to the prophets' attributes, divine decree, Allah's knowledge, resurrection, monotheism, and gratitude towards the Benefactor. These principles lay the groundwork for obedience through belief and action, from which the entire Sharia branches out, affirming rewards for good and evil with diverse evidence from both the universe and the self.

BRIEF SŪRAH SUMMARY

Verses 1-12	Introductory verses about the Qur'ān and the responses of the different types of people who listen to it.
Verses 13-32	The story of the city with three Messengers and the warning of the man who came from the other side of town.
Verses 33-49	Indicators and evidences of Allah's greatness and power.
Verses 50-83	A discussion about reward and punishment in the hereafter on Judgment Day.

سُورَةُ الصَّافَّاتِ

AL-ṢĀFFĀT (37)

Those Arranged in Ranks

VERSES
182

WORDS
860

LETTERS
3,816

REVEALED IN
MAKKAH

REVEALATION ORDER
56

It is said to have been revealed after al *An'ām* and before Luqmān during the fourth or fifth year after the Prophethood. It is the only *Sūrah* to mention the near sacrifice of Ismā'īl. It begins and ends with the mention of the angels *(1-3; 165-166)*

✦ **Main theme:** The honoring of Allah's allies & humiliation of His enemies; exalting Allah above what polytheists attributed to Him; and debunking their claims regarding angels and jinn.

Objectives of the Sūrah:

- Affirming the oneness of Allah, he presented numerous pieces of evidence of His sole act of creating magnificent creations, such as the celestial and earthly realms and everything within them.
- Discussing some of the polytheists' stances, such as their denial of the resurrection, accusing the Prophet (ﷺ) of sorcery, and responding to his call with mockery and ridicule.
- Establishing the reality of the resurrection and the ensuing recompense, the text describes the state of polytheists on that day, the painful punishment prepared for them, and the bliss of believers and what has been prepared for them from the finest food, drink, and spouses.
- It presents the stories of messengers with their people, how Allah supported His messengers, elevated their status, blessed them, and described the fate of nations that denied them.
- Clarifying the corruption of polytheists' beliefs in divinity, their association of partners with Allah, their claim that angels are daughters of Allah, and elucidating the status and reality of angels.

BRIEF SŪRAH SUMMARY

Verses 1-70	Discussion about the shayateen and angels, those who deny the judgment and divine recompense followed by the description of the blisses of paradise and the punishment of the hellfire. Verses 12, 17, 35, 36, 69, 70 mention many reasons that the *Kuffar* are destroyed, such as: mocking Allah's signs; aversion to sincere advice; false claims against the message; rejection of the hereafter; sheer arrogance; insulting the Prophet ﷺ; blind loyalty to one's ancestors.
Verses 71-148	Examples of how Allah aided the Messengers & their followers; the stories of eight prophets, beginning with the reminder that there have always been the likes of the current disbelievers amongst the previous nations. Punishments were sent as signs to prove the final outcome of each group. Allah has mentioned the people of sincerity, goodness and belief many times throughout this section, particularly: (1.) the people of sincerity are mentioned five times (v. 40, 74, 128, 160, 169); (2.) the people of *iḥsān* are mentioned five times (v. 80, 105, 110, 121, 131); the people of *īmān* are mentioned four times (v. 81, 111, 122, 132). The test of Ibrāhīm is especially relevant to the theme of the *Sūrah* in as much as that his love for his son was examined against his love of Allah, upon which his love for Allah was found to be greater.
Verses 149-182	Brings the original mention of the devils and angels to the forefront; how Allah has aided His Messengers & believing servants; this triumph comes after some time, after a period of purification; conclusion with salam on the messengers and praise of Allah.

سُورَةُ صٓ
ṢĀD (38)
The Letter Sad

VERSES
88

WORDS
732

LETTERS
3,067

REVEALED IN
MAKKAH

REVEALATION ORDER
38

It is said to be the 38th in its sequence of revelation, having been revealed after *al-Qamar* and before al *'Araf*. It is estimated to have been revealed toward the end of Abu Ṭalib's life, roughly three years before the *hijrah*.

Some also call it Sūrah Dawūd because it mentions unique aspects of Dawūd's story that are unmentioned elsewhere.

✦ **Main Theme:** Constantly returning to the truth. The story is named "Sad" because it begins with this isolated letter as a form of challenge and a sign of its miraculous nature.

Objectives of the Sūrah:

- Highlighting the significance of the Qur'ān, reproaching the polytheists for their denial and obstinance towards the Prophet (ﷺ), their astonishment at the revelation being sent down to him, and refuting their claims regarding the Prophet's humanity and the denial of the oneness of divinity. This includes drawing parallels for those arrogant among the Quraysh polytheists with previous defiant nations.
- Mentioning the stories of some prophets as a consolation for the Prophet (ﷺ) for what he faced from his people, to follow the examples of the prophets before him, and to show Allah's mercy towards His messengers with the care, favor, and blessings He bestowed upon them. All of this is in response to the disbelievers' wonder at Muhammad (ﷺ) being chosen as a messenger among them.
- Discussing some of the horrors of the Day of Judgment, the compensation of the righteous believers, and their counterparts among the tyrannical wrongdoers.
- The story of Adam and Iblis's refusal to prostrate to him indicates that the polytheists' arrogance and refusal to accept the revelation to the Prophet over themselves were influenced by Iblis and that their actions reflected the characteristics he adorned for them.

As Makkan *Suwar* overwhelming does, the *Sūrah* clarifies that the three foundations of unbelief are:

(1.) Polytheism. See verse 5: *"Has he made the deities into one single deity? This is something truly shocking."*

(2.) Belying the Messengers and their revelation, as is addressed in verse 4: "*They were amazed that a warner should come to them from themselves. The disbelievers said this man is a sorcerer and a liar.*"

(3.) The denial of the Hereafter, as is addressed at the end of the passage, beginning with verse 49 and concluding with verse 56.

BRIEF SŪRAH SUMMARY

Verses 1-7	The first seven verses of the *Sūrah* deal with the topic of *Tawḥīd* and renouncing all forms of polytheism.
Verses 8-48	From verse 8 to verse 48, the *Sūrah* discusses the belief in divine revelation and the importance of Prophethood, specifically that of Muḥammad ﷺ. Within this section, there are intermittent narratives about past nations who rejected Allah's Messengers and the punishments that were inflicted upon them. These nations include the people of Nuḥ, 'Aad, Pharaoh, Thamūd, Lūṭ, and the dwellers of al Aykah. Additionally, the *Sūrah* mentions that those who reject Prophet ﷺ are expecting a catastrophic wind to destroy them, just as the previous nations were destroyed. The *Sūrah* then addresses something important of the stories of three Prophets, namely, Dawūd, Sulaymān and Ayyub. It then briefly mentions the names of six others, Ibrāhīm, Isḥaq, Ya'qūb, 'Ismā'īl, Yasa', Dhul Kifl—each of whom were from the righteous elect.
Verses 49-63	The issue of belief in the Hereafter is addressed. This passage concludes with the debate between the people of the hellfire.
Verses 64-88	The *Sūrah* then mentions the inception of Shayṭan's misguidance of humankind, narrating the story of Ādam and Iblīs. While addressing the three main themes, the Sūrah also provides logical evidence for the Oneness of Allah, in order to strengthen the connection between His servants and Him. *(See verses 10, 27, and 65)*

CONTEMPLATE, COMPREHEND, APPLY: SŪRAH YASIN (36)

Contemplation Insights from Page 440 [Yasin 1-12]

- Acting according to the Qur'ān and fearing Allah are reasons for entering Paradise.
- The virtue of a righteous child and ongoing charity benefits the believing servant.
- For those doomed to punishment, warning does not benefit them, "Indeed, the word has become true upon most of them, so they do not believe."
- If you fear an oppressor's injustice, say, "And We have placed before them a barrier, and behind them a barrier, and covered them, so they do not see."

Contemplation Insights from Page 441 [Yasin 13-27]

- The importance of stories in calling to Allah.
- Superstition and pessimism are acts of disbelief.
- Advising the people of truth is a duty.
- Loving goodness for people is a trait of believers.

Contemplation Insights from Page 442 [Yasin 28-40]

- How insignificant creation is to Allah when they disobey Him, and how honored they are if they obey Him.
- Among the evidence of resurrection is bringing dead land to life with green plants and producing grain from it.
- Evidence of monotheism: Creating creatures in the heavens and the earth and their regulation by decree.

Contemplation Insights from Page 443 [Yasin 41-54]

- Among Allah's methods of educating His servants is placing signs that they use to deduce benefits for their religion and worldly life.
- Allah empowered His servants, giving them the strength to perform commands and avoid prohibitions. Their failure to do what they are commanded is their choice.
- On the Day of Judgment, believers will experience mercy from their Lord beyond their imagination.

Contemplation Insights from Page 444 [Yasin 55-70]

- The people of Paradise are delighted with all that souls desire, eyes find pleasing, and aspirations reach.
- The one with a heart is purified by the Qur'ān, gaining knowledge and action.
- The human body parts will testify against him on the Day of Judgment.

Contemplation Insights from Page 445 [Yasin 71-83]

- Among Allah's favors and blessings to people is making animals subservient to them, utilizing them for various benefits.
- Abundant rational evidence for the Day of Judgment and the disbelievers' disregard for it.
- Allah's attributes include His encompassing knowledge of all His creations in all their states at all times, knowing what the earth diminishes of the dead bodies and what remains, and knowing the unseen and the witnessed.

SŪRAH AL-ṢĀFFĀT 37

Contemplation Insights from Page 446 [Al-Ṣāffāt 1-24]

- Adorning the nearest heaven with stars for benefits, including beautification and protection against rebellious devils.
- Affirming the existence of the Sirat, a bridge stretched over Hell through which the people of Paradise will cross, and the feet of the people of Hell will slip.

Contemplation Insights from Page 447 [Al-Ṣāffāt 25-51]

- The disbelievers' punishment is due to their reprehensible deeds, such as polytheism and sins.
- Part of the bliss for the people of Paradise is enjoying gatherings and meetings, which contributes to complete joy.

Contemplation Insights from Page 448 [Al-Ṣāffāt 52-76]

- Attaining the bliss of Paradise is the greatest victory, and for such a reward, workers should strive.
- The food of the people of Hell is Zaqqum, which has a bitter, unpleasant taste and smell, is difficult to swallow and is painful to eat.

Contemplation Insights from Page 449 [Al-Ṣāffāt 77-102]

- Manifestations of favor upon Noah include saving him and those who followed him, making his progeny the basis for human races and ethnicities, and preserving a positive remembrance and praise.
- Allah created human actions that the servant performs out of choice.
- According to these verses and their sequence, the sacrifice is Ismail; he was the first to be given glad tidings, while Ishaq was informed of after Ismail.
- Ismail's saying, "You will find me, if Allah wills, of the patient," was the reason Allah gave him patience, for he left the matter to Allah.

Contemplation Insights from Page 450 [Al-Ṣāffāt 103-126]

- "When they both submitted" proves that Ibrahim and Ismail were in complete submission to Allah's command.
- One of the purposes of the legislation is to free people from the servitude of other humans.
- Good praise and positive mention are part of the immediate bliss in this world.

Contemplation Insights from Page 451 [Al-Ṣāffāt 127-153]

- Allah's unchanging tradition: saving the believers and destroying the disbelievers.
- It is necessary to take lessons from the fate of those who denied the messengers to prevent similar outcomes.
- The legitimacy of drawing lots is evidenced by the following: "So they cast lots, and he was among the losers."

Contemplation Insights from Page 452 [Al-Ṣāffāt 154-182]

- Allah's tradition is to support His messengers and their successors with argument and dominance, offering great glad tidings to those characterized as Allah's soldiers, assuring their ultimate victory and support.
- These verses demonstrate the impotence of polytheists and their deities in misleading anyone and glad tidings to Allah's sincere servants that by His power, He will save them from the misguidance of the misguided.

SŪRAH SAD (38)

Contemplation Insights from Page 453 [Sad 1-16]

- Allah swears by the magnificent Qur'ān, emphasizing the necessity of accepting it with faith and delving into its meanings.

- Materialistic perspectives predominated the polytheists' minds and desired revelation to descend upon the leaders and nobles.
- The disbelievers' aversion to faith stems from arrogance, tyranny, and haughtiness in accepting the truth.

Contemplation Insights from Page 454 [Sad 17-26]

- The virtues of Prophet Dawud and the special signs Allah bestowed upon him.
- Prophets are infallible in what they convey from Allah; the purpose of the message cannot be achieved otherwise. However, they might act upon natural inclinations, forgetting or overlooking a ruling, but Allah promptly corrects and guides them with His grace.
- Observing etiquette when entering upon people of virtue and status is appropriate.

Contemplation Insights from Page 455 [Sad 27-42]

- Encouragement to ponder upon the Qur'ān.
- The verses indicate that the remembrance and benefit from the Qur'ān depend on the heart's purity and the individual's keenness.
- The verses support the well-known rule: "Whoever abandons something for the sake of Allah, Allah will compensate them with something better."

Contemplation Insights from Page 456 [Sad 43-61]

- Those who patiently endure harm will be rewarded by Allah both in this life and hereafter, and their supplications will be answered when they call upon Him.
- The verses provide evidence that a husband may discipline his wife with a non-severe beating for educational purposes, as Prophet Ayyūb did swear to beat his wife and then fulfilled his oath.

Contemplation Insights from Page 457 [Sad 62-83]

- Reasoning and juristic effort in the presence of a clear text is a flawed approach.
- Iblis's disbelief was out of stubbornness and arrogance.
- Those whom Allah has sincerely devoted to His worship are beyond the reach of Satan.

Contemplation Insights from Page 458 [Sad 84-88]

- A caller to Allah expects reward only from Him and does not seek compensation from people for calling them to the truth. - If you can avoid asking for any reward for your call except from Allah (عَزَّوَجَلَّ), do so.
- Pretentiousness is not part of the religion.

CONTEMPLATION STUDY QUESTIONS

Sūrah YaSīn Questions

Verses 2-3: What are the strongest proofs of the Prophet's message (ﷺ)? *[Al-Sa'dī]*

Verse 5: Why does the verse end with these two noble names: "the Almighty, the Most Merciful"? *[Al-Sa'dī]*

Verse 12: Explain the rank of calling to Allah through this verse.

Verse 13: What is the best way to deal with the ambiguity in the Qur'ān? And why? *[Al-Sa'dī]*

Verse 21: Why does the verse end with His saying: "and they are guided"? *[Al-Sa'dī]*

Verse 28: Discuss human weakness through this verse. *[Al-Sa'dī]*

Verses 37-40: What are the most prominent divine attributes indicated by these verses? *[Al-Sa'dī]*

Verse 39: Why is the time of dispute specified over other times? *[Al-Sa'dī]*

Verse 52: Does the disbelievers' saying, "Who will resurrect us from our place of rest?" contradict the punishment of the grave? *[Al-Sa'dī]*

Verse 60: Who is included in this rebuke mentioned in this verse? *[Al-Sa'dī]*

Verse 68: What is meant by informing about the reversal of humans in their old age? *[Al-Sa'dī]*

Verse 76: What is meant by Allah's informing about Himself that He knows what the disbelievers conceal and reveal? *[Ibn Kathīr]*

Verse 79: Explain the breadth of Allah's knowledge through the verse. *[Ibn Kathīr]*

Verse 80: How is this verse used as evidence for the resurrection? *[Al-Sa'dī]*

Sūrah al-Ṣāffāt Questions

Verses 4-5: Why did Allah mention lordship after mentioning divinity? *[Al-Sa'dī]*

Verse 25: Why did Allah mention the question of the people of Hell without mentioning their response? *[Al-Sa'dī]*

Verses 41-49: Why was there detailed mention of the bliss of the people of Paradise when the phrase "in gardens of delight" encompasses all of that? *[Al-Sa'dī]*

Verse 48: How does the verse indicate the perfection of men's beauty in Paradise? *[Al-Sa'dī]*

Verses 50-51: The people of knowledge have a special delight in Paradise through their conversation; what is it?

Verse 64: What is learned from the description of the tree as emerging from the base of Hell? *[Al-Sa'dī]*

Verse 65: How was the fruit of the Zaqqum tree likened to something unknown, namely the heads of devils? *[Al-Sa'dī]*

Verses 67-68: What is the relationship between these successive verses? *[Al-Sa'dī]*

Verse 78: How does the verse instill fear and terror in the disbelievers? *[Al-Sa'dī]*

Verse 102: What is the benefit of attributing Ismail's patience to the will of Allah? *[Al-Sa'dī]*

Verse 103: How was the vision fulfilled when he did not sacrifice his son? *[Ibn Kathīr]*

Verse 106: This event was a test and a purification for the heart of Ibrahim - explain this. *[Al-Sa'dī]*

Verse 107: What is the reason for describing the sacrifice as great? *[Al-Sa'dī]*

Verses 139-140: What do you gain from knowing that a prophet was punished for a sin he committed? *[Al-Sa'dī]*

Verse 158: What is the purpose behind informing about the jinn that they will be present for the reckoning? *[Al-Sa'dī]*

Verse 180: Why did the Sūrah end with Allah glorifying Himself? *[Al-Sa'dī]*

Sūrah Ṣad Questions

Verses 1-2: Mention the impediments that prevent benefiting from the Qur'ān in the verse *[Ibn Kathīr]*

Verse 6: Explain through this verse how to respond to those who criticize the intentions of scholars and preachers. *[Al-Sa'dī]*

Verse 17: Indeed, Allah (عَزَّوَجَلَّ) loves strength in His obedience; explain that through His description of Dawud (عَلَيْهِ ٱلسَّلَامُ) as "Dhu al-Ayd," meaning the one with strength. *[Al-Sa'dī]*

Verse 20: What do you benefit from Allah's favor upon Dawud by granting him wisdom? *[Al-Sa'dī]*

Verses 24-25: Through the verse: What is the importance of prayer in expiating sins? *[Al-Sa'dī]*

Verse 44: Whoever is truthful in fearing Allah (عَزَّوَجَلَّ), Allah will make a way out for him. Explain this from the verse *[Ibn Kathīr]*

Verse 50: The verse indicates a great blessing Allah bestows upon the people of Paradise; what is it? *[Al-Sa'dī]*

Verse 52: Describing the Houri as "modestly lowering their gaze" indicates a characteristic that a Muslim woman should embody in this world; perhaps it will be a reason for her entry into Paradise; what is it? *[Al-Sa'dī]*

Verse 65: Why did Allah (عَزَّوَجَلَّ) associate His attributes "the One, the Prevailing" together? *[Al-Sa'dī]*

Verse 67: Knowing that the Day of Resurrection and Reckoning is tremendous news and a serious matter, what should you do? *[Al-Sa'dī]*

Verses 79-81: What divine attribute do you learn from Allah's (عَزَّوَجَلَّ) response to Iblis's request for respite? *[Ibn Kathīr]*

Verse 86: Abdullah bin Mas'ud deduced a manner from the manners of seeking knowledge through his contemplation of the verse; what is it? *[Ibn Kathīr]*

Verse 87: What is the most recurring commandment in the Sūrah? Mention two benefits from that. *[Al-Sa'dī]*

Day 23: al-Zumar - Fussilat

The portion of reading for **Day 23** is *Sūrah al-Zumar, Sūrah Ghāfir* and *Sūrah Fuṣṣilat.* The main theme of *al-Zuma*r is pure *Tawḥīd.* The main theme of *Ghāfir* and all of the *ḤawāMīm* (i.e., the chapters that start with *Ḥa Mīm* from *Ghāfir* to *al Aḥqāf*) is inviting to Allah and cautioning against the most common obstacles to the truth.

سُورَةُ الزُّمَرِ

AL-ZUMAR (39)

The Troops

VERSES	75
WORDS	1,172
LETTERS	4,980
REVEALED IN	MAKKAH
REVEALATION ORDER	59

It is said to have been revealed after *Sūrah Saba'* and before *Sūrah Ghāfir*, in year five after the Prophethood, before the *hijrah* to Abbysinia. It is also called Sūrah al *Ghuraf* because of the 20th verse, which mentions the mansions of Paradise.

An authentic hadīth mentions that the Prophet (ﷺ) recited *Isra'* and *Zumar* nightly before sleeping. It is named Az-Zumar because Allah mentioned in it the groups (Zumar) of the blissful, who are the people of Paradise, and the groups of the wretched, who are the people of Hell.

✦**Main Themes:** The first main theme addressed by the *Sūrah* is *Tawḥīd.* The *Sūrah* presents simple arguments with logical proofs to support the concept of monotheism. These proofs include the creation of the heavens and the earth, the alternation of night and day, the movements of the Sun and the Moon, the stages of human development in the womb, and other brilliant examples.

These proofs establish the Oneness of Allah and reinforce the idea that He deserves to be worshipped. The *Sūrah* clarifies the great difference between one who worships a single Deity and those who worship multiple deities. The first is like a servant to a single master, and the other is like a servant to many masters who argue and fight over him.

The **second main theme** the Sūrah addresses is the belief in the Hereafter. Throughout the *Sūrah,* Allah explains the punishment of disbelievers and polytheists in the Hereafter when they are enveloped in fire from above and below. Allah awakens and excites the believers' hearts with glad tidings interspersed throughout *(See verses 17-18, 23, 36; and verse 45, in contrast, to see what causes the disbeliever's heart to rejoice).* This theme is the most prominent one in the last section of the *Sūrah*, such as verses 54-55, verse 60, and the lengthy concluding passage, one of the most notable passages detailing the description of Judgment Day.

The **third main theme** (based on frequency of mention) is the belief in revelation and the Prophethood. The *Sūrah* outlines the arguments and logical evidence supplied to the Prophet (ﷺ) to repudiate the doubts of the unbelievers. There are five main instances of this, each of which begins with "Say:" These are verses 11, 38, 39, 44, and 64. Regarding the status of the revelation sent to the Prophet (ﷺ), the *Qur'ān* is mentioned in seven places with many excellent descriptions *(See verses 1, 2, 23, 27, 41, 55, 59).*

Sūrah al-Zumar explains what makes the believers excellent and exceptional in contrast to the disbelievers. It shows us that there are essential key differences between their hearts and actions, contrasting between both factions (Zumrah) of humankind—those who are commendable and those who are contemptuous. Below is a list of thirteen key differences between the hearts of righteous believers and those unlike them:

(1.) Verse 7: Allah is pleased with *gratitude* for His servants and is displeased with ingratitude.

(2.) Verse 9: The people of *knowledge* and *worship* are exceptional and have excellence above all others.

(3.) Verses 13, 15, 17, 18: The one who worships Allah while refraining from harmful urges and passions is unlike those who pursue such things and chase their desires.

(4.) Verse 19: The people of *goodness and righteousness* are unlike those who disobey and behave poorly.

(5.) Verse 22: There is no equivocation between one whose *heart is open and comfortable with faith* and those who are contrary to that.

(6.) Verse 24: There is no similarity between *one who can shield his face from the hellfire* on judgment day and those who risk subjecting their faces to it.

(7.) Verse 29: There is no equivalency between the monotheist and the pagan, believer and disbeliever.

(8.) Verses 32-33: There is no equality between the people of truth and falsehood.

(9.) Verse 38: There is no similarity between One who causes both benefit and harm and those who have no control over benefit and harm for themselves or others.

(10.) Verses 45-46: The difference between the heart of the *Muwaḥḥid* and that of the *Mushrik*.

(11.) Verse 49: The contrast between people's behavior in good times and during hardship.

(12.) The Verses surrounding verse 49 describe the difference between those who rush to Allah's forgiveness and mercy and those who stray further into misguidance.

(13.) The final passage of the *Sūrah* separates the People of Paradise from the People of the Hellfire. See verses 71 and 73 and the surrounding verses.

Objectives of the Sūrah:

- Mentioning a doubt raised by the polytheists in their worship of deities other than Allah, refuting that doubt, and denying forms of polytheism, their turn to Allah when calamity strikes.
- Clarifying the evidences and proofs of the oneness of the Lord of the worlds in the creation of the heavens and the earth, the alternation of night and day, the subjugation of the sun and the moon, the amazing creation of humans, and the creation and variation of cattle, all being clear proofs of Allah's power and His oneness, which deserve gratitude, not denial.
- Directing the Prophet (ﷺ) to proclaim pure monotheism, declare his fear of disobeying Allah and his commitment to His path, contrasting the state of the polytheists with that of the sincere believers, and depicting the condition of both groups in this life and the Hereafter.
- Highlighting the importance of the Qur'ān as a revelation from Allah, inviting reflection and consideration upon it.
- Demonstrating the difference between those who worship Allah and those who worship other deities, informing the polytheists that they and their partners are insignificant to Allah and His Messenger (ﷺ), engaging them in the futility of their supposed deities, warning them of facing what befell the polytheistic nations of the past, emphasizing the enormity of polytheism, and its fearfulness, and that it nullifies all deeds.
- Describing the Day of Judgment, explaining the condition of the believing affirmers and the disbelieving deniers.

BRIEF SŪRAH SUMMARY

Verses 1-7	*Tawḥīd* and a repudiation of polytheism; how the world itself is an evidence of that; negating that Allah has counterparts or children.
Verses 8-52	The human condition: guidance and misguidance; belief and disbelief; knowledge and ignorance; pleasure and displeasure, etc., alongside encouragement to improve and discouragement from holding on to evil traits.
Verses 53-66	Encouragement to repent and to hasten in turning to Allah in devotion.
Verses 67-75	A powerful passage about the Day of Judgment.

سُورَةُ غَافِر

GHĀFIR (40)

The Forgiver

VERSES
85

WORDS
1,199

LETTERS
4,960

REVEALED IN
MAKKAH

REVEALATION ORDER
60

It is said to have been revealed after *al-Zumar* and before *Fuṣṣilat*. It is called *Ghāfir*; it is also sometimes called *al-Ṭawl, al Mu'min*, and *ḤaMīm al Mu'min.*

✦ **Main Theme**: The importance of calling to Allah and various effective ways to do so. It begins by mentioning the argumentative nature of the disbelievers and what shall become of them *(verse 5)*. This is repeated throughout. It concludes by mentioning their delusion and their outcome *(verse 83). "They rejoiced at what knowledge they already possessed."* This is an indispensable lesson for all of humankind. As such, this is repeated throughout the *Sūrah (see verses 4-5, 35, 56, 69.)*

Abu Bakr is said to have recited a portion of verse 28, "Do you kill a man because he says my Lord is Allah?" when the Quraysh assembled to physically attack the Prophet (ﷺ).[18] This was said to be three years before the Hijrah after the deaths of Abu Ṭālib and Khadījah.

Objectives of the Sūrah

- It challenges the stubborn deniers in proving the truth of the Qur'ān; it explains that their disputing about it is for nothing but troublemaking, driven by envy. It invites people to abandon their stubbornness, denial, arguing, and threatening the deniers, the stubborn, and the disputers about Allah's verses.
- Discussing some spectacles of the Day of Judgment and its horrors: people emerging for Allah, hearts reaching the throats, and discussing the criminals as they argue in the fire of Hell, and depicting their scene in Hell as humbled, asking the keepers of Hell to pray to Allah to lighten their torment.
- It mentions the story of Mūsā with Pharaoh, representing a stance of tyranny and arrogance against the call of truth. It depicts what a believer should be like in admonishing his people, in the story of the believer of the family of Pharaoh, speaking the truth softly, cautiously, and with a wide range of warning.

18 see Ṣaḥīḥ al Bukhārī 3643.

- Mentioning the creational signs indicating the greatness of this universe, evidencing the oneness of the Creator and His power, and the argument for the possibility of resurrection, and drawing a comparison between the believer and the disbeliever.
- Clarifying the end of the deniers and tyrants, whom Allah seized with a seizure of One Mighty, Powerful, and depicting the condition of the deniers of the Prophet (صَلَّى ٱللَّهُ عَلَيْهِ وَسَلَّمَ) like the condition of nations that denied Allah's messengers before him.

BRIEF SŪRAH SUMMARY

Verses 1-22	The opening of the *Sūrah* begins with a mention of Allah's Beautiful Names (refer to *Tafsīr* Sa'di for a magnificent benefit). The *Sūrah* briefly mentions those who dispute about the signs of Allah, despite their clarity and truth. It goes on to highlight how the angels are preoccupied with supplicating to Allah for forgiveness of the believers. This is in contrast to the disbelievers who are more hated by Allah and the angels than they are by themselves, due to their polytheistic beliefs. Therefore it is incumbent upon them to single out Allah with worship. The Sūrah then encourages them to reflect upon the demise of those who came before them.
Verses 23-55	These verses mention the message of Mūsā and how the Pharaoh opposed it. It then describes how a believer from the Pharaoh's family defended Tawḥīd in a remarkable way. This segment concludes with a reference to the dispute between the inhabitants of hellfire, specifically between the weak and the tyrannical. The *Sūrah* returns to the message and prophethood of Mūsā, and Allah commands His Prophet (H) to be patient, just as Mūsā had been.
Verses 56-77	These passage provides a series of creational proofs for the Oneness of Allah, including the creation of the heavens and the earth, the alternation of night and day, and the stages of human development. These proofs are presented in response to those who dispute about Allah's signs without any proof. Amidst these evidences, Allah commands sincere worship and forbids polytheism. These passage conclude with a reminder to be patient with the mistreatment and abuse from people. It emphasizes that Allah is the ultimate helper and punisher of those who deny His existence, both in this world and the next.
Verses 78-85	These eight verses provide comfort for the Prophet ﷺ by reminding him that Allah sent many messengers before him.It describes how Allah destroyed the deniers from previous nations, who did not believe in their prophets and were ungrateful for Allah's blessings. This nation must learn from the lessons of history and recognize the ultimate defeat of those who rejected Allah's messengers, as that is the way of Allah. The *Sūrah* concludes with this message.

سُورَةُ فُصِّلَتْ

FUṢṢILAT (41)

Explained in Detail

VERSES
54

WORDS
796

LETTERS
3,350

REVEALED IN
MAKKAH

REVEALATION ORDER
61

Main Themes: Establishing the Evidence for *Tawḥīd* (Allah's Oneness) and Allah's Power through His detailed and clear signs. The second main subject of the Sūrah is the Day of Judgment. Explaining how to deal gently with those who turn away from the Qur'ān by clarifying that the Qur'ān is the truth and the consequences of turning away.

It begins by mentioning the book's status and that Allah has detailed it for the servants (Verses 2-3). It concludes by mentioning that none are more astray than those who go against the truth *(Verse 52).*

The main subject of *Tawhīd* is mentioned in the beginning (see Verse 6 and how it explains that the entirety of the revelation is *Tawhīd* so be upon *istiqamah* and make *istighfar*), middle (37: don't prostrate to the sun and moon) and end (47: where are your *Shuraka'*).

Its main objectives:

- Highlighting the Qur'ān and its guidance, affirming its truthfulness and its protection from falsehood, establishing the reality of the Messenger (ﷺ) as a human to whom Allah revealed to be a guide and a caller to His true religion, and threatening those who deny the Qur'ān's verses.
- Discussing the creation of the heavens and the earth, rebuking the polytheists and criticizing them for their disbelief in the Creator of the heavens and the earth, with what is in their creation of evidence of His unique divinity, reminding them of the ends of those who denied before them, threatening them with the punishment of the hereafter, and warning them against the companions who adorn disbelief for them from among the jinn and humans, and contrasting all that with the honor for the monotheists with Allah.
- Reinforcement of the Prophet (ﷺ) and the believers with Allah's support, directing the believer to repel with what is better, to be patient with the opponents' aversion, and to repel evil by seeking refuge from the cursed devil.
- Mentioning the signs of Allah's unique creation of magnificent creatures, such as the sun and the moon, what He has placed of signs in the horizons and the selves, and the evidence of the

possibility of resurrection, and threatening those who deviate from those clear signs or turn a blind eye to them, thus disbelieving in them.

BRIEF SŪRAH SUMMARY

Verses 1-36	The *Qurā'n,* its revelation, its eloquence and irreplaceable nature; the unwillingness of the disbelievers to benefit from the *Qurā'n* has sealed their hearts *(v. 5)*; the threat of punishment in this life (the punishment of *'Aad* and *Thamud* despite their power; their testimony against their selves on Judgment Day; the source of their misguidance is the devils of jinn and mankind who beautified their evil works *(see verse 26).*
Verses 37-54	The universal evidences for Allah's Oneness and for the Day of Judgment; the sentiments of the *Mulhideen* in response to these signs; their blindness to the unmistakable truth; The carrying of the message by this Ummah like those who preceded it; how the earlier nations forgot the foundations of the religion; Allah alone knows the unseen; the reality of people in hardship and difficulty.

CONTEMPLATE, COMPREHEND, APPLY

Contemplation Insights from Page 458 [Az-Zumar 1-5]

◆ Seeking means to Allah should only be through His names, attributes, faith, and righteous deeds.

◆ Allah (عَزَّوَجَلَّ) only accepts sincere worship, so ensure all your deeds are such, {So worship Allah, being sincere to Him in religion}.

◆ Condemning lying and attributing falsehood to Allah, His Messenger, and the believers, {Indeed, Allah does not guide the one who is a liar, ungrateful}.

Contemplation Insights from Page 459 [Az-Zumar 6-10]

◆ Allah's care for humans in their mother's womb.

◆ Affirming the attributes of self-sufficiency and contentment for Allah.

◆ A disbeliever's acknowledgment of Allah in hardship and denial in ease is evidence of their confusion and instability.

◆ Fear and hope are attributes of the believers.

Contemplation Insights from Page 460 [Az-Zumar 11-21]

- Sincere worship of Allah is a condition for its acceptance.
- Sins necessitate Allah's punishment and His wrath.
- Guidance to faith is in Allah's hands, not in the hands of the Messenger ﷺ.

Contemplation Insights from Page 461 [Az-Zumar 22-31]

- Those of faith and piety are the ones who feel awe at hearing the Qur'ān, whereas those of sin and abandonment are those who do not benefit from it.
- Denying what the messengers brought is a cause for punishment to descend either in this life, the Hereafter, or both.
- The Qur'ān leaves nothing concerning the affairs of this life and the Hereafter except that it clarifies it, either summarily or in detail, and sets parables for it.

Contemplation Insights from Page 462 [Az-Zumar 32-40]

- The great danger of fabricating lies against Allah and attributing to Him what does not befit Him or His law.
- The affirmation of Allah's protection of the Prophet (صَلَّىٰ ٱللَّٰهُ عَلَيْهِ وَسَلَّمَ) from harm by his enemies.
- Acknowledging the Lordship of Allah alone without the worship of Him does not save one from the punishment of Hell.

Contemplation Insights from Page 463 [Az-Zumar 41-47]

- Sleep and awakening are daily lessons about death and resurrection.
- When Allah alone is mentioned before the disbelievers, they feel distressed because it reminds them of what Allah commands and prohibits, which they ignore.
- A disbeliever would ransom himself with everything he possesses on the Day of Judgment despite his miserliness in this life, but it will not be accepted.

Contemplation Insights from Page 464 [Az-Zumar 48-56]

- Blessings on a disbeliever are a form of entrapment.
- The vastness of Allah's mercy to His creation.
- Beneficial regret occurs in this world and is followed by sincere repentance.

Contemplation Insights from Page 465 [Az-Zumar 57-67]

- Arrogance is a despicable and ominous trait that prevents reaching the truth.

- The blackening of faces on the Day of Judgment is a sign of the misery of its owners.
- Polytheism nullifies all righteous deeds.
- Affirming the attributes of seizing and the right-hand

Contemplation Insights from Page 466 [Al-Zumar 57-67]

- Arrogance is a despicable and ominous trait that prevents one from reaching the truth.
- The darkening of faces on the Day of Judgment is a sign of the misery of its owners.
- Associating partners with Allah nullifies all righteous deeds.
- Establishing the grasp and the right hand for Allah (سُبۡحَانَهُۥ وَتَعَالَىٰ) without likening or representation.

Contemplation Insights from Page 467 [Al-Zumar 68-74]

- The establishment of the two trumpet blasts.
- Explaining the humiliation that the disbelievers will face and the honor with which the believers will be received.
- The eternal abode of disbelievers in Hell and the eternal bliss of the believers.
- Good deeds lead to good compensation.

Contemplation Insights from Page 468 [Al-Zumar 75]

- Combining the encouragement towards Allah's mercy and the warning of His severe punishment is a good approach.
- The end scene shows the dwellers of Hell, among the disbelievers and the wicked, settling in Hell, and the dwellers of Paradise, among the believing, pious, and righteous, in Paradise, the abode of the righteous.
- Every deed is sealed with praise; Allah the Creator began with praise, saying, "Praise be to Allah, who created the heavens and the earth," and ended with praise, saying, "Praise be to Allah, Lord of the worlds."

Contemplation Insights from Page 467 [Ghafir 1-7]

- Praising Allah by affirming His Oneness and glorifying Him with His praise is one manner of supplication.
- The honor of the believer with Allah, where He made angels seek forgiveness for him

Contemplation Insights from Page 468 [Ghafir 8-16]

- The acceptance of repentance is in this worldly life.
- The benefit of warning is specific to those who turn repentantly to their Lord.

- The believer's steadfastness is not affected by the disbelievers' rejection of his religion.
- The submission of tyrants and unjust rulers to Allah on the Day of Judgment

Contemplation Insights from Page 469 [Ghafir 17-25]

- Reminding of the Day of Judgment is one of the greatest deterrents against sins.
- Allah's encompassing knowledge of His servants' deeds, whether hidden or apparent.
- The command to travel through the land to take heed from the condition of the polytheists who were destroyed.

Contemplation Insights from Page 470 [Ghafir 26-33]

- The believers resort to their Lord for protection from the plot of his enemies.
- The permissibility of concealing faith for a prevailing benefit or to ward off harm.
- Advising people is one of the characteristics of people of faith

Contemplation Insights from Page 471 [Ghafir 34-40]

- Arguing to invalidate the truth and establish falsehood is a reprehensible trait characteristic of the misguided.
- Arrogance prevents guidance to the truth.
- The failure of the disbelievers' plots and their cunning to invalidate the truth.
- The obligation to prepare for the Hereafter and not to be distracted by this worldly life.

Contemplation Insights from Page 472 [Ghafir 41-49]

- The importance of reliance on Allah.
- The salvation of the one who calls to the truth from the plots of his enemies.
- The establishment of the punishment of the grave.
- The desperate clinging of disbelievers to any means to relieve them from the Fire, even for a limited time, although that will never happen.

Contemplation Insights from Page 473 [Ghafir 50-58]

- Allah's support for His messengers and the believers is a constant divine tradition.
- The excuse of the oppressor on the Day of Judgment will not benefit him.
- The importance of patience in facing falsehood.
- The creation of the heavens and the earth indicates resurrection, for He who created what is great can bring life back to what is less.

Contemplation Insights from Page 474 [Ghafir 59-66]

- Supplication is considered an act of worship that should be directed solely to Allah, for supplication is the essence of worship.
- Allah's blessings require gratitude from His servants.
- The affirmation of Allah's attribute of eternally living.
- The importance of sincerity in action.

Contemplation Insights from Page 475 [Ghafir 67-77]

- Gradual creation is a divine norm from which people learn to progress gradually.
- The horror of rejoicing over falsehood.
- The importance of patience in people's lives, especially for the callers to faith.

Contemplation Insights from Page 476 [Ghafir 78-85]

- Allah has messengers other than those mentioned in the Qur'ān, in whom we believe generally.
- Among Allah's blessings is His clarification of the signs that indicate His Oneness.
- The danger of rejoicing over falsehood and its bad consequences for the one who does it.
- The invalidity of belief when witnessing the destructive punishment.

Contemplation Insights from Page 477 [Fussilat 1-11]

- The disbelievers' disavowal of guidance leads to their persistence in disbelief.
- Clarifying the status of Zakat and stating that it is a pillar of Islam.
- The universe's submission to Allah and compliance with His command (سُبۡحَانَهُۥ وَتَعَالَىٰ) in everything within it.

Contemplation Insights from Page 478 [Fussilat 12-20]

- Turning away from the truth is a cause of destruction in both this life and the hereafter.
- Pride and being deluded by power prevent submission to the truth.
- Disbelievers will face the punishment of this world and the punishment of the hereafter.
- The limbs will testify against their owners on the Day of Judgment.

Contemplation Insights from Page 479 [Fussilat 21-29]

- Suspecting Allah's wisdom is a characteristic of disbelief.
- Disbelief and sins are reasons for the domination of devils over humans.

- Followers wishing their leaders to receive the severest punishment on the Day of Judgment.

Contemplation Insights from Page 480 [Fussilat 30-38]

- The status of steadfastness with Allah is great.
- Allah's honor for His believing servants, taking care of their affairs and the affairs of their successors.
- The status of calling to Allah, and that it is the best of deeds.
- Patience in the face of harm and repelling it with what is better are essential qualities for those calling to Allah.

Contemplation Insights from Page 481 [Fussilat 39-46]

- Allah has preserved the Qur'ān from alteration and corruption, and He (سُبْحَانَهُ وَتَعَالَىٰ) has taken upon Himself this preservation, unlike the previous scriptures.
- The argument was conclusively made against the Arab polytheists by revealing the Qur'ān in their language.
- Denying injustice from Allah and affirming His justice.

Contemplation Insights from Page 482 [Fussilat 47-54]

- The knowledge of the Hour is with Allah alone.
- The disbeliever's handling of Allah's blessings and afflictions is marked by confusion and turmoil.
- Allah's encompassing knowledge and power over everything.

CONTEMPLATION STUDY QUESTIONS

Sūrah al-Zumar Questions

Verse 1: This verse informs about the greatness of the Qur'ān; explain that. *[Al-Sa'dī]*

Verse 6: Why were these eight pairs specified rather than other animals? *[Al-Sa'dī]*

Verse 10: Why mention the vastness of His earth after stating that every doer of good has a reward in this world? *[Al-Sa'dī]*

Verse 12: The Noble Qur'ān encourages strong adherence to religion; explain that through the noble verse. *[Al-Sa'dī]*

Verse 15: If the sinners enter the Fire with their families on the Day of Resurrection, will they be happy with them? *[Ibn Kathīr]*

Verse 21: How do you judge a person to be of sound and balanced mind? *[Al-Sa'dī]*

Verse 23: Some meanings may be repeated in the Qur'ān in many places; what is the wisdom behind this repetition? *[Al-Sa'dī]*

Verse 24: What is the reason for the people of the Fire to shield themselves with their faces from the punishment? *[Al-Sa'dī]*

Verse 33: What is the relationship between piety and truthfulness in the truth and belief in it? *[Al-Sa'dī]*

Verse 42: How do you reconcile that Allah takes the souls at death and that the Angel of Death is the one who does it? *[Al-Sa'dī]*

Verse 52: How can a lack of provision be a reason for Allah's kindness and mercy to His servants? *[Al-Sa'dī]*

Verse 62: How do you respond to those who claim that some creations are ancient? And what is the flaw in that? *[Al-Sa'dī]*

Verse 64: What is the reason for describing the polytheists with ignorance? *[Al-Sa'dī]*

Verse 66: What is the reason for concluding the verse with the saying of Allah (عَزَّوَجَلَّ): "And be among the grateful"? This verse directs towards removing arrogance and vanity that may afflict some of those who do righteous deeds; explain the reason for that. *[Al-Sa'dī]*

Verse 69: What is the proof that people will first be gathered in darkness? And what is the reason for combining the verse with the hadiths that indicate Allah's light burns whatever His sight reaches of His creation? *[Al-Sa'dī]*

Verse 73: What is the benefit of omitting the response to the conditional statement in this verse? *[Al-Sa'dī]*

Verse 75: Why is the expression "وقيل" (it was said) used instead of "قالوا" (they said) in the noble verse? *[Ibn Kathīr]*

Sūrah Ghāfir Questions

Verse 3: Why are forgiveness and punishment paired together in this verse and others? *[Ibn Kathīr]*

Verse 8: In this verse, there is encouragement to associate with the righteous. Explain this. Why do they conclude their prayer with these two attributes: "the Almighty, the Wise"? *[Al-Sa'dī]*

Verse 8: Why are fathers, spouses, and offspring specifically mentioned? *[Ibn Kathīr]*

Verse 19: What practical benefit can a Muslim take from this verse? *[Al-Sa'dī]*

Verse 25: Why does the verse end with the general phrase "and the plot of the disbelievers" instead of ending with "and the plot of Pharaoh" or "and their plot"? *[Al-Sa'dī]*

Verse 30: This verse offers high guidance to those inviting to Allah not to lose hope. Explain it. *[Al-Sa'dī]*

Verse 35: Those whom scholars and the righteous despise are in a difficult situation and must rectify themselves. Explain this through the verse. *[Al-Sa'dī]*

Verse 46: How can this verse be used as proof of the existence of the punishment of the grave? *[Ibn Kathīr]*

Verse 50: List some disadvantages that befall disbelievers due to their disbelief. *[Al-Sa'dī]*

Verse 60: Compare asking Allah to asking people. Discuss the concept of "the recompense is of the same nature as the act" in the context of this verse. *[Al-Sa'dī]*

Verse 75: What is commendable joy, and what is condemnable joy? *[Al-Sa'dī]*

Verse 82: When is it beneficial to pass by the remnants of the communities that Allah has destroyed, and when is it detrimental? *[Al-Sa'dī]*

Verse 83: When are certain sciences deemed reprehensible? Discuss in light of this verse. *[Al-Sa'dī]*

Sūrah Fuṣṣilat Questions

Verse 2: Highlight the greatest manifestations of Allah's mercy on this Ummah. *[Al-Sa'dī]*

Verse 3: What do you benefit from His saying, "Its verses are detailed"? *[Al-Sa'dī]*

Verse 14: Explain the similarity in the arguments of the disbelievers through the verse. *[Al-Sa'dī]*

Verse 17: Why was Thamud specifically mentioned with guidance even though Allah (عَزَّوَجَلَّ) called all humanity to guidance? *[Al-Sa'dī]*

Verse 20: Why were these three organs specifically mentioned rather than others? *[Al-Sa'dī]*

Verse 26: In the verse, there is a testimony from the disbelievers to the truth; what is the basis of this testimony? *[Ibn Saadi]*

Verse 33: The truthful preacher has a sign; what is it? *[Ibn Kathīr]*

Verse 35: Why was this state only affirmed for those who were patient and those of great fortune? The verse indicated a sign among the signs of Allah's special creation; what is it? *[Al-Sa'dī]*

Verse 36: How do we repel the enemy from the jinn? *[Al-Sa'dī]*

Verse 40: What is meant by Allah informing us that these atheists are not hidden from Him? *[Ibn Kathīr]*

Verse 43: Why do many verses combine forgiveness and punishment as in this verse? *[Ibn Kathīr]*

Verse 49: You are weak in your body and heart; explain this through the verse and how to remedy it. *[Al-Sa'dī]*

Verse 51: What state should a believer be in during ease or hardship? *[Al-Sa'dī]*

Verse 54: Some of those who believe in the Day of Resurrection show through their condition that they are in doubt and skepticism about it, explain that *[Ibn Kathīr]*

DAY 24. AL-SHŪRĀ - AL AHQĀF

The *Qurā'n* reading for **day 24** is the remaining ḤawāMīm, *al-Shūrā; al-Zukhruf, al-Dukhān; al Jāthiyah; al Aḥqāf.* The overall theme of the chapters beginning with *ḤaMīm* is inviting to Allah and outlining the common obstacles to accepting the truth.

سُورَةُ الشُّورَىٰ
AL-SHURA (42)
The Consultation

VERSES
53

WORDS
860

LETTERS
3,588

REVEALED IN
MAKKAH

REVEALATION ORDER
62

It is said to have been revealed near the eighth year of the Prophethood when the rain stopped in Makkah. The end of its revelation is said to have been in year nine after the first *bay'ah* of *'Aqabah.*

Main Theme: The obligation of unity upon the message of truth, its virtue, and means. From the greatest of which is *al-Shura.* Sūrah Ash-Shura (The Consultation) is named for its depiction of the believers as those who conduct their affairs through mutual consultation, highlighting this trait as commendable and worthy of mention and praise.

Objectives of the Sūrah:

- To affirm the source of revelation and the unity of religious principles from the earliest prophecies to the final message, illustrating Allah's selection of the last of His prophets, upon whom be peace, by revealing the Qur'ān to him and prescribing for him the religion He commanded the prophets before him; to warn creation.
- To sternly warn those who oppose and argue with falsehood, cautioning those who deny the Qur'ān and disbelieve in the Resurrection, mentioning the punishment awaiting the polytheists on the Day of Reckoning and the honor awaiting the believers.
- To denounce the polytheists for attributing falsehood to the Prophet (ﷺ) and to console the Messenger (ﷺ) with the assurance that Allah is the recompenser of their deeds.
- To present evidence of monotheism and signs of divine power in the creation of this universe, remind of Allah's blessings, warn against causing these blessings to cease through wicked actions, encourage striving for success in the hereafter, and urge immediate action before it's too late.

- This section highlights some of the believers' qualities that reflect the nobility of this religion's values. It shows they are devoted to obeying Allah, avoiding His prohibitions, and treating His creation kindly.

It begins by mentioning the revelation and its source and concludes similarly *(verses 3 and 52)*. This is repeated differently throughout *(verses 7, 13, 14, 48, 51, 52)*.

It mentions the *Ayāt* of Allah throughout *(see Verses 28-29, 32-33)*. Verses 36-40 mention the attributes of the righteous believers.

BRIEF SŪRAH SUMMARY

Verses 1-26	This section discusses the revelation and prophethood and what is relevant to that. It emphasizes the continuity and unity of the message that was conveyed to all the Prophets. The Arabic *Qur'ān* was revealed to the Prophet (صَلَّى ٱللَّهُ عَلَيْهِ وَسَلَّمَ) with the intention of warning the people of the mother of all towns and its surrounding areas. Had He so willed, he would have unified mankind upon the truth. He legislated the same for all Messengers and peoples: establish the religion and be not divided therein. As such humankind is divided into two factions: one in Paradise and the other in Hell *(verses 3 and 13)*. This passage also highlights the unity of the message between the greatest messengers.
Verses 27-53	Evidences of *Tawḥīd (v. 27-35);* Many essential traits of the believers *(v. 36-43);* Conclusion: the reason for the sending of the Prophet (صَلَّى ٱللَّهُ عَلَيْهِ وَسَلَّمَ) is guiding to Allah's straight path and to warn them of the reality that all shall return to Him for Judgment.

سُورَةُ الزُّخرُف

AL-ZUKHRUF (43)

The Ornaments of Gold

VERSES
89

WORDS
733

LETTERS
3,400

REVEALED IN
MAKKAH

REVEALATION ORDER
63

It is said to have been revealed after *al-Shūrā* and before *al-Dukhān.*

✦**Main Theme:** A warning against the temptations of the world.

At the beginning of the Sūrah (Verse 9), Allah establishes that He is the creator of the universe. Toward its end, He establishes He is its owner (Verse 57). Sūrah [Al-Zukruf (The Gold Adornments)] addresses various themes and messages to guide and warn its audience.

Sūrah al-Zukhruf is centered around the main subjects of the Makkan chapters: *Tawḥīd,* Revelation & Prophethood, and Eternal reward and punishment. The heads of the tribes of Makkah and 'Ṭāif objected to the possibility that revelation would be sent to someone of lower standing than them. Allah establishes that wealth and status are commonly used to divert from the truth and unite people upon falsehood (see verses 31-35); therefore, be firm on the straight path. Some of the previous nations are mentioned, and special mention is given to the message of Ibrāhīm because the Arab polytheists and *Ahlul Kitāb* wrongly claimed him. Special attention is also given to the story of Mūsā with Fir'awn. Like the tribal chieftains of Makkah and Ṭā'if, Fir'awn was deluded by his status: *"Isn't the authority of Egypt mine?" (verse 51).* It also gives mention to ʿĪsā and the doubts of people about him.

Objectives of the Sūrah:

- To demonstrate the polytheists' acknowledgment of monotheistic lordship, which logically necessitates the recognition of monotheistic deity, expressing astonishment at their condition, they confess that Allah is their Creator and the Creator of all beings, yet they ascribe powerless partners to Him.
- To invalidate the polytheists' beliefs regarding angels, whom they considered to be Allah's daughters and worshipped, despite their belief that daughters were less esteemed than sons,

based merely on the tradition of their forefathers, and their false claim of following Prophet Ibrāhīm's religion.

- To clarify that worldly life is not a measure of Allah's love for a servant, the polytheists found it improbable for the revelation to be sent to Muhammad ﷺ due to his being an orphan and poor, preferring instead a wealthy and influential man, which the Qur'ān refutes, highlighting the fallacy of such earthly values.
- To narrate the stories of Mūsā and 'Īsā, peace be upon them, in their call to monotheism to their respective peoples, who then divided into sects, and their eventual fate; comforting the Messenger ﷺ regarding the opposition and arrogance of his people's leaders towards his selection for prophethood, their pride in false values, and their disregard for him.
- The text depicts the state of people on the Day of Judgment to warn of the sudden arrival of the Hour. It describes the believers' situation upon entering Paradise and contrasts it with the criminals in Hell. It reminds them that their deeds, recorded by angels, cause their suffering.

BRIEF SŪRAH SUMMARY

Verses 1-7 and 23-45	The revelation and prophethood.
Verses 8-22	Simple logical proofs establishing the message of *Tawḥīd*.
Verses 46-56	The story of Mūsā in debating with *Fir'awn*. *Fir'awn's* delusions of grandeur and refusal to accept any sign and demanding alternative ones connected to wealth and status (an entourage of angels, golden bangles).
Verses 57-65	Īsā is Allah's servant and Messenger; He will return before the final hour; Allah will judge between His servants as relates to that which they differ about.
Verses 66-89	*Targhīb* and *Tarhīb*, challenging and threatening the disbelievers of all times and places, lest they suffer the fate of those like them in the past.

سُورَةُ الدُّخَانِ

AL-DUKHĀN (44)

The Smoke

VERSES
59

WORDS
346

LETTERS
1,431

REVEALED IN
MAKKAH

REVEALATION ORDER
64

Main Theme: A warning to the common folk from being deluded by those in authority and power.

It begins by mentioning that it is a warning and concludes by mentioning that it is a reminder *(verses 2-3 and 58).*

Allah may delay the destruction of the disbelievers, but they may still be afflicted until they recant *(verses 10-16).*

Verses 18-31 mention how Pharaoh was deluded by his power until Allah seized him with punishment. What befell him befell his army. Neither the heavens nor the earth wept for them, nor shall they be granted respite.

The remainder of the *Sūrah* outlines what shall become of the believers and the disbelievers in the Hereafter.

BRIEF SŪRAH SUMMARY

Verses 1-16	The excellence of the *Qurā'n,* its revelation from the controller of the universe; the impending threat of punishment for those who reject it.
Verses 17-36	The singular outcome of oppression in every time and place, similar to that which befell Fir'awn and his people. This is what awaits anyone of the sort.
Verses 38-59	The truth for which the heavens and earth were created. A vivid description of the punishments of the hellfire (*zaqqum*) and of the paradise.

سُورَةُ الجَاثِيَة

AL JĀTHIYAH (45)

The Crouching

VERSES
37

WORDS
488

LETTERS
2,191

REVEALED IN
MAKKAH

REVEALATION ORDER
65

Main Theme: A warning against arrogance and following one's desires. It covers the three main topics, giving the most attention to Tawḥīd. It begins by mentioning how the arrogant are rendered deaf by their arrogance, unable to hear the truth (verses 7-8). It concludes by mentioning Allah's exclusivity to greatness to the exception of all else *(verse 37)*. The reality of the arrogant is repeated throughout *(see verses 11, 21-24, 31-34)*.

Objectives of the Sūrah:

- To affirm Allah's exclusive divinity with evidence of His power and uniqueness in His creation of humans, animals, the heavens, the earth, the reviving of the earth through rain, and the alternation of night and day. This serves as a reminder of Allah's great blessings upon creation, necessitating gratitude towards the Benefactor and monotheism towards the Creator.
- To reassure and console the Messenger ﷺ that his experience with his people is similar to Mūsā's mission, indicating that opposition does not detract from the truth of the message or its bringer. It emphasizes not being concerned with the deniers, no matter their number, and draws a parallel between those who neglected to consider Allah's signs and opposed the Prophet (صَلَّى ٱللَّهُ عَلَيْهِ وَسَلَّمَ) and the Children of Israel who disputed their book after receiving knowledge, leading Allah to empower their enemies over them.
- Denouncing materialists who denied the existence of the Great Creator, disbelieved in resurrection after death, claimed that time alone causes destruction, and believed in no resurrection, reckoning, or recompense, and to describe some of the horrors of the Day of Recompense, thereby frightening with the punishment prepared for the disbelievers.

BRIEF SŪRAH SUMMARY

Verses 1-23	The *Qurā'n,* its origin, and how it is faced with rejection and arrogance. The threat against the disbelievers & the mention of Allah's clear creational signs.
Verses 24-37	The day of judgment, those who deny it and what awaits of reward and punishment. It concludes with praise for Allah just as it began.

سُورَةُ الأَحْقَاف
AL AḤQĀF (46)
The Curved Sandhills

VERSES
35

WORDS
644

LETTERS
2,595

REVEALED IN
MAKKAH

REVEALATION ORDER
66

Main Theme: Allah guides whom He chooses to answer His call. Verses 29-32 mention the Jinn accepting Islam and inviting their people to faith. They begin by mentioning the status of the Qur'ān and conclude by mentioning the Jinn's reaction to hearing the *Qurā'n*.

Its objectives include:

- It shares many of Al-Jathiya's objectives but with some variations. It opens similarly to Al-Jathiya, indicating the miraculous nature of the Qur'ān as evidence that Allah reveals it. The argument is made through the perfection of the creation of the heavens and the earth to demonstrate Allah's exclusive divinity and to affirm the recompense for deeds. It points to the occurrence of compensation after the resurrection and that this world is destined for extinction. It invalidates claims of counterparts in divinity, arguing their lack of divine attributes.
- It refutes the possibility that the Qur'ān is the work of anyone other than Allah. It confirms the message of Muhammad (ﷺ) and Allah's (سُبْحَانَهُ وَتَعَالَى) testimony to the truth of his message, along with the testimony of a witness from the Children of Israel. It praises those who believed in the Qur'ān, mentioning some of their commendable qualities and contrasting them with the qualities of the disbelievers and their envy, which drove them to deny it.
- It mentions the miracle of the jinn's faith in the Qur'ān. The chapter concludes by affirming the truthfulness of the Prophet (ﷺ). Included in this is the treatment of parents and offspring, which is from the character of the believers. It mentions some characteristics of those who are astray. The lesson from their misguidance despite their power, Allah seized them for their disbelief, making them a lesson for the deniers, while all their false gods availed them not.

BRIEF SŪRAH SUMMARY

Verses 1-14	The status of the *Qur'ān*, the message of *Tawḥīd*, the debate between the Messenger and the disbelievers.
Verses 15-19	Parable of the righteous son and the wicked son.

Verses 20-27	The story of the people of Hūd (the people of the *Aḥqāf*)
Verses 28-35	The delegation of the *Jinn* who accepted Islam. This section also mentions the beginning and end of humankind, who will all eventually believe, but not until it is too late. The command: "Be patient as were the *Ulul 'Azm* (i.e., the Prophets of highest resolve)," *(verse 35)* is an amazing conclusion to the seven Ḥawāmīm chapters whose main theme was inviting to Allah despite adversity and harm.

CONTEMPLATE, COMPREHEND, APPLY

Contemplation Insights from Page 483 [Ash-Shura 1-10]

- Allah's greatness is evident in everything.
- Angels pray for the well-being of those with faith.
- The Qur'ān and Sunnah are references for believers in all their affairs, especially in matters of disagreement.
- The focus is on warning the people of Mecca and its surroundings; they are the primary audience in response to their denial of the Prophet's (ﷺ) message, which was sent to all humanity as stated: "We have not sent you except comprehensively to mankind..."

Contemplation Insights from Page 484 [Ash-Shura 11-15]

- The religion of the prophets, at its core, is one.
- The importance of unity and the danger of division.
- Successful da'wah (calling to Allah) relies on correct principles, steadfastness, avoiding caprices, justice, focusing on commonalities, avoiding futile arguments, and reminding of the shared destiny.

Contemplation Insights from Page 485 [Ash-Shura 16-22]

- The believer's fear of the Day of Judgment aids in preparation for it.
- Allah's kindness to His servants can be expressed by expanding or restricting the best provision for them.
- The danger of preferring the worldly life over the hereafter.

Contemplation Insights from Page 486 [Ash-Shura 23-31]

- The one who calls to Allah does not seek compensation from people.
- Expansion and restriction in provision are subject to divine wisdom that may be hidden from many.
- Sins and disobedience are reasons for calamities.

Contemplation Insights from Page 487 [Ash-Shura 32-44]

- Patience and gratitude are reasons for success and reflection on Allah's signs.
- The position of consultation in Islam is significant.
- It's permissible to retaliate against injustice equivalently, but forgiveness is better.

Contemplation Insights from Page 488 [Ash-Shura 45-51]

- The obligation to hasten in obeying Allah's commands and avoiding His prohibitions.
- The Messenger's role is to convey that the outcomes are in Allah's hands.
- Allah bestows sons, daughters, or both according to His wisdom in what is best for His servants, without any preference for males over females.
- Allah reveals to His prophets in various ways for reasons known to Him alone.

Contemplation Insights from Page 489[Ash-Shura 52-53]

- Revelation is called 'spirit' due to its significance in guiding people, akin to the spirit's role in the body.
- The guidance attributed to the Messenger ﷺ is that of directing and not of ensuring success. Reflect on the worldly or otherworldly benefits that your contemplation of the Qur'ān revives in you.

Contemplation Insights from Page 489 [Al-Zukruf 1-10]

- The Qur'ān's nobility and superiority over previous scriptures.
- Human extravagance in polytheism and corruption does not preclude admonishing, advising, and guiding them.
- The historical pattern of messengers being mocked by their people.
- The destruction of the strong is evidence that those less than them are more deserving of destruction, especially with their severe disbelief.
- There is a possibility that those who indulge in heedlessness could become beneficial to Muslims if guided.
- The polytheists' acknowledgment of monotheistic lordship offers no benefit on the Day of Judgment.

Contemplation Insights from Page 490 [Al-Zukruf 11-22]

- Every blessing demands gratitude.
- The injustice of polytheists in their perceptions of Allah when they attributed daughters to Him, despite their disdain for having daughters themselves.
- The invalidity of using predestination as an excuse for committing sins.
- Witnessing as a foundation for establishing truths.

Contemplation Insights from Page 491 [Al-Zukruf 23-33]

- Blind imitation as a cause of misguidance in previous nations.
- The necessity of disassociating from disbelief and disbelievers.
- Divine distribution of sustenance based on wisdom.
- The insignificance of worldly life to Allah; if it had the weight of a mosquito's wing, He would not have given a disbeliever even a sip of water.

Contemplation Insights from Page 492 [Al-Zukruf 34-47]

- The danger of ignoring the Qur'ān.
- The Qur'ān is an honor for the Prophet (ﷺ) and his Ummah (nation).
- The agreement of all messengers on rejecting polytheism.
- Mocking the truth is a characteristic of disbelief.

Contemplation Insights from Page 493 [Al-Zukruf 48-60]

- Breaking covenants is a trait of disbelievers.
- The light-minded are easily mocked by those seeking to deride them.
- Allah's wrath entails loss.
- People of misguidance attempt to distort Qur'ānic texts to suit their desires.

Contemplation Insights from Page 494 [Al-Zukruf 61-73]

- 'Īsā' descent is one of the major signs of the Hour.
- The cessation of relationships with the wicked on the Day of Judgment, while relationships among the righteous endure.
- Allah's glad tidings and reassurance to believers about their past in the worldly life and what awaits them in the Hereafter.

Contemplation Insights from Page 495 [Al-Zukruf 74-89]

- The great danger of detesting the truth.
- The plots of disbelievers turn against them eventually.
- Increased knowledge of Allah leads a servant to greater trust in Allah and submission to His law.
- The exclusive knowledge of the Hour's timing belongs to Allah.

Contemplation Insights from Page 496 [Al-Dukhān 1-18]

- The revelation of the Qur'ān on Laylat al-Qadr, which is abundant in blessings, signifies its immense value.
- The sending of messengers and the revelation of the Qur'ān are manifestations of Allah's mercy to His servants.
- The prophets' messages liberate the oppressed from the grip of the arrogant.

Contemplation Insights from Page 497 [Al-Dukhān 19-39]

- A believer must seek refuge with his Lord to protect him from the cunning of his enemy.
- The legitimacy of praying against the disbelievers when they do not respond to the call and when they fight against its people.
- The universe does not grieve for the death of a disbeliever due to his insignificance to Allah.
- The creation of the heavens and the earth is for a profound wisdom unknown to atheists.

Contemplation Insights from Page 498 [Al-Dukhān

- Combining physical and psychological punishment for the disbeliever.
- The great success is to be saved from the Fire and to enter Paradise.
- Allah makes the pronunciation and meanings of the Qur'ān easy for His servants.

Contemplation Insights from Page 499 [Al-Jathiya 1-13]

- Lying, persisting in sin, arrogance, and mocking Allah's signs are characteristics of the misguided, and Allah has threatened those who exhibit them.
- Allah's blessings on His servants are numerous, including making what is in the universe subservient to them.
- Blessings require the servants to be thankful to the deity who granted them.

Contemplation Insights from Page 500 [Al-Jathiya 14-22]

- Pardoning and overlooking oppressors' wrongdoing, if they do not manifest corruption on Earth and transgress Allah's limits, is a noble character Allah commanded the believers to have if they believe it leads to a positive outcome.
- The obligation to follow the divine law and avoid following human whims.
- Just as believers and disbelievers are not equal in traits, they are not equal in recompense.
- Allah created the heavens with profound wisdom unknown to material atheists.

Contemplation Insights from Page 501 [Al-Jathiya 23-32]

- Following whims leads to destruction and veils one from the path of success.
- The terror of the Day of Judgment.
- Assumptions are of no avail against the truth, especially in matters of belief.

Contemplation Insights from Page 502 [Al-Jathiya 33-37]

- Mocking Allah's signs constitutes disbelief.
- The danger of being deluded by the pleasures and desires of worldly life.
- The attribute of majesty belongs exclusively to Allah (سُبْحَانَهُ وَتَعَالَى).

Contemplation Insights from Page 502 [Al-Ahqaf 1-5]

- The Prophethood of Muhammad ﷺ is affirmed by stating the Qur'ān is a revelation from Allah.
- It rejects the notion that Allah engaged in futile actions in creating the heavens, the earth, and everything in between, emphasizing that everything He does and says is purposeful.
- An irrefutable reality that those who cannot create should not be worshipped.
- Highlights the folly of calling upon entities (idols, graves, trees) that cannot respond, contrasting it with the concept of dua (supplication) as a clear sign of Allah's existence and deservingness of worship.

Contemplation Insights from Page 503 [Al-Ahqaf 6-14]

- All worshipped besides Allah will disown their worshippers among the disbelievers.
- The Prophet (صَلَّى ٱللَّهُ عَلَيْهِ وَسَلَّمَ) did not have knowledge of the unseen except what Allah revealed to him.
- Evidence of Muhammad's (صَلَّى ٱللَّهُ عَلَيْهِ وَسَلَّمَ) prophethood is present in previous scriptures.
- Highlights the virtue of steadfastness and the reward for its adherents.

Contemplation Insights from Page 504 [Al-Ahqaf 15-20]

- Emphasizes the importance of dutifulness towards parents, especially the mother, and warns against disobedience.
- Warns against indulgence in worldly pleasures as they distract from the Hereafter.
- Describes the severe warning for those who are arrogant and commit transgressions.

Contemplation Insights from Page 505 [Al-Ahqaf 21-28]

- Messengers do not have knowledge of the unseen except what Allah reveals to them.
- This is the story of the people of Hud, who mistook the approaching punishment for rain and failed to repent before it was too late.
- Despite the strength of the Ad people surpassing that of Quraish, Allah destroyed them, serving as a lesson that wisdom lies in heeding warnings from others' fates rather than enduring the same oneself.

Contemplation Insights from Page 506 [Al-Ahqaf 29-35]

- Good manners include listening attentively to the speaker.
- The quick response of the rightly guided jinn to the truth serves as an encouragement for humans.
- Responding to the truth necessitates hastening to invite others to it.
- Patience is a virtue exemplified by the prophets.

CONTEMPLATION STUDY QUESTIONS

Sūrah al-Shura Questions

Verse 10: How does this verse indicate the validity of consensus? *[Al-Sa'dī]*

Verse 13: What is the greatest blessing that Allah has bestowed upon you? *[Al-Sa'dī]*

Verse 14: What is the benefit of this information about the people of earlier scriptures? *[Al-Sa'dī]*

Verse 15: The verse warns of the danger of innovation; explain it. *[Al-Sa'dī]*

Verse 18: What is the reason for the believers' fear of the Hour? *[Al-Sa'dī]*

Verse 19: Why is provision mentioned after mentioning kindness to His servants? *[Al-Sa'dī]*

Verse 23: What is the aspect of good news for the believers in this verse? *[Ibn Kathīr]*

Verse 25: Why does the verse end with "He knows what you do"? *[Al-Sa'dī]*

Verse 38: Establishing prayer and giving zakat are included in responding to the Lord, so why are they mentioned after mentioning the response? The consultation among Muslims indicates another great matter: what is it? *[Al-Sa'dī]*

Verse 40: What is the reason for mentioning reform after forgiveness? What do you benefit from making the reward of the forgiver on Allah? *[Al-Sa'dī]*

Verse 47: What is the blameworthy hope? And is it permissible to delay action? *[Al-Sa'dī]*

Verse 48: What is the difference between a Muslim and a disbeliever viewing previous blessings? *[Ibn Kathīr]*

Sūrah al-Zukhruf Questions

Verse 4: Why did Allah inform about this book's honor and high status with the highest assembly? *[Ibn Kathīr]*

Verse 14: Often, our worldly affairs indicate the hereafter conditions; explain that through the previous verses *[Ibn Kathīr]*

Verses 16-19: There is a clear contradiction in the statement of the polytheists; explain it. *[Al-Sa'dī]*

Verse 26: How do luxury and tyranny impact the belief in monotheism? *[Al-Sa'dī]*

Verse 30: What do you understand from the state of the polytheists from their saying, "This is magic"? *[Al-Sa'dī]*

Verses 31-32: Why mention the provision division after they suggested the Qur'ān should have been revealed to a man from the two cities? *[Al-Sa'dī]*

Verses 34-35: The verse indicates that it is from His mercy, may He be exalted, to sometimes prevent His servants from some of the adornments of the world; explain that. *[Al-Sa'dī]*

Verse 37: Do the misguided have an excuse since they thought they were guided but were not? *[Al-Sa'dī]*

Verse 49: The community cannot do without scholars and worshippers; explain this through the verse. *[Al-Sa'dī]*

Verse 51: There is great ignorance in Pharaoh's praise of himself; explain that. *[Al-Sa'dī]*

Verse 67: What is the reason for the permanence of friendship on the Day of Judgment? *[Ibn Kathīr]*

Verses 77-78: What is the benefit of saying, "Indeed, we have come to you with the truth," after saying, "You will remain"? *[Ibn Kathīr]*

Sūrah al-Dukhān Questions

Verse 3: What is meant by the blessed night? And why is it described as blessed? *[Al-Sa'dī]*

Verse 18: The verse condemns innovation and initiating; explain it. *[Al-Sa'dī]*

Verses 21-22: What made Mūsā transition from inviting them to praying against them? *[Al-Sa'dī]*

Verse 29: What causes the sky and the earth to cry over the servants? *[Al-Sa'dī]*

Verse 53: In Paradise, there is not the slightest type of humiliation; explain that through the verse. *[Al-Sa'dī]*

Verse 58: Speak about the preference of the Arabic language over other languages through the verse *[Ibn Kathīr]*

Sūrah al Jāthiyah Questions

Verses 3-5: Explain why faith is presented first, then certainty, then reason in the description of the believers. *[Ibn Kathīr]*

Verse 5: Why did Allah call rain a provision? *[Ibn Kathīr]*

Verses 16-17: These verses are about the Children of Israel; what can we, the nation of Islam, benefit from these two verses? *[Ibn Kathīr]*

Verse 28: What is the reason for the nations' kneeling on the Day of Judgment? *[Al-Sa'dī]*

Verses 36-37: What are the pillars of worship, and from what do they arise? *[Al-Sa'dī]*

Sūrah al Aḥqāf Questions

Verses 2-3: Why is the creation of the heavens and the earth, and what is between them mentioned after mentioning the revelation of the Book? *[Al-Sa'dī]*

Verse 8: Allah always pairs encouragement and intimidation in His book; explain that through this verse. *[Ibn Kathīr]*

Verse 11: What is the difference between the statement of the polytheists and the statement of Ahlus-Sunnah wal-Jama'ah regarding the companions? *[Ibn Kathīr]*

Verse 15: What guidance is indicated by the verse for those who reach forty years? *[Ibn Kathīr]*

Verse 15: Why should a person be grateful for the blessings that Allah has bestowed upon his parents? *[Al-Sa'dī]*

Verse 26: Material strength is of no benefit if Allah decides to punish its people; explain that. *[Al-Sa'dī]*

Verse 29: What manners did the jinn exhibit when they listened to the Qur'ān? And are there messengers among the jinn? *[Ibn Kathīr]*

Verse 30: Why did the jinn say, "Revealed after Mūsā," and not say, "Revealed after 'Īsā"? *[Ibn Kathīr]*

Verse 30: In the arrangement of the jinn's speech, there is an important da'wah benefit; explain it. *[Al-Sa'dī]*

Section 04

The Mufaṣṣal

Day 25: Muḥammad - Dhāriyāt
Day 26: al-Ṭur - Ḥadīd
Day 27: Juz' Qad Sami'
Day 28: Juz' Tabārak
Day 29: Juz' 'Ammā

DAY 25: MUHAMMAD - DHĀRIYĀT

The Qurā'n reading for **day 25** is from *Sūrah Muḥammad* to *Sūrah al-Dhariyāt*. It concludes the chapters of the third greatest length and begins the last section of the *Qur'ān*, the most detailed shorter chapters, called the *Mufaṣṣal* (most of which were revealed in Makkah).

سُورَةُ مُحَمَّدٍ

MUḤAMMAD (47)

Muḥammad

VERSES
38

WORDS
539

LETTERS
2,349

REVEALED IN
MADINAH

REVEALATION ORDER
95

Main Theme: encouraging the believers to fight those obstructing Allah's path. **Objectives of the Sūrah:**

- Encouragement to combat the transgressing disbelievers, with Allah's promise to reward the believers for their deeds and rectify their condition, leading them to Paradise and outlining the believers' duty to support Allah's religion and counter the enemies' plots. Allah promises them victory over their enemies and the stabilization of their footing in battle if they support Allah's religion and honor His law.
- It illustrates the reality of disbelief and faith by describing the characteristics of those following both paths, comparing believers and disbelievers in their goals, conditions, and outcomes, and detailing the characteristics of Paradise, its bliss, and Hell and its torment.
- Describing the schemes of the hypocrites, revealing their plots and morals, indicating their connection with the Jews, their lack of contemplation on the Qur'ān, their alliance with the polytheists, threatening them by informing the Messenger ﷺ of their signs, and warning Muslims not to be deceived by the hypocrites' duplicity.

Verses 1-2	The futility of the efforts of the disbelievers and the reward of the believers.
Verses 3-15	The reward of the believers and the exhortation to fight the oppressors.
Verses 16-31	Exposing the *Munāfiqūn* in detail.
Verses 32-38	The final abode of the believers and of the disbelievers.

سُورَةُ الفَتْحِ
AL FATḤ (48)
The Victory

VERSES
29

WORDS
560

LETTERS
2,348

REVEALED IN
MADINAH

REVEALATION ORDER
111

It is said to be one of the very last in order of its revelation, revealed in the year six after the peace treaty of al *Ḥudaybiyyah.*

Main Theme: The divine promise to grant victory and strength to the Prophet (ﷺ) and the believers who truly support the religion, to calm their hearts after the disbelievers stopped them from entering Makkah and after the *Munafiqīn* attacked their morale.

Objectives of the Sūrah:

- Glad tidings to the believers about the favorable outcome of the Treaty of Hudaybiyyah, as a victory and conquest that brought tranquility to the believers' hearts, informing them that the outcome was for them and that adversity would afflict the polytheists and the hypocrites.
- Allah's protection of His sincere allies when they were called to jihad, promptly pledging allegiance to the Prophet (ﷺ) for battle, thereby protecting them from the disbelievers of Mecca, and His (سُبْحَانَهُ وَتَعَالَىٰ) kindness to the oppressed believers in Mecca by not permitting the Muslims to fight the polytheists at that time to protect those oppressed.
- Denouncing those who refrained from accompanying the Prophet (ﷺ) to Mecca, thinking he and the believers would not return, only to be disappointed by Allah returning the Prophet (ﷺ) and the believers to Medina, honoring them with this conquest, and promising them a near victory over the Jews of Khaybar.
- Praising the believers who followed the Prophet (ﷺ) through hardships and ease, outlining their characteristics, urging them to adopt these traits, illustrating their impact on their conduct, and honoring them with forgiveness and a great reward.

Ibn Shihāb al-Zuhrī (رَحِمَهُ ٱللَّهُ) famously said:

فَمَا فُتِحَ فِي الْإِسْلَامِ فَتْحٌ قَبْلَهُ كَانَ أَعْظَمَ مِنْهُ، إِنَّمَا كَانَ الْقِتَالُ حَيْثُ الْتَقَى النَّاسُ، فَلَمَّا كَانَتِ الْهُدْنَة ووضعت الْحَرْب أَوزارها وَأمن النَّاس كلم بَعْضُهُمْ بَعْضًا وَالْتَقَوْا فَتَفَاوَضُوا فِي الْحَدِيثِ وَالْمُنَازَعَةِ، فَلَمْ يُكَلَّمْ أَحَدٌ فِي الْإِسْلَامِ يَعْقِلُ شَيْئًا إِلَّا دَخَلَ فِيهِ، وَلَقَدْ دَخَلَ فِي تِيْنَكِ السَّنَتَيْنِ مِثْلُ مَنْ كَانَ دَخَلَ فِي الْإِسْلَامِ قَبْلَ ذَلِكَ أَوْ أَكْثَرُ

"There was no victory in Islām greater than the peace treaty at al Ḥudaybiyah before it. There had been fighting whenever the people encountered each other (i.e. when the polytheists encountered the believers). When the peace treaty happened, the conflict laid its burdens, and people could feel at peace with one another, and then people engaged in conversation and disputation. No one with the slightest sense was spoken to about Islam except that they entered into it. In those two years, the equivalent of or more than the number of those who entered before entered Islam.

BRIEF SŪRAH SUMMARY

Verses 1-9	Glad tidings to the believers after their disappointment at the events surrounding the peace treaty at *al Ḥudaybiyah*.
Verses 10-26	The *Ba'yah* of *Riḍwān* (the oath taken by the companions after the peace treaty); exposing those who broke their word to Prophet (ﷺ); exposing the Bedouins who offered weak excuses for not going with the Prophet (ﷺ); explaining that the Prophet (ﷺ) would not invade Makkah out of concern for the safety of the Muslim minority that were still there; the dream of the Prophet (ﷺ) after the peace treaty that they would safely enter Makkah in the near future.
Verses 26-29	The prerequisites of victory and the description of the Ṣaḥābah.

سُورَةُ الحُجُرَات
AL ḤUJURĀT (49)
The Dwellings

VERSES
18

WORDS
343

LETTERS
1,476

REVEALED IN
MADINAH

REVEALATION ORDER
106

It is said to have been revealed between *Sūrah al-Taḥrīm* and *Sūrah al Mujādalah* in the year of the delegations, year nine after the *Hijrah* during the visit of the delegation of *Banū Tamīm.*

✦ **Main Theme:** Cultivating within the believers the correct manners of speaking to achieve the ideal level of faith and strengthen the bond of faith. This theme was revealed at a time of utmost importance, as many new peoples of different persuasions and characteristics entered Islam in the year of the delegations.

Main Objectives of the Sūrah:

- Educating and guiding the believers to honor Allah's command and the command of His Messenger (ﷺ) as a requirement of faith and teaching them the proper etiquette in dealing with and addressing the Prophet (ﷺ).
- Purifying the Muslim community from vile morals leads to division and hatred, such as mockery, name-calling, suspicion, spying, and backbiting.
- He explained the wisdom behind creating people as diverse nations and tribes and stated that superiority with Allah is through righteousness.
- It highlights the greatness of faith, showing it is not merely a claim made by a person but something that settles in the heart, affirmed by words, actions, and striving for the cause of Allah.

BRIEF SŪRAH SUMMARY

Verses 1-5	Good conduct with Allah and His Messenger (ﷺ)
Verses 6-13	Good dealings between the Muslims.
Verses 14-18	An encouragement for new Muslims to work toward the mandatory level of faith that guarantees success in both worlds.

سُورَةُ قٓ

QĀF (50)

The Letter Qaf

VERSES
50

WORDS
357

LETTERS
1,494

REVEALED IN
MAKKAH

REVEALATION ORDER
34

It is said to be around the 34th Sūrah revealed after *Sūrah al Mursalāt* and most of the shorter chapters in *Juz' Amma.*

Main Theme: Admonishing the hearts with the spectacles of death and judgment in the hereafter *(see the last verse).* Named Qaf for its opening with this letter from the disconnected letters at the beginnings of the Sūrahs, indicative of the Qur'ān's inimitability.

Objectives of the Sūrah:

- Mentioning the stance of those who deny the message and resurrection, and the reason for their denial, and arguing the affirmation of resurrection with tangible evidence such as the creation of the heavens and the earth and everything on it, reviving the earth after its death with rain from the sky, and the sprouting of trees and fruits.
- Demonstrating Allah's encompassing knowledge of the hidden aspects of things and thoughts of souls, and that every individual is under Allah's watchfulness from birth until death.
- Reminding the disbelievers of the nations before them who were destroyed for being mightier than them, alerting them to Allah's power to create magnificent creations effortlessly, and consoling the Prophet (صَلَّىٰ ٱللَّٰهُ عَلَيْهِ وَسَلَّمَ) for their denial of him.

BRIEF SŪRAH SUMMARY

Verses 1-5	Those who disbelieve in the Hereafter and Judgment Day.
Verses 6-11	Evidences from the universe to substantiate belief in the Hereafter.
Verses 12-14	The final abode of those who disbelieve in Allah, the Messenger (صَلَّىٰ ٱللَّٰهُ عَلَيْهِ وَسَلَّمَ) and the Hereafter.
Verses 15-25	Some frightening events of Judgment Day.
Verses 26-45	A final admonition about the fates of the past nations and that which awaits all who disbelieve.

سُورَةُ الذَّارِيَاتِ
AL-DHĀRIYĀT (51)
The Wind that Scatters

VERSES
60

WORDS
360

LETTERS
1,236

REVEALED IN
MAKKAH

REVEALATION ORDER
67

It is said to be the 66th *Sūrah* revealed before *Sūrah al Ghāshiyah.*

✦ **Main Themes:** This Surah acquaints people with the truth that the Sustaining Provider is the only one who deserves to be fled to and worshipped (see verses 22, 50, 56-58). It is centered around the three main subjects of the Qur'ān. It is Named Adh-Dhariyat for its uniqueness and opening with the oath by the scattering winds, which scatter dust and other things.

The opening of the *Sūrah* cites various things subjected to our service (the winds, clouds, ships, angels). It mentions the story of Ibrāhīm's hospitality towards the angels, which sets an example of generosity to others and gratitude to the Giver of Sustenance. It also mentions the tales of the destroyed nations as a threat to the disbelievers of imminent punishment.

Objectives of the Sūrah:

- Affirming the occurrence of resurrection and recompense, refuting the claims of the deniers of it and the prophethood of Muhammad (صَلَّى ٱللَّهُ عَلَيْهِ وَسَلَّمَ), highlighting their confusion regarding the afterlife, and threatening the deniers with punishment on the Day of Judgment, contrasting it with the promise of bliss for the believers, and mentioning some of their qualities.
- Stating the fate of tyrannical nations that denied Allah's messengers, whom Allah destroyed with various types of punishment and destruction, as a warning to the polytheists that they may face the same fate as those deniers and illustrating the similarity between the polytheists of Mecca and the deniers among the previous nations in their accusations against the messengers, and consoling the Prophet (صَلَّى ٱللَّهُ عَلَيْهِ وَسَلَّمَ) by ordering him to turn away from them.
- Arguing the oneness of Allah with observable and tangible evidence of His power (سُبْحَانَهُ وَتَعَالَىٰ) in constructing the heavens and leveling the earth and explaining the wisdom behind creation, which is to devote worship exclusively to Allah (سُبْحَانَهُ وَتَعَالَىٰ).

BRIEF SŪRAH SUMMARY

Verses 1-23	The five things by which Allah swore that the reward and punishment of the next life are true and real. It establishes that the *da'wah* of the Prophet ﷺ is the truth, and any false claims against it are inherently contradictory. Despite this, most will remain deluded until they taste the fire. It mentions the descriptions of the believers and draws attention to the signs of the truth in the world around us and within ourselves. The first 14 verses discuss the day of judgment. Verses 15-23 mention the creational signs of Allah.
Verses 24-46	The destruction of six nations who rejected Allah's Messengers.
Verses 47-60	Emphasis upon the evidences of *Tawḥīd* and the final result of disbelief, as found in the beginning of the Sūrah.

CONTEMPLATE, COMPREHEND, APPLY

Contemplation Insights from Page 507 [Muhammad 1-11]

- Harming the enemy through combat is an optimal means of subjugation.
- Alms, ransom, killing, and enslavement are options in Islam for dealing with the captive disbeliever at the discretion of legal authorities, from which what serves the interest is chosen.
- The immense virtue of martyrdom in the cause of Allah.
- Allah's support for the believers is conditional upon their support for His religion.

Contemplation Insights from Page 508 [Muhammad 12-19]

- The disbeliever's sole concern is to enjoy fleeting pleasures in this world.
- The contrast between the rewards of believers and disbelievers illustrates the vast difference between them, guiding the wise to choose faith and the foolish to choose disbelief.
- Highlighting the bad manners of the hypocrites towards the Messenger of Allah (صَلَّى ٱللَّهُ عَلَيْهِ وَسَلَّمَ).
- Knowledge precedes speech and action.

Contemplation Insights from Page 509 [Muhammad 20-29]

- The obligation of jihad in the cause of Allah distinguishes the hypocrites from the ranks of the believers.
- The importance of contemplating the Book of Allah and the danger of turning away from it.
- Corruption on earth and severing kinship ties are among the reasons for failure and distance from Allah's mercy.

Contemplation Insights from Page 510 [Muhammad 30-38]

- The inner malice and deceit of the hypocrites are apparent on their faces and in their manner of speaking.
- Testing is a divine tradition that distinguishes between believers and hypocrites.
- Allah's support for His believing servants with victory and guidance.
- Allah's kindness to His servants includes not asking them to spend all their wealth on His cause.

Contemplation Insights from Page 511 [Al-Fath 1-9]

- The Treaty of Hudaybiyyah began a great victory opening for Islam and Muslims.
- Tranquility is a result of faith, bringing calmness and steadiness.
- The danger of harboring ill thoughts about Allah, for He deals with people according to their perception of Him.
- The obligation to honor and revere the Messenger of Allah (ﷺ).

Contemplation Insights from Page 512 [Al-Fath 10-15]

- The Pledge of Ridwan has great status in Allah's sight, and its participants are among the best people on earth.
- Harboring ill thoughts about Allah can lead to sin and potentially disbelief.
- The weak in faith are few in times of fear and many in times of greed.

Contemplation Insights from Page 513 [Al-Fath 16-23]

- The Qur'ān's foretelling of future events - such as the Islamic conquests - is undeniable proof that the Qur'ān is from Allah.
- The rulings of Sharia are based on kindness and ease.
- The reward for the people of the Pledge of Ridwan includes immediate and deferred rewards in the hereafter.
- The triumph of truth and its people over falsehood and its adherents is a divine tradition.

Contemplation Insights from Page 514 [Al-Fath 24-28]

- Preventing people from Allah's way is a crime deserving severe punishment.
- Allah's planning for His servants' affairs surpasses their limited knowledge.
- The warning against replacing the bond of religion with tribal or pre-Islamic loyalties.
- The emergence of Islam is a divine tradition and promise fulfilled.

Contemplation Insights from Page 515 [Al-Fath 29]

- Mercy is prescribed for the believers and harshness for the warring disbelievers.
- Cohesion and cooperation characterize the Prophet's companions.
- Harboring hatred towards the noble companions is feared to lead to disbelief.

Contemplation Insights from Page 515 [Al-Hujurat 1-4]

- Muslims should not place their opinions or *ijtihād* above the Qur'ān and Sunnah, except without a text from the Qur'ān or Sunnah. If one exerts makes *ijtihād* (i.e., reaches an approximate ruling by exercising their best effort), it must be closest to the intent of Allah and His Messenger, aligning with the Sharia. If a text from the Qur'ān or Sunnah becomes apparent after *ijtihād*, one must immediately and without hesitation return to the Qur'ān and Sunnah, abandoning their opinion or *ijtihād*.
- Since the Prophet's death (ﷺ), we should lower our voices when he is mentioned among us or his hadith is mentioned; we must behave respectfully, not laugh, raise our voices, or show disregard or carelessness, as was the guidance of the *Salaf*, or else we fear our deeds will be nullified without us realizing.
- The Prophet (ﷺ) holds a great status; hence, a Muslim must show respect when his name is mentioned, sending blessings upon him, "O you who have believed, do not raise your voices above the voice of the Prophet or be loud to him in speech."
- Intellect is found alongside having good manners.
- It is obligatory to respect the Messenger of Allah (ﷺ), his Sunnah, and his successors (the scholars).

Contemplation Insights from Page 516 [Al-Hujurat 5-11]

- Verifying the accuracy of the news, especially those transmitted by someone unknown or accused of immorality.
- The obligation to reconcile between fighting Muslims and the legitimacy of fighting a group that insists on aggression and refuses peace. Muslims are obliged to cooperate in disciplining any group that transgresses and aggresses until it returns to the truth.
- The necessity of repentance and turning back to Allah.

- The essentiality of Islamic brotherhood and the obligation to realize it in word and deed. The obligation of judging justly in cases among Muslims and others.
- Rights of the brotherhood of faith: Reconciling between disputants and avoiding hurtful behaviors like mockery, defamation, and name-calling.
- The love of faith and righteous deeds and the dislike of disbelief, immorality, and disobedience are favors Allah grants to whom He wills among His servants, so supplicate for that.

Contemplation Insights from Page 517 [Al-Hujurat 12-18]

- The obligation to avoid all suspicion without strong evidence or circumstance to justify it. Harboring ill-suspicion of good people is a sin, while exercising caution towards malicious individuals through suspicion is permissible.
- The prohibition of spying, i.e., seeking out the faults of Muslims and exposing them to others.
- The prohibition of backbiting and slander. Slander is relating the injurious speech of some to those about whom it was said to ruin and worsen what is between them. It's permissible to mention someone in their absence in cases like seeking redress by mentioning the wrong done to remove an injustice, seeking help from others in changing a wrong by mentioning the transgressor, asking for a religious verdict like saying someone wronged me, warning Muslims of evil by mentioning its doer so they may beware. Also, public display of sin removes the prohibition of backbiting and identifying someone by a nickname that contains something unpleasant known only by it.
- The unity of human origin necessitates the rejection of boasting about lineages. The prohibition of boasting about lineages and the obligation of getting to know each other for cooperation. The diversity of nations and tribes is for mutual acquaintance and love, not for spreading division and differences and stirring up rivalries. It is ignorance and mindlessness to think that superiority among people is based on anything other than righteousness. There is no nobility or honor except through the nobility and honor of piety.
- Faith is not merely a verbal declaration without belief; it is belief in the heart, affirmation by the tongue, and action by the limbs.
- If Allah has favored you with the opportunity to do good, praise Allah for the blessing and do not boast about it; He can deprive you.
- Divine guidance and success are in Allah's hands alone and are a grace from Him, not a right to which anyone is entitled.

Contemplation Insights from Page 518 [Qaf 1-15]

- The polytheists deem prophecy too significant for humans and attribute divinity to stones!
- The creation of the heavens and the earth, the descent of rain, the revival of the arid earth, and the first creation are all proofs of resurrection.

- Denying the messengers is a tradition of previous nations, and the punishment of the deniers is a divine tradition.

Contemplation Insights from Page 519 [Qaf 16-35]

- Allah's knowledge of what occurs in the souls of good and evil.
- The danger of neglecting the Hereafter.
- The attribute of justice is affirmed for Allah (عَزَّوَجَلَّ).

Contemplation Insights from Page 520 [Qaf 36-45 & Adh-Dhariyat 1-6]

- Taking lessons from historical events is of concern to those with conscious hearts.
- Allah created the universe in six days for reasons He knew, possibly including demonstrating the principle of progression.
- The Jews' poor manners in claiming Allah grew tired after creating the heavens and the earth in disbelief in Allah.

Contemplation Insights from Page 521 [Al-Dhāriyyāt 7-30]

- Good deeds and sincerity towards Allah lead to entering Paradise.
- The virtue of night prayer is that it is among the best acts of devotion.
- Among the etiquettes of hosting: returning greetings more beautifully, preparing the meal secretly, getting ready for guests before they arrive, not excluding anything from the meal, overseeing its preparation, hastening it, presenting it to the guests, and addressing them gently.

Contemplation Insights from Page 522 [Al-Dhāriyyāt 31-51]

- Faith is a higher degree than Islam.
- Allah's destruction of the denying nations serves as a lesson for all people.
- Fearing Allah entails rushing towards Him with good deeds, not running away from Him.

Contemplation Insights from Page 523 [Al-Dhāriyyāt 52-60]

- Disbelief is one nation even if its means and the diversity of its people, places, and times differ.
- Allah's testimony to His Messenger Muhammad (صَلَّىٱللَّهُعَلَيْهِوَسَلَّمَ) for delivering the message.
- The wisdom behind creating jinn and humans is to realize the worship of Allah in all its forms.

CONTEMPLATION STUDY QUESTIONS

Sūrah Muhammad Questions

Verse 4: What is the trial that is based on the polytheists' victory over Muslims in some situations? *[Al-Sa'dī]*

Verse 11: If the disbelievers' protectors are the tyrants, what is meant by them having no protector? *[Al-Sa'dī]*

Verse 19: What are the prerequisites of seeking forgiveness for believing men and women? *[Al-Sa'dī]*

Verse 25: What causes some of those affiliated with Islam to revert to disbelief? *[Al-Sa'dī]*

Verse 30: Why didn't Allah (عَزَّوَجَلَّ) reveal to the Muslims all the hypocrites? *[Ibn Kathīr]*

Verse 35: What results from Allah being with the Muslims? The verse clarifies the Muslims' stance towards their enemy when they are strong, so what is their stance when they are weak? *[Ibn Kathīr]*

Sūrah Al-Fath Questions

Verses 1-2: Why did Allah link victory to forgiving the Prophet's past and future sins? *[Al-Sa'dī]*

Verse 15: What is the real reason for depriving the hypocrites of the spoils of Khaybar? *[Al-Sa'dī]*

Verse 29: Why mention their prayer after mentioning their harshness towards the disbelievers and their mercy towards the believers? *[Al-Sa'dī]*

Sūrah Al-Hujurat Questions

Verse 1: What is the ruling on following the words of others besides the Prophet (صَلَّى ٱللَّهُ عَلَيْهِ وَسَلَّمَ) when the statement of the Prophet is clear and apparent? *[Al-Sa'dī]*

Verse 4: What is the relationship between etiquette and intellect through this verse? *[Al-Sa'dī]*

Verse 15: Why did Allah combine faith and jihad for the true believer in this verse?

Sūrah Qaf Questions

Verse 1: The Qur'ān is glorious; what warrants this description? *[Al-Sa'dī]*

Verse 6: Why did Allah describe the sky as above them, despite everyone knowing it is above them? *[Al-Sa'dī]*

Verse 16: What is the wisdom behind specifically mentioning the jugular vein? And what do we benefit from that? *[Al-Sa'dī]*

Verse 33: Why is the mention of fear in the unseen specified? *[Al-Sa'dī]*

Verse 37: What does someone who does not listen to the Qur'ān with his heart and does not pay attention benefit from it? *[Al-Sa'dī]*

Verses 39-40: What is the wisdom behind the command to glorify Allah after the command to be patient? *[Al-Sa'dī]*

Verse 45: What specifically is the duty of a preacher? *[Al-Sa'dī]*

Sūrah Adh-Dhariyat Questions

Verse 16: What is the sign of the righteous in this world? *[Al-Sa'dī]*

Verse 50: Why is returning to Allah described as fleeing? *[Al-Sa'dī]*

Verse 57: What is the relevance of mentioning the attribute of strength after the attribute of provision? *[Al-Sa'dī]*

Day 26: Al-Tūr - al Hadīd

The Qurā'n reading for **day 26** is from *Sūrah al-Ṭūr* to *Sūrah al Ḥadīd*. These chapters were revealed at various stages of the Makkan phase before the *Hijrah.*

سُورَةُ الطُّورِ

AL-ṬŪR (52)

The Mount

VERSES
49

WORDS
312

LETTERS
1,500

REVEALED IN
MAKKAH

REVEALATION ORDER
76

Main Theme: Presenting proofs and arguments to refute the disbelievers' doubts drives them toward voluntary submission. It is Named At-Tur for its opening with the oath by the mount, the mountain where Allah spoke to Mūsā.

This surah discusses the resurrection and its details and subsequently describes the state of disbelievers and believers on the Day of Judgment. It extensively talks about Paradise and the eternal bliss reserved for the righteous. Then, it addresses the polytheists, debating their corrupt beliefs. The surah concludes with advice to the Prophet (ﷺ) and the believers following his call. The surah begins with an oath affirming the certainty of Allah's punishment. It concludes by reiterating the certainty of Allah's punishment for the wrongdoers. This emphasis on warning, threat, and promise of retribution significantly impacts the human psyche.

Objectives of the Sūrah:

- Threatening with the actualization of punishment on the Day of Judgment, through the swearing by a number of His creations on that, depicts the state of the criminals when they are driven to Hell and what they will face of punishment, contrasting that with the description of the state of the people of bliss and what they will encounter from various honors prepared by Allah for the believers.
- Consoling the Prophet (ﷺ) by nullifying the polytheists' claims against him, their accusation of fabricating the Qur'ān, challenging them to produce something like it, and responding to a series of their lies, such as denying the recreation, the belief in multiple gods, and their mockery of the warning.

BRIEF SUMMARY OF SŪRAH

Verses 1-14	Allah swears by five of His tremendous creations that His punishment will arrive and is unstoppable.
Verses 15-28	The final favorable outcome for the righteous believers; the detailed description of the blisses of Paradise.
Verses 29-34	Response to false claims about the Prophet (صَلَّى ٱللَّهُ عَلَيْهِ وَسَلَّمَ).
Verses 35-43	Response to the false claims with fifteen challenge questions for the disbelievers.
Verses 44-49	Final admonition for the disbelievers and advice for the Prophet (صَلَّى ٱللَّهُ عَلَيْهِ وَسَلَّمَ).

سُورَةُ النَّجْمِ

AL-NAJM (53)

The Stars

VERSES
62

WORDS
360

LETTERS
1,405

REVEALED IN
MAKKAH

REVEALATION ORDER
23

Main Theme: Demonstrating the truth of the revelation to establish the foundation of *Tawḥīd* and weaken paganism's influence.

It praises knowledge and what knowledge yields in guidance and concern for the hereafter while dispraising speculative and unfounded approaches to religion—establishing that such approaches result in misguidance, blindness, and clinging greedily to the world.

Named "An-Najm" because it begins with an oath by the star. The star is mentioned in various contexts throughout the Qur'ān, not only in oaths.

Objectives of the Sūrah:

- It affirms the truthfulness of the Prophet's (صَلَّى ٱللَّهُ عَلَيْهِ وَسَلَّمَ) message and clears him of the accusations made by the polytheists. It emphasizes that the Qur'ān is a revelation from Allah, delivered through Gabriel, and references the event of Isra and Mi'raj, detailing what the Prophet (صَلَّى ٱللَّهُ عَلَيْهِ وَسَلَّمَ) saw.
- To refute the polytheists' claims of divinity for their idols, their assertion that angels are Allah's daughters, and their myths about idols' intercession.
- Asserting that knowledge of the unseen belongs only to Allah, dismissing the polytheists' analogy of the unseen world to the observable world, indicating that all creation's fate rests with Allah, who manages all their affairs, affirming resurrection and just recompense, warning them by drawing attention to the fate of nations that denied their messengers, and hinting at the nearness of the Day of Judgment and its significance.

BRIEF SŪRAH SUMMARY

Verses 1-18	The message and Prophethood; some details of the *Mi'rāj*; the truthfulness of the Messenger ﷺ and his exoneration from the false claims of the disbelievers.
Verses 19-28	A refutation of polytheism and the polytheists' delusions.
Verses 29-32	Advice for those who invite to Allah; a reminder of Allah's forgiveness and an advice about seeking forgiveness.
Verses 33-49	The effects of Allah's power and the evidence for His Oneness.
Verses 50-62	The punishments that befell the previous nations. The *Sūrah* concludes with a *Sajdah* after instilling veneration in the heart of the listener to such an extent that the polytheists prostrated when the Prophet ﷺ recited it at the *Haram* in the Makkan phase *(see Bukhārī 1070 and Muslim 576).*

سُورَةُ القَمَر

AL QAMAR (54)
The Moon

VERSES
55

WORDS
342

LETTERS
1,423

REVEALED IN
MAKKAH

REVEALATION ORDER
37

The miracle of the splitting of the moon is said to have occurred in between the year of sorrow (i.e., the deaths of Abū Ṭālib and Khadījah) and the night journey.

✦ **Main Theme:** The verse repeats throughout, reminding us of the blessing of the Qur'ān's simplicity and its clear proofs and warnings.

Named "Al-Qamar" for the incident of the moon's splitting, a miracle with which Allah supported Prophet ﷺ.

Objectives of the Sūrah:

- To warn of the Day of Judgment's approach and the hardships people will face upon resurrection, emerging from their graves like scattered locusts.
- To urge the polytheists to reflect on the scenes of punishment and torment that befell the tyrants of the past for denying Allah's messengers, warning them that they will face the same fate, and cautioning them about the greater horrors of the Day of Judgment and its terrors.

BRIEF SŪRAH SUMMARY

Verses 1-5	The message and Prophethood; some details of the *Mi'rāj*; the truthfulness of the Messenger ﷺ and his exoneration from the false claims of the disbelievers.
Verses 6-8 and 16-55	The hereafter and being resurrected for Judgment.
Verses 9-42	The destruction of five disbelieving nations.
Verses 43-55	A threat to those who come after them that they would not be spared from similar punishment as what befell the disbelieving tyrants; a concluding encouraging passage mentioning the imminent reward of the righteous believers.

سُورَةُ الرَّحۡمَٰن
AL-RAḤMAN (55)
The Most Gracious

VERSES
78

WORDS
351

LETTERS
1,636

REVEALED IN
MADINAH

REVEALATION ORDER
97

It is said to be approximately the 43rd in the order of revelation (between *Sūrah al Furqān* and *Sūrah Fāṭir*).

Main Theme: A reminder of Allah's amazing favors and the clear effects of His mercy in this world and the next; it mentions the beautiful ayāt of Allah in this world and the beauty of Paradise to encourage belief and warn against disbelief, which is caused by ingratitude.

Named "Al-Raḥmān" for beginning with this Beautiful Name of Allah, the surah reminds us of Allah's numerous blessings, all of which are manifestations of His mercy bestowed upon His servants, reminding them of the duty of gratitude.

Objectives of the Sūrah:

- Mentioning a series of Allah's blessings and magnificent signs, apparent in His beautiful creation and management of existence, all results of Allah's mercy poured upon His servants, reminding them of the duty to be grateful.
- Threatening both jinn and humans, it prepares them for the horrors of the Day of Judgment and its account, mentioning the punishment of the wretched and the bliss of the fortunate.

BRIEF SŪRAH SUMMARY

Verses 1-25	Reflecting upon what Allah has created and his blessing of creating mankind equipped for knowledge and establishing justice.
Verses 26-45	Death, the end of this world and judgment in the hereafter.
Verses 46-61	The two gardens of Paradise for those nearest and dearest to Allah.
Verses 61-78	The two gardens of Paradise for most of the remaining people of faith.

سُورَةُ الوَاقِعَةِ

AL WĀQI'AH (56)

The Event

VERSES
96

WORDS
378

LETTERS
1,703

REVEALED IN
MAKKAH

REVEALATION ORDER
46

Main Theme: It establishes belief in Judgment Day and describes the different types of people on that day. It is called *al Wāqi'ah* because it will happen for certainty, and nothing can stop it. It ends with the fact that it is a certain truth (*verses 95-96).* Everything in between is evidence for that inevitable day. It is one of the Sūrahs that caused the Prophet (ﷺ) to have gray hairs. (See the authentic hadīth and explanation of al Qurṭubī in the summary of Sūrah Hūd.) Named "Al-Waqi'ah" because it opens with the event: the Day of Resurrection, with the surah filled with the description of that day's events and severe terrors.

Objectives of the Sūrah:

- It reminds us of the Day of Resurrection and affirms its occurrence. It describes the transformations this earthly realm will undergo at the moment of resurrection, mentioning the condition of the people of Paradise, their bliss, and the punishment of Hell.
- Affirming resurrection and recompense, arguing for Allah's power to recreate creation, as demonstrated through His initial creation of existences from nothing.
- Emphasizing that the Qur'ān is a revelation from Allah, a blessing bestowed upon people.

BRIEF SŪRAH SUMMARY

Verses 1-56	The next life: the day of Judgment; the three types of people in the Hereafter; detailed description of the reward of the first two types and the punishment of the third.
Verses 57-96	How what we have in this life serves as evidence for the Hereafter and Divine Judgment; what will happen at the moment of death.

سُورَةُ الحَدِيدِ
AL ḤADĪD (57)
The Iron

VERSES
28

WORDS
544

LETTERS
2,476

REVEALED IN
MAKKAH*

REVEALATION ORDER
94

There is a known difference over whether it was revealed in Makkah or Madīnah. What appears to be most correct is that it was revealed in the middle of the Makkan phase. From the evidence for this is the statement of Ibn Mas'ūd (رَضِيَ اللَّهُ عَنْهُ):[19] "Only four years passed between our Islām and the revelation of this verse: '*Has not the time come for those who believe that their hearts should be humbled by the remembrance of Allah...*" *(Verse 16)*

✦ **Main Themes:** Uplifting the soul to believe, to spend in Allah's path, and to aid the religion, freeing the soul from all barriers to this objective. *Imān* and its derivatives are mentioned 14 times therein. Spending is also mentioned throughout. The *Sūrah* is named after iron, the greatest fighting tool. *(See verse 25).* Named "Al-Hadid" for mentioning iron within its context, highlighting its strong nature and the numerous benefits it provides to people.

Objectives of the Sūrah:

- Reminding of the majesty of Allah (عَزَّوَجَلَّ) and His grand attributes, the vastness of His power and dominion, His comprehensive management, extensive knowledge, commanding belief in Allah and what His Messenger (صَلَّى ٱللَّهُ عَلَيْهِ وَسَلَّمَ) brought forth, and urging spending in the way of Allah.
- It mentions what is prepared for believing men and women on the Day of Judgment of Good and the punishment for hypocritical men and women.
- It reminds us of resurrection, explains the reality of the afterlife, calls for asceticism in the transient, fleeting life, commands patience in adversity, and highlights the wisdom behind sending messengers and revealing scriptures.
- Illustrating the similarity between the message of Muhammad (صَلَّى ٱللَّهُ عَلَيْهِ وَسَلَّمَ) and those of Noah and Ibrāhīm (عَلَيْهِمَا السَّلَامُ) and the prophets who followed them, including 'Īsā, as they were all sent with the law of Islam. Among these nations, some were guided, while others were defiant and disobedient. Similarly, among the Prophet's (صَلَّى ٱللَّهُ عَلَيْهِ وَسَلَّمَ) nation, there are believers and

19 [Ṣaḥīḥ Muslim 3027].

disbelievers, calling people to fear Allah, believe in His Messenger, and what Allah has prepared for them as compensation for that.

BRIEF SŪRAH SUMMARY

Verses 1-6	Allah's greatness: Twenty two evidences from Allah's names, attributes and tremendous creation are mentioned in these initial verses.
Verses 7-19	Believe and spend; spending is an evidence of faith.
Verses 20-24	The reality of this worldly life; the exhortation to race to Paradise.
Verses 25-28	The message, the Prophethood and the physical means to establish it.

CONTEMPLATE, COMPREHEND, APPLY

Contemplation Insights from Page 523 [At-Tur 1-14]

- The state of the universe will change on the Day of Judgment.

Contemplation Insights from Page 524 [At-Tur 15-31]

- Gathering parents and children in Paradise at the same rank, even if some of their deeds fall short, is an honor to them all to complete joy.
- The wine of the Hereafter does not lead to any harm.
- Those who fear their Lord in this world will be in comfort in the Hereafter.

Contemplation Insights from Page 525 [At-Tur 32-49]

- Tyranny is a cause of misguidance.
- The importance of logical argumentation in proving religious truths.
- The existence of punishment in the Barzakh (the interval between death and the Day of Resurrection).

Contemplation Insights from Page 526 [An-Najm 1-26]

- The perfection of the Prophet's (صَلَّى ٱللَّهُ عَلَيْهِ وَسَلَّمَ) manners, as his gaze did not swerve nor transgress beyond the limit while he was in the seventh heaven.

- The foolishness of the polytheists for worshiping something that neither harms nor benefits, attributing to Allah what they dislike and choosing for themselves what they love.
- Intercession will not occur except with two conditions: permission for the intercessor and approval of the one being interceded for.

Contemplation Insights from Page 527 [An-Najm 27-44]

- The division of sins into major and minor.
- The danger of attributing statements to Allah without knowledge.
- The prohibition of self-purification.

Contemplation Insights from Page 528 [An-Najm 45-62 & Al-Qamar 1-6]

- Not being affected by the Qur'ān is a bad omen.
- The danger of following desires on oneself in this world and the Hereafter.
- Not taking lessons from the destruction of nations is a characteristic of disbelievers.

Contemplation Insights from Page 529 [Al-Qamar 7-27]

- The legitimacy of praying against a disbeliever who insists on disbelief.
- The destruction of the deniers and the salvation of the believers is a divine tradition.
- The Qur'ān was made easy to memorize, reflect upon, and heed.

Contemplation Insights from Page 530 [Al-Qamar 28-49]

- The encompassing punishment includes the direct perpetrator of a crime and those who consent to it.
- Thanking Allah for His blessings is a reason for safety from punishment.
- The Qur'ān's foretelling of the disbelievers' defeat on the day of Badr before it occurred is a form of informing about the unseen, proving the Qur'ān's truthfulness.
- The necessity of belief in destiny.

Contemplation Insights from Page 531 [Al-Qamar 50-55 & Al-Raḥmān 1-16]

- The recording of deeds, both small and large, in the scrolls of deeds.
- The commencement of Al-Raḥmān with the mention of its blessings starting with the Qur'ān signifies the Qur'ān's nobility and the greatness of Allah's favor upon creation with it.
- The significance of justice in Islam.
- Allah's blessings require our recognition and gratitude, not denial and ingratitude.

Contemplation Insights from Page 532 [Al-Raḥmān 17-40]

- The merging of the salty and fresh seas without mixing is a manifestation of Allah's power.
- All creations are destined to perish, and only Allah remains eternal, encouraging servitude solely to Him.
- Affirming the attribute of the Face of Allah in a manner befitting His majesty without likening Him to His creation.
- The variation in the punishment of disbelievers.

Contemplation Insights from Page 533 [Al-Raḥmān 41-67]

- The importance of fearing Allah and the dread of standing before Him.
- Praising the women of Paradise for their chastity highlights the virtue of this trait.
- The principle is that deeds are rewarded in kind.

Contemplation Insights from Page 534 [Al-Raḥmān 68-78 & Al-Waqi'ah 1-16]

- Constantly remembering Allah's blessings and signs obligates magnifying Allah and obeying Him properly.
- The disbelief of disbelievers ceases upon witnessing the events of the Day of Judgment.
- The degrees of Paradise's inhabitants vary according to their deeds.

Contemplation Insights from Page 535 [Al-Waqi'ah 17-50]

- Righteous deeds are the cause of attaining bliss in the Hereafter.
- Luxury and indulgence are reasons for falling into sins.
- The danger of persisting in sin.

Contemplation Insights from Page 536 [Al-Waqi'ah 51-76]

- The first creation indicates the ease of resurrection.
- The descent of rain, the growth of the earth, and the fire that benefits people are blessings that require gratitude towards Allah, for He can withdraw them at any time.
- Believing that stars influence rain is disbelief, a practice of ignorance.

Contemplation Insights from Page 537 [Al-Waqi'ah 77-96 & Al-Hadid 1-3]

- The agonies of death are intense, and humans are incapable of repelling them.
- Humans typically do not see angels unless Allah wills for divine wisdom.

- Allah's names (The First, The Last, The Loftiest, The Near) necessitate glorifying Allah and being mindful of Him in visible and hidden deeds.

Contemplation Insights from Page 538 [Al-Hadid 4-11]

- Wealth belongs to Allah, and humans are merely trustees over it.
- The degrees of believers vary according to their precedence in faith and righteous deeds.
- Spending in the way of Allah is a cause for the blessing and growth of wealth.

Contemplation Insights from Page 539 [Al-Hadid 12-18]

- Allah's favor upon the believers by giving them a light that runs before them and by their right hands.
- Sins and hypocrisy lead to darkness and destruction on the Day of Judgment.
- Waiting to betray the believers, doubting the resurrection, being deluded by vain desires, and being deceived by Satan are traits of the hypocrites.
- The danger of heedlessness leads to the hardening of hearts.

Contemplation Insights from Page 540 [Al-Hadid 19-24]

- Asceticism in this worldly life and its fleeting pleasures and encouragement towards the everlasting bliss of the hereafter assist in adhering to the straight path.
- The necessity of believing in divine decree.
- One of the benefits of believing in divine decree is not grieving over lost worldly fortunes.
- Stinginess and commanding stinginess are reprehensible traits not befitting a believer.

Contemplation Insights from Page 541 [Al-Hadid 25-29]

- The truth requires strength to protect and spread it.
- The importance of justice in divine laws.
- Kinship with people of faith and righteousness benefits an individual only if they are believers.
- The prohibition of innovating in religion.

CONTEMPLATION STUDY QUESTIONS

Sūrah At-Tur Questions

Verse 16: Why is the outcome of the righteous mentioned after the outcome of the deniers? *[Al-Sa'dī]*

Verse 20: In describing the couches as "lined up," it signifies matters, explain them. *[Al-Sa'dī]*

Verse 26: When is fear of Allah and the Hereafter beneficial for a person? *[Al-Sa'dī]*

Verse 46: What is the difference between the plotting of the disbelievers in this world and their plotting in the Hereafter? *[Al-Sa'dī]*

Sūrah An-Najm Questions

Verses 1-2: What is the relevance between the stars and the prophethood of the Prophet (صَلَّى ٱللَّهُ عَلَيْهِ وَسَلَّمَ)? *[Al-Sa'dī]*

Verses 3-4: Explain how this verse clarified the status of the Sunnah. *[Al-Sa'dī]*

Verse 27: What emboldened the polytheists to oppose Allah and His Messenger and to speak falsely about the angels? *[Al-Sa'dī]*

Verses 29-30: How does this verse indicate the virtue of Sharia knowledge? *[Al-Sa'dī]*

Verse 62: How do you understand from this verse the status of prostration among acts of worship? *[Al-Sa'dī]*

Sūrah Al-Qamar Questions

Verse 8: What do we learn from the news that that day will be difficult for the disbelievers? *[Al-Sa'dī]*

Verse 10: This verse hints at the importance of supplication in calling to Allah (عَزَّوَجَلَّ). Explain that *[Ibn Kathīr]*

Verse 47: Illustrate two forms of the criminals' misguidance in this world. *[Al-Sa'dī]*

Verse 48: In Allah's punishment of the criminals in this manner, there is physical and psychological pain; explain that through your understanding of the verse. *[Al-Sa'dī]*

Verse 51: Why did Allah narrate to us the stories of the destruction of previous nations? *[Al-Sa'dī]*

Sūrah Al-Raḥmān Questions

Verse 14: The verses indicate the greatness of man and his favor over the jinn; what is the reason for that? *[Al-Sa'dī]*

Verses 35-36: How is mentioning Hell a blessing for the believers? *[Al-Sa'dī]*

Verses 43-45: Allah mentioned the punishment of the criminals in Hell, then showed favor upon them by saying: "So which of the favors of your Lord would you deny?" How does He show favor upon His servants by punishing the criminals? *[Ibn Kathīr]*

Verse 54: What does the beauty of the couches' linings indicate? *[Al-Sa'dī]*

Verse 60: What is the significance of Allah's statement in the first two gardens: "Is there any reward for good other than good?" and why is it not mentioned in the latter two? *[Al-Sa'dī]*

Sūrah Al-Waqi'ah Questions

Verse 10: Why are these the foremost in the Hereafter? *[Ibn Kathīr]*

Verses 13-14: These verses indicate the favor of the earlier generations over others and clarify the basis for this indication. *[Al-Sa'dī]*

Verse 16: This verse indicates the purity of hearts of the people of Paradise and the removal of resentment and malice from their hearts; explain that. *[Al-Sa'dī]*

Verses 43-44: What is meant by denying cold and hospitality from the shade of the fire? *[Al-Sa'dī]*

Verse 80: Why did Allah describe Himself as the Lord of the worlds after mentioning the revelation of the Noble Qur'ān? *[Al-Sa'dī]*

Sūrah Al-Hadid Questions

Verse 4: What type of companionship is mentioned in this verse? *[Al-Sa'dī]*

Verse 10: What is the wisdom behind mentioning Allah's statement: "And to Allah belongs the inheritance of the heavens and the earth," after commanding to spend? *[Ibn Kathīr]*

Verse 20: If you knew the state of this world, what would your stance towards it be? If you knew that the Hereafter is either punishment or forgiveness, how should your stance towards this world be? *[Al-Sa'dī]*

Verse 25: Why was the mention of sending down the scriptures placed before sending down iron? *[Ibn Kathīr]*

Verse 27: When were the Christians softer-hearted towards the believers? *[Al-Sa'dī]*

Day 27: Mujādilah - Tahrīm

The Qurā'n reading for **day 27** is *Sūrah al Mujādilah* to *Sūrah al-Taḥrīm*. These chapters were revealed at different stages of the Madīnah phase, mostly between the years 4-8 (except for *Sūrah al-Taghābun*, which was most likely revealed in Makkah).

سُورَةُ المُجَادِلَة

AL-MUJĀDILAH (58)

The Pleading Woman

VERSES
21

WORDS
473

LETTERS
1,792

REVEALED IN
MADINAH

REVEALATION ORDER
105

It is approximately 103rd in its order of revelation (after *Sūrah al Munāfiqūn* and before *Sūrah al-Taḥrīm* and *Sūrah al Ḥujurāt*). **Main Theme:** a manifestation of Allah's Omniscience, teaching the creation to respect Him and be mindful of His watchfulness so that they are warned from opposing Him.

This Sūrah explains the Islamic ruling on nullifying zihar and its expiation, as one of the laws that Allah refuted and condemned from the practices of the Age of Ignorance. It mentions the delusions of the hypocrites, such as their private consultations, inappropriate greetings to the Prophet (صَلَّى ٱللَّهُ عَلَيْهِ وَسَلَّمَ), alliances with the Jews, and oaths to falsehood. It forbids the believers from adopting their manners, teaching them the etiquette of assembly and interaction with the Prophet (صَلَّى ٱللَّهُ عَلَيْهِ وَسَلَّمَ), and explaining the reality of love and hatred for the sake of Allah, which is the strongest bond of faith, completed by opposing Allah's enemies. This quality belongs to those whose faith Allah has settled firmly in their hearts and whom He has supported with His aid, and they are the successful ones.

Verses 1-6	The ruling of the practice from the pre-Islamic times known as *al-Ẓihār*
Verses 7-8	Some of the plotting of the disbelievers in Madīnah.
Verses 9-13	A number of instructions for the believers to be distinct from the disbelievers as relates to the purposes, etiquettes and rulings of private and public gatherings and conversations.
Verses 14-21	The reality of loving for Allah's sake and disavowal for Allah's sake.

سُورَةُ الحَشْر
AL ḤASHR (59)
The Gathering

VERSES
13

WORDS
348

LETTERS
1,510

REVEALED IN
MADINAH

REVEALATION ORDER
101

It was revealed right after *Banū Naḍīr* was expelled from their lands after conspiring to kill the Prophet (ﷺ) in the year four after *Hijrah.*

Main Themes: The expulsion of *Banū Naḍīr.* Allah's strength and might in aiding the believers and weakening the disbelievers and hypocrites while exhibiting their humiliation and splitting; concurrently, Allah demonstrates the connectedness of the believers. This is to strengthen the believers' hearts and weaken the morale of the disbelievers and hypocrites. The *Sūrah* is concluded with His names to excite them to venerate Allah (which is the cause of their brotherhood and unity). **Objectives include:**

Illustrating Allah's power and majesty, His support for the Prophet (ﷺ) by the exile of the Banu Nadir despite their strongholds, detailing the laws concerning the spoils of war, glorifying the status of the Prophet's companions, highlighting the virtues of the Migrants and the Helpers, mentioning some hypocrites' traits, revealing their ill intentions, drawing parallels between the hypocrites' deception of the Jews with their false promises of support, and Satan's deception of the disbelievers, resulting in their eternal damnation.

It advises believers to be mindful of God, reminds them of the Day of Judgment, contrasts the dwellers of Paradise with those of Hell, emphasizes the Qur'ān's greatness, and concludes with mentioning some of Allah's Beautiful Names, indicating His majesty, perfection, and transcendence.

Verses 1-5	The banishing of *Banū Naḍīr.*
Verses 6-7	Distribution of *al Fay* (property left by the enemy).
Verses 8-10	The selflessness and goodwill of the believers toward each other generationally.
Verses 11-17	A rebuke of the *Munafiqūn* for their affinity with the disbelievers of *Banū Naḍīr* despite their treachery.
Verses 18-20	A powerful admonition for the believers to fear Allah and not be like those who forgot Allah.
Verses 21-24	The tremendous effect of the *Qur'ān* and the mention of Allah's beautiful names.

سُورَةُ المُمتَحنَة

AL MUMTAḤANAH (60)

The Woman to be examined

VERSES
13

WORDS
348

LETTERS
1,510

REVEALED IN
MADINAH

REVEALATION ORDER
91

It is estimated to have been revealed in the sixth year after the *Hijrah* (between *Sūrah al Mā'idah* and *Sūrah al-Nisā'*).

Main Theme: Warning the believers against allying with the disbelievers. It contains the command to take Ibrāhīm as our example in freeing ourselves from the disbelievers.

Named "Al-Mumtahina" for mentioning the verse that tests the migrating women from Mecca to Medina.

Objectives include:

It warns believers against befriending enemies, highlights the enemies' exploiting opportunities to cause division among them, and states that kinship ties are irrelevant against religious enmity. It mandates the testing of believing women who migrate, detailing the implications of their successful test, the conditions of their pledge of allegiance, and the requirements of this pledge.

BRIEF SŪRAH SUMMARY

Verses 1-9	Important instructions about loving for Allah and disavowing the disbelievers; the encouragement to take Ibrāhīm as one's example in doing so.
Verses 10-12	Instructions for the Prophet ﷺ and the believers as relates to taking in and accepting the *bay'ah* (pledge of allegiance) from women who accepted Islam and migrated to al Madīnah.
Verse 13	A reiteration of the obligation to disassociate with the disbelievers.

سُورَةُ الصَّفِّ
AL-ṢAFF (61)
The Ranks

VERSES
14

WORDS
221

LETTERS
900

REVEALED IN
MADINAH

REVEALATION ORDER
109

Main Theme: Encouraging believers to support the true religion of Allah. See verses 4 and 14 at its two ends. It is named "As-Saff" because it mentions the term in the context of believers fighting for the cause of Allah as though they were a solidly constructed wall.

Objectives encompass urging towards jihad for Allah's sake, steadfastness therein, promising good rewards and victory for sincere faith and struggle, calling believers to support the religion and to follow the example of the truthful, such as the disciples of 'Īsā when he asked for their support for the sake of Allah, and they responded. It warns against harming the Messenger (ﷺ), consoling the Prophet (ﷺ) by comparing the treatment he received to that of Mūsā and 'Īsā by the Jews, pointing out God's tradition of supporting His religion, prophets, and allies, and illustrating the stance of the religion's enemies by likening their efforts to extinguish God's light to one attempting to blow out the sun with his breath.

BRIEF SŪRAH SUMMARY

Verses 1-9	The subject of aiding Allah's religion: how the nations of Mūsā and 'Isā neglected to aid Allah's religion; the Prophet (ﷺ) was sent with beneficial knowledge and righteous deeds, on account of which his religion is preeminent over all others.
Verses 10-14	Allah's bargain with the believers and glad tidings of victory; the example of the disciples of 'Isā

سُورَةُ الجُمُعَة
AL JUMU'AH (62)
Friday

VERSES
11

WORDS
80

LETTERS
720

REVEALED IN
MADINAH

REVEALATION ORDER
110

✦ **Main Theme:** the blessing of the Prophethood upon this Ummah so that we obey the Prophet (ﷺ) and unite around that obedience; a warning from opposing him and resembling *Ahlul Kitāb* who cast off the responsibility of carrying the trust and opposed the Messengers. From the excellence of this Ummah is the Day of a*l Jumu'ah* and their attachment to it. It is from the exceptional aspects of this nation that unify it (similar to what is mentioned in the *Sūrah* before it).

Objectives of the Sūrah:

- It highlights the role of the Prophet (ﷺ) in rescuing the Arabs from the darkness of polytheism and honoring humanity.
- Discussing the deviation of the Jews from God's law, refuting their claim of being Allah's chosen ones, and likening them to a donkey carrying valuable books but benefiting from none, leading to ultimate misery and wretchedness.
- Mentioning several rulings regarding Friday prayer.

BRIEF SŪRAH SUMMARY

Verses 1-4	The status of the message and the Messenger ﷺ.
Verses 5-8	The failure of the *Yahūd* to benefit from what they knew due to their excessive love of this world.
Verses 9-11	The command to hasten to attend the *khuṭbah* and prayer of *al Jumu'ah*. The warning to those who prefer amusement and trade over what is with Allah of reward.

سُورَةُ المُنَافِقُونَ
AL MUNĀFIQŪN (63)
The Hyprocrites

VERSES
11

WORDS
180

LETTERS
975

REVEALED IN
MADINAH

REVEALATION ORDER
104

It is understood to have been revealed in the year five after the *Hijrah*, after the Battle of Banī Muṣṭaliq, when Abdullah bin Ubayy, the head of the hypocrites, said what is mentioned in verse eight.

Main Theme: The reality of the *Munafiqīn* and their traits and a warning against their schemes.

The *Munafiqūn* are described in detail in (1.) al Baqarah: 8-20; (2.) the second half of Aāli 'Imrān due to their weakening of morale after the Day of Uḥud; (3.) Sūrah al-Nisā' ; (4.) Sūrah al-Tawbah ; (5.) Sūrah al Aḥzāb; and (6.) *Sūrah al Munāfiqūn.*

It is named "Al-Munafiqun" because it discusses the hypocrites, their characteristics, statements, and their stance towards our noble Prophet (صَلَّى ٱللَّهُ عَلَيْهِ وَسَلَّمَ) and the believers.

Objectives of the Sūrah:

- The Surah exposes the disgrace of the hypocrites by mentioning their reprehensible traits, conspiracies against the Prophet (صَلَّى ٱللَّهُ عَلَيْهِ وَسَلَّمَ) and the companions, ugliness of their inner selves, and some of their appalling statements about the Prophet (صَلَّى ٱللَّهُ عَلَيْهِ وَسَلَّمَ).
- Warning the believers against being distracted by worldly allurements from obeying Allah and worship, urging them to spend their money in the way of Allah, seeking His pleasure before it's too late, and regretting when it does not benefit them.

BRIEF SŪRAH SUMMARY

[I.]	The first half mentions them and their evil traits.
[II.]	The second half is a warning against resembling them by being preoccupied with wealth and children from remembering Allah and withholding from spending in His path.

سُورَةُ التَّغَابُنِ
AL-TAGHĀBUN (64)
Mutual Loss & Gain

VERSES
18

WORDS
241

LETTERS
1,070

REVEALED IN
SCHOLARS DIFFER

REVEALATION ORDER
108

Main Themes: a warning against the greatest causes of loss on the Day of Judgment by showing the dreadfulness of disbelief and the great loss of the disbeliever; directing the Muslims to prepare themselves materially and spiritually to avert such loss and to face the people of falsehood by refining bad traits.

Named "At-Taghabun" because it mentions this term, one of the names for the Day of Judgment – when differences among people become apparent, and disbelievers suffer loss by forsaking faith –unique to this Sūrah. **Objectives of the Sūrah:**

- Warning against denying Muhammad's ﷺ message, inviting to learn from the fate of nations that denied their messengers and rejected the signs, resulting in their punishment and ruin due to their disbelief, stubbornness, and misguidance.
- Denouncing the polytheists for their disbelief in the resurrection, threatening them with facing the consequences of their deeds upon resurrection, clarifying that salvation lies in believing in Allah alone, acknowledging His messenger ﷺ, and adhering to the Book he brought.
- Warning the believers against the enmity of some kin lest they deter them from faith, migration, and jihad; advising them on patience towards such kin and regarding their seized wealth; commanding them to spend in virtuous causes; fearing Allah; obeying Him; and warning them against stinginess and miserliness.

Verses 1-6	Allah's perfection and His great purpose for creating; a warning to those who fail to live up to this purpose.
Verses 7-13	Repudiation of those who deny that they will be resurrected for judgment; a reiteration of *Tawḥīd*.
Verses 14-18	Warning the believers against the distractions of their spouses, children and wealth away from remembering Allah; an exhortation to be generous in spending.

سُورَةُ الطَّلَاقِ
AL-ṬALĀQ (65)
The Divorce

VERSES
12

WORDS
249

LETTERS
1,060

REVEALED IN
MADINAH

REVELATION ORDER
96

Ibn Mas'ūd called it "The shorter *Sūrah al-Nisā'*."[20] **Main Themes:** The seriousness of divorce and its boundaries while emphasizing the results of having *Taqwā* and cautioning against transgressing Allah's bounds. It concludes by threatening those who violate Allah's commandments and with a beautiful reminder about Allah's perfect knowledge and power. It is named "At-Talaq" because it details the rulings on divorce, its process, the consequent waiting period ('iddah), provisions, and residency.

Objectives of the Sūrah:

- Clarifying the rulings on divorce, its aftermath concerning the waiting period, types of 'iddah, and related matters of breastfeeding, maintenance, and residency.
- Commanding adherence to Allah's limits, not defying His commands, calling for God-consciousness, warning against crossing His boundaries, exemplifying past nations who rebelled against Allah's command, hence suffering torment and punishment.

BRIEF SŪRAH SUMMARY

Verses 1-3	Divorcing in the proper frame of time in a correct manner. These verses are interspersed with admonitions and promises from Allah to encourage justice and to calm troubled and broken hearts during a divorce.
Verses 4-5	The waiting period *(al 'iddah)*. These two verses conclude with similar promises from Allah that He will ease matters for those who fear Him.
Verses 6-7	Rulings pertaining financial maintenance and providing shelter during the waiting period.
Verses 8-10	The threat of Allah's punishment for those who oppose His laws.
Verse 11	The blessing of Allah sending the Messenger ﷺ and the reward for following him.
Verses 12	Concluding reminder about Allah's perfect knowledge and power.

[20] Bukhārī 4532

سُورَةُ التَّحْرِيم

AL-TAḤRĪM (66)

The Prohibition

VERSES
12

WORDS
247

LETTERS
1,060

REVEALED IN
MADINAH

REVEALATION ORDER
107

It is said to have been revealed in approximately year seven after the *Hijrah.*

Main Themes: raising believing households to venerate Allah's boundaries and prioritize pleasing Him. It mentions the story of the Prophetic household to serve as a foundation for preparing the Muslim family and society.

Named "At-Tahrim" for mentioning the Prophet's (ﷺ) self-imposed prohibition of something Allah made lawful for him, starting with a reproof for such prohibition.

Objectives of the Sūrah:

- Educating the Muslim household, preparing an ideal model for a happy family through prohibiting the disclosure of secrets between spouses, advising wives not to annoy their husbands excessively, urging believers to educate their families and encourage them, and working on their salvation from the Hereafter's punishment.
- This is to alert all servants, especially women, that no one can benefit another in the Hereafter, nor will lineage or rank avail if the individual's deeds are not righteous. An example is a disbeliever married to a believer and vice versa.

BRIEF SŪRAH SUMMARY

Verses 1-5	Advice to the Prophet ﷺ and his wives about an incident between he and his wives.
Verses 6-12	Advice to save oneself and ones family from the fire; an encouragement for all to sincerely repent; two examples of righteous women and two examples of wicked women.

CONTEMPLATE, COMPREHEND, APPLY

Contemplation Insights from Page 542 [Al-Mujadila 1-6]

- Allah's kindness towards the oppressed among His servants is evident in answering their prayers.
- The variety of expiations for "Dhihar" according to one's capability is from Allah's mercy to relieve the servant from hardship.
- The conclusion of the verses on "Dhihar" mentions the disbelievers, indicating that such practices are from their deeds, followed by some descriptions of the disbelievers' conditions.

Contemplation Insights from Page 543 [Al-Mujadila 7-11]

- Though Allah is Exalted above His creation, He is all-knowing of them, and nothing is hidden from Him.
- Since many people sin through private consultations, Allah commands the believers that their secret counsels should be in righteousness and piety.
- Among the etiquette of gatherings is making space for others.

Contemplation Insights from Page 544 [Al-Mujadila 12-21]

- Allah's grace towards His Prophet (ﷺ) is shown by teaching his companions not to overburden him with excessive private consultations.
- The allegiance of Jews is characteristic of hypocrites.
- The ultimate loss of disbelievers and the victory of believers is a divine tradition that may be delayed but is never absent.

Contemplation Insights from Page 545 [Al-Mujadila 22 & Al-Hashr 1-3]

- Love that does not make a Muslim denounce a disbeliever's religion and dislike it is prohibited. Natural love, like a Muslim's love for their non-Muslim relative, is permissible.
- The bond of faith is the strongest link among the people of faith.
- The ascendancy of falsehood may seem unending until their defeat comes unexpectedly.
- Allah's decree includes alleviating calamities through lesser hardships.

Contemplation Insights from Page 546 [Al-Hashr 4-9]

- Acting in a harmful way to achieve a greater benefit does not constitute corruption on Earth.
- One of Islam's beauties is considering the needy when allocating wealth, directing the spoils of war to them rather than the self-sufficient wealthy.

◆ Preferring others over oneself is a noble trait vividly demonstrated by the Ansar (the Helpers).

Contemplation Insights from Page 547 [Al-Hashr 10-16]

◆ The bond of faith is unaffected by the passage of time or change of place.

◆ The hypocrites' friendship with Jews and others is a superficial bond that dissolves during hardships.

◆ Jews are described as cowards in battle, relying on their fortifications and weapons for protection.

Contemplation Insights from Page 548 [Al-Hashr 17-24]

◆ A sign of Allah's guidance is a believer's self-accountability before the Day of Judgment.

◆ The profound impact of the Qur'ān on a great mountain reminds us that humans, being more susceptible, should be even more moved.

◆ The names (the Creator, the Originator, the Fashioner) reflect the stages of creation, from decreeing to bringing into existence to giving it a unique form. Mentioning one implies the others.

Contemplation Insights from Page 549 [Al Mumtahanah 1-5]

◆ Leaking the news of Muslims to the disbelievers is a major sin.

◆ The hostility of the disbelievers is deep-rooted and is not affected by their allegiance.

◆ Ibrahim's seeking forgiveness for his father was due to a promise he made to him. However, when Allah forbade him from doing so because his father died in disbelief, he ceased to seek forgiveness for him.

Contemplation Insights from Page 550 [Al Mumtahanah 6-11]

◆ In Allah's transformation of the heart from hostility to affection and from disbelief to faith, there is a sign that the servants' hearts are between two of His fingers (سُبْحَانَهُ وَتَعَالَىٰ). Therefore, the servant should ask Him for steadfastness in faith.

◆ Differentiating in judgment between the hostile disbelievers and those who are peaceful.

◆ The prohibition of a man marrying a disbeliever who is not from Ahl al Kitāb, both initially and permanently, and the prohibition of a Muslim woman marrying a disbeliever, both initially and permanently.

Contemplation Insights from Page 551 [Al Mumtahanah 12-13 & Al-Ṣaff 1-5]

◆ The legitimacy of pledging allegiance to the ruler is based on listening, obedience, and righteousness.

◆ The necessity of honesty in actions and their consistency with words.

- Allah has shown the servant the path of good and evil. If the servant chooses deviation and misguidance and does not repent, then Allah punishes him by increasing his deviation and misguidance.

Contemplation Insights from Page 552 [Al-Ṣaff 6-14]

- The prophecy of our Prophet (صَلَّى ٱللَّهُ عَلَيْهِ وَسَلَّمَ) in the previous messages is a testament to the truth of his prophethood.
- Empowering religion is a divine tradition.
- Faith and jihad in the cause of Allah are among the reasons for entering Paradise.
- Allah may hasten the believer's reward in this world or reserve it for him in the Hereafter, but He does not discard it.

Contemplation Insights from Page 553 [Al-Jumu'ah 1-8]

- The immense favor of the Prophet (صَلَّى ٱللَّهُ عَلَيْهِ وَسَلَّمَ) on humanity in general, and the Arabs in particular, as he rescued them from the darkness of ignorance and loss.
- Guidance is a favor from Allah alone, sought from Him and attracted by obedience to Him.
- The claim of the Jews that they are Allah's allies is refuted; they are challenged to wish for death if they are truthful in their claim because a true ally yearns for their beloved.

Contemplation Insights from Page 554 [Al-Jumu'ah 9-11 & Al-Munafiqun 1-4]

- The obligation to hasten to attend Friday prayer after the call and the prohibition of worldly activities except for a valid excuse.
- A surah specifically dedicated to the hypocrites highlights their danger and their concealed nature.
- The real value is in the righteousness of the inner self, not in the beauty of appearance or eloquence of speech.

Contemplation Insights from Page 555 [Al-Munafiqun 5-11]

- Ignoring advice and arrogance are characteristics of hypocrites.
- The economic blockade of Muslims by the enemies of the religion is one of their strategies.
- The danger of wealth and children if they distract from the remembrance of Allah.

Contemplation Insights from Page 556 [At-Taghabun 1-9]

- It is by Allah's decree that people are divided into the wretched and the blissful.
- Remembering the loss of people on the Day of Judgment aids in righteous deeds.

Contemplation Insights from Page 557 [At-Taghabun 10-18]

- The messengers' role is to convey the message from Allah; guidance is in the hands of Allah.
- Belief in destiny brings tranquility and guidance.
- Obligations are proportional to the capacity of the person.
- Spending in Allah's way multiplies the reward.

Contemplation Insights from Page 558 [At-Talaq 1-5]

- The address to the Prophet (صَلَّىٰٱللَّهُعَلَيْهِوَسَلَّمَ) is for his Ummah unless a specific exclusivity is proven.
- Providing accommodation and maintenance is mandatory for a revocably divorced woman.
- Encouragement towards witnessing to prevent disputes.
- The many benefits and greatness of piety.

Contemplation Insights from Page 559 [At-Talaq 6-12]

- No obligation for a pregnant woman to breastfeed if divorced.
- Obligations are only within one's capability.
- Belief in Allah's power and His comprehensive knowledge brings contentment and tranquility to the heart.

Contemplation Insights from Page 560 [At-Tahrim 1-7]

- The legitimacy of expiation for oaths.
- The Prophet's (صَلَّىٰٱللَّهُعَلَيْهِوَسَلَّمَ) esteemed position before his Lord and His defense of him.
- The Prophet's (صَلَّىٰٱللَّهُعَلَيْهِوَسَلَّمَ) kindness towards his wives involved overlooking some mistakes to maintain affection.
- The believer's responsibility for himself and his family.

Contemplation Insights from Page 561 [At-Tahrim 8-12]

- Sincere repentance is the cause of all goodness.
- Combining the struggle of knowledge and evidence with the struggle of the sword highlights their importance, indicating that neither can be dispensed with.
- Kinship by blood or marriage benefits no one on the Day of Judgment if they are separated by religion.
- Modesty and avoiding suspicion are traits of righteous-believing women.

CONTEMPLATION STUDY QUESTIONS

Sūrah Al-Mujadila Questions

Verse 1: Why did the verse conclude with these two noble names? *[Al-Sa'dī]*

Verse 11: Talk about the principle of "the reward is of the same nature as the action" found in the verse. *[Al-Sa'dī]*

Verse 11: Is making room for your brother in a gathering a diminution of your right? *[Ibn Kathīr]*

Verse 13: Why were these two acts of worship specifically mentioned and not others? Why follow obedience with the description of Him being All-Knowing of what we do? *[Al-Sa'dī]*

Verse 18: How are the hypocrites' conditions in the Hereafter similar to their conditions in this world? *[Al-Sa'dī]*

Verse 22: What is the relationship between belief in Allah and the Last Day and detesting those who oppose Allah and His Messenger? *[Al-Sa'dī]*

Verse 22: Explain the reason for Allah's pleasure with the believers and their pleasure with Him through the verse *[Ibn Kathīr]*

Sūrah Al-Hashr Questions

Verse 2: The verse encourages reliance on Allah (عَزَّوَجَلَّ) and not to lean on causes. Explain that. *[Al-Sa'dī]*

Verse 2: What is the lesson learned from the story of Banu Nadir? *[Ibn Kathīr]*

Verse 9: Which is better: preferring others over oneself or giving money despite love for it? *[Ibn Kathīr]*

Verse 9: How does protecting oneself from stinginess lead to success? *[Al-Sa'dī]*

Verse 10: Mention a virtue of faith indicated by this verse. *[Al-Sa'dī]*

Verse 13: What is the sign of a servant's understanding? *[Al-Sa'dī]*

Verse 18: Talk about self-accountability in light of this verse. *[Al-Sa'dī]*

Sūrah Al-Mumtahina Questions

Verse 1: Why is there a prohibition against befriending the disbelievers? *[Al-Sa'dī]*

Verse 5: How can a Muslim be a trial for a disbeliever? *[Al-Sa'dī]*

Verse 7: Why did Allah mention His power after stating that the hostility of the disbelievers can turn into friendship? *[Al-Sa'dī]*

Verse 10: Can certain knowledge about some people's faith be attained? *[Ibn Kathīr]*

Sūrah As-Saff Questions

Verse 1: What does the believer calling to faith benefit from this verse? *[Al-Sa'dī]*

Verse 8: Clarify the metaphorical image indicated by this verse. *[Ibn Kathīr]*

Verse 11: The verse connects faith and jihad, so what is their relationship? *[Al-Sa'dī]*

Verse 14: Is Allah's support limited to a specific time or aspect? *[Al-Sa'dī]*

Sūrah Al-Jumu'ah Questions

Verse 1: Is the glorification of Allah by His creation limited to animate, speaking creatures? *[Ibn Kathīr]*

Verse 5: Is a Qur'ān memorizer who does not understand it, contemplate it, or act upon it considered among the people of the Qur'ān? *[Ibn Kathīr]*

Verse 10: How did Irak ibn Malik (رَضِيَ اللَّهُ عَنْهُ) embody this verse? *[Ibn Kathīr]*

Verse 11: Why does this verse end with the command to remember Allah after ordering to spread in the land and seek provision? *[Al-Sa'dī]*

Sūrah Al-Munafiqun Questions

Verse 4: Why did Allah describe the hypocrites as true enemies? *[Al-Sa'dī]*

Verse 9: What is the benefit of the preposition "from" indicating partiality in this verse? *[Al-Sa'dī]*

Verse 10: Is regret at the time of death exclusive to disbelievers? And what do you benefit from that? *[Ibn Kathīr]*

Sūrah At-Taghabun Questions

Verse 4: What benefits a wise person from knowing that Allah is All-Knowing of the thoughts in the chests? *[Al-Sa'dī]*

Verse 11: If you know that calamities are from Allah, what effect does that have? *[Al-Sa'dī]*

Verse 16: What do you benefit from specifying piety as per one's ability? *[Al-Sa'dī]*

Sūrah At-Talaq Questions

Verse 2: For those who do not fear Allah, how are their conditions in crises and hardships? *[Al-Sa'dī]*

Verse 10: Why is piety mentioned after the story of the punished village? *[Al-Sa'dī]*

Sūrah At-Tahrim Questions

Verse 11: Why was "near unto You" mentioned before "a house" by the wife of Pharaoh? *[Ibn Kathīr]*

Day 28. Juz' Tabārak

The Qurā'n reading for **day 28** is *Juz' Tabārak* (from *Sūrah al Mulk* to *Sūrah al Mursalāt*). *Juz' Tabārak* consists of chapters revealed at various parts of the Makkan phase of *Da'wah.*

سُورَةُ المُلْك

AL MULK (67)

The Dominion

VERSES
31

WORDS
330

LETTERS
1,313

REVEALED IN
MAKKAH

REVEALATION ORDER
77

Main Theme: Exhibiting Allah's perfect dominion and power to instill reverence and fear of Him and as a warning against opposing Him and earning His punishment. As such, it is recommended to recite it every night.

It is named "The Dominion" because it opens with the sanctification of Allah, to whom belongs the dominion and sovereignty and who has power over everything, and mentions matters that can only pertain to one with complete sovereignty and absolute control, which is Allah (سُبْحَانَهُ وَتَعَالَىٰ).

Objectives of the Sūrah:

- Mentioning many of Allah's magnificent attributes, such as His unique sovereignty and complete power, the creation of the heavens with utmost precision, adorning them with bright stars, reminding of the grace of creating the terrestrial world, the precision of its system and its suitability for human life, all of which is evidence of Allah's oneness in divinity.
- Warning people against the plots of devils, clarifying that salvation is in following the Prophet (صَلَّى ٱللَّٰهُ عَلَيْهِ وَسَلَّمَ) and loss is in denying him, alerting the obstinate to Allah's knowledge encompassing all creatures, and comparing the fates of disbelievers and believers, following the Qur'ānic method of combining intimidation and encouragement.
- Discouraging the polytheists from relying on idols for support or sustenance, rebuking them for denying Allah's grace and hastening the Prophet's (صَلَّى ٱللَّٰهُ عَلَيْهِ وَسَلَّمَ) death, and threatening them with the punishments of this world and the torment of the hereafter.

The *Sūrah* establishes 13 simple logical proofs for belief in Allah's Oneness, Power, and Greatness. These are interspersed with reminders of Allah's reward and punishment. Allah informs us of seven of these directly, and six (beginning with verse 23) begin with *"Say to them ..."*

سُورَةُ القَلَمِ
AL QALAM (68)
The Pen

VERSES 52

WORDS 300

LETTERS 1,256

REVEALED IN MAKKAH

REVEALATION ORDER 2

It is said to be one of the earliest chapters revealed (preceded by *al 'Alaa, al Mudaththir,* and *al Muzammil*).

Main Themes: Commending the Prophet (ﷺ) for his phenomenal character —from the greatest proofs for his prophethood—while dispraising the disbelievers for having vile character. It was revealed in defense and support of the Prophet (ﷺ) and as a threat to the transgressing disbelievers. It contains the story of the stingy people of the orchard and their remorse and repentance after earning punishment. It contains a threat of worldly punishment for the polytheists and encourages them to repent. Named "The Pen" for its opening with an oath by the pen, highlighting the significance of the pen and the civilizational advancement it brings to nations through the knowledge of writing.

Objectives of the Sūrah:

- Consoling the Prophet (ﷺ) for the harm he suffered from the polytheists, instructing him to be patient with them, clarifying his high status, nobility, and perfect guidance, showing the misguidance of his opponents, mentioning their ugly traits as a warning against obeying them.
- Threatening the polytheists with the torment of the hereafter and the calamities of this world by presenting the story of the owners of the garden as an example of their ingratitude towards Allah's blessings, where their arrogance and wealth led them to deny Allah's favors and withhold the rights of the poor, resulting in Allah removing His blessings, contrasting this with the state of the righteous followers, combining encouragement and intimidation.

- Discussing the Day of Resurrection and its horrors, demonstrating the impotence of the polytheists' gods, which are of no avail in this world or the hereafter, mentioning the condition of the criminals on that dreadful day, and warning that their current state of blessings is but a deception, leaving them without excuse for opposing the Prophet's (صَلَّى ٱللَّهُ عَلَيْهِ وَسَلَّمَ) call.

BRIEF SŪRAH SUMMARY

Verses 1-9	Absolving the Prophet (صَلَّى ٱللَّهُ عَلَيْهِ وَسَلَّمَ) of what the disbelievers falsely attributed to him while praising him for his excellent character.
Verses 10-16	A description of the evil traits of his detractors.
Verses 17-32	The story of the people of the orchard and how their stinginess incurred upon them Allah's anger.
Verses 33-43	Repudiation of the doubts of those who denied the truth of the message.
Verses 44-52	Comforting the Prophet (صَلَّى ٱللَّهُ عَلَيْهِ وَسَلَّمَ) by ordering him with patience and informing him what happened with Yunus when he gave up on his people; the fact that the Prophet (صَلَّى ٱللَّهُ عَلَيْهِ وَسَلَّمَ) was sent to all of the creation.

سُورَةُ الحَاقَّةِ

AL ḤĀQQAH (69)

The Reality

VERSES
52

WORDS
256

LETTERS
1,034

REVEALED IN
MAKKAH

REVEALATION ORDER
78

Main Theme: Emphasizing that the day of judgment is without doubt and the truthfulness of the *Qurā'n*. It contains an unmistakable threat for the disbelievers and their ultimate regret, as well as a promise of reward for the believers and their ultimate happiness. The beginning and end of the *Sūrah* contain the concept of *al ḥaqq*. Named "The Inevitable Reality" for its opening with the term Al-Haqqah, which refers to the Day of Resurrection when the promise and threat become reality, the term is repeated in the Sūrah three times to emphasize its importance.

Objectives of the Sūrah:

- Magnifying the Day of Resurrection, threatening the deniers with its occurrence, reminding them of the punishment that befell previous denying nations in this world, describing the horrors of the Day of Judgment, and mentioning the conditions of the fortunate and the wretched on that day.
- Highlighting the significance of the Qur'ān, the solemn oath affirming the truthfulness of the Prophet (ﷺ), refuting the polytheists' claims that the Qur'ān is sorcery or soothsaying, explaining that the Qur'ān is a mercy for believers and a source of regret for disbelievers, and it contains warnings of the fulfillment of the threats it contains.

BRIEF SŪRAH SUMMARY

Verses 1-12	Reinforcing belief by describing the Day of Judgment in a broad way and then mentioning the punishment of the disbelievers in this world, nation after nation.
Verses 13-37	A more detailed description of the Day of Judgment.
Verses 38-52	The truth of the message and the Messenger (H).

سُورَةُ المَعَارِج

AL MA'ĀRIJ (70)

The Ascending Stairways

VERSES
44

WORDS
224

LETTERS
929

REVEALED IN
MAKKAH

REVEALATION ORDER
79

Main Theme: Emphasizing imminent punishment to befall the polytheists and the bliss enjoyed by those who believe in the day of judgment. It completes the themes of *Sūrah al Ḥāqqah*. Named "The Ascending Stairways" for mentioning the ascent of angels and the spirit from the Earth to the heavens at the beginning of the Sūrah.

Objectives of the Sūrah:

- Threatening disbelievers with the punishment of the Day of Resurrection, depicting their condition on that terrible day, affirming the Prophet (صَلَّى ٱللَّهُ عَلَيْهِ وَسَلَّمَ), and consoling him from what he faces from the mocking disbelievers.
- Describes human nature of being impatient in adversity and arrogant in prosperity, contrasting this with the deeds of the believers that have earned them the abode of honor.
- Emphasizing with an oath that resurrection and judgment are an undeniable truth.

BRIEF SŪRAH SUMMARY

Verses 1-18	Refutation of those who deny the Hereafter and Day of Judgment.
Verses 19-35	The nature of most people; the exceptionality of the righteous believers who are described with nine excellent characteristics.

سُورَةُ نُوحٍ
NŪḤ (71)
Noah

VERSES
28

WORDS
224

LETTERS
999

REVEALED IN
MAKKAH

REVEALATION ORDER
71

Main Themes: The patience of those who invite others to Allah by narrating the story of Nūḥ and his people to encourage the Prophet (ﷺ) and believers and to warn the disbelievers. Named Noah for recounting the story of Prophet Noah, his dealings with his people, the details of his call to them, and his prayers from beginning to end.

Objectives of the Sūrah:

- He mentions Noah's message and his charge to convey the call, sets an example for the polytheists with his people, as they were the first polytheists among Adam's progeny, details his call to worship Allah alone and to shun idol worship, reminds of the Day of Resurrection, warns of punishment, and uses the wonders of Allah's creation as evidence of His unique divinity.
- Nūḥ asks his people why they don't revere and respect Allah in verse 13. This statement is central to the theme of the Sūrah. Immediately before and after this pivotal statement, Nūḥ uses two methods to instill this reverence for Allah in those with sound minds. (1.) He leads up to this statement—in verses 10-12—by appealing to their emotions, mentioning five tremendous incentives they will benefit from by accepting his message. (Note: these incentives are the fuller details of what is mentioned in verse 4). (2.) Immediately after—in verses 14-20— Nūḥ establishes seven simple yet powerful evidences for Allah's Oneness and Greatness.

BRIEF SŪRAH SUMMARY

Verses 1-9	The sincere *da'wah* of Nūḥ and the arrogant response of his people.
Verses 10-20	Establishing Allah's greatness.
Verses 21-20	The lengthy supplication of Nūḥ against his people after 950 years of patience and advice.

سُورَةُ الجِنّ
AL JINN (72)
The Jinn

VERSES
28

WORDS
285

LETTERS
870

REVEALED IN
MAKKAH

REVEALATION ORDER
40

It was revealed in the tenth year of Prophethood, during the year of sadness, as the Prophet (ﷺ) was returning to Makkah following his being turned away and abused by the chieftains and people of al-Ṭā'if. The Jinn accepting Islām was a means to comfort the Prophet (ﷺ) during this time of difficulty.

Main Theme: Commending the believing Jinn in their responsiveness to the Da'wah of truth while rebuking the polytheists for their aversion to the truth and their worship of Jinn. Named The Jinn for its mention of some of their conditions, sayings, amazing stories, and their connection with humans.

- This Sūrah affirms an honor for the Prophet by showing that his message reached the jinn, who believed immediately upon hearing the Qur'ān, called their people to faith, dedicated worship solely to Allah, and sanctified Him from having a consort or offspring.
- It also strongly denounces those who attribute things to Allah without knowledge, denying the resurrection, invalidating the worship of jinn, guarding the heavens against the jinn's eavesdropping, nullifying soothsaying, and reaching the knowledge of the unseen to anyone other than the messengers whom Allah informs of what He wills.

BRIEF SŪRAH SUMMARY

[I.]	*al-Tawḥīd* (see verses 2, 3, 18, 20, 22).
[II.]	The Day of Judgment (see verses 7, 15, 17, 23).
[III.]	Revelation and the message (see verses 1, 13, 19, 27).

سُورَةُ المُزَّمِّل
AL MUZAMMIL (73)
The One wrapped in Garments

VERSES
20

WORDS
285

LETTERS
830

REVEALED IN
MAKKAH

REVEALATION ORDER
3

Main Themes: clarifying the means that aid in carrying the mantle of Da'wah, especially the night prayer—which is the spiritual provision of the worshipper in confronting hardships and difficulties in life to comfort the Prophet ﷺ and to serve as a threat to the disbelievers.

Objectives of the Sūrah:

- Highlighting the heavy burden of the revelation charged to the Prophet (صَلَّىٱللَّهُعَلَيۡهِوَسَلَّمَ) by Allah, ordering him to seek strength through night worship, affirming him in this duty, instructing him to turn away from the disbelievers' denial and to be patient with their harm.
- Advising the polytheists with the fate of Pharaoh's people for denying Allah's messenger to them, threatening them with punishment, calamity, and terror on the Day of Resurrection.
- Praising a group of believers who adhered to night prayers, ordering the continual establishment of prayer, giving zakat, and the promise of great reward for good deeds.

BRIEF SŪRAH SUMMARY

Verses 1-9	The command to pray in the night (before the obligation of the five daily prayers) and to recite the *Qur'ān;* taking advantage of the best times to recite.
Verses 10-19	The command to be patient with the mistreatment of the disbelievers and to leave them to Allah who will protect His Prophet ﷺ and punish those deny the clear truth; a warning to the disbelievers lest that they be destroyed like Fir'awn and his people for rejecting the Messenger.
Verse 20	In the last verse Allah lightens the responsibility of the night prayer and makes it a recommended deed in order to accommodate the growing number of believers.

سُورَةُ الْمُدَّثِّر

AL MUDATHTHIR (74)

The One Enveloped

VERSES
56

WORDS
255

LETTERS
1,010

REVEALED IN
MAKKAH

REVEALATION ORDER
4

Main Themes: The command to undertake *da'wah* and warning; the importance of relying on divine assistance when faced with ridicule and rejection from non-believers; and their ultimate punishment.

It completes the theme of *Sūrah al Muzammil* by highlighting the means of carrying out the *da'wah*. Just as *al Muzammil* begins with the command to stand and pray, *al Mudaththir* begins with the command to stand and warn. The first *Sūrah* prepares the Prophet (صَلَّىٱللَّهُعَلَيۡهِوَسَلَّمَ) to warn, and the second dispatches him.

BRIEF SŪRAH SUMMARY

Verses 1-7	Charging the Prophet (H) with the heavy duty of being Allah's Messenger and conveying the message; how this requires sacrificing sleep and comfort.
Verses 8-10	The difficulty of Judgment Day on the disbelievers.
Verses 11-30	A rebuke of al Walīd bin Mughīrah and every person thereafter who deems themself without need of guidance and believes themself to be self-sufficient because of wealth, family and status.
Verses 31-37	The hellfire and the nineteen angels who guard it; how this number of angels was responded to by believers and disbelievers.
Verses 38-47	How the righteous will ask those who enter Hellfire what led them to their destruction: four reasons are mentioned.
Verses 47-56	Allah mentions how a main motivation for the disbelievers' apathy and aversion to the truth was envy.

سُورَةُ القِيَامَةِ
AL QIYĀMAH (75)
The Resurrection

VERSES
39

WORDS
199

LETTERS
652

REVEALED IN
MAKKAH

REVEALATION ORDER
31

Main Theme: It exhibits Allah's omnipotence and ability to resurrect and gather the servants for judgment. It disproves the denial of the day of judgment and comforts the Prophet (H) as he conveys the message. It shows that it was simply upon him to convey, and Allah has guaranteed to preserve what is conveyed.

It is Named The Resurrection because it opens with an oath on the Day of Resurrection, magnifying it and affirming its certainty.

Objectives of the Sūrah:

1. It affirms the concept of resurrection, emphasizing the certainty and reality of being brought back to life after death.

2. It serves as a reminder of the Day of Judgment and mentions its signs, aiming to prepare individuals for this inevitable event.

3. It confirms the compensation based on the deeds performed by people in this worldly life, highlighting the principle of divine justice.

4. It contrasts the conditions of the fortunate and the unfortunate, honoring those who achieve happiness through their righteous deeds.

5. It reminds people of death as the first stage of the hereafter, urging them to reflect on their mortality and the transient nature of this world.

6. It discourages prioritizing the immediate benefits of worldly life over the eternal bliss promised to the righteous in the hereafter.

سُورَةُ الإِنسَانِ
AL INSĀN (76)
Man

VERSES
31

WORDS
240

LETTERS
1,054

REVEALED IN
MADINAH

REVEALATION ORDER
98

Main Theme: It reminds mankind of his origin, the wise purpose of his existence, and his ultimate abode in one of two worlds. It describes the perfect bliss of paradise while comforting the Prophet (H) and encouraging the disbelievers to recant and repent. It is Named Man for its opening mention of man, his creation from nothing, and the provision of Earth's bounties for him.

Objectives of the Sūrah:

•It demonstrates Allah's power in creating man and preparing him to fulfill his duties of worship by granting him hearing sight, and senses. It states that man is commanded to worship Allah alone in gratitude to his Creator, warns against polytheism, and affirms that reward or punishment follows either action.

- He describes the bliss prepared in the hereafter for the righteous, mentioning some of their traits, such as fulfilling vows, feeding the poor for Allah's pleasure, and fearing His punishment.
- Strengthening the resolve of the Prophet for carrying the responsibilities of his message, ordering him to be patient in this path, warning against compliance with disbelievers, and acknowledging his selection for the message as a great blessing to be thanked through devotion to Allah day and night.

Verses 1-3	Human origin and their final destination.
Verses 4-22	More than half of the *Sūrah* describes the traits and rewards of the successful believers.
Verses 23-26	Encouraging the Prophet ﷺ and strengthening his resolve.
Verses 27-31	A stern reminder of the difficulty of Judgment Day; the *Qur'ān* is a reminder for mankind.

سُورَةُ المُرسَلَات

AL MURSALĀT (77)

Those sent forth

VERSES
50

WORDS
180

LETTERS
816

REVEALED IN
MAKKAH

REVEALATION ORDER
33

Main Theme: The Sūrah exposes the plight of non-believers on the day of judgment and presents convincing arguments to invalidate their rejection of the Qur'an after it has unmistakably clarified the truth: "In which narrative after this will they then believe?" (verse 50).

Objectives of the Sūrah:

Arguing for the occurrence of resurrection following the world's end, mentioning some descriptions of that day, presenting evidence of Allah's power to resurrect humans after death, addressing the punishment for deniers in this world, detailing their fate in the hereafter, discussing the righteous in contrast, and mentioning the honors Allah prepared for them.

BRIEF SŪRAH SUMMARY

Verses 1-14	Allah swears by five great things that He created about the undeniable truth of the Day of Judgment.
Verses 16-19	The demise of past nations.
Verses 20-24	The origin of human life and creation.
Verses 25-28	The earth and its being an abode for mankind in life and after death.
Verses 29-40	On Judgment Day, disbelievers will face punishment and condemnation, unable to speak or provide excuses. They are challenged to find a way to avoid punishment if they are truthful.
Verses 41-45	The reward of the righteous.
Verses 46-50	A final warning to the disbelievers.

CONTEMPLATE, COMPREHEND, APPLY

Contemplation Insights from Page 562 [Al-Mulk 1-12]

- Recognizing the wisdom behind the creation of death and life necessitates hastening toward good deeds before death.
- Hell's fury and rage against the disbelievers stem from jealousy for Allah (سُبۡحَانَهُۥ وَتَعَالَىٰ).
- Jinn had preceded humans in space exploration, and any of them exceeding their limits would be met with surveillance and punishment.
- Obedience to Allah and fearing Him in secrecy are reasons for forgiveness and entry into Paradise.

Contemplation Insights from Page 563 [Al-Mulk 13-26]

- Allah's awareness of the secrets within His servants' hearts.
- Disbelief and sins are reasons for enduring Allah's punishment in this world and the hereafter.
- Disbelief in Allah results in darkness and confusion, whereas faith in Him brings light and guidance.

Contemplation Insights from Page 564 [Al-Mulk 27-30 & Al-Qalam 1-15]

- The morals of the Qur'ān characterize the Prophet (صَلَّى ٱللَّهُ عَلَيۡهِ وَسَلَّمَ).
- The characteristics of disbelievers are reprehensible, and believers should avoid them and their obedience.
- Those who frequently swear diminish their standing before the Most Merciful and among people.

Contemplation Insights from Page 565 [Al-Qalam 16-42]

- Denying the rights of the poor leads to the destruction of wealth.
- Hastening the punishment in this world indicates a desire for the servant to repent and return to righteousness.
- The believer and the disbeliever do not equate in compensation, just as their traits do not.

Contemplation Insights from Page 566 [Al-Qalam 43-52 & Al-Haaqqa 1-8]

- Patience is a commendable trait necessary for callers to Allah and others.
- Repentance erases previous sins and is one reason Allah selected the servant, making him among His righteous servants.
- The variety of punishments Allah sends to disbelievers and the disobedient demonstrates His perfect power and justice.

Contemplation Insights from Page 567 [Al-Haaqqa 9-34]

- Gratitude is due for the favor bestowed upon a parent by a child.
- Feeding the needy and encouraging others to do so is a means of protection from the fire's punishment.
- The severity of the punishment of the Day of Judgment necessitates precaution through faith and righteous deeds.

Contemplation Insights from Page 568 [Al-Haaqqa 35-52 & Al-Ma'arij 1-10]

- The Qur'ān is exonerated from poetry and soothsaying.
- The danger of speaking about Allah without knowledge and fabricating lies against Him (سُبۡحَانَهُۥ وَتَعَالَىٰ).
- Beautiful patience, which seeks reward from Allah without complaining to others, is emphasized.

Contemplation Insights from Page 569 [Al-Ma'arij 11-39]

- The intense torment of Hell makes its inhabitants wish to escape it by any means familiar from worldly methods.
- Prayer is among the greatest deeds for expiating sins in this world and protection from the Hellfire.
- Fear of Allah's punishment motivates righteous deeds.

Contemplation Insights from Page 570 [Al-Ma'arij 40-54 & Nuh 1-10]

- The danger of being heedless about the Hereafter.
- Worshipping Allah and fearing Him lead to the forgiveness of sins.
- Continuously preaching and diversifying its methods is a necessary and obligatory duty for callers to Allah.

Contemplation Insights from Page 571 [Nuh 11-28]

- Seeking forgiveness is a cause for rain to descend, wealth to increase, and offspring to multiply.
- The role of the elite in leading the lesser ones astray is evident and observable.
- Sins are a reason for destruction in this world and punishment in the hereafter.

Contemplation Insights from Page 572 [Al-Jinn 1-13]

- The profound impact of the Qur'ān on those who listen to it with a sincere heart.
- Seeking aid from jinn is associating partners with Allah, and those who do so are punished with the opposite of their intentions in this world.

- The practice of soothsaying was invalidated with the Prophet's (صَلَّى ٱللَّٰهُ عَلَيْهِ وَسَلَّمَ) mission.
- It's part of a believer's etiquette not to attribute evil to Allah.

Contemplation Insights from Page 573 [Al-Jinn 14-28]

- Oppression is a reason for entering Hell.
- The importance of steadfastness in achieving good objectives.
- The protection of revelation from the interference of devils.

Contemplation Insights from Page 574 [Al-Muzzammil 1-19]

- The significance of night prayer, Qur'ānic recitation, remembrance of Allah, and patience for a caller to Allah.
- The heart's emptiness at night affects memorization and understanding.
- Enduring obligations requires strict training.
- Luxury and indulgence deter from the path of Allah.

Contemplation Insights from Page 575 [Al-Muzzammil 20 & Al-Muddathir 1-17]

- Hardship brings facilitation.
- The necessity of cleanliness from both visible and invisible impurities.
- Bestowing favor upon the wicked is a form of entrapment, not honor.

Contemplation Insights from Page 576 [Al-Muddathir 18-47]

- The danger of arrogance, as it diverted Walid ibn Mughira from faith after the truth was clear to him.
- Individuals are responsible for their actions in this world and the hereafter.
- Failing to feed the needy is one of the reasons for entering Hell.

Contemplation Insights from Page 577 [Al-Muddathir 48-56 & Al-Qiyama 1-19]

- A servant's will is subject to Allah's will.
- The Prophet's (صَلَّى ٱللَّٰهُ عَلَيْهِ وَسَلَّمَ) eagerness to memorize the revelations of the Qur'ān and Allah's guarantee to compile it in his chest and protect it completely ensure that he forgets none.

Contemplation Insights from Page 578 [Al-Qiyama 20-40 & Al-Insan 1-5]

- The danger of loving this world and turning away from the Hereafter.
- The affirmation of human choice is a form of Allah's honor for him.

- Gazing upon Allah's Noble Face is among the greatest delights.

Contemplation Insights from Page 579 [Al-Insan 6 - 25]

- Fulfilling vows, feeding the needy, sincerity in deeds, and fearing Allah are reasons for salvation from Hell and entry into Paradise.
- If the state of the youths serving in Paradise is so beautiful, what about the state of the Paradise inhabitants themselves?

Contemplation Insights from Page 580 [Al-Insan 26-31 & Al-Mursalat 1-19]

- The danger of being attached to this world and forgetting the Hereafter.
- A servant's will follows Allah's will.
- The destruction of denying nations is a divine tradition.

Contemplation Insights from Page 581 [Al-Mursalat 20-50]

- Allah's care for humans in their mother's womb.
- The earth's expanse for the living and the dead.
- The severe threat and punishment for those who deny Allah's signs.

CONTEMPLATION STUDY QUESTIONS

Sūrah Al-Mulk Questions

Verse 13: What is the reason for concluding the verse with the description of Allah as All-Knowing of what is in the breasts? *[Al-Sa'dī]*

Verse 15: What does attributing provision to Himself signify about Allah (عَزَّوَجَلَّ)? *[Ibn Kathīr]*

Verse 23: What does ending the verse with "little do you give thanks" indicate? *[Ibn Kathīr]*

Verse 29: Trust is part of faith, so why did Allah mention it among all other deeds?

Sūrah Al-Qalam Questions

Verse 7: What is the benefit of mentioning His knowledge, may He be exalted, of those who are astray and guided? *[Al-Sa'dī]*

Verse 10: Why are we advised against following the one who swears a lot? *[Ibn Kathīr]*

Verse 17: Are wealth and poverty indicators of Allah's love for the wealthy servant and His displeasure with the poor? *[Al-Sa'dī]*

Verse 42: Why were they prevented from prostrating on that day? *[Ibn Kathīr]*

Verse 51: This verse is used as evidence that the evil eye is real; explain that *[Ibn Kathīr]*

Sūrah Al-Haaqqah Question

Verse 34: Why are the wretched described as those who do not believe in the Great Allah and do not encourage feeding the poor? *[Al-Sa'dī]*

Sūrah Al-Ma'arij Questions

Verses 6-7: More than 1400 years have passed since the revelation of this verse, so how is the Day of Judgment described as near despite this long duration? *[Al-Sa'dī]*

Verses 7-8: What is the benefit of mentioning the changing of the skies and the mountains? *[Al-Sa'dī]*

Sūrah Nuh Questions

Verse 27: Why did Noah pray against his people? *[Al-Sa'dī]*

Verse 28: Why were the parents mentioned before the believers in the prayer? *[Al-Sa'dī]*

Sūrah Al-Jinn Questions

Verse 22: The verse indicates the misguidance of those whose hearts are worshipfully attached to the "awliya" and the righteous; explain that.

Verses 26-27: Is access to some of the unseen exclusive to human messengers? And do angels know the unseen? *[Ibn Kathīr]*

Sūrah Al-Muzzammil Question

Verse 6: What distinguishes night recitation from day recitation? *[Ibn Kathīr]*

Sūrah Al-Muddathir Questions

Verse 4: What is meant by purifying the garments in the verse? *[Al-Sa'dī]*

Verse 13: What is the blessing in a man's children being witnesses for him? *[Ibn Kathīr]*

Verse 31: The verse indicates the necessity of certainty in all matters of religion; explain that. *[Al-Sa'dī]*

Verse 56: If you know that Allah is worthy of forgiving sins, what should your practical stance be? *[Ibn Kathīr]*

Sūrah Al-Qiyamah Questions

Verses 16-19: What is the etiquette of seeking knowledge derived from the verse? *[Al-Sa'dī]*

Verses 20-21: What causes humans to love the immediate life and neglect the bliss of the Hereafter? *[Ibn Kathīr]*

Verse 27: Why did they search for a sorcerer to treat the dying, and why didn't they look for treating physicians? *[Al-Sa'dī]*

Sūrah Al-Insan Questions

Verses 2-3: This verse explains how humans can rid themselves of arrogance, explain that *[Ibn Kathīr]*

Verse 7: What does Allah's praise for the righteous in fulfilling their vows indicate? *[Al-Sa'dī]*

Verse 24: What is the benefit of associating patience with Allah's decree? *[Ibn Kathīr]*

Verse 24: Why command the remembrance of Allah's name in the morning and the evening after ordering patience for Allah's decree? *[Al-Sa'dī]*

Verse 26: How does the verse encourage frequent night prayer? *[Al-Sa'dī]*

Verse 28: How is this life used as evidence of resurrection on Judgment Day? *[Al-Sa'dī]*

Sūrah Al-Mursalat Questions

Verses 32-33: Through your contemplation and understanding of the verse, what is the color of the fire? And is it dark, or does it contain some light? *[Al-Sa'dī]*

Verses 48-49: Talk about the status of prayer through your contemplation of the verse. *[Al-Sa'dī]*

Day 29: Juz' Ammā

The final day of *Qur'ān* reading is *Juz' 'Ammā*, the last 30th of the *Qur'ān*. Most of these chapters, especially the shortest of them, were revealed in Makkah during the first three years of the prophethood when the Prophet (صَلَّى ٱللَّهُ عَلَيْهِ وَسَلَّمَ) was focused primarily on inviting his kinsmen and those most receptive to *Islām* before the command to proclaim the message in the fourth year openly. *Sūrah al Muṭafiffīn* (83) is said to be the last Sūrah revealed in Makkah, before the *Hijrah*.

سُورَةُ النَّبَإِ
NABA' (78)
The Great News

VERSES	40
WORDS	173
LETTERS	173
REVEALED IN	MAKKAH
REVEALATION ORDER	80

Main Theme: Affirming the news of the *Qurā'n* about the judgment and recompense by using simple logical evidence, serving as a refutation and warning for the disbelievers and as a solace and divine promise in favor of the believers. Named The Tidings for its opening with a question posed by the polytheists about the "great news," which is the Day of Resurrection. It discusses the Resurrection, revival, and compensation, mentioning the stance of those who deny the resurrection and their threat, establishing proofs and evidence of Allah's power to resurrect creation after death, describing the horrors of the Day of Resurrection, mentioning the torment prepared for the disbelievers and the bliss prepared for the righteous believers, in the Qur'ān's manner of combining encouragement and deterrence.

Some Key Benefits:[21]

- This highlights that the appointed day by Allah for judgment among the servants is the Day of Distinction.
- Informing that the trumpet will be blown on that day.
- People will arrive in groups from every direction, the skies will open and become portals, and the firm mountains will turn into a mirage.

[21] Adapted from Al Burhan al Muhkam by 'Abd al 'Azīz al-Salmān (رَحِمَهُ ٱللَّهُ).

- Clarifying the fate of tyrannical disbelievers on this difficult day for them, as Hell has been prepared for them, where they will reside for long, renewable periods.
- Describes the drink of the people of Hell as boiling water that scorches faces and severs intestines and the pus of Hell's inhabitants, which is extremely foul-smelling and distasteful.
- Clarifying that this is a just recompense proportional to their deeds and stances, as they denied Allah's signs without considering the consequences and did not believe in the Day of Reckoning and Punishment, Allah has enumerated everything, offering a warning and inducing fear, urging reflection and return to Allah.
- Describes the fate of the righteous on the Day of Distinction and what Allah has prepared for them of honor and everlasting bliss, contrasting with the fate of disbelievers and what awaits them of Hell, scalding drink, and painful punishment. This motivates lofty ambitions to persist in good deeds and increase acts of closeness and obedience while also distressing the souls of denying wrongdoers, encouraging them to turn away from their misguidance.
- Informing about Allah's greatness and majesty, He is the Lord of the heavens, the earth, and all between them, and He is the Merciful whose mercy encompasses everything. Clarifying that on that day, no one will be able to speak without His permission and that whatever is spoken must be true,
- Mentioning the stance of those close to Allah, silent and speaking only with His permission, fills hearts with awe, reverence, and fear, urging a return to Allah. Clarifying that day is the Day of Truth and just, decisive judgment, where secrets are revealed and intentions uncovered.
- Encouraging righteous deeds that bring one closer to Allah and grant His honor, with reward on that day. Warning the imminent punishment and life from beginning to end is a short journey.
- On that great day, one will see the outcome of their good or bad deeds,
- Informing that on that day, filled with hardships, fears, troubles, and horrors, the disbeliever will wish, in distress and trouble, to be dust,
- The verses mentioned earlier are evidence of Allah's greatness, power, majesty, and gentleness towards His servants, and a warning that urges reflection and consideration for the clear destiny that only those whom Allah has guided to faith in Him and His messengers can escape from its terror.

Verses 1-16	Provides an answer to those inquiring about Judgment Day, while also threatening and rebuking those who reject it. The following ten verses present nine proofs of Allah's power evident in creation.
Verses 17-20	Changing of the heavens and earth for Judgment Day.
Verses 21-30	Punishment awaiting the disbelievers on Judgment Day.
Verses 31-36	Everlasting bliss awaiting the righteous believers.
Verses 36–40	Description of Judgment Day and its frights.

سُورَةُ النَّازِعَاتِ
AL-NĀZI'ĀT (79)
Those who Pull Out

VERSES
46

WORDS
197

LETTERS
753

REVEALED IN
MAKKAH

REVEALATION ORDER
81

Main Theme: Presenting spectacles of death, resurrection, and judgment to frighten the tyrannical disbelievers and as a reminder for the believers *(see verses 8-9)*. The Sūrah uses divine oaths to emphasize resurrection and recompense, refutes the polytheists' skepticism about the feasibility of resurrection, and depicts the Day of Resurrection and the condition of people therein.

Some of its main objectives and benefits:[22]

- Mentioning evidence and proofs that affirm the resurrection and its simplicity for Allah.
- Rebuking and denying those who deny the resurrection.
- Drawing the attention of those who deny and find the occurrence of resurrection improbable to the creation of the heavens and the earth, which is greater than the creation of humans.
- Explaining how the sky was created with its wonders, perfect exactitude, beautiful form, strong composition, and solid construction without cracks, bends, or disturbances despite its vastness and height. And to the creation of the earth that was spread out and made habitable, prepared for living and moving upon, with means of sustenance for humans and animals, water that gives life to everything, plants that sustain humans and animals, and mountains anchored to prevent it from swaying, to make them realize that the One who created them from a humble origin can easily resurrect them.
- Clarifying the wisdom of what is created for human and livestock benefit.
- Warning of the approaching day of doom, the great calamity, and describing the horrors, hardships, troubles, fears, and disturbances of that day.
- On that day, humans will recall their efforts, but recalling and considering will not increase good deeds nor decrease bad deeds. Regret will follow if they were righteous for not doing more good, and if they were wrongdoers, they would despair and imagine the punishment and calamity ahead.
- Hell will be made apparent on that day.

---

[22] Ibid..

- Warning against tyranny and exceeding the limits set by Allah.
- Warning against preferring worldly life over the Hereafter.
- Informing that those who prefer the worldly life will have Hell as their dwelling, a wretched place to stay.
- Urging to fear Allah and stand before Him.
- Encouraging to restrain oneself from desires.
- Warning against following desires.
- Explaining the abode of those who feared standing before their Lord and restrained themselves from desires.
- Mentioning the disbelievers' mocking and challenging questions to the Prophet (ﷺ) about the Hour's arrival and the response that only Allah knows its time.
- Highlighting the Prophet's (ﷺ) mission.
- Emphasizing the fleeting nature of worldly life as if it were just an evening or morning, showing how brief and insignificant worldly life is compared to the eternal life hereafter.

BRIEF SŪRAH SUMMARY

Verses 1-14	Allah swears by five groups of angels to affirm the truth of Judgment Day. He depicts the humbling fate of non-believers on that day when the Earth expels them for their final reckoning, leaving no option but to believe. This description serves as a reminder for all to prepare for that day.
Verses 15-26	A brief mention of the story of Mūsā with Pharaoh, who denied Allah's Oneness, rejected His Prophet, and disbelieved in the Day of Judgment, and who was destroyed and made a lesson out of for all time.
Verses 27-33	Reminders of Allah's power and what He has created of blessings for our benefit and for the benefit of our livestock such as the sky, the earth, water, plant-life, foliage, and the mountains.
Verses 34-46	The Day of Judgment and what will happen of bliss or misery according to whether or not a person was fearful of standing for judgment.

سُورَةُ عَبَسَ
'ABASA (80)
He Frowned

VERSES
40

WORDS
180

LETTERS
816

REVEALED IN
MAKKAH

REVEALATION ORDER
12

Main Theme: The Qur'an's significance in guiding and purifying individuals, distinguishing those who benefit from it from those who reject it and will face consequences in the afterlife. After outlining a tremendous principle about prioritizing the most deserving in da'wah, this Sūrah focuses on the three main subject matters of the Meccan Suwar: Tawḥīd, the Message and Prophethood, and the Day of Judgment. **Main objectives and benefits:**[23]

- Expressing reproach towards the Prophet (صَلَّى ٱللَّهُ عَلَيْهِ وَسَلَّمَ) for his reaction to the blind Muslim who, driven by a sense of fearing Allah, sought enlightenment and guidance, in contrast with his engagement with a wealthy man.
- Encouraging preaching and guidance, warning against favoring disbelievers over believers, advising against neglecting a poor Muslim in favor of engaging with wealth, and highlighting the need for extra care, gentleness, and compassion toward a blind Muslim.
- This explicit admonition to the Prophet (صَلَّى ٱللَّهُ عَلَيْهِ وَسَلَّمَ) serves as clear proof of the Prophet's fair-mindedness and truthfulness in conveying what he received from his Lord. It indicates that the Qur'ān is from Allah, not the Prophet himself. This is also evidenced by verses indicating that the Prophet (صَلَّى ٱللَّهُ عَلَيْهِ وَسَلَّمَ) has no control over matters and highlighting the incident where he was not allowed to take captives until after a significant victory.
- Guidance on prioritizing known duties over speculative ones and not forsaking a certain benefit for an uncertain one. The importance of focusing on those eager for knowledge.
- It is evidence that knowledge of the unseen is exclusive to Allah, and the Prophet (صَلَّى ٱللَّهُ عَلَيْهِ وَسَلَّمَ) only knows what Allah reveals to him. The Prophet's (صَلَّى ٱللَّهُ عَلَيْهِ وَسَلَّمَ) role is merely to convey the message, while guidance and inspiration are in Allah's hands.
- Encouraging contemplation of the Qur'ān's verses, taking lessons from them, and acting according to their guidance.
- Affirming both divine will and choice for humans after explaining the path of guidance and misguidance, truth and falsehood. Responding to fatalists who claim that humans have no real will or action and are compelled in their deeds by affirming that humans have will and capability.

[23] Ibid.

- Highlighting the significance of the reminder, the Qur'ān, and its noble status despite its ease and simplicity. The reminder is preserved in honored, venerated, revered, and purified scrolls. The scrolls are in the hands of noble emissaries, honored by Allah, virtuous, and trustworthy, faithfully obedient to Him. Emphasizing the respect and honor due to the Qur'ān, keeping it away from places of disrespect, and removing any disrespectful images surrounding its text. It is necessary to believe in the Qur'ān, accept it, and act upon it.
- Condemning those who deny Allah, rebel against His commands, and fail to fulfill what Allah has mandated, depicting their actions as vile. Expressing astonishment at the extent of their disbelief despite abundant evidence supporting monotheism and faith.
- Drawing attention to human origin, to cease defiance, and clarifying that Allah has delineated the straight path, facilitated its pursuit, endowed humans with the capacity to follow it, given them intellect to distinguish between beneficial and harmful actions, and sent messengers with clear guidance and scriptures calling to righteousness and warning against evil and its proponents.
- Highlighting the honor Allah bestowed upon humans by providing a grave for burial, distinguishing them from being discarded or consumed by predators.
- It reminds us that humans are not neglected or left without purpose, accountability, or recompense. It urges preparedness for resurrection and accountability.
- Highlighting that humans are utterly deficient; they do not adequately recognize their origin, appreciate their Creator, fulfill their earthly journey in preparation for the hereafter, utilize the various provisions Allah has made available for sustenance, or appreciate the temporary nature and purpose of such blessings.
- These provisions are detailed, including the descent of rain, the splitting of the earth to facilitate plant growth, and the listing of various types of plants provided for nourishment and enjoyment. The wisdom behind the creation of these resources.
- Warning of the Day of Judgment, its terrifying events, and the importance of being mindful of its outcomes, prompting diligent preparation and caution against sinfulness.
- Highlighting the brevity of worldly life compared to the eternal hereafter, the text urges a focus on deeds that secure divine favor and salvation while warning against the temporary allure of worldly gains.

Verses 1-10	The Prophet being subtly rebuked for turning away from Ibn Umm Maktūm because of being preoccupied with inviting the heads of *Quraysh* to Islām.
Verses 11-16	The Message, its intended effect and its status.
Verses 17-32	Evidences for *Imān* and *Tawḥīd* from birth to death and the blessings enjoyed in between.
Verses 33-42	The frightening condition of mankind on Judgment Day to such an extent that each would flee from the nearest and dearest of people to him.

سُورَةُ التَّكْوِيرِ
AL-TAKWĪR (81)
The Overthrowing

VERSES 29

WORDS 104

LETTERS 530

REVEALED IN MAKKAH

REVEALATION ORDER 7

It is one of the earliest *Suwar* revealed, approximately the seventh in order of revelation. (after *al Fātiḥah* and before *al 'Alā*).

Main Theme: Reminding of the spectacles of Judgment Day as an unmistakable proof of the truthfulness of the revealed message and to frighten the disbelievers. The Prophet (ﷺ) said:

{من سره أن ينظر الى يوم القيامة كأنه راي العين فلقراء...}

"Whoever would like to see the Day of Judgment as though with his own eyes, then let him recite (al-Takwīr, al Infiṭār and al Inshiqāq."

Some Objectives & Benefits of the Sūrah:[24]

- Informing about the Day of Judgment, its precursors, hardships, calamities, and horrors.
- Illustrating how, on that day, the sun will be folded up, the stars will scatter, and mountains will be uprooted.
- The ceasing of pregnancies and the disregard for treasures due to the overwhelming situation, as individuals are preoccupied with their survival. Stating that wild beasts will gather together due to the terrifying conditions, forgetting their natural habitats and fears of each other.
- Seas becoming aflame.
- Souls are paired with their bodies after resurrection. Indicating that souls persist from death until resurrection when they are rejoined with their bodies.
- Reproaching those who buried their daughters alive. Querying the buried girl about her death.
- Unfolding the record of deeds allows every individual to see their actions and accounts.
- The sky is peeled away.

[24] Ibid.

- Hell is exhibited and ignited for the enemies of Allah. Paradise is brought near for the allies of Allah.
- Highlighting that with these events, every soul will find the outcome of their deeds, whether good or bad; it urges preparation for this day by doing deeds that bring one closer to Allah and the hereafter.
- Stating that Allah swears by the retreating stars, the night as it darkens, and the dawn as it breathes, asserting that the Qur'ān is the word of a noble messenger, Gabriel, who is described with five qualities:
    1. Noble in character, making him the highest among angels.
    2. He possesses immense strength, demonstrated by his destruction of the people of Lut.
    3. Holding a distinguished position before Allah.
    4. Being obeyed in the highest assembly of angels due to his closeness to Allah.
    5. Trustworthy with the revelation of his Lord.
- These attributes collectively emphasize the Qur'ān's nobility, elevation, and abundance of goodness, benefits, and wisdom.

BRIEF SŪRAH SUMMARY

Verses 1-14	A detailed description about the transformation of the world above and below at the beginning of the Day of Judgment and major subsequent events therein. Twelve major happenings are mentioned, the first six of which occur as the world is coming to an end (see verses 1-6), and the last six of which occur during the day of Judgment *(see verses 7-14).*
Verses 15-29	The second half *of Sūrah al Takwīr* is a description of the Revelation and a number of things related to it such as: the Angel who brought it, the Messenger who received it, the description of the *Qur'ān;* the description of those for whom the *Qur'ān* was revealed. This half opens with Allah swearing by a number of His greatest creations that what He revealed of the *Qur'ān* is the truth. The *Sūrah* closes by disproving the opponents of truth and explaining why the *Qur'ān* does not affect them.

سُورَةُ الانفِطَار
AL INFIṬĀR (82)
The Cleaving

VERSES
19

WORDS
80

LETTERS
327

REVEALED IN
MAKKAH

REVEALATION ORDER
82

It is said to be the 82nd Sūrah revealed, just as it is the 82nd in the order of the Muṣḥaf.

Main Theme: Shared with *Sūrah al-Takwīr.* Named The Cleaving for its opening, mentioning the sky's cleaving, splitting, and disruption of its order as one of the Day of Resurrection's horrors. It describes the scene of transformation occurring at the Hour's establishment and what follows of accounting and compensation, dividing people in the afterlife into two groups, the righteous and the wicked, and the outcome for each. It criticizes human denial of Allah's blessings upon him, awakening the polytheists from their neglect of monotheism, considering the signs of resurrection and recompense, and reminding them of the recording angels noting their deeds.

Some Objectives & Benefits:[25]

1. Detailing the events preceding the Day of Resurrection, including the Trumpet-blowing of Destruction followed by the Trumpet-blowing of Resurrection, where creations are gathered, deeds are accounted, records distributed, deeds weighed, and the Ṣirāṭ (bridge) set, leading to either Paradise or Hell.

2. Warning against leaving behind a bad precedent, for its sins are recorded against the person even in their grave.

3. Warning against being deluded and deceived by the devil's agents from both humans and jinn.

4. Cautioning against denying the resurrection and compensation, as it is a major factor of evil and corruption in the world and a leading cause of punishment on the Day of Judgment.

5. Affirming the belief in the recording of deeds, both good and bad, and the accountability based on them on the Day of Judgment by two noble angels assigned to every responsible individual, as per the authentic hadith about the alternation of angels by night and day.

[25] Adapted from Al Muyassar.

سُورَةُ المُطَفِّفِين

AL MUṬAFIFFĪN (83)

Those Who Deal in Fraud

VERSES
36

WORDS
169

LETTERS
730

REVEALED IN
MAKKAH

REVEALATION ORDER
86

Approximately the 86th in order of revelation (after *al 'Ankabūt* and before *al Baqarah*).

Main Themes: The Surah explains how people will fare upon being weighed and recompensed hereafter. It serves as a threat to the Muṭafiffeen who berate the believers, how their standing will be utterly downgraded in the hereafter, and as a cause of solace for the vulnerable believers and how their standing will be exalted. Some say that the subject matter of al Muṭafiffeen is like the completion of al *Infiṭār* and elaborates on what it briefly mentioned without much detail.

Some Objectives and Benefits of the Sūrah:[26]

- Rebuke and severe warning to those who give short measures. Explanation of their actions that warranted this warning. They are those who, when buying for themselves, demand full measure, but when selling to others, they give less than due, ensuring their profit at the expense of others.
- Warning, fear induction, and astonishment at their audacity in doing so. The reason behind their fraudulent actions is their disbelief in the Hereafter,
- That day was described as great due to the significant events of resurrection, gathering, accounting, the bridge, the scale, the recompense for deeds, paradise, and hell.
- Warning against giving short measures and fraud; urging deterrence from such acts, disbelief, and negligence of the Day of Reckoning.
- Mentioning the abode of the wicked in Sijjin, Highlighting its significance and the distress contained within it due to their vile deeds.
- Threatening those who deny the resurrection and recompense for deeds,
- Characterizing those who deny the Day of Judgement as transgressors.
- Among their traits, when the Qur'ān is recited to them, they claim it is "Ancient tales." The reason for their claim that the Qur'ān is an ancient tale is their abundance of sins and wrongdoing, which have sealed their hearts and confused truth and falsehood for them.

[26] Adapted from Al Burhān al Muḥkam.

- Warning against sins: They cover the heart gradually until its light is extinguished, flipping realities and making falsehood seem true, and vice versa.
- Clarifying that disbelievers and wicked individuals will be veiled from seeing their Lord on the Day of Judgement, Evidence that Allah will be seen in the Hereafter by the believers, Increasing the punishment for the wicked as, after being veiled from seeing their Lord, they are destined for hell, enduring long-term punishment. Issuance of a divine rebuke and reproach.
- Informing that the record of the righteous, detailing their good deeds, is in the highest places. Stating that noble angels witnessed and attended to this record, honoring them and elevating their status. In contrast, the purpose of placing the record of the wicked in the lowest depths is to demean and disgrace them, indicating they are unworthy of concern or attention. Magnifying the status of 'Illiyyin and emphasizing its significance,
- Describes the condition of the righteous, obedient to Allah, and the immense bliss prepared for them, affecting their souls, hearts, and bodies. Describing the bliss and its heavenly nature, including their sitting on thrones.
- They will behold Allah (سُبْحَانَهُ وَتَعَالَىٰ) and the delights prepared for them, Highlighting the impact of this bliss on the inhabitants of paradise,
- Describing their drink, pure and refined wine without impurities or bitterness, not causing headaches or intoxication, Noting that their vessels are sealed with musk,
- Emphasizing the honor bestowed upon the believers deserving this bliss and reward.
- Encouraging righteous deeds to attain this honor, everlasting bliss, and abundant favor, Suggesting that competition should aim for this enduring, magnificent bliss, not for fleeting, troubled pleasures.
- Detailing another aspect of the righteous' drink, mixed from a spring called Tasnim, elevated both physically and in status, the noblest and highest beverage of paradise, pure for the closest to Allah, and mixed for the righteous,
- Recalling how disbelievers mocked believers in the worldly life, ridiculing their faith and deeming them misguided, despite the disbelievers not being guardians or caretakers of the believers.
- Foretelling of a situation where, in the Hereafter, believers rejoice over disbelievers, who are then in a state of disgrace, overwhelmed by punishment, contrasting their previous mockery in the world.

سُورَةُ الانْشِقَاقِ
AL INSHIQĀQ (84)
The Splitting Asunder

VERSES 25

WORDS 107

LETTERS 430

REVEALED IN MAKKAH

REVEALATION ORDER 83

Approximately 83rd in the order of revelation (before *Sūrah al-Rūm*).

Main Themes: See *Sūrah al-Takwīr* and *al Infiṭār.*

Named Al-Inshiqaq due to its opening with the mention of the splitting of the sky, one of the events of the Day of Judgment.

Objectives of the Sūrah:

Describes spectacles of the Hereafter, signaling the changes that will occur in the world at the Hour's advent, detailing the differing states of creation on that day: those in bliss honored, receiving their books with their right hands, and those in misery, taking their books behind their backs. It accuses the polytheists of their disbelief despite the clarity of the Qur'ān's signs and its evident proofs, promising them painful punishment in Hell.

Some Key Benefits:

- Affirmation of belief in resurrection and recompense by detailing the precursors in transforming the universe.
- Clarification of the inevitability of a person meeting their Lord. Every person endowed with reason and maturity is inevitably a doer and earner until they die and meet their Lord.
- The people of faith and piety are subjected to an easy account. Those scrutinized in their accounting are doomed and punished, for they possess no excuse or justification.
- Man is headed towards situations and terrors, one after another, until they end up in either Paradise or Hell.
- People's disbelief in their Lord invites astonishment.
- Allah's knowledge of what a person conceals in their heart and harbors in their soul is a reminder for the servant to be mindful of their Lord, harboring only faith in their heart and bearing only goodness in their soul, devoid of malice, envy, doubt, hostility, or hatred.

سُورَةُ البُرُوجِ
AL BURUJ (85)
The Big Stars

VERSES
22

WORDS
109

LETTERS
465

REVEALED IN
MAKKAH

REVEALATION ORDER
27

This *Sūrah* mentions the devastating punishment of Allah against the wicked who persecute the believers.

Main Theme: It portrays Allah's power and the threat of those who lay in wait to ambush the believers; it serves as a warning to the disbelievers and solace for the believers. It is Named Al-Burooj for its opening with an oath by the constellations in the sky, referring to the stars that move in their orbits.

Some of its objectives & benefits:

- Allah swears a divine oath by the sky adorned with constellations—either the stars or the twelve known zodiac signs—and by the promised Day, which is the Day of Judgment, by the witness, which is Friday, and the witnessed, which is the Day of Arafah. The response to the oath, [Cursed be the companions of the trench], means the companions of the trench are cursed, with the trench being a rectangular excavation in the earth. The story of the companions of the trench is a long and well-known one.
- In the story of the companions of the trench, there is a lesson, a reminder of the punishment in the Hereafter, and a deterrence and rebuke for the tyrants who inflict various tortures on the believers.
- It points to the hardness of their hearts, the ferocity of their manners, and the absence of mercy within them. It highlights the strength of endurance, fortitude, and steadfastness of the believers in their faith and the firmness of their belief.
- It clarifies that the reason the tyrants burned the believers was only because they believed in Allah alone, which everyone should adhere to and invite others to, which is faith in Allah, the Mighty, the Praiseworthy.
- This is an affirmation of Allah's description of perfect glory. It is proof that Allah, had He willed, could have prevented the tyrants from harming the believers with His might and power. However, if He delays punishing the wrongdoers in this world, it does not mean He has neglected them. Rather, He has postponed their punishment to a day when eyes will stare in horror.

- An explanation of the painful punishment prepared for the disbelievers as a recompense for the evils they committed, including harming the believers.
- A warning and alert to those who persecute believing men and women who follow the Book of Allah and the Sunnah of His Prophet, forcing them to renounce Islam, threatening them with the burning fire of Hell if they do not cease from their oppression, falsehood, and tyranny.
- This explains Allah's beautiful reward and generous bounty for the believers. It also provides information that Allah's vengeance upon the tyrants, the oppressors, and the transgressors is of extreme severity and finality. The disbelievers are severely intimidated. It consolates the Prophet (ﷺ) and the believers with him.
- Guidance for the worshipers that Allah initiates creation and then repeats it.
- A mention of four divine attributes: (1.) that He is the Forgiver for those who repent and return to Him; (2.) that He is the Loving One, He loves the believers, and they love Him, a love unmatched by anything; (3.) He is the owner of the majestic throne; (4.) He does whatever He wills, whatever He intends to do; there is no repeller of His action, no one to question His decrees due to His greatness, power, dominance, and justice.
- This is another reminder of what happened with Pharaoh Thamud, their armed forces, their rebellion, and the divine punishment that befell them, which no one could avert. There is a lesson and a moral in how they denied the messengers, how the punishment descended upon them, how the messengers were patient, and how they were victorious.
- A reiteration of consolation for the Prophet (ﷺ) and the believers. A severe threat to the disbelievers who are under Allah's control and might.
- Evidence that disbelievers in every era are alike, and their situation with their prophets does not change or alter; they are uniformly obstinate and arrogant, just like the teeth of a comb. The people of the Prophet (ﷺ) are not an exception among the nations; previous nations faced divine retribution, which serves as a lesson for those who reflect.
- Affirmation of Allah's power, knowledge, encompassment (*iḥāṭah*) of everything.
- Responding to those who denied the Qur'ān or claimed it was the legends of the ancients. The information that the Qur'ān is a magnificent, noble, lofty, and vastly beneficial Book, with vast and profound meanings, abundant in goodness and blessings. Is there anything more majestic, elevated, noble, and venerable than the word of Allah, the Most High, the Magnificent?

Ibn al Qayyim (رَحِمَهُ ٱللَّهُ) says about the moral of the main story in this Sūrah:

وهذا شأن أعداء الله دائمًا، ينقمون على أوليائه ما ينبغي أن يُحَبُّوا ويُكْرَمُوا لأجله

"This is the affair of Allah's enemies; they resent and criticize His allies for the very reason that they should love and honor them."

He mentions many historical examples of this, which are summarized below:

(1.) Ahl al Kitāb resent and criticize the Muslims for their faith. [see al Mā'idah: 59].

(2.) The homosexuals resented and detested Lūṭ because he remained pure of their abomination. [see al 'Arāf: 82].

(3.) The polytheists resent and have a problem with the people of Tawḥīd because they worship Allah exclusively.

(4.) Ahl al-Bida resents and has a problem with Ahl al-Sunnah because they restrict themselves to the Sunnah while abandoning what opposes it.

(5.) The Mu'aṭṭilah (those who negate Allah's attributes) resent and despise those who affirm Allah's Divine Attributes.

(6.) The Rāfiḍa resent and criticize Ahl al-Sunnah because of the latter's love for the Ṣaḥāba.

(7.) Those who adhere to human opinion resent the people of ḥadīth for holding fast to the aḥādīth.

وكلُّ هؤلاء لهم نصيبٌ من هذه الآية ، وفيهم شَبَهٌ من أصحاب الأخدود، وبينهم نسبٌ قريبٌ أو بعيدٌ

All of them incur a portion of and have a resemblance to the Aṣḥāb al Ukhdūd, and they all share a close or distant lineage with them."

BRIEF SŪRAH SUMMARY

Verses 1-7	Allah swears that the *Aṣḥāb al Ukhdūd* (those who reveled in the torment of the believers in a previous nation) are destroyed and accursed. He attests to this by swearing by: (1.) the heavens, (2.) the Day of Judgment, (3.) every witness and (4.) every matter requiring testimony.
Verses 8-11	Allah warns against persecuting believers and promises to be their ally. The faithful are encouraged to remain patient and trust that Allah will ultimately reward them.
Verses 12-22	Allah concludes the story of *Aṣḥāb al Ukhdūd* by mentioning: (1.) His universal norm of exacting retribution against the wicked; (2.) He mentions His severe striking against the tyrants and describes Himself with five magnificent divine attributes; (3.) He provides examples of previous peoples against whom divine retribution was exacted; (4.) He concludes by praising the *Qur'ān* and challenging those who disbelieve in it.

سُورَةُ الطَّارِقِ
AL-ṬAARIQ (86)
The Night-Comer

VERSES
17

WORDS
61

LETTERS
239

REVEALED IN
MAKKAH

REVEALATION ORDER
36

Main Theme: This Surah demonstrates Allah's far-reaching power concerning humankind's creation, His watchfulness over them, and His recreating them for judgment. It serves as a warning for the scheming disbelievers and a reinforcement for the believers.

Some objectives & benefits of this Sūrah:

- Explaining that Allah (تَبَارَكَ وَتَعَالَى) swore by the sky and its luminous stars that souls are not left without purpose nor neglected. Every soul is under the watch of a guardian from its Lord, who preserves its deeds and tallies its good and evil actions.
- This serves as a directive and attention-grabber for people to contemplate the creation of the sky and its celestial bodies. Their conditions, shapes, balanced orbits, risings, and settings hold wonders and marvels that, upon reflection, unmistakably point to a Creator and Organizer—Wise, Knowledgeable, All-Aware, Hearing, Seeing, and Powerful, who manages their affairs without a partner or assistant in this creation and craftsmanship.
- This includes a warning for the disbelievers and consolation for the Prophet (صَلَّى اللَّهُ عَلَيْهِ وَسَلَّمَ) and his companions, as Allah has accounted for the disbelievers' deeds and will repay them accordingly.
- Urging vigilance, self-accountability, and encouragement towards obedience.
- Drawing human attention to deliberate, ponder, and infer, to realize that the One who initiated their creation from a drop can surely resurrect them. This first creation attests to His power and precise planning and management.
- Describes that ejaculatory fluid emerges from between the spine and ribs, from the man's backbone and the woman's chest area.
- Informing that the One capable of initially creating humans from this substance can undoubtedly resurrect them after death, as the initial creation attests to His power and meticulous planning.
- Clarifying the return time, the Day of Judgment, when secrets are unveiled, hidden intentions are exposed, and the pure is distinguished from the impure.

- Informing that on that day, humans will be stripped of all power and support,
- Another oath by the sky and the earth that the Qur'ān is a decisive statement, truth without doubt, serious and not frivolous, with no room for jest or triviality.
- Highlighting the stance of the disbelievers and their plots against believers, their harm, their turning away, the malice within their hearts, and how Allah is ever-watchful over them.

BRIEF SŪRAH SUMMARY

Verses 1-4	Allah swears that there are angels recording all that we do.
Verses 5-10	Just as Allah can create us from seminal fluid, He can recreate us for judgment.
Verses 11-17	Allah swears that the *Qur'ān* is the truth and that the plots of the disbelievers will be turned against them.

سُورَةُ الأَعْلَى
AL 'ALA (87)
The Most High

VERSES 19

WORDS 72

LETTERS 291

REVEALED IN MAKKAH

REVEALATION ORDER 8

Main Themes: Reminding people of Allah's highest favor (the message of guidance), connecting them to the hereafter, and detaching them from this worldly life. This theme is emphasized by verse 9 until the end of the *Sūrah*.

Objectives of the Sūrah:

- Sanctify Allah and point to His Oneness because He is unique in creating humans and what sustains them on Earth.
- Supporting and steadying the Prophet (ﷺ) in receiving revelation.
- That Allah has given him a lenient law and a Book by which those with pure souls who fear their Lord can reflect, whereas those doomed to wretchedness, who prefer the life of this world and pay no heed to the eternal life, turn away from it.
- What has been revealed to him is affirmed by the scriptures of the prophets before him, all of which diminish what he encounters from the polytheists' disregard.

BRIEF SŪRAH SUMMARY

Verses 1-5	*Tawḥīd* and some of its creational evidences.
Verses 6-8	The revelation of the *Qur'ān* and the importance of maintaining diligence in learning it so that it is not forgotten.
Verses 9-19	Allah's reward for those who benefit from the *Qur'ān* and embrace guidance. The punishment of Allah for those who fail to do so.

سُورَةُ الغَاشِيَةِ
AL GHĀSHIYAH (88)
The Overwhelming

VERSES
26

WORDS
92

LETTERS
381

REVEALED IN
MAKKAH

REVEALATION ORDER
68

Main Theme: Reminding about the spectacle of torment and bliss in the hereafter, it then looks at the simple evidence of Allah's amazing power to fill the souls with fear and yearning. *Sūrah al 'Ala* focuses more on encouraging, incentivizing, and attaching the souls to Allah and the hereafter, whereas *al Ghāshiyah* focuses more on instilling fear of divine punishment and disconnecting souls from their attachment to this world.

Some of its objectives:

- Magnifying the Day of Resurrection and the punishment of a group with a deformed state and the reward of a group in bliss, with a general approach that either terrifies or entices.
- Hinting at what clarifies this generality, by denouncing people who were not guided by the signs of Allah's creations that are right before their eyes, to acknowledge His uniqueness in divinity, so the listeners know that the threatened group are the polytheists.
- The possibility of His resurrecting some of His creations anew after death on the Day of Resurrection.
- Steadying the Prophet (ﷺ) in calling to Islam and not to care about their disregard. Clarifying that all will be resurrected and returned to Allah, who will repay them for their disbelief and disregard.

BRIEF SŪRAH SUMMARY

Verses 1-16	The Day of Judgment and the two factions of mankind on that day; a description of some of the blisses of paradise
Verses 17-20	Four signs within the creation proving Allah's Oneness and Power.
Verses 21-26	Conveying the Message of Islam and knowing that the ultimate return is to Allah.

سُورَةُ الفَجْرِ

AL FAJR (89)

The Dawn

VERSES 29

WORDS 139

LETTERS 597

REVEALED IN MAKKAH

REVELATION ORDER 10

Main Theme: Presenting spectacles of divine greatness and omnipotence in the universe and the human condition, serving primarily as a warning for the deceived disbelievers and a solace for the calm believers. It sends respect and fearful veneration into disbelieving souls while inspiring peace within the believing heart.

Its objectives include:

- Setting an example for the polytheists of Mecca in their refusal to accept their Lord's message by comparing them to the people of 'Ad, Thamud, and the followers of Pharaoh. Warning them of the punishment in the Hereafter.
- Affirming and reassuring the Prophet (ﷺ), along with the promise of the eventual disappearance of his enemies.
- Invalidating the delusion of the Meccan polytheists who believed that their prosperity was a sign of Allah's favor and that the believers' hardships indicated Allah's disdain. Highlighting their ingratitude towards Allah's blessings, as they did not share them with the needy and were only driven by greed for more.
- They would regret on the Day of Judgment for not having forwarded good deeds for themselves that could benefit them on a day when neither wealth nor children would avail, except for one's faith and belief in the promise of their Lord. This will benefit the believers by leading them to Paradise.

BRIEF SŪRAH SUMMARY

Verses 1-14	Allah swears by the best times and places in which mankind worship Him that He is watching the wicked and is not heedless of them. He mentions how their worldly accomplishments resulted in nothing but their ruin as a warning to all who disbelieve in the Prophets and their Message.
Verses 15-20	The common fallacy of looking at material wealth and social status, or the lack thereof, as evidence of Allah's honor or dishonor towards individuals.
Verses 21-30	These verses contain a short yet vivid description of the major occurrences of Day of Judgement and how some will be doomed and remorseful while others will return to Allah in eternal peace.

سُورَةُ البَلَد
AL BALAD (90)
The City

VERSES
20

WORDS
82

LETTERS
320

REVEALED IN
MAKKAH

REVELATION ORDER
35

Main Theme: Focuses on the fact that humankind is created in a state of toil and hardship to constantly remind him of divine omnipotence. The only way to overcome this is by ascending through guidance to achieve Allah's mercy in both worlds.

Objectives of the Sūrah:[27]

• Highlighting the significance of Mecca, the Prophet's (ﷺ) status, and the blessings he brought to its inhabitants.

• Mentioning the Prophet's (ﷺ) ancestors from Mecca who were among the prophets, such as Ibrāhīm and Ismail, or followers of the monotheistic religion, such as Adnan and Mudar.

- It moves on to condemn the behavior of the polytheists, their denial of the resurrection, their exaggerated boasting, and their negligence in appreciating the blessings of senses, speech, thought, and guidance. They failed to show gratitude through benevolence and fell short in aspects of faith and its morals.
- Warning the disbelievers and giving glad tidings to those with conviction.

[27] Adapted from al Muyassar.

Some of its benefits:

- Highlighting the honor of Mecca, as Allah (عَزَّوَجَلَّ) swore by Mecca, which He honored, making it a sacred and secure sanctuary, and placing within it the Sacred House, which He made a place of return for people whose longing calls back to visit repeatedly, and made within it the Kaaba, the Qibla for Muslims, and established the Station of Ibrāhīm,
- Drawing attention to Adam and his offspring, for they are among the most astonishing of Allah's creations on earth due to their remarkable creation, marvelous making, and their ability to express, reason, and plan,
- Clarifying the subject of the oath - that which is sworn upon, as Allah (عَزَّوَجَلَّ) said: "Indeed, We have created man into hardship." Highlighting that human life involves hardship and struggle: carrying, birth, breastfeeding, weaning, growing up, earning a livelihood, living, and dying.
- There is consolation for the Prophet (H) and his followers in this.
- The rhetorical question and the warning against being deceived by fleeting strength,
- Encouraging constant mindfulness of Allah at all times,
- Mentioning some of Allah's great blessings and generous favors that require the servant to fulfill the rights of Allah, be thankful for them, and not use them in disobedience, including 1—That He made for him two eyes for beauty and sight. 2—He made for him a tongue and two lips, a tongue with which to speak and lips to aid in articulation and to cover his mouth.
- Clarifying the path of good and evil. Encouragement towards the liberation of slaves and freeing them from bondage. Encouragement to feed the needy orphan who is close in relation. Encouragement to feed the indigent, Clarifying the evidence that acts of righteousness are beneficial only with faith.
- Encouragement to advise one another to be patient in obedience to Allah, and to be patient with Allah's painful decrees. Encouragement to advise one another to be merciful to Allah's servants,
- It clarifies the outcome for those who perform these acts of righteousness, Clarifying the fate of those who disbelieve in Allah's signs.

سُورَةُ الشَّمْسِ
AL-SHAMS (91)
The Sun

VERSES
15

WORDS
54

LETTERS
247

REVEALED IN
MAKKAH

REVEALATION ORDER
26

Main Theme: Those who work to purify themselves are successful; all others are ruined.

From the objectives of the Sūrah:

Pointing to the conditions of people and their ranks in the paths of guidance and misguidance, happiness and misery, and emphasizing this with a divine oath by the universe itself, which indicates the marvelous creation of Allah (سُبْحَانَهُ وَتَعَالَى) and His uniqueness in divinity.

Some of its benefits:

- Demonstrating the manifestations of divine power in the signs by which the Lord (سُبْحَانَهُ وَتَعَالَى) swore.
- Explaining what leads to success and what leads to loss.
- Encouraging belief and righteous deeds and warning against polytheism and disobedience.
- Clarifying that a servant's salvation from the fire and entry into Paradise depends on purifying oneself and cleansing it from the filth of sins and disobedience and that a servant's misery and loss are caused by defiling oneself with polytheism and sins, and all this is from the laws of Allah in causes and effects.
- It warns against tyranny, which is excess in evil and corruption. It is destructive and ruinous, leading to devastation in this world and punishment in the Hereafter.
- Consoling the Messenger ﷺ and alleviating his burden as the tribe of Thamud and other nations like the people of Madyan, the people of Lut, and Pharaoh had denied their messengers before the Quraysh.
- Warning the disbelievers of Quraysh of the consequences of polytheism, denial, and sins such as oppression and aggression.

سُورَةُ اللَّيْلِ

AL-LAYL (92)
The Night

VERSES
21

WORDS
71

LETTERS
310

REVEALED IN
MAKKAH

REVEALATION ORDER
9

Main Theme: Focuses on the human condition related to belief and effort and how valid belief and diligent striving lead to ease in both worlds, whereas disbelief and sinfulness lead to utter hardship.

Some benefits of the Sūrah:

- Clarifying Allah's greatness, power, and knowledge necessitates His lordship, requiring His worship alone without any partners.
- Affirming the divine decree and predestination, every person is facilitated for what they were created for, whether happiness or misery. It is affirmed that whoever is guided to act pleasing to Allah is a sign that they are as happy if they die upon what they were guided to of righteous deeds. And whoever is guided to act in a way that angers Allah, it is a sign that their misery is written if they die upon that.
- From Allah's universal ways in His creation, success (tawfīq) in obeying Allah depends, according to Allah's decree, on the servant's desire and pursuit, eagerness for it, choosing it over others, and mobilizing oneself and limbs towards it. Similarly, success in corrupt action is based on what was mentioned regarding righteous deeds: the servant's choice, pursuit, eagerness, and mobilization of oneself and limbs towards it.
- It clarifies that Allah, the Exalted, has established the path of guidance by sending messengers and revealing the scripture to clarify and elucidate the path.
- This noble Surah clarifies that the dominion of this world and the Hereafter belongs only to Allah, the Exalted, so whoever desires them or one of them should seek it from Allah, the Exalted. The Hereafter is sought through faith and piety, and this world is sought through following Allah's laws in acquiring it. This noble Surah highlights the virtue of Abu Bakr Al-Siddiq and that he is given glad tidings of Paradise.

سُورَةُ الضُّحَىٰ

AL-ḌUḤA (93)
The Night

VERSES
11

WORDS
40

LETTERS
72

REVEALED IN
MAKKAH

REVEALATION ORDER
11

Main Theme: Allah's care for his Prophet (and the believers by extension) throughout his life and his favor upon him via the revealed message to encourage thankfulness.

The early days of Prophethood were very difficult as the Prophet (صَلَّى ٱللَّهُ عَلَيْهِ وَسَلَّمَ) adjusted to carrying the mantle of the Message. Allah withheld the revelation of the new *Surahs* for a brief period as the Prophet (صَلَّى ٱللَّهُ عَلَيْهِ وَسَلَّمَ) was feeling unwell. When he did not stand to pray during the night for two or three days, this caused some of the disbelievers to scoff at the Prophet (صَلَّى ٱللَّهُ عَلَيْهِ وَسَلَّمَ) and say that Allah had forsaken him and hated him. Allah revealed this *Sūrah* in response to them. Allah informed the Prophet that He had not forsaken and loved him. Allah reminded him that He had always cared for him throughout his life and commanded him to care for others in need.[28] **Some benefits from the Sūrah:**[29]

- The divine oath is mentioned as a form of affirmation and reassurance to the Prophet ﷺ that Allah has not forsaken his Messenger ﷺ nor detested him, Encouragement towards asceticism in this worldly life, and lightening its burden. Clarification that the Hereafter is better than this fleeting world.
- Glad tidings for the Prophet ﷺ. This is a reference to the Prophet's ﷺ personal development and his economic status until Allah honored him with the message. It confirms Allah's favor upon him when his father died, and he remained an orphan. Allah provided refuge for him first through Abdul Muttalib, and then when he died, Allah made his uncle a guardian and protector who defended him.
- Among Allah's favors to His Messenger ﷺ is guiding him after he was unaware of what the Book and faith were; that among Allah's favors to His Messenger ﷺ is enriching him after he had been poor; Reminding of the favors to be thankful for them, and encouraging this so that the grateful may receive more.
- Directions to honor the orphan prohibit oppressing, humiliating, and breaking their spirit. Prohibiting the scolding of the seeker and being harsh to him, but rather to give him even if it is

[28] *See Ṣaḥīḥ al Bukhārī, Kitāb al-Tafsīr.*

[29] Adapted from al Burhan al Muhkam.

little or to respond with a kind refusal, and if he is a seeker of knowledge, he should not be rebuked harshly and coldly but answered with what one knows kindly, gently, and with an open heart so that he becomes enthusiastic and strengthens his resolve, increasing his eagerness for knowledge. Commanding to speak of Allah's blessings because speaking of them is an act of gratitude, especially when coupled with praising and glorifying Allah.

سُورَةُ الشَّرْحِ
AL-SHARḤ (94)
The Opening Forth

VERSES
8

WORDS
34

LETTERS
105

REVEALED IN
MAKKAH

REVEALATION ORDER
28

Main Theme: The completion of Allah's favor by removing hardship and distress and their causes (both are said to have been revealed after the incident at *al Ta'if)*. This Sūrah was revealed soon after *Sūrah al-Ḍuḥā* to reiterate the special favor of Allah upon His Prophet. Allah had opened his heart, honored his mention, purified him from all sin, and gave him glad tidings of success in his Da'wah. In this Sūrah, Allah instructs him and the believers to devote themselves to worship after attending to their worldly work and family responsibilities to make the religion easy. **From the Objectives of the Sūrah:**

It mentions Allah's care for His Messenger (صَلَّى ٱللَّٰهُ عَلَيْهِ وَسَلَّمَ) by expanding his chest with faith, purifying him from sins, and elevating his status in this world and the hereafter, comforting the Messenger (صَلَّى ٱللَّٰهُ عَلَيْهِ وَسَلَّمَ) from the harm he faces from the wicked and giving him glad tidings of ease after hardship. It also reminds him (صَلَّى ٱللَّٰهُ عَلَيْهِ وَسَلَّمَ) to devote himself to worship Allah after completing the delivery of the message as gratitude to Allah for the blessings He bestowed.

From the Benefits of the Sūrah:

- Affirming the great favor of Allah upon His Messenger (صَلَّى ٱللَّٰهُ عَلَيْهِ وَسَلَّمَ) by expanding his chest for the laws of Islam, the call to Allah, embodying noble characteristics, focusing on the Hereafter, and asceticism towards this worldly life.
- That Allah relieved the Prophet (صَلَّى ٱللَّٰهُ عَلَيْهِ وَسَلَّمَ) of his burden, meaning the sin that weighed heavily on his back,
- Allah elevated the mention of His Prophet (صَلَّى ٱللَّٰهُ عَلَيْهِ وَسَلَّمَ), so Allah is not mentioned without mentioning His Messenger (صَلَّى ٱللَّٰهُ عَلَيْهِ وَسَلَّمَ) alongside, as in entering Islam, in the call to prayer (Adhan), the Iqama (the second call to prayer), the Tashahhud (testification of faith during prayer), sermons, and other matters with which Allah elevated the mention of His Messenger (صَلَّى ٱللَّٰهُ عَلَيْهِ وَسَلَّمَ).

- The great glad tidings that with every hardship comes ease,
- Encouragement to diligence and striving in the work for the Hereafter.
- Encouragement to persist in good deeds.
- Encouragement to ask Allah.
- Encouragement to thank Allah.

سُورَةُ التِّين
AL-TIN (95)
The Fig

VERSES 8

WORDS 36

LETTERS 152

REVEALED IN MAKKAH

REVEALATION ORDER 16

Main Themes: Allah's wisdom in honoring mankind by creating him to receive guidance. Those who refuse this honor will plummet to the lowest of the low. To this end, Allah swore upon the locations of the greatest revealed scriptures.

Allah swears by four things about four geographical places known for four of the greatest Messengers:[30]

(1.) Figs, likely an allusion to the mountain above which the Ark of Noah rested; (2.) Olives, understood to be a geographical allusion to the Bayt al Maqdis and thus the message of 'Isā; (3.) Mount Sinai is an obvious reference to where Allah spoke to Mūsā (4.) The safe land, Makkah, is an allusion to the Prophethood of Muḥammad (صَلَّى ٱللَّهُ عَلَيْهِ وَسَلَّمَ).

- He swears by these four things: He created man in the best of stature, upright in form, with well-proportioned limbs, beautifying and distinguishing him from others with the gifts of speech, discernment, planning, and thinking; this is a reference to the state of youth.
- He informs him that He will return him after that to the lowest of the low, to the fire, if he does not obey Allah and follow the messengers. Allah makes an exception for those who believe and do righteous deeds, informing them that for them, it is with Allah an enduring reward.
- Allah then issues a rhetorical question that reproaches rebukes and establishes the argument against those who deny the resurrection and the compensation for actions.
- This establishes that man is to acknowledge that Allah, the Exalted, is the Wisest of judges in His creations and actions and that there is no flaw or disorder in any of them. Does His wisdom

[30] *See Ibn al Qayyim, Hidāyah al Ḥayāra; al Burhān al Muhkam by al-Salmān.*

entail neglecting His creation aimlessly, without command, prohibition, reward, or punishment? Certainly not; rather, there must be resurrection, gathering, and recompense.

سُورَةُ العَلَقِ
AL 'ALAQ (96)
The Clot

VERSES
19

WORDS
92

LETTERS
280

REVEALED IN
MAKKAH

REVEALATION ORDER
1

Main Themes: The ideal human state is achieved by knowledge of and submission to the truth. It then contrasts between the highest exemplar of that (the Prophet ﷺ) and the greatest embodiment of its opposite (Abu Jahl). This is an honor for those who follow the truth and a humiliation for those who revel in ignorance and arrogance.

This *Sūrah* mentions the beginning of the *Qur'ān's* revelation in its first five verses; the remainder of the *Sūrah* is about how wicked people of wealth and status were typically the opponents of the Messengers. It contrasts the commendation of the Prophet (صَلَّى ٱللَّهُ عَلَيْهِ وَسَلَّمَ) for his diligence upon guidance and the condemnation of Abu Jahl due to his hostility to the message. Allah clarified that no matter how much he denied the truth and forsook the Prophet (صَلَّى ٱللَّهُ عَلَيْهِ وَسَلَّمَ), Allah would support the truth, His Prophet, and those who call to the truth. The *Sūrah* closes by issuing a severe threat to Abu Jahl and any who follow his way. Those who act threateningly to the truth and its people at any time or place are sternly threatened by Allah, who does not discriminate in His universal laws of reward and punishment. Shaykh al Islām Ibn Taymiyyah (رَحِمَهُ ٱللَّهُ) said:

فَسُورَةُ (اقْرَأْ) هِيَ أَوَّلُ مَا نَزَلَ مِنْ الْقُرْآنِ؛ وَلِهَذَا افْتُتِحَتْ بِالْأَمْرِ بِالْقِرَاءَةِ وَخُتِمَتْ بِالْأَمْرِ بِالسُّجُودِ وَوُسِّطَتْ بِالصَّلَاةِ الَّتِي أَفْضَلُ أَقْوَالِهَا وَأَوَّلُهَا بَعْدَ التَّحْرِيمِ هُوَ الْقِرَاءَةُ وَأَفْضَلُ أَفْعَالِهَا وَآخِرُهَا قَبْلَ التَّحْلِيلِ هُوَ السُّجُودُ؛

"It is the first of the Qur'ān to be revealed. As such, it opens with the command to recite and concludes with the command to prostrate. The Ṣalāt—whose best and first statement after the opening takbīr is recitation, and whose best and final action before its conclusion is prostration—(as mentioned) in the middle."

Some objectives and benefits of the Sūrah:[31]

---

[31] Al Burhan al Muhkam.

- Allah commanded His Prophet (ﷺ) to read in the name of his Lord and to call Him by His beautiful names. To honor the name is to honor the named because the name mentions the One named with what is specific to Him. So, one cannot honor it except by its meaning. Only those who understand its meaning and believe in worshiping Him can truly honor Allah's name.
- Allah created humans from a clot of congealed blood. Specifying humans in mention honors them because of their unique creation and wondrous making.
- This is an encouragement to praise and thank Allah for His abundant blessings. It is evidence of Allah's generosity and goodness, of Allah's kindness and care for His creation.
- One of Allah's blessings on His servants is that He taught them by the pen, which preserves knowledge, secures rights, and serves as messengers among people. So, all praise and thanks are due to Him. He taught humans what they did not know. Evidence of the importance of reading, writing, and knowledge.
- Humans are urged to reflect on their journey from the lowest ranks to the highest and most noble levels. This requires the administering of a wise, capable, and knowledgeable One who perfected everything He created, majestic and holy.
- The real reason for human tyranny and arrogance is seeing oneself as self-sufficient and beyond need, which leads to transgression, oppression, and pride in worldly life. This focus on acquiring status and wealth and establishing power on earth blinds one's insight, making them forgetful of their Creator and what is due to Him in terms of reverence, appreciation, and glorification.
- Warning and cautioning against the consequences of tyranny and arrogance. Threats and warnings against harming any of Allah's servants, especially stopping them from praying. Warning against denying Allah and His Messenger and turning away from faith.
- Strengthening the Prophet (ﷺ) in his calling. Warning, frightening, and threatening the criminals and the arrogant.

سُورَةُ القَدْرِ

AL QADR (97)

The Night of Decree

VERSES
5

WORDS
30

LETTERS
112

REVEALED IN
MAKKAH

REVEALATION ORDER
25

Main Themes: The greatness and significance of the *Laylatul Qadr*: Traversing on the ark of salvation in the ocean of fate.

There is a strong connection between this *Sūrah* and the preceding one. This is found in the first verse, with the use of two pronouns about Allah and the *Qur'ān*, without Allah or the *Qur'ān* being mentioned beforehand: "WE (meaning Allah in His Greatness) revealed IT (meaning the *Qur'ān*) in *Laylat al Qadr*." Allah described Himself and His Book in the previous *Sūrah*, sufficing thereby from repeating it in this *Sūrah*. Allah mentions three amazing attributes of *Laylat al Qadr:* (1.) worship performed during it is better than a thousand months of worship outside of it; (2.) the descent of the angels to the earth on the annual occasion of *Laylat al Qadr*; (3.) it is a night of exceptional tranquility and peace.

Some of its benefits:

- Pointing to the time of the Qur'an's revelation to the Messenger of Allah (ﷺ).
- Guiding the servants to the great significance of this night so they strive in it, as the question form used indicates magnification and glorification of its importance.
- Indicating that its nobility is known only to Allah.
- This clarifies the extent of its virtue, as the deeds performed on the Night of Decree are better than those performed in a thousand months without the Night of Decree, and a thousand months is eighty-three years and four months.
- Mentioning some of the merits of this blessed night,
- Clarifying that its end and beginning are known.

سُورَةُ البَيِّنَةِ

AL BAYYINAH (98)

The Clear Proof

VERSES
8

WORDS
94

LETTERS
399

REVEALED IN
SCHOLARS DIFFER

REVEALATION ORDER
100

Main Themes: The perfection of the message and its clear veracity; how people respond and their recompense. Shaykh al Islām Ibn Taymiyyah mentions how these three *Sūrahs—al 'Alaq, al Qadr,* and *al Bayyinah*—are connected to each other. He says:

فهذه السُّوَرُ الثَّلَاثُ مُنْتَظِمَةٌ لِلْقُرْآنِ أَمْرًا بِهِ وَذِكْرًا لِنُزُولِهِ وَلِتِلَاوَةِ الرَّسُولِ لَهُ عَلَى الْمُنْذَرِينَ

"These three *Sūrahs* are connected in their theme to the *Qur'ān*: commanding (that it be recited) [as is found in *Sūrah al 'Alaq*], mentioning its revelation [as is found in *Sūrah al Qadr*] and Messenger's recitation of it to those issued divine warning [as is found in *Sūrah al Bayyinah*]."

Some of its benefits:

- This affirms the condition of the People of the Book and the polytheists before the Prophet's (ﷺ) mission, as each clung to their beliefs, unwilling to deviate until clear evidence came to them.
- Clarifying the evidence that showed them the path of truth, a messenger from Allah reciting a pure, sacred Book explaining the path they should follow.
- Rebuking the People of the Book and criticizing them for their separation and disputes was not due to confusion but after the truth and correctness became clear.
- Clarifying that what came to them was not subject to disagreement or conflict; they were commanded to worship Allah alone, dedicating religion sincerely to Him, maintaining the straight path without deviating, establishing prayer, and giving zakat, the upright religion and the correct way.
- Clarifying the fate of the People of the Book and the polytheists in the hereafter, which is eternal dwelling in the fire of Hell, never to exit from it.
- They are described as the worst of creation, worse than thieves for stealing descriptions of the Prophet (ﷺ) from the scriptures and hiding them, worse than highway robbers for blocking the path of truth and preventing people from following it, and worse than rude ignorants for their actions and arrogance preventing them from acting on their knowledge.

- Placing the People of the Book before the polytheists in this threat implies that their crime against the Prophet (ﷺ) was greater. They internally recognized his mission and used it to triumph over the polytheists, but they denied him upon his arrival despite their knowledge; thus, their crime was more severe.
- Great glad tidings for those who believed in Allah and affirmed the messengers were described as the best of creation, in contrast to the description of disbelievers as the worst of creation. Allah will admit them into the gardens of Eden, beneath which rivers flow. They will never exit from them. Allah is pleased with them, and they are pleased with Him, which is the ultimate achievement sought by those of understanding.

سُورَةُ الزَّلْزَلَةِ
AL-ZALZALAH (99)
The Earthquake

VERSES	8
WORDS	35
LETTERS	139
REVEALED IN	SCHOLARS DIFFER
REVEALATION ORDER	93

Main Theme: The terrors of Judgment Day and its meticulous reckoning to encourage righteous acts and discourage wicked acts. This *Sūrah* mentions the major earthquakes that will completely transform the Earth for Judgment Day, upon which people will emerge from their graves resurrected for judgment. It is a powerful appeal to do good deeds and a warning against evil deeds.

Shaykh al Islām Ibn Taymiyyah (رَحِمَهُ ٱللَّهُ) says about the common theme of *Sūrah al-Zalzalah, al 'Aadiyāt, al Qār'iah,* and *al-Takāthur:*

ثُمَّ سُورَةُ (الزَّلْزَلَة) و (الْعَادِيَات) و (الْقَارِعَة) و (التَّكَاثُر) مُتَضَمِّنَةٌ لِذِكْرِ الْيَوْمِ الْآخِرِ وَمَا فِيهِ مِنْ الثَّوَابِ وَالْعِقَابِ وَكُلُّ وَاحِدٍ مِنْ الْقُرْآنِ وَالْيَوْمِ الْآخِرِ قِيلَ هُوَ النَّبَأُ الْعَظِيمُ.

Sūrah Zalzalah, al 'Aadiyāt, al Qāri'ah, and *al-Takāthur* comprise the mention of the Last Day and what it contains of reward and punishment. Both the *Qu'rān* and the Last Day are said to be what is meant by *Al-Naba' al 'Aẓīm* "The Great News."[32]

Some benefits of the Sūrah:

[32] Meaning that the preceding three *Sūrahs* were about the *Qur'ān* whereas these are about the Day of Judgment, and these two meanings are the explanation of the scholars for 'the great news' mentioned in *Sūrah al-Naba'*.

- Pointing to the Day of Resurrection, it's horrors, disturbances, upheavals, and reckoning, where the earth shakes, trembles, collapses, and splits open, releasing its dead and treasures and all its burdens.
- Informing that the human observer of these earthquakes, which baffles the mind in understanding their causes, will be astonished by what they see and perceive.
- It informs us that at the time of the earthquake, the earth will testify about the deeds of those who worked upon it, bearing witness for those who obeyed on its surface and against those who disobeyed Allah on it.
- After what is mentioned occurs, people will be scattered to see their deeds.
- Guiding the servants not to belittle bad deeds, no matter how small and insignificant they may seem.
- Guiding the servants towards good deeds, encouraging them to seize these opportunities, and not to neglect them, no matter how minor and insignificant they may seem.

سُورَةُ العَادِيَات
AL-'ĀDIYĀT (100)
Those That Run

VERSES
11

WORDS
40

LETTERS
169

REVEALED IN
MAKKAH

REVEALATION ORDER
14

Main Themes: Allah warns man against denying the truth, reminds him of what Allah has created for his use, and fears him from the hereafter. Allah swears by the steeds of war concerning what people strive to achieve. This is to rebuke him and remind him of his true purpose. These eleven verses contain three groupings of verses (see below).

Some benefits:

- Allah (سُبْحَانَهُ وَتَعَالَىٰ) swore by the horses for what they possess of amazing signs, obvious blessings, and their intense charge when they are set to raid, their breath panting, sparks flying from their hooves striking the stones, dust swirling, and charging into the midst amidst the raided.
- Clarifying the truth that man is ungrateful to his Lord and His blessings upon him, he remembers the calamity when it strikes him but forgets the blessings that have enveloped him unless he believes and does righteous deeds.
- Clarifying that man loves wealth intensely unless refined by faith and righteous deeds.

- Rebuking man for stinginess, denying Allah's blessings, and other base morals, urging him towards what pleases Allah, reminding him of Allah's blessings upon him, surrounding him with his deeds, and holding him accountable for them in the hereafter.
- Affirming the belief in resurrection and recompense.

Verses 1-5	In the first five verses, Allah swears by three amazing descriptions of the steeds of war.
Verses 6-8	By swearing upon these remarkable creatures, Allah bears witness to the truth that humanity, in both its words and actions, is largely ungrateful toward Him.
Verses 9-11	Allah concludes by mentioning that what is concealed in the graves will be exposed just as what is hidden in the hearts will be divulged, as Allah has intricate knowledge of all matters, large and small.

سُورَةُ القَارِعَةِ
AL QĀRI'AH (101)
The Striking Hour

VERSES 8

WORDS 36

LETTERS 152

REVEALED IN MAKKAH

REVEALATION ORDER 30

Main Theme: Shaking the hearts to imagine the dreadfulness of Judgment Day. This *Sūrah*, like those before and after, speaks about Judgment Day and describes its frightening occurrences.

Some of its benefits:

- Warning and alerting to the Day of Resurrection, its horrors, and its severity.
- The question is posed to magnify and emphasize its importance,
- Explaining when it will occur and what will happen then, as people, due to the terror of that day and its hardships, disturbances, and calamities, will scatter like moths, spreading out and dispersing in their confusion and panic from what they see and hear. The moth, an insect that flies and falls into fire and light, is used as a metaphor for recklessness and chaos,
- That the solid, firm mountains will be removed from their places, becoming light as carded wool,

- This is a lesson and warning for people of intellect upon emerging from their graves: how they will be astonished, disturbed, and bewildered! And that what they know to be solid and firm will disintegrate and dissolve, becoming soft and gentle, light as scattered wool due to the intense horrors of the Day of Resurrection,
- Informing about the outcome of the workers' deeds on that day and what they will become of honor or degradation according to their deeds, there will be two groups: one whose scales are heavy, these are the fortunate ones whose destination is peace and contentment, and the other group whose scales are light, these are the wretched ones whose abode and dwelling is Hell, also known as the Abyss. They resort to it as a child resorts to its mother.

سُورَةُ التَّكَاثُرِ
AL-TAKĀTHUR (102)
The Piling Up

VERSES	8
WORDS	28
LETTERS	120
REVEALED IN	MAKKAH
REVEALATION ORDER	16

Main Themes: Reminding those who compete to accumulate worldly possessions of death and divine reckoning. Ibn al Qayyim (رَحِمَهُ ٱللَّهُ) says:[33]

أُخْلِصَتْ هذه السورة للوعد والوعيد والتهديد، وكفى بها موعظةً لمن عقلها.

"This *Sūrah* has been exclusively devoted to divine promise and the divine threat of punishment, and it is sufficient as an admonition for anyone who comprehends it."

Some of its benefits:

- Denunciation and rebuke are directed at the listeners for their involvement in competing for more wealth and children and boasting about it, which consumes them to the extent that it prevents them from contemplating death and what follows it, to the point where they will not cease their ways until they die.
- There is evidence for the affirmation of resurrection, heaven, and hell, given that graves are places of visitation and that the visitor must return to his abode, either to heaven or hell.
- Reproach and threats are issued against such behavior.
- A threat following another in the context of reproach and rebuke.
- Enlightening and making them aware, for they will know with certainty that they were mistaken.

[33] *al Fawā'id.*

- Informing that if they knew with certain knowledge, without doubt, or suspicion, that would occupy them away from competing and boasting, and they would hasten towards what benefits them in righteous deeds.
- Encouraging to keep the Hereafter, its horrors, and its punishment in mind so that a person becomes alert and strives in what saves him from Hell.
- Informing that a person will be questioned about the bliss he enjoyed.
- Highlighting the importance of earning lawful sustenance.
- Warning against the unlawful.

سُورَةُ الْعَصْرِ
AL 'AṢR (103)
The Time

VERSES 3

WORDS 14

LETTERS 68

REVEALED IN MAKKAH

REVEALATION ORDER 13

Main Theme: The necessary components for salvation and success.

It is one of only three Sūrahs containing three verses, the other two being *Sūrah al Kawthar* and *Sūrah al-Naṣr.* This Sūrah contains the four traits needed to avoid most people's loss: knowledge-based faith, righteous deeds, sincere religious advice, and patience.

Imām Al-Shafi'ī (رَحِمَهُ ٱللَّهُ) famously said:

"لو ما أنزل الله حجة على خلقه إلا هذه السورة لكفتهم."

"If Allah had revealed no proof upon His creation except for this Sūrah, it would have sufficed them."

Shaykh al Islām Ibn Taymiyyah said about the common theme of the chapters from *Sūrah al 'Aṣr* to *Sūrah Masad:*

ثُمَّ سُورَةُ (الْعَصْرِ) و (الْهُمَزَةِ) و (الْفِيلِ) و (لِإِيلَافِ) و (أَرَأَيْت) و (الْكَوْثَرِ) و (الْكَافِرُونَ) و (النَّصْرِ) و (تَبَّتْ) مُتَضَمِّنَةٌ لِذِكْرِ الْأَعْمَالِ حَسَنِهَا وَسَيِّئِهَا وَإِنْ كَانَ لِكُلِّ سُورَةٍ خَاصَّةٌ.

"Sūrah al 'Aṣr, al Humazah, al Fīl, li'Ilāf (i.e., Quraysh), al Mā'ūn, al Kawthar, al Kāfirūn, al-Naṣr, and Masad contain the mention of good and evil deeds, although each chapter has something unique of a theme."

The benefits of Sūrah al 'Aṣr are vast and incalculable and thus deserve daily reflection, Sh. 'Abdul 'Azīz al-Salmān (d. 1422 AH رَحِمَهُ ٱللَّهُ) explains:[34]

"Sūrah Al-Asr holds the greatest indication of the Qur'ān's miracle because, despite its few letters, it indicates all people need in religion regarding knowledge and action. In His statement, "And advise each other to the truth," there is evidence for enjoining good.

1. This indicates a prohibition against evil; that prohibiting it is advising with the truth.
2. Calling to the oneness of Allah; because it is part of advising with the truth.
3. Calling to justice and fairness because it is part of advising with the truth.
4. Commanding prayer upon children and neighbors is part of advising with the truth.
5. Encouraging the giving of Zakat because it is part of advising with the truth.
6. Commanding fasting and encouraging it upon children, neighbors, and others because it is part of advising with the truth.
7. Encouraging Hajj because it is part of advising with the truth.
8. Encouraging dutifulness to parents because it is part of advising with the truth.
9. Maintaining ties of kinship is part of advising with the truth.
10. Encouraging the remembrance of Allah because it is part of advising with the truth.
11. Encouraging acting according to the Qur'ān is part of advising with the truth.
12. Encouraging striving in the way of Allah because it is part of advising with the truth.
13. Encouraging feeding the needy and showing compassion towards them because it is part of advising with the truth.
14. Encouraging kindness to the orphan because it is part of advising with the truth.
15. Encouraging kindness to the neighbor because it is part of advising with the truth.
16. Encouraging the pursuit of knowledge because it is part of advising with the truth.
17. Encouraging giving respite to the indebted; because it is part of advising with the truth.
18. Encouraging the reconciliation of relationships is part of advising with the truth.
19. Encouraging and urging to keep trusts and fulfill them because it is part of advising with the truth.
20. Encouraging performing the prayer in congregation because it is part of advising with the truth.
21. Encouraging fair measurement and warning against shortchanging because it is part of advising with the truth.
22. Encouragement and urging towards the fear of Allah are part of advising with the truth.

[34] He was from the foremost student of Imam al-Sa'dī. This is adapted from his book *al Burhan al Muḥkam*.

23. Encouraging and motivating patience in obeying Allah, refraining from disobeying Allah, and enduring Allah's painful decrees because it is part of advising with the truth.
24. Advising to fulfill promises is part of advising with the truth.
25. Advising to seek lawful earnings is part of advising with the truth.
26. Advising to be kind to the traveler because it is part of advising with the truth.
27. Encouraging the construction of masjids because it is part of advising with the truth.
28. Encouraging self-accountability because it is part of advising with the truth.
29. Encouraging repentance and turning back to Allah is part of advising with the truth.
30. Encouraging contemplation of the creation of the heavens and the earth is part of advising with the truth.
31. Encouraging the glorification and sanctification of Allah because it is part of advising with the truth.
32. Advising moderation in affairs because it is part of advising with the truth.
33. Encouraging seeking guidance from Allah because it is part of advising with the truth.
34. Advising against extremism and harshness in religion is part of advising with the truth.
35. Encouraging forgiveness and pardon is part of advising with the truth.
36. Encouraging truthfulness is part of advising with the truth.
37. Encouraging seeking help from Allah because it is part of advising with the truth.
38. Encouraging following the path of the believers; is part of advising with the truth.
39. Commanding justice among wives because it is part of advising with the truth.
40. Encouraging emancipation and motivating towards it because it is part of advising with the truth.
41. Encouraging people to do good and not to forget themselves is part of advising them with the truth.
42. Encouraging marriage because it is part of advising with the truth.
43. Encouraging good treatment of women because it is part of advising with the truth.
44. Encouraging eating from the wholesome because it is part of advising with the truth.
45. Encouraging prioritizing what benefits one in the hereafter because it is part of advising with the truth.
46. Encouraging sincerity in deeds for Allah because it is part of advising with the truth.
47. Encouraging excellence in action, which is following the Prophet (ﷺ), because it is part of advising with the truth.
48. Encouraging taking adornment at every masjid because it is part of advising with the truth.

49. Encouraging humility in prayer and when reciting the Holy Qur'ān is part of advising with the truth.
50. Encouraging holding firmly to Allah because it is part of advising with the truth.
51. Encouraging trust in Allah's promise because it is part of advising with the truth.
52. Commanding to repel the wrongdoer with what is better because it is part of advising with the truth.
53. Commanding seeking refuge from Satan is part of advising with the truth.
54. Encouraging verification of a report from a sinner because it is part of advising with the truth.
55. Encouraging handing over properties to orphans when they reach maturity as part of advising with the truth.
56. Commanding the caller to the way of Allah to call with wisdom and good instruction is part of advising with the truth.
57. Advising what Ibrahim and Ya'qub advised their children because it is part of advising with the truth.
58. Encouraging patience in hardship is part of advising with the truth.
59. Encouraging patience in times of conflict is part of advising with the truth.
60. Encouraging self-composure during calamities is part of advising with the truth.
61. Commanding the believer to avoid ostentation because commanding its abandonment is part of advising with the truth.
62. Commanding the believer to avoid usury because commanding its abandonment is part of advising with the truth.
63. Commanding the believer to avoid backbiting because commanding its abandonment is part of advising with the truth.
64. Commanding the believer to avoid lying because commanding its abandonment is part of advising with the truth.
65. Commanding the believer to avoid envy because commanding its abandonment is part of advising with the truth.
66. Commanding the believer to avoid vindictiveness and grudge holding because commanding its abandonment is part of advising with the truth.
67. Commanding the believer to avoid gossip because the command to abandon it is part of advising with the truth.
68. Commanding the believer to refrain from spying on Muslims because the command to abandon it is part of advising with the truth.

69. Commanding the believer to forsake harmful forbidden desires because the command to abandon it is part of advising with the truth.
70. Commanding the believer to avoid characteristics of hypocrisy is important because the command to abandon them is part of advising with the truth.
71. Encouraging advising for the sake of Allah, His Book, His Messenger, the leaders of Muslims, and their common folk because encouraging it and commanding it is part of advising with the truth.
72. Thank Allah and praise Him because the command to do so is part of advising with the truth.
73. Commanding to bear witness and preserve it because it is part of advising with the truth.
74. Commanding to follow the path of the believers is part of advising with the truth.
75. Commanding to abandon deceit and fraud because the command to abandon them is part of advising with the truth.
76. Commanding to forsake bribery and to stay away from it because it is part of advising with the truth.
77. Commanding to abandon engaging in frivolities and vices because the command to abandon them is part of advising with the truth.
78. Commanding to avoid depicting living beings because the command to abandon it is part of advising with the truth.
79. Commanding to forsake smoking, both consuming and selling, because the command to abandon it is part of advising with the truth.
80. Commanding to forsake betrayal because the command to abandon it is part of advising with the truth.
81. Commanding to spend wealth in defense of the religion because the command to do so is part of advising with the truth and part of enjoining good.
82. Commanding the believer and encouraging them to seek a righteous companion is part of advising with the truth.
83. Commanding the believer to avoid bad company because the command to abandon it is part of advising with the truth.
84. Commanding the believer to be humble and encouraging it because it is part of advising with the truth.
85. Commanding the believer to be forbearing because it is part of advising with the truth.
86. Commanding the believer to avoid imitating disbelievers in their dress and appearance because the command to do so is part of advising with the truth.

87. Commanding the believer to stay away from oppression and corruption because command to stay away from them is part of advising with the truth and part of enjoining good.
88. Commanding the believer to avoid aggression without right and severing ties because the command to abandon and stay away from them is part of advising with the truth.
89. Commanding the believer to stay away from distractions that divert from obedience to Allah because the command to do so is part of advising with the truth.

I'll stop here to avoid lengthiness for the reader, and anyone seeking more can generalize from the judgments they receive under Allah's statement: "And advise each other to the truth and advise each other to patience." From what has been mentioned, the profound understanding of Imam Al-Shafi'i (رَحِمَهُ ٱللَّهُ) becomes apparent when he says: If people contemplated this Sūrah, it would suffice them, meaning Sūrah Al-Asr."

سُورَةُ الهُمَزَة
AL HUMAZAH (104)
The Slanderer

VERSES 9

WORDS 30

LETTERS 103

REVEALED IN MAKKAH

REVEALATION ORDER 32

Main Theme: Warning those who show arrogance and mock the people of faith.

Some of its benefits:[35]

- A severe threat and warning against slandering people's honors, diminishing their status, belittling their deeds and characteristics, attributing misdeeds to them, and denying their present or absent virtues.
- Reprimand and rebuke, clarifying the error in their speculations.
- Clarification of the punishment prepared for them.
- Magnifying the matter of *Al-Hutamah* (the Crushing Fire) and emphasizing its significance.
- Describing it after obscuring its matter and attributing it to Allah for magnification and emphasis.
- Describing it as contrary to the fire of this world in that it penetrates from the bodies to the hearts.
- Describing it as enveloping them.

[35] Ibid.

- What has been mentioned evokes fear and alarm and encourages diligence and effort in performing righteous deeds.

BRIEF SŪRAH SUMMARY

Verses 1-3	The Sūrah issues a severe threat for those who possess the evil traits of scoffing and making fun of the believers with their speech and behavior, thinking themselves to be superior to them because of what they own of wealth.
Verses 4-9	It concludes by mentioning the exact punishment, describing the hellfire with four brief yet vivid descriptions.

سُورَةُ الفِيلِ
AL FIL (105)
The Elephant

VERSES 5

WORDS 20

LETTERS 95

REVEALED IN MAKKAH

REVEALATION ORDER 19

Main Theme: Allah's protection of His house is a blessing for the Prophet (ﷺ) and the believers.

Some of its benefits:

• Reminding the listeners, in the context of warning and frightening, of Allah's punishment upon the People of the Elephant.

• This signifies the magnificence of His power, the perfection of His knowledge, and His wisdom, as Allah (سُبْحَانَهُ وَتَعَالَىٰ) said: "Have you not considered how your Lord dealt with the people of the elephant?" This includes astonishment at what Allah did to them.

• Clarifying the situation they found themselves in, where Allah nullified their planning and thwarted their efforts. Detailing the plan to foil their plot.

سُورَةُ قُرَيْشٍ
QURAYSH (106)
Quraysh

Main Theme: Allah's favor upon the keepers of His house—the Quraysh—to establish the mandate of monotheistic worship and gratitude upon them.

Sūrah al Fīl and *Sūrah Quraysh* read like a single *Sūrah*. 'Amr bin Maymūn reported that 'Umar recited them in the second *Rak'ah* of the *Maghrib* prayer. They are coupled together in their theme. Allah miraculously protected the *Ka'bah* and restored security and well-being to the *Quraysh* before the advent of Islām so that Allah would be worshipped alone in Makkah and beyond without any counterpart or rival.

VERSES 4

WORDS 17

LETTERS 73

REVEALED IN MAKKAH

REVEALATION ORDER 29

Some of its benefits:

- Reminding Quraysh of Allah's blessings upon them.

- Calling them to worship Allah alone.
- Urging them to be grateful for Allah's blessings, who fed them in hunger and provided them security from fear.
- That it is Allah who feeds and provides sustenance.
- That security from fear and other things is in the hands of Allah.

سُورَةُ المَاعُون
AL MĀ'ŪN (107)
Small Kindnesses

VERSES	7
WORDS	25
LETTERS	125
REVEALED IN	MAKKAH
REVEALATION ORDER	17

Main Theme: Clarifying the traits of those who disbelieve in the day of judgment.

Some of its benefits:

1. Questioning to express astonishment at the state of those who deny the religion.
2. They describe their characteristics, including that they harshly repel the orphans and push them away when seeking help.
3. They do not encourage others to feed the needy, and it is even more likely that they do not do it themselves.
4. This directs our attention to the fact that if we cannot help the needy, we should strive to encourage and urge others to do so.
5. Warning against denying the religion.
6. Warning against harshly repelling and pushing away the orphan.
7. Warning against stinginess with wealth.
8. Warning against stinginess with status.
9. Evidence that denying the hereafter encourages people to commit sins in this world.
10. There is evidence that denying the hereafter hardens hearts toward the weak and the poor when they feel secure in recompense and accountability.
11. This clarifies that the essence of religion is not merely a word spoken in judgment but a transformation in the heart that drives one towards kindness, compassion, generosity, doing good to needy brethren, and care and protection. Actions demonstrate the truthfulness of faith.

12. A severe and definite threat to those who neglect and become heedless of their prayers until their time expires.
13. Warning against showing off.
14. Encouraging sincerity.
15. Encouraging giving what is customarily not withheld, which does not harm to give, and is asked for by both the rich and the poor, attributing its withholding to the meanness of spirit and flawed character.

سُورَةُ الكَوثَر
AL-KAUTHAR (108)
A River in Paradise

VERSES
3

WORDS
14

LETTERS
68

REVEALED IN
MAKKAH

REVEALATION ORDER
103

Main Theme: Defense of the Prophet (صَلَّى ٱللَّهُ عَلَيْهِ وَسَلَّمَ) and a promise of unimaginable reward and ample good. It is the shortest Sūrah in the Qur'ān in its words and letters. It has been reported from a number of the Salaf held that it was a Madinan Sūrah, revealed after the Treaty of al Ḥudaybiah to comfort the Prophet (صَلَّى ٱللَّهُ عَلَيْهِ وَسَلَّمَ). (This is reported from al Ḥasan al Baṣrī, Mujāhid, Qatādah, and 'Ikrimah). Perhaps the mention of prayer followed by slaughtering, an allusion to the 'Eid al Aḍḥā supports this view. And Allah knows best.

Some of its benefits:

- Glad tidings and reassurance to the Prophet (صَلَّى ٱللَّهُ عَلَيْهِ وَسَلَّمَ) with the granting of abundant goodness and bountiful favor, including the river named Al-Kawthar, the basin, and the watering place. The command to be grateful for these blessings,
- Turning the plotter's plan against him and clarifying that the truly cut-off person is the Prophet's enemy.
- Among the evidence of the Prophet's (صَلَّى ٱللَّهُ عَلَيْهِ وَسَلَّمَ) truthfulness and the validity of his prophethood is his knowledge of what was in the hearts of his enemies and what was uttered by their tongues, which he had not heard from people, yet it happened as he informed.
- The inability of all Arabs and others to produce a surah like this despite its brevity.
- Muhammad spread the religion of Allah, elevating his status, increasing his remembrance, and growing his supporters and followers.
- Encouraging sincerity in deeds.

سُورَةُ الكَافِرُونَ
AL-KĀFIRŪN (109)
The Disbelievers

VERSES
6

WORDS
26

LETTERS
94

REVEALED IN
MAKKAH

REVEALATION ORDER
18

Main Theme: Disassociation with disbelief those who adhere to it, and making a complete distinction between Islam and disbelief. Shaykh al Islām Ibn Taymiyyah (d. 728 AH رَحِمَهُ ٱللَّهُ) said:

"فيها التوحيد القصدي العملي".

"The Sūrah contains the Tawḥīd of intention and action (i.e., singling out Allah sincerely with worship)."

Elsewhere, he wrote in response to some heretical people who claimed that this *Sūrah* meant approving of other religions:

"وهي كلمة تقتضي براءته من دينهم، وأن ديني لي وأنتم بريئون منه، ودينكم لكم وأنا بريء منه."

"It (i.e., the last verse) is a statement that necessitates one freeing their self from their religion: my religion is mine, and you are free of it, and your religion is yours, and I am free of it."

From the objectives of the surah:

Clarifying the distinction and separation between the worship of Allah and the worship of others, stating that they cannot coexist and that the religion of Islam does not mix with any aspect of the religion of polytheism. It also dispels any hope polytheists might have that the Messenger ﷺ would agree with them on any aspect of their disbelief.

From the benefits of the surah:

1. Affirming the belief in divine decree and that the disbeliever has disbelieved by destiny, and the believer has believed by destiny.

2. The guardianship of Allah (سُبْحَانَهُ وَتَعَالَىٰ) over His Messenger, protecting him from accepting the false suggestions of the polytheists.

3. Establishing a clear distinction between the people of faith, the people of disbelief, and polytheism.

سُورَةُ النَّصْرِ
AL-NAṢR (110)
The Help

VERSES
3

WORDS
17

LETTERS
77

REVEALED IN
MADINAH

REVEALATION ORDER
114

Main Theme: Giving the Prophet (ﷺ) glad tidings of victory and the conclusion of the message and what should be done after blessing. No full *Sūrah* was revealed after it, although the remaining segments of other *Sūrahs* were revealed. Islam is the religion of success and victory. Only after achieving total victory and success did Allah cause the Prophet's life to draw to an end.

Shaykh al Islām Ibn Taymiyyah (ﷺ) said:[36]

"فدخل الناس في دين الله أفواجا بعد الفتح، فما مات (ﷺ) وفي بلاد العرب كلها موضع لم يدخله الإسلام."

"So the people entered Allah's religion in droves after the conquest (of Makkah). He (صلى الله عليه وسلم) did not die while there was still a single place in the 'Arab lands in which Islam had not entered."

Some of its benefits:

- Glad tidings for the Prophet (ﷺ) with victory, conquest, honor, and empowerment.
- This means that people will enter into Allah's religion in groups, one after another.
- The command to glorify Allah.
- The command to seek forgiveness.
- This surah is a sign of the approaching end of the Messenger of Allah's (ﷺ) life, which his Lord (تَبَارَكَ وَتَعَالَىٰ) informed him about.
- Encouraging repentance and seeking forgiveness for sins and wrongdoings.
- Encouraging praise of Allah and gratitude to Him.
- It is appropriate for those who feel their end is near to increase in glorifying and praising Allah, seeking forgiveness extensively, and repenting from sins.

[36] Al Jawāb al-Ṣaḥīḥ 6/78; Dār al 'Aaṣimah 1999/1422.

سُورَةُ المَسَد
AL MASAD (III)
The Palm Fiber

VERSES
5

WORDS
20

LETTERS
77

REVEALED IN
MAKKAH

REVEALATION ORDER
6

Main Themes: The utter loss of those who use influence or family status to advocate for disbelief and show hostility to the religion, specifying Abu Lahab as the first to do so. This was revealed in support of the Prophet (صَلَّى ٱللَّهُ عَلَيْهِ وَسَلَّمَ). *Sūrah al Masad* is from the miracles of the *Qur'ān* because many of those who were the early enemies of Islām eventually entered Islam. Allah knew that Abu Lahab would never accept Islam and would die in disbelief.

Ibn Taymiyyah (رَحِمَهُ ٱللَّهُ) said:[37]

"وليس في القرآن ذم من كفر به (صلى الله عليه وسلم) باسمه إلا هذا وامرأته، ففيه أن الأنساب لا عبرة بها، بل صاحب الشرف يكون ذمه على تخلفه عن الواجب أعظم."

"There is no explicit mention in the Qur'ān of dispraise of someone by name who disbelieved in the Prophet, except for him and his wife. Within this is the fact that no consideration is to be assigned to blood ties, but rather someone of status is more deserving of blame for failing to carry out their obligation."

Some of its benefits:

- Informing that Abu Lahab will face loss and destruction as a reward for his opposition to the Prophet's (صَلَّى ٱللَّهُ عَلَيْهِ وَسَلَّمَ) message. Abu Lahab was a vehement enemy and caused significant harm to the Prophet (صَلَّى ٱللَّهُ عَلَيْهِ وَسَلَّمَ), as did his wife, who spared no effort in evil and harm against the Prophet (صَلَّى ٱللَّهُ عَلَيْهِ وَسَلَّمَ).
- Clarifying that his wealth and earnings did not shield him from Allah's punishment, detailing his punishment in the hereafter, as Allah (سُبْحَانَهُ وَتَعَالَىٰ) said: "He will burn in a Fire of blazing flame."
- Informing that his wife would also be punished with him because she supported him in opposing and harming the Prophet (صَلَّى ٱللَّهُ عَلَيْهِ وَسَلَّمَ) and engaged in spreading rumors and discord.
- The surah signifies the truthfulness of the Prophet (صَلَّى ٱللَّهُ عَلَيْهِ وَسَلَّمَ) and the authenticity of his prophethood, as he predicted that Abu Lahab would die in disbelief, and it occurred as he stated.

[37] Majmū al Fatāwā 16/602.

سُورَةُ الإِخْلَاصِ
AL IKHLAṢ (112)
Sincerity

VERSES
4

WORDS
17

LETTERS
73

REVEALED IN
MAKKAH

REVEALATION ORDER
22

Main Theme: Singling out Allah as the possessor of absolute perfection and absolving him of offspring or equals.

Named "Al-Ikhlas" because it encompasses the monotheism of Allah (سُبۡحَانَهُۥ وَتَعَالَىٰ) dedicating worship solely to Him, seeking recourse only in Him, and exalting Him above any deficiency and polytheism.

Objectives of the surah:

Affirming the uniqueness of Allah (سُبۡحَانَهُۥ وَتَعَالَىٰ) in divinity and perfection, exalting Him above any equal or likeness, and that none but He is sought for needs, refuting those who attribute a father or son to Allah the Exalted.

Some benefits of the Sūrah:

- Affirming the oneness of Allah.
- The perfection of His self-sufficiency and the creation's need for Him.
- Refuting those who claim that Allah has a child, holy is Allah far above their statements.
- Exalting Allah above any resemblance to His creations.
- Denying all forms of associating partners with Allah.
- Refuting those who said that the Qur'ān is the speech of Muhammad.
- Denying that Allah has a spouse.

سُورَةُ الفَلَق
AL FALAQ (113)
The Daybreak

VERSES
5

WORDS
23

LETTERS
74

REVEALED IN
MAKKAH

REVEALATION ORDER
20

Main Theme: Seeking Allah's protection from external and outward evils.

From the objectives of the surah:

Affirming the oneness of Lordship and Divinity by teaching the Prophet (ﷺ) and his Ummah to attach their hearts to Allah and seek refuge in Him from the evils of His creation, that He is the One who suffices a person from the harm of every harmful being, and protects him from all evil and dislike.

Some benefits of the surah:

- The obligation to seek refuge in Allah and His sanctuary from every fear one cannot repel due to its hidden nature or inability to do so.
- Seeking refuge from the evil of darkness when it spreads.
- Seeking refuge from the evil of witches who blow on knots in their magic spells.
- Prohibiting blowing on knots as it is part of sorcery. Sorcery is disbelief, and the punishment for a sorcerer is execution by the sword.
- Prohibiting envy, which is a dangerous disease that led the son of Adam to kill his brother and Yūsuf's brothers to plot against him.
- Seeking refuge from the evil of the envier when he envies, the envier wishes for Allah's blessings to be removed from others.
- Admiring or wanting what others have while being happy for them is not considered envy. In line with the authentic hadith, "Envy is only permissible in two cases," envy refers to being happy for others' blessings.

سُورَةُ النَّاسِ

AL-NĀS (114)

Mankind

VERSES
6

WORDS
20

LETTERS
79

REVEALED IN
MADINAH

REVEALATION ORDER
21

Main Theme: Seeking Allah's protection from internal and hidden evils.

From the objectives of the surah:

Affirming the oneness of Lordship and Divinity by teaching the Prophet (ﷺ) and his Ummah to turn to Allah and seek refuge in Him to protect them from the evil of the whisperers among humans and jinn, who beautify the path of evil.

From the benefits of the surah:

- The necessity of seeking refuge in Allah (عَزَّوَجَلَّ) from the devils of humans and jinn.
- Divine instruction to seek refuge in Allah, the Lord of everything and its King, from the evil of the whisperer who withdraws, who is the root of all evils and their agent, and that is the devil.
- Affirming the Lordship and Divinity of Allah (عَزَّوَجَلَّ).
- Clarifying the place of his whispering, which is in people's chests.
- Clarifying that the whisperers are of two kinds: jinn and human.
- Clarification of the phrase for seeking refuge, which is "I seek refuge in Allah from the accursed devil," as indicated by the authentic Sunnah when two men quarreled in the Prophet's masjid, and the Prophet (ﷺ) said, "I know a phrase which, if he said it, what he feels (i.e., the anger) would go away: 'I seek refuge in Allah from the accursed devil.'"
- Allah's kindness to His servants by guiding them to the means of their protection.

Ibn Taymiyyah says about Sūrah al Ikhlāṣ and the Mu'awwidhatayn:[38]

وَأَمَّا سُورَةُ (الْإِخْلَاصِ و (الْمُعَوِّذَتَانِ فَفِي الْإِخْلَاصِ الثَّنَاءُ عَلَى اللَّهِ وَفِي الْمُعَوِّذَتَيْنِ دُعَاءُ الْعَبْدِ رَبَّهُ لِيُعِيذَهُ ،

"As for *Sūrah al Ikhlāṣ* and the *Mu'awwidhatayn* (i.e., *Sūrahs al-Nas and al Falaq*): In Sūrah al Ikhlāṣ is the praise of Allah and in the Mu'awwidhatayn is the worshipper invoking his Lord to grant him refuge.

[38] *Majmū' al Fatāwā 16/478-479.*.

وَالثَّنَاءُ مَقْرُونٌ بِالدُّعَاءِ كَمَا قَرَنَ بَيْنَهُمَا فِي أُمِّ الْقُرْآنِ الْمَقْسُومَةِ بَيْنَ الرَّبِّ وَالْعَبْدِ: نِصْفُهَا ثَنَاءٌ لِلرَّبِّ وَنِصْفُهَا دُعَاءٌ لِلْعَبْدِ وَالْمُنَاسَبَةُ فِي ذَلِكَ ظَاهِرَةٌ؛

Here, praising (Allah) is coupled with *du'ā* just as He coupled the two together in (the *Fātiḥah*), apportioned in two halves between the Lord and the slave. Half of it is praise for the Lord, and half is *du'ā* made by the worshipper. The similarity and connection (between the beginning and end of the Qur'ān) is obvious.

فَإِنَّ أَوَّلَ الْإِيمَانِ بِالرَّسُولِ الْإِيمَانُ بِمَا جَاءَ بِهِ مِنْ الرِّسَالَةِ وَهُوَ الْقُرْآنُ

Indeed, the first part of belief in the Messenger is in what he came with of the message, the Qur'ān (i.e., *Sūrah al 'Alaq, al Qadr, and al Bayyinah*].

ثُمَّ الْإِيمَانُ بِمَقْصُودِ ذَلِكَ وَغَايَتُهُ وَهُوَ مَا يَنْتَهِي الْأَمْرُ إلَيْهِ مِنْ النَّعِيمِ وَالْعَذَابِ: وَهُوَ الْجَزَاءُ

That is followed by believing in the goal and ultimate purpose for all of that, the outcome of reward or punishment, which is the compensation [i.e., *Sūrah Zalzalah, al 'Aadiyāt, al Qāri'ah and al-Takāthur*].

ثُمَّ مَعْرِفَةُ طَرِيقِ الْمَقْصُودِ وَسَبَبُهُ وَهُوَ الْأَعْمَالُ: خَيْرُهَا لِيَفْعَلَ وَشَرُّهَا لِيَتْرُكَ.

That is followed by knowing the path and the means to reach the goal, namely, the deeds: the good to implement them and the evil to avoid them. [Ibn Taymiyyah is referring here to Sūrah al 'Aṣr, al Humazah, al Fīl, Quraysh, al Mā'ūn, al Kawthar, al Kāfirūn, al-Naṣr, and Masad].

ثُمَّ خَتَمَ الْمُصْحَفَ بِحَقِيقَةِ الْإِيمَانِ وَهُوَ ذِكْرُ اللَّهِ وَدُعَاؤُهُ كَمَا بُنِيَتْ عَلَيْهِ أُمُّ الْقُرْآنِ

Then (Allah) concludes the Muṣḥaf with the reality of faith, which is remembrance of Allah and supplicating for Him, as *Sūrah al Fātiḥah* is structured upon this.

فَإِنَّ حَقِيقَةَ الْإِنْسَانِ الْمَعْنَوِيَّةَ هُوَ الْمَنْطِقُ وَالْمَنْطِقُ قِسْمَانِ: خَبَرٌ وَإِنْشَاءٌ

Undoubtedly, an individual's spiritual reality resides within their reasoning, composed of two fundamental components: information and conduct.

وَأَفْضَلُ الْخَبَرِ وَأَنْفَعُهُ وَأَوْجَبُهُ مَا كَانَ خَبَرًا عَنْ اللَّهِ كَنِصْفِ الْفَاتِحَةِ وَسُورَةِ الْإِخْلَاصِ

The most noble, advantageous, and obligatory knowledge one can possess is that which pertains to Allah, such as half of the Fātiḥah and Sūrah al Ikhlāṣ.

وَأَفْضَلُ الْإِنْشَاءِ الَّذِي هُوَ الطَّلَبُ وَأَنْفَعُهُ وَأَوْجَبُهُ مَا كَانَ طَلَبًا مِنْ اللَّهِ كَالنِّصْفِ الثَّانِي مِنْ الْفَاتِحَةِ وَالْمُعَوِّذَتَيْنِ

The most virtuous, beneficial way one should conduct oneself, which is one's pursuit, is what one wants from Allah, such as the second half of the Fātiḥah and the Mu'awwidhatayn."

CONTEMPLATE, COMPREHEND, APPLY

Contemplation Insights from Page 582 [An-Naba 1-30]

- Allah's perfection in creation signifies His ability to resurrect.
- Tyranny leads to Hell.
- The punishment for disbelievers is multiplied.

Contemplation Insights from Page 583 [An-Naba 31-40 & An-Nazi'at 1-15]

- Piety is the reason for entering Paradise.
- Remembering the horrors of the Day of Judgment motivates good deeds.
- The soul of the disbeliever is taken forcefully and violently, while the soul of the believer is taken gently and softly.

Contemplation Insights from Page 584 [An-Nazi'at 16-46]

- Gentleness is required when addressing one being invited to Islam.
- Fear of Allah and restraining oneself from whims are reasons for entering Paradise.
- The knowledge of the Hour is of the unseen, known only to Allah.
- Allah details the creation of the heavens and the earth.

Contemplation Insights from Page 585 [Abasa 1-42]

- Allah's admonition to His Prophet regarding Abdullah bin Umm Maktum shows that the Qur'ān is from Allah.
- Paying attention to the seeker of knowledge and guidance.
- The severe horrors of the Day of Judgment are where no one is concerned except for themselves; even prophets say: "Myself, Myself."

Contemplation Insights from Page 586 [At-Takwir 1-29]

- A person will be gathered with those alike in good or evil.
- If the buried girl is asked, what about the one who buried her? This indicates the magnitude of the situation.
- The will of the servant follows the will of Allah.

Contemplation Insights from Page 587 [Al-Infitar 1-19] - Al-Mutaffifin 1-7

- Warning against arrogance that prevents following the truth.
- Greed is a reprehensible trait in merchants, and one is only safe from it who fears Allah.
- Remembering the terror of the Day of Judgment is one of the greatest deterrents against sin.

Contemplation Insights from Page 588 [Al-Mutaffifin 7-34]

- The danger of sins on hearts.
- Disbelievers will be deprived of seeing their Lord on the Day of Judgment.
- Mocking the people of religion is a characteristic of disbelievers.

Contemplation Insights from Page 589 [Al-Mutaffifin 35-36 & Al-Inshiqaq -1-25]

- The heavens and the earth submit to their Lord.
- Every person strives towards either good or evil.
- Taking the book with the right hand is a sign of bliss on the Day of Judgment, and taking it with the left is a sign of misery.

Contemplation Insights from Page 590 [Al-Burooj 1-22]

- The trial of a believer is proportional to their faith.
- Preferring the safety of faith over the safety of the body is a sign of salvation on the Day of Judgment.
- Repentance, with its conditions, demolishes what was before it.

Contemplation Insights from Page 591 [At-Tariq 1-17 & Al-A'la 1-10]

- Angels safeguard people and their deeds, good and bad, for accountability.
- The plots of disbelievers weaken when faced with the plan of Allah (عَزَّوَجَلَّ).
- Fear of Allah leads to admonition.

Contemplation Insights from Page 592 [Al-A'la 11-19 & Al-Ghashiyah 1-22]

- The importance of purifying the self from both apparent and hidden vices.
- Using creation as evidence of the Creator's existence and greatness.
- The caller's duty is to call; guiding people to the right path is in Allah's hands.

Contemplation Insights from Page 593 [Al-Ghashiyah 23-26 & Al-Fajr 1-23]

- The virtue of the first ten days of Dhul-Hijjah over other days of the year.
- The coming of Allah (عَزَّوَجَلَّ) on the Day of Judgment is affirmed in a manner befitting His majesty, without likening Him to His creation nor denying His attributes.
- A believer remains patient during trials and grateful when blessed.

Contemplation Insights from Page 594 [Al-Fajr 24-30 & Al-Balad]

- Freeing slaves, feeding the needy during hard times, having faith in Allah, and advising each other to be patient and merciful are among the reasons for entering Paradise.
- One of the signs of prophethood is the Prophet's (صَلَّى ٱللَّهُ عَلَيْهِ وَسَلَّمَ) prediction that Mecca would become lawful for him for a moment during the day.
- As Allah narrowed the paths to enslavement, He expanded the ways to emancipation, making freeing slaves a means of drawing closer to Allah and a form of expiation.

Contemplation Insights from Page 595

- The importance of purifying the soul.
- Those who collaborate in sin share the guilt.
- Sins are a cause for worldly punishments.
- Everyone is facilitated for what they were created for; some are obedient, and some are disobedient.

Contemplation Insights from Page 596

- The Prophet's status with his Lord is unmatched.
- Gratitude for blessings is a duty to Allah from His servant.
- The obligation of mercy towards the weak and gentleness towards them.

Contemplation Insights from Page 597

- Seeking Allah's pleasure is the highest goal.
- The significance of reading and writing in Islam.
- The danger of wealth if it leads to arrogance and distancing from the truth.
- Denying good deeds is a characteristic of disbelief.
- Sins weighed heavily on the Prophet (صَلَّى ٱللَّهُ عَلَيْهِ وَسَلَّمَ), so what about the rest of creation?

Contemplation Insights from Page 598

- The virtue of Laylat al-Qadr over other nights of the year.
- Sincerity in worship is a condition for its acceptance.
- Disbelievers are the worst of creation, while believers are the best.
- The agreement of religions in their fundamentals is a reason to accept the message.

Contemplation Insights from Page 599

- Fearing Allah leads to His pleasure with His servant.
- The Earth will testify to the deeds of Adam's children.

Contemplation Insights from Page 600

- The danger of boasting and showing off wealth and children.
- The grave is a temporary visit before moving to the eternal hereafter.
- On the Day of Judgment, people will be asked about the luxuries Allah bestowed upon them in this life.
- Humans are inherently inclined to love wealth.

Contemplation Insights from Page 601

- Those who do not possess faith, perform righteous deeds, advise each other in truth, and advise each other in patience are at a loss.
- Slandering and backbiting people are prohibited.
- Allah defends His Sacred House, which is among the security He decreed for it.

Contemplation Insights from Page 602

- The importance of security in Islam.
- Showing off is a disease of the heart that nullifies deeds.
- Responding to blessings with gratitude increases them.
- The Prophet's (صَلَّى ٱللَّهُ عَلَيْهِ وَسَلَّمَ) honor with his Lord and His protection and honor of him in this life and the hereafter.

Contemplation Insights from Page 603

- Severing ties with disbelievers.
- Responding to blessings with gratitude.

- Sūrah Al-Masad is evidence of prophethood since it decreed Abu Lahab would die as a disbeliever, and he died ten years later as such.
- The validity of marriages among disbelievers.

Contemplation Insights from Page 604

- Affirming Allah's attributes of perfection and negating imperfections from Him.
- The existence of magic and its cure.
- The cure for whispers is in remembering Allah and seeking refuge from Satan.

CONTEMPLATION STUDY QUESTIONS

Sūrah An-Naba Questions

Verse 9: What is the reason for sleep being a blessing that Allah bestows upon His servants? *[Al-Sa'dī]*

Verse 21: What can be understood from Hell being a place of ambush? *[Ibn Kathīr]*

Verse 29: What is the wisdom behind recording the servants' deeds? *[Al-Sa'dī]*

Verse 35: The verse mentions spiritual bliss in Paradise; explain it. *[Ibn Kathīr]*

Sūrah An-Nazi'at Questions

Verse 26: Who benefits from the Qur'ānic warnings, and who does not? *[Al-Sa'dī]*

Verses 27-33: What do these significant verses mentioned by Allah (عَزَّوَجَلَّ) indicate? And why is the mention of recompense followed after these verses? *[Al-Sa'dī]*

Sūrah 'Abasa Questions

Verses 1-10: The verses benefit the preacher in prioritizing his call to Allah; explain that. *[Al-Sa'dī]*

Verses 11-16: Allah described the angels entrusted with the Qur'ānic scrolls with characteristics; how can the Qur'ān memorizer and bearer benefit from these characteristics? *[Ibn Kathīr]*

Verse 21: How is burial a blessing Allah bestows upon His servants? *[Al-Sa'dī]*

Sūrah Al-Infitar Questions

Verse 13: Obedience leads to bliss and happiness in three stages a person goes through; what are they? *[Al-Sa'dī]*

Verses 10-12: How do you feel about the angels who record your deeds? And what does this feeling drive you to do? *[Al-Sa'dī]*

Sūrah Al-Mutaffifin Question

Verse 31: Explain the great misconduct Allah revealed about these polytheists. *[Al-Sa'dī]*

Sūrah Al-Inshiqaq Question

Verse 13: When is joy condemned? *[Ibn Kathīr]*

Sūrah Al-Burooj Questions

Verse 9: What is the wisdom behind Allah (عَزَّوَجَلَّ) mentioning His sovereignty of the heavens and the earth after mentioning the situation of the tyrants of the trench?

Verse 14: What is the secret in associating Allah's name Al-Wadud (the Loving) with His name Al-Ghafur (the Forgiving)? *[Al-Sa'dī]*

Verse 11: From where can Allah's generosity and His great existence be deduced through the verse? *[Ibn Kathīr]*

Verses 21-22: Talk about the status of the Noble Qur'ān with Allah (عَزَّوَجَلَّ) through the verses. *[Al-Sa'dī]*

Sūrah At-Tariq Question

Verses 16-17: The disbelievers and those in misguidance plot against Islam and Muslims at every moment, so who prevails through your contemplation of this verse? *[Al-Sa'dī]*

Sūrah Al-A'la Questions

Verse 8: Deduce the leniency and ease of Islam through this noble verse *[Ibn Kathīr]*

Verse 9: Allah's statement "Indeed, the reminder benefits" indicates an etiquette among the etiquettes of seeking knowledge; what is it? *[Ibn Kathīr]*

Sūrah Al-Fajr Questions

Verse 5: What is the importance of intellect for a Muslim? *[Al-Sa'dī]*

Verses 12-13: What practical stance do you take from knowing Allah monitors all actions? *[Ibn Kathīr]*

Verses 15-17: Wealth and poverty can be blessings or trials; explain that through the verses. *[Al-Sa'dī]*

Verse 18: What prevents a person from feeding the poor and needy? *[Al-Sa'dī]*

Sūrah Ash-Shams Question

Verse 7: Allah swears by His magnificent creations, so what is the aspect of greatness in the soul He swore by? *[Al-Sa'dī]*

Sūrah Al-Layl Question

Verse 3: What is the wisdom behind Allah (عَزَّوَجَلَّ) creating creatures in two types? *[Al-Sa'dī]*

Sūrah Ad-Duha Question

Verse 11: Is the prohibition of scolding the seeker only for those asking for money? Explain. *[Al-Sa'dī]*

There are no contemplation questions for the short Sūrahs. Instead, refer to the detailed synopses of the short Sūrahs above and reflect on the benefits.

May Allah send peace and salutations upon our beloved Prophet, his family, and followers until the Day of Judgment.

Primary Sources:

•Al Jāmi' li Kalām al Imām Ibn Taymiyyah fil-Tafsīr; Dār Ibn al Jawzī (1422).

•Majmū' al Fatāwā; collection Ibn Taymiyyah's writings gathered by 'Abd al-Rahmān b. Muhammad b. Qāsim (1425).

•Badā'i al-Tafsīr limā Fassarahul Imam Ibn Qayyim al Jawziyyah; Dār Ibn al Jawzī (1427)

•Tafsīr Ibn Kathīr

•Naẓm Al-Durar fī Tanāsub al Ayāt wal-Suwar; and Maṣā'id al-Naẓr by Imam al Biqā'ī (d. 885 AH).

•Basā'ir Dhawi-Tamyīz li Fayruz Abādī (d. 817 AH).

•Marāsid al Matāli' by Jalāl al-Dīn al-Suyūtī (d. 911 AH).

•Tafsīr Al-Sa'dī (Taysir al Karīm al-Rahmān)

•Al-Tahrīr wal-Tanwīr Ibn 'Ashūr; al-Dār al Tunisiyyah lil-Nashr (1984).

•Al Muyassar fi-l-Tafsīr Majma' Al Malik Fahad

•Al Muktasar fī Tafsīr al Qur'ān al Karīm. Compiled by a team of tafsir scholars. Markaz Tafsīr lil-Dirāsāt al Qur'āniyyah, 6th edition. (1441).

•Muhtawayāt Suwar Al Qur'ān Al Karim; Ahmad Tawīl; Madār Al Watan, Riyādh (1434).

•Ma'ālim al-Suwar, by Fāyiz al-Sariyḥ (5th edition)

•Al Qur'ān, Tadabbur wa 'Amal; Markaz al Minhāj lil Ishrāf wal-Tadrīb al-Tarbawī (1442)

Printed in Great Britain
by Amazon

43951250R00205